THE THIRD EYE

Race, Cinema, and Ethnographic Spectacle

Fatimah Tobing Rony

An earlier version of a section of the conclusion originally appeared
in "Victor Masayesva, Jr. and the Politics of Imagining Indians," *Film
Quarterly* 48, no. 2, copyright 1994 by the Regents of the University of
California. An earlier version of sections of chapters 1 and 2 originally
appeared in "Those Who Sit and Those Who Squat: The 1895 Films of
Felix-Louis Regnault," *Camera Obscura* 28 (1992). "The Venus Hottentot" from *The Venus Hottentot*, by Elizabeth Alexander (Charlottesville:
University Press of Virginia, 1990). Used with permission of the Univer-
sity Press of Virginia.

THE THIRD EYE ─────

DUKE UNIVERSITY PRESS   *Durham and London 1996* —————

This book is dedicated to my parents,
Mr. Abdul Kohar Rony and Mrs. Minar Tobing Rony,
and to the memory of my Ompung, Mrs. H. L. Tobing,
and my late uncle, Mr. R. A. P. L. Tobing

CONTENTS

List of Illustrations   ix

Acknowledgments   xi

Introduction. The Third Eye   3

I. INSCRIPTION

1. Seeing Anthropology:
Félix-Louis Regnault, the Narrative of Race, and
the Performers at the Ethnographic Exposition   21

2. The Writing of Race in Film:
Félix-Louis Regnault and the Ideology of
the Ethnographic Film Archive   45

II. TAXIDERMY

3. Gestures of Self-Protection:
The Picturesque and the Travelogue   77

4. Taxidermy and Romantic Ethnography:
Robert Flaherty's *Nanook of the North*   99

III. TERATOLOGY

5. Time and Redemption in the "Racial Film" of
the 1920s and 1930s   129

viii   Contents

6. *King Kong* and the Monster in
Ethnographic Cinema   157

Conclusion. Passion of Remembrance:
Facing the Camera/Grabbing the Camera   193

Notes   219

Bibliography   265

Index   289

LIST OF ILLUSTRATIONS

1. Still from *King Kong* (1933).   2
2. Dayak family group, Smithsonian Institution.   11
3. Charles Comte and Félix-Louis Regnault, "Negress walking with a light weight on her head" (1895).   22
4. Printed illustration in Félix-Louis Regnault's "De la fonction préhensile du pied."   31
5. Printed illustration in Félix-Louis Regnault's "Les déformations crâniennes dans l'art antique."   34
6. Printed illustration in Félix-Louis Regnault's "Exposition Ethnographique de l'Afrique Occidentale au Champs-de-Mars à Paris: Sénégal et Soudan Français."   37
7. Charles Comte and Félix-Louis Regnault, "Jump by three Negroes" (1895).   50
8. Charles Comte and Félix-Louis Regnault, "Walk" (1895).   50
9. Charles Comte and Félix-Louis Regnault, "Run" (1895).   51
10. Charles Comte and Félix-Louis Regnault, "Run" (1895).   52
11. Charles Comte and Félix-Louis Regnault, "Three clothed men walk" (1895).   53
12. Charles Comte and Félix-Louis Regnault, "Negress walks" (1895).   55
13. Photographic reproduction, "Malagasy carrying a palanquin on their shoulders" (1895).   56
14. Printed illustration of Colonel Gillon carried in a palanquin by four Malagasy men.   57
15. Printed illustration of Commandant de Raoul walking *en flexion*.   60
16. Printed illustration of diagrams depicting Commandant de Raoul walking and running *en flexion*.   60
17. "Doctor Regnault walks," Institut de physiologie.   60

18. Lorna Simpson, *Easy for Who to Say* (1989).   72
19. Léon Busy, "Village performers—Ha-noi—Tonkin" (1916).   81
20. Still from Burton Holmes's *Sights of Suva* (1918).   86
21. Still from Gaston Méliès's *Captured by Aborigines* (1913).   87
22. Osa Johnson and unidentified actors on location in Osa and
    Martin Johnson's *Cannibals of the South Seas* (1917).   88
23. Still from Osa and Martin Johnson's *Simba* (1928).   89
24. Edward Sheriff Curtis, "Bridal group" (1914).   96
25. Edward Sheriff Curtis, "Masked dancers in canoes" (1914).   97
26. Still from *Nanook of the North* (1922).   103
27. Elisha Kent Kane, Joe, and Hanna, Smithsonian Institution
    life group (1873).   106
28. Still from *Nanook of the North* (1922).   112
29. Original drawing on paper, most likely by Wetalltok, from
    the Belcher Islands, 1916, of Flaherty and Inuit camera crew.   119
30. Still from *Qaggiq/The Gathering Place* (1989).   125
31. Still from *Grass* (1925).   134
32. Still from *Chang* (1927).   136
33. Still from *Moana* (1926).   139
34. Still from *The Silent Enemy* (1930).   142
35. Still from *White Shadows in the South Seas* (1929).   145
36. Photograph from Margaret Mead's book *Balinese Character*
    (1942).   147
37. Still from *Goona Goona* (1932).   149
38. Still from *Tabu* (1931).   150
39. Still from *Tabu* (1931).   152
40. Photograph of Ota Benga (1904).   158
41. Still from *Island of Lost Souls* (1933).   168
42. Still from *Trader Horn* (1931).   173
43. Still from *Blonde Venus* (1932).   174
44. Still from *King Kong* (1933).   183
45. Still from *King Kong* (1933).   185
46. Still from *King Kong* (1933).   187
47. Coco Fusco and Guillermo Gómez-Peña in "The Couple in
    the Cage" (1992).   190
48. Still from *Zou Zou* (1932).   201
49. Still from Zora Neale Hurston's films of 1928–29.   205
50. Still from *Itam Hakim, Hopiit* (1985).   214

ACKNOWLEDGMENTS

Many people have contributed to the completion of this book. My earliest debts are to Angela Dalle Vacche and David Rodowick for their crucial encouragement and assistance at all stages of this project. I would also like to thank Esther da Costa Meyer and Mary Miller who provided much needed critical advice.

I would like to thank the following people and institutions in North America for their kind assistance in facilitating my research: Marta Braun, Emilie de Brigard, Samba Diop, and Faye Ginsburg; Hazel V. Carby, Anne Coffin Hanson, Brigitte Peucker, and Sara Suleri at Yale University; Elaine Charnov, Joel D. Sweimler, and David Wells at the American Museum of Natural History; Paul Spehr, Arlene Balkansky, Cooper Graham, Patrick Loughney, Madeline Matz, and David Parker at the Library of Congress; Wendy Shay, Jake Homiak, and Pam Wintle at the Human Studies Film Archives; Mary Corliss, Terry Geesken, and Charles Silver at the Museum of Modern Art; the National Archives; Christraud Geary at the National Museum of African Art; Paula Fleming at the National Museum of Natural History; Robert Fleegal at the National Geographic Society; Sterling Memorial Library; Audrey Kupferberg, Sharon Della Camera, and Michael Kerbel at the Yale Film Studies Center; Barbara Adams, Mary Carrano, Susan Emerson, Rose Gibbons, and Marie Kuntz at the History of Art department at Yale; Joanasie Kanawuk at the Inuit Broadcasting Corporation; and Charlie Adams of Taqramiut Nipingat, Incorporated, Inukjuak, Nunavut.

In France I received generous aid and advice from Jean Rouch. I would also like to thank Noëlle Giret, Vincent Pinel, Alain Marchand, and the late Olivier Meston of the Cinémathèque française; Eric Vivié for graciously allowing me to view his collection of films from the Marey Institute at the Archives du film; Michelle Aubert, Andrei Dyja, and Eric Le Roy at the Archives du film; Françoise Foucault, Jean Jamin, Michelle Fontan, P. Pitoeff, and Christiane Rageau at the Musée de l'homme; Jean-Dominique Lajoux at CNRS; Jeanne Beausoleil, Nathalie Bonnet, and Marie Corneloup at the Collection Albert Kahn; Christine Delangle at the Collège de France; Aicha Kherroubi at the Musée d'Orsay; Jean-Michel Bouhours of the Centre Georges Pompidou; and Emmanuelle Toulet at the Bibliothèque de l'arsénale. I would also like to thank Claude Blanckaert, Amy and Robert Fienga, Richard Leacock, Valérie Lalonde, Philippe Lourdou, Marc Piault, Chantal Riss, and Vittorio Tosi. Research was also conducted at the Bibliothèque nationale in Paris.

Those in the United Kingdom, I would like to thank include Penny Bateman and Ben Burt at the Museum of Man, and Elaine Burrows and Jackie Morris at the National Film Archive of the British Film Institute. I am grateful to Hoos Blotkamp, Rogier Schmeele, and Marÿke von Kester at the Nederlands Filmmuseum in Holland. In Germany, Dr. Dolezel and Dr. Franz Simon at the Institut für den Wissenschaftlichen Film, Dr. Markus Schindlbeck at the Museum für Völkerkunde in Berlin, the Museum für Völkerkunde in Hamburg, and the Staatliches Museum für Völkerkunde in Munich all guided me to important research materials.

Research for the book was made possible by grants from the Council for European Studies, the Samuel H. Kress Foundation, the Yale Center for International Area Studies, the History of Art department at Yale, and the American Association of University Women. I would like to thank M. Eric Vivié, the Archives du film du centre national de la cinématographie, and the Cinémathèque française for permission to reproduce images.

I would also like to extend my thanks to those who invited me to give talks on various sections of my book, thus providing me with the invaluable feedback needed to conduct revisions: John Hanhardt at the Whitney Museum of American Art; Karen Newman and Elizabeth Weed at the Pembroke Center for Teaching and Research on Women at Brown University; Youssef El-Ftouh and the Institut du monde arabe in Paris; Edward Branigan, Constance Penley, and Charles Wolfe at the University of California, Santa Barbara; Vicente Rafael at the University of California, San Diego; Susan Douglas, Jacqueline Hayden, and Sherry Milner at Hampshire College; and Margaret Daniels, David Eng, Peter Feng, Marina Heung, Trang Kim-T. Tranh, Sandra Liu, and Michelle Materre.

I am indebted to the University of California President's Postdoctoral Fellowship program for providing me the support needed to complete the book. I especially want to thank Valerie Smith and Raymond Paredes, and the UCLA James S. Coleman African Studies Center, in particular its director Edmond J. Keller. Teshome Gabriel and Billy Woodberry provided invaluable advice and insightful comments. I also thank the professional staff at the Coleman Center: Alice Nabalamba and Muadi Mukenge; Donna Jones, Ethel Enoex, and Imogene Moncrief; Jonas Admassu, Caseline Kunene, Terrence Rose, and Bridget Teboh; and Maxine Harris at Bunche Hall. I would also like to thank Don Nakanishi, Enrique dela Cruz, Catherine Castor, Maria J. Ventura, and Christine Wang of the UCLA Asian American Studies Center for their support.

Very special thanks go to César José Alvarez, Lisa Cartwright, Allan deSouza, Jodi Hauptman, Kellie Jones, Ming Yuen-S. Ma, Yong Soon Min, Carol Ockman, Dawn Suggs, William Valerio, and Clyde Woods for their intellectual enthusiasm and extraordinary concern. I am also grateful to Ken Wissoker at Duke University Press for his careful guidance and attention at each step. I would like to express my gratitude to Joseph H. Saunders who edited several full drafts, provided invaluable comments, and contributed countless hours of his time. To him I give my deepest thanks for his critical engagement in this project.

Last, I can never thank my parents Mr. Abdul Kohar Rony and Mrs. Minar Tobing Rony enough for their unconditional support and intellectual sustenance. I give thanks to the beloved dead as well as the living: the late Mrs. H. L. Tobing, the late Mr. R. A. P. L. Tobing, Mr. Ismail Rony, Mrs. Chadidjah Rony, Dorothy Fujita Rony who sustained me with her brilliant sisterly wit, and Elice Loembantobing who kept on insisting that this book be finished *dengan kepuasan hati,* and the rest of my family who are scattered across several continents and archipelagos all over the globe. *Horas!*

My views may diverge from those who have helped me; I take full responsibility for all errors. Note also that all translations are mine unless stated otherwise.

Travel books tell us that the thing to do is attract the attention of the main party by firing a shot.—Claude Lévi-Strauss, *Tristes Tropiques* (1955)

For every native of every place is a potential tourist, and every tourist is a native of somewhere. . . . But some natives—most natives in the world—cannot go anywhere. They are too poor. They are too poor to go anywhere. They are too poor to escape the reality of their lives; and they are too poor to live properly in the place where they live, which is the very place you, the tourist, want to go—so when the natives see you, the tourist, they envy you, they envy your ability to leave your own banality and boredom, they envy your ability to turn their own banality and boredom into a source of pleasure for yourself. —Jamaica Kincaid, *A Small Place* (1988)

But you cannot possibly know what I have done or why I have done it if you think of me as a savage.—James Baldwin, *A Rap on Race* (1971)

THE THIRD EYE ———

1. Still from *King Kong* (1933).
(Courtesy of the Museum of Modern Art)

INTRODUCTION

THE THIRD EYE

How I Became a Savage: Seeing Anthropology

Sometimes, there are moments in watching a film when the illusion of entering another space, another time, another experience is shattered. A tropical island. A prehistoric land. Fay Wray. Island Savages. King Kong.

The Savages are speaking my language. Tidak. Bisa. Kau. Like King Kong and the Islanders, I was born in two places, Sumatra and the United States: the daughter of a Batak mother from North Sumatra, and a father from Palembang, in South Sumatra. I am watching myself being pictured as a Savage. I am the Bride of Kong.

Several years after seeing *King Kong* for the first time, I had another occasion to be reminded of my Savagery. One gray rainy afternoon in Paris, I sat with cold feet conducting research in a deep cavern of a library with tall stone ceilings and coughing tweed-clad scholars at long tables. I was reading the writings of a certain doctor in Paris who was interested in pathological anatomy and movement; that is, the anatomy of criminals, circus freaks, and people of color. Savages squat whereas Civilized people sit, explained the doctor: a Batak, because of this, is akin to a monkey.[1] I come across this passage:

> All savage peoples make recourse to gesture to express themselves; their language is so poor it does not suffice to make them understood: plunged in darkness, two savages, as travelers who often witness this fact affirm, can communicate their thoughts, coarse and limited though they are.
>
> With primitive man, gesture precedes speech. . . .
>
> The gestures that savages make are in general the same everywhere, because these movements are natural reflexes rather than conventions like language.[2]

According to the doctor, a Batak from North Sumatra would be able to speak to a Wolof, an Inuit, an Igorot, through the language of gesture.

The doctor, Félix-Louis Regnault, went on to make what have been considered the first ethnographic "films."[3] Regnault believed not only that film could furnish documents for the study of race, but also that by capturing the physical form in motion, film could serve as an unimpeachable scientific index of race. Under the shadow of the Eiffel Tower, that supreme symbol of progress, Regnault filmed West African performers at an 1895 Ethnographic Exposition in Paris. As in other "native village" displays at world's fairs, these West African performers who danced, and conducted animal sacrifices and other rituals for coin-throwing French spectators, were inscribed in film in order to study the language of gesture, the language of race.

Thinking back on it now, I believe that the doctor may have been correct. Perhaps we Savages, plunged in darkness, do understand each other. What we share is the ability to see with the "third eye." In conventional terms, the third eye refers to the experience one has when, during an argument with one's lover, for example, one has the feeling that a third eye has floated out of one's body and is observing the altercation with the dispassionate air of a zoologist examining a specimen. "I am watching myself and my lover act out a conventional lover's quarrel." Or, "I've heard those words before, they're my mother's." Most everybody has had this experience of the third eye. But for a person of color growing up in the United States, the experience of viewing oneself as an object is profoundly formative. Reflecting on an indelible childhood memory, W. E. B. Dubois describes the double consciousness that a young person of color is forced to develop. Dubois explains that one day, a young white girl gave him a glance, and in that glance he recognized that he was marked as an Other. As Dubois describes it, the internalization of this recognition gives one the "sense of always looking at one's self through the eyes of others,"[4] or of seeing "darkly as through a veil."[5] The experience of the third eye suggests that Dubois's insight can be taken one step further—the racially charged glance can also induce one to see the very process which creates the internal splitting, to witness the conditions which give rise to the double consciousness described by Dubois. The veil allows for clarity of vision even as it marks the site of socially mediated self-alienation.

The movie screen is another veil. We turn to the movies to find images of ourselves and find ourselves reflected in the eyes of others. The intended audience for dominant Hollywood cinema was, of course, the "American," white and middle-class. Not Hopi, Sumatran, or Dahomeyan, or even African American, but "American." Thus Frantz Fanon is describing a third eye experience when he writes, "I cannot go to a film without seeing myself. I wait for me. In the interval, just before the film starts, I wait for me. The people in the theater are watching me, examining me, waiting for me. A Negro groom is going to appear. My heart makes my head swim."[6] Born in Martinique of African descent, Fanon writes eloquently of the humiliation of being forced to identify with images of blacks on the screen as servile and inferior: in *Black Skin, White Masks* he explodes at his objectification, fixed as if by a dye under the gaze of commercial cinema and the white audience.

But there is yet another form of identification which Fanon describes. A black schoolboy, he writes, deluged by Tarzan stories and other such adventure narratives, "identifies himself with the explorer, the bringer of civilization, the white man who carries truth to savages—an all-white truth."[7] How can it be otherwise? How can any viewer identify with the "savage," a being represented as having scarcely a shred of subjectivity? Indeed, in the Tarzan literature, jungle animals at times receive more sympathetic treatment than the African "native." If the "Negro groom" is a straitjacketing image issuing from white racism, the "native" is even more Other—represented as trapped in some deep frozen past, inarticulate, not yet evolved, seen as Primitive, and yes, Savage.

This book has two primary objectives. First, I offer a sustained critique of the pervasive form of objectification of indigenous peoples which I somewhat tendentiously, though with clear purpose, will label Ethnographic. I seek to subject representations of the "Native" to the kind of critical analysis that Edward Said has applied to representations of the "Oriental."

At present, a silence surrounds the stereotype of non-white indigenous peoples. Landscaped as part of the jungle mise-en-scène, or viewed as the faithful Man Friday to a white Robinson Crusoe, or perhaps romanticized as the Noble Savage struggling to survive in the wild, the individual "native" is often not even "seen" by the viewer but is taken for real: as when the barker outside the fair tent calls potential spectators to come in and "see real Indians," or the excitement over Kevin Costner's recent *Dances with Wolves* (1991) as a film employing "real Lakota Indians." It is as if the distance between the signifier and the referent in the construction of native peoples collapses. In *Tristes Tropiques* (1955), Claude Lévi-Strauss muses that explorers, anthropologists, and tourists voyage to foreign places in search of the novel, the undiscovered. What they find, he tells us, apart from their own trash thrown back in their faces, is what they already knew they would find, images predigested by certain "platitudes and commonplaces."[8] It is thus impossible to view the "native" with fresh eyes. Lévi-Strauss himself explains that part of the motivation for his voyage to meet the Tupi of the Brazilian Amazon was to reenact the 1560 meeting between the Tupi and Montaigne.[9] Similarly, when the average museum goer views a life group of Hopi dancers handling snakes, or a display of Wolof pottery, or an ethnographic film about trance and dance in Bali, he or she does not see the images for the first time. The exotic is always already known.

My first objective is thus to begin to uncover the conditions of possibility of this conventional framing of ethnographic visualization and to analyze the forms it took in cinema prior to World War II.

The second objective of the book, which intersects with but ultimately moves away from the ideological critique of representations of the Ethnographic, is to use the experience of the third eye to address the dilemma so eloquently outlined by Fanon: although the non-white child nourished on stories of *Tarzan* cannot grow up forever identifying with the white explorer, what does one become when one sees that one is not fully recognized as Self by the wider society but cannot fully identify as Other? I believe that understanding how the "native" is represented in film—how ethnographic cinema forces us to "see" anthropology—is crucial to people of color currently engaged in developing new modes of self-representation. I am speaking not only of artists and filmmakers in major metropolitan cities of the West, but also of those who are creating national cinemas in formerly colonized countries, as well as of minority groups who are producing independent film and maintaining indigenous broadcasting corporations. The modes of representation of ethnographic cinema, of course, need not be and often are not always rejected in their entirety: ideas from anthropology and modes of representation taken from ethnographic cinema can be appropriated by people of color in many different ways, both conservative and oppositional. It is only by understanding what ethnographic cinema is, and how it works, that the powerful potential of the third eye can be more fully realized.

"Ethnographic Cinema" Defined

"Ethnography" is, in the first place, an invention of anthropology, its defining practice. In cultural anthropology, ethnography refers both to the actual process of fieldwork and to the final product, the written ethnography. Anthropologist Susan Slyomovics explains:

> The classic ethnography by a social anthropologist trained via Malinowski, Lévi-Strauss, would be a work in which the life of a tribe would be encapsulated into a volume, divided very clearly into certain topics:

life cycle, economics, land tenure, social organization of the village
notables as opposed to the various classes. In the appendix you would
put a section on folk tales. For the most part, there would be no investigation of individual lives. . . . The traditional model would be to
encode the account so that it is implicit that you have been there,
without actually stating it.[10]

The encyclopedic coverage of the written ethnography occurs also in cinema. In the popular imagination an "ethnographic film" is akin to a National Geographic special which purports to portray whole cultures within
the space of an hour or two. The viewer is presented with an array of subsistence activities, kinship, religion, myth, ceremonial ritual, music and
dance, and—in what may be taken as the genre's defining trope—some form
of animal sacrifice. Like a classic ethnography which encapsulates a culture
in one volume, an "ethnographic film" becomes a metonym for an entire
culture.

As historian of anthropology George W. Stocking Jr. explains, anthropology's historical unity lies in its subject matter: dark-skinned people known
as "savages" or "primitives."[11] Visual anthropologist Jay Ruby also points
out that ethnographic film is most often defined by subject matter. He
writes, "The vast majority of films described as ethnographic are concerned
with exotic, non-Western people."[12] The boundaries of anthropology have
broken down recently, perhaps in response to the fact that descendants of
so-called Primitives are doing ethnography, and the fact that the European
myth of first contact can no longer be sustained in a postcolonial world.
Founded in the late nineteenth century, the discipline of anthropology has
undergone a series of transformations and is now more self-reflexive about
the ethics and politics of its own "customs and manners."

Nevertheless, the category of "ethnographic film," at least in the popular
imagination, is still by and large *racially* defined. The people depicted in an
"ethnographic film" are meant to be seen as exotic, as people who until only
too recently were categorized by science as Savage and Primitive, of an
earlier evolutionary stage in the overall history of humankind: people without history, without writing, without civilization, without technology,
without archives. In other words, people considered *"ethnographiable,"* in
the bipolar schema articulated by Claude Lévi-Strauss, as opposed to people
classified as *"historifiable,"* the posited audience of the ethnographic film,
those considered to have written archives and thus a history proper. The
historian Michèle Duchet has explained that Enlightenment thinkers Joseph François Lafitau, Comte Buffon, and Jean-Jacques Rousseau located

the study of non-Western indigenous peoples as a subfield of natural history, a discipline which, Duchet explains, was essentially descriptive. Physical and cultural anthropology were born out of this eighteenth-century refusal to regard indigenous peoples as *"historifiable."*[13]

The term "ethnographic" literally comes from "ethnos," a people, and "graphos," the describing or writing. The term, however, although at times used by anthropologists as a synonym for the objective description of a people, instead is a category which describes a relationship between a spectator posited as Western, white, and urbanized, and a subject people portrayed as being somewhere nearer to the beginning on the spectrum of human evolution. Although there is no English word which fully captures the notion of the *ethnographiable*, even the seemingly innocent word "ethnographic" has resonances of the *ethnographiable/historifiable* dichotomy. I assume those resonances in my use of the word "ethnographic."

Let me be clear that when I refer in this way to the "ethnographic" in cinema, I do not mean to implicate all of what others call ethnographic film. Some may challenge my definition of the "ethnographic" as anachronistic.[14] U.S. visual anthropologist Faye Ginsburg defines ethnographic film as a medium "intended to communicate something about that social or collective identity we call 'culture,' in order to mediate (one hopes) across gaps of space, time, knowledge, and prejudice."[15] Ethnographic filmmakers like Jean Rouch and David and Judith Macdougall have made increasingly reflexive and collaborative cinema in an effort to get beyond scientific voyeurism. Their use of handheld cameras, direct address, and elicitation of the participation of the peoples filmed expresses a modernist sensibility toward the precarious statuses of truth and realism. I am not concerned here with how best to envision an ideal of ethnographic cinema of the kind that Ginsburg, Rouch, and others are pursuing. Instead, I seek to explain what I see as the pervasive "racialization" of indigenous peoples in both popular and traditional scientific cinema.[16] I thus use the term "ethnographic cinema" to describe the broad and variegated field of cinema which situates indigenous peoples in a displaced temporal realm. I include within the category works now elevated to the status of "art," scientific research films, educational films used in schools, colonial propaganda films, and commercial entertainment films. Ethnographic cinema so defined, I would contend, has proved staunchly resilient.

Finally let me emphasize that I couple "ethnographic" with the word "cinema" rather than with "footage" or "films" because I wish to stress the institutional matrix in which the images are embedded. Cinema is not only a technology, it is a social practice with conventions that profoundly shape its forms. My particular interest, of course, is that cinema has been a primary means through which race and gender are visualized as natural categories; cinema has been the site of intersection between anthropology, popular culture, and the constructions of nation and empire.

Fascinating Cannibalism: History, Cinema, and Race

Phil Rosen brilliantly delineates how, in the nineteenth century in Europe and North America, history was enshrined as the "sovereign science of mankind" and an explicitly historical consciousness came to pervade everyday life.[17] This was the century of Leopold von Ranke and Jules Michelet, of the growth of museums, of architectural and artistic revivals, and of the invention of archeology and anthropology. Our present century reverberates with the resultant discourses. If the nineteenth century is the century of history, however, the twentieth century is the century of the image, of cinema. The twentieth century is characterized by the accessibility, circulation, and popularization of mechanically reproduced images. If the nineteenth century was obsessed with the past, the twentieth century is, in the words of Walter Benjamin, characterized by "the desire . . . to bring things 'closer' spatially and humanly . . . overcoming the uniqueness of every reality by accepting its reproduction."[18]

Cinema appears to bring the past and that which is culturally distant closer; likewise, anthropology, which posits that indigenous peoples are remnants of earlier ages, has been largely concerned with the description and preservation or reconstruction of the spatially and historically distant.

Rosen contends that classical Hollywood cinema is superior to photography as a means of controlling and managing time and the past. Using Roland Barthes's notion of the *punctum*—the potentially threatening and hallucinatory detail in the photograph—Rosen explains that photography's status as document, its particular subjective nature, disrupts realism; but the detail in cinema, subjugated to diegesis, more easily results in socially mediated meanings.[19] The shared experience of viewing a film allows for a high degree of ideological control—cinema is after all an industry—whereas photography elicits a more solipsistic engagement between viewer and photograph, an engagement which leaves open the possibility of unconventional readings. Early-twentieth-century cinema is thus a privileged locus for the investigation of the coming together of the nineteenth-century obsession with the past, and the twentieth-century desire to make visibly comprehensible the difference of cultural "others."

As V. Y. Mudimbe explains, in anthropology's construction of the Savage,

"an explicit political power presumes the authority of a scientific knowledge and vice versa."[20] In such diverse genres as colonial propaganda film,
Tarzan movies, and scientific films seen as positivist recordings, ethnographic cinema is often harnessed to ideologies of nationalism and imperialism; it has been an instrument of surveillance as well as entertainment,
linked like the written ethnographies of cultural anthropology to a discourse of power, knowledge, and pleasure.

It is impossible to speak of the ethnographic without speaking of race.
"Race" as we now know it—the general color-coded configuration of
"white," "red," "black," and "yellow"—was an invention of the nineteenth
century and became the defining problem for early anthropology.[21] In evolutionary terms, "race" consciously or unconsciously implies a competition
involving time, and both cinema and anthropology enabled the viewer to
travel through dimensions of space, time, and status.[22] Johannes Fabian
explains that anthropology is premised on notions of time which deny the
contemporaneity—what he calls coevalness—of the anthropologist and the
people that he or she studies. Anthropology, asserts Fabian, is a time machine.[23] At the height of the age of imperialism during the late nineteenth
and early twentieth century in the United States and Europe, there was a
tremendous proliferation of new popular science entertainments visualizing the "ethnographic," such as the dioramas and bone collections of the
natural history museum, the exhibited "native villages" of the world's fair
and the zoo, printed representations such as the postcard and stereograph or
carte de visite, popular science journals such as *National Geographic,* and,
of course, photography and cinema. These entertainments too were time
machines: to see the subjects portrayed was to see a nexus between race and
a past of origins. Even Walter Benjamin's insight that the appeal of media
like photography stemmed from the masses' desire to bring distant things
closer does not adequately capture the masses' voracious appetite for the
images of peoples of color which these entertainments made possible. In
order to understand the early history of how indigenous peoples of color
were represented in film, it is necessary to examine the obsession with and
anxiety about race manifested in both science and popular culture.

The obsessive consumption of images of a racialized Other known as the
Primitive is usefully labeled *fascinating cannibalism.*[24] By "fascinating
cannibalism" I mean to draw attention to the mixture of fascination and
horror that the "ethnographic" occasions: the "cannibalism" is not that of
the people who are labeled Savages, but that of the consumers of the images
of the bodies—as well as actual bodies on display—of native peoples offered
up by popular media and science.

2. Dayak family group, Smithsonian Institution. (Smithsonian Institution photo no. 28321, used by permission of the Smithsonian Institution, National Anthropological Archives)

Although ethnographic film is often seen as a subgenre of scientific film—and hence is assumed to be inherently dry, boring, and uninteresting—there are at least three reasons why such film, and the broader field in which I situate it, deserve close scrutiny. First, such a study reveals how inextricably early cinema is linked to discourses of race. In the historiography of cinema, D. W. Griffith's *The Birth of a Nation* (1915) is hailed as an early monument of dominant Hollywood film; its equivalent in status for documentary and ethnographic film is Robert Flaherty's *Nanook of the North* (1922).[25] Film historians call the formal aesthetic qualities of both films revolutionary, yet both films focus upon the racialized body, an Other whose race is an immediate marker of a problematic difference—whether it be Griffith's racist portrayal of the African American in the post–Civil War South, or Flaherty's portrayal of the Inuit hero Nanook as a kind of archetypal "natural" and Primitive Everyman.[26] Griffith's film celebrates the birth of History, whereas Flaherty's film extols the birth of Ethnography. The two films, hardly ever compared, were made only seven years apart; they both impose a stereotyped vision of the meaning of the past, and both smooth over anxieties about difference through ideologies of race. The dominant subject position of the spectator, the ideal viewer of the films—white, masculine, the bearer of History—is alternately frightened and soothed by the narratives of the Ku Klux Klan as saviors of the nation, and of the Inuit hunter as raw-flesh–eating but smiling Savage.

Second, the will to perceive ethnographic cinema as scientific and objectively voyeuristic—a common trope of early ethnographic cinema is that the peoples who were filmed were ignorant of film technology—is in need of interrogation. It is not only that film is seen as a positivist tool for recording reality; it is also that indigenous peoples are seen as natural, more *authentic* humanity. Just as mainstream Hollywood cinema depicts Western peoples in obviously scripted narrative films, the Primitive is constructed in a genre of film akin to the nature film. Film studies has begun to examine the construction of race in classical Hollywood cinema, but has largely ignored any film associated with science, including the body of work conventionally labeled "ethnographic." The current scholarship on and criticism of such films is scarce, and is comprised of mostly self-reflexive accounts by visual anthropologists eager either to find *totemic ancestors*[27] or to slay and denounce the colonial complicity of Oedipal fathers (and, when Margaret Mead is the target, mothers). Many anthropologists, although acknowledging particular ethnocentric biases of the filmmakers, still do not dispute the status of ethnographic film as empirical record. It is astonishing how often the constructed nature of the ethnographic film is ignored; yet, just as *The Birth of a Nation* reveals mainstream fears of miscegenation and thus weaves a web of myths around race, ethnographic film reveals an obsession with race and racial categorization in the construction of peoples always already Primitive. Of equal significance, scholars have largely overlooked the ways in which standard ethnographic film is linked to popular media entertainments and Hollywood spectacle.

Finally, a study of ethnographic cinema is crucial to understanding issues of identity. The anthropologist Lila Abu-Lughod describes how even today the Self/Other opposition is integral to anthropology:

> Anthropological discourse, with its roots in the exploration and colonization of the rest of the world by the West, is the discourse of the self. It defines itself primarily as the study of the other, which means that its

selfhood was not problematic. Some would even argue that the Western civilized self was constituted in part through this confrontation with and picturing of the savage or primitive other. Even when anthropology is in crisis, as many would argue it is today, and even when the focus of that crisis is precisely the self/other problem, as it is in reflexive anthropology and the new ethnography, the divide tends to remain unquestioned.[28]

One result of this ever present division between Historical Same—Western subjectivity—and Primitive Other is a speaking for and thus a silencing of the peoples depicted in ethnographic cinema, an assumption of voice made especially dangerous because of the perception that film is a window onto reality. In this setting, the critic may become the unwitting propagator of a new postcolonial form of fascinating cannibalism, a reification that further entrenches the categories of Same and Other, Western and Indigenous. I acknowledge the precariousness of my position. Against this danger, however, and in an attempt to negotiate new ways of thinking about the relationship between the camera and the peoples filmed in ethnographic cinema, I turn at various points in the text to reflections on how the people of color who performed and acted in these films experienced the process. The evidence suggests that many of them also saw with a "third eye." Although my efforts are tentative, I believe that approaching the images with this understanding produces a new way of looking at the images, one that can begin to bring the people who inhabit them out of their bondage of silence and into the present, one that acknowledges performance rather than empirically represented Primitives in timeless picturesques.

Regnault, Nanook of the North, King Kong: Science, Taxidermy, and the Monster

This book does not purport to offer a comprehensive survey of early film conventionally labeled ethnographic or, indeed, of the broader field I have labeled "ethnographic cinema." It is structured as a triptych, each part dedicated to a distinct modality in early ethnographic cinema: (1) the positivist mode of the scientific research film, represented here by the 1895 chronophotographie or time motion studies of Félix-Louis Regnault; (2) the taxidermic mode of the lyrical ethnographic film, represented here by Robert Flaherty's 1922 Nanook of the North; and (3) the postmodern mode of the commercial entertainment film, represented here by Merian Cooper and Ernest Schoedsack's 1933 King Kong.

I have chosen Regnault's work and Flaherty's *Nanook* because they have been described by historians of visual anthropology as two moments of origin of ethnographic film. Regnault's time motion studies or *chronophotographie* of West African performers in the Paris Ethnographic Exposition of 1895 represents the supposed moment of origin of a particular type of ethnographic film: the scientific research film. Regnault believed that by filming the movements—walking, running, climbing, jumping—of West Africans, and comparing them with films of the movements of Europeans, one could establish an evolutionary typology of the races. Human history could be read in locomotion. The peoples filmed were perceived as raw data, and the films were meant to be studied both in themselves and to aid comparative studies of the physiologies of different races, much the way the microscope was used by other scientists. As people pictured as "ethnographic," the West African performers who Regnault filmed were literally *written* into film as racialized bodies, transformed into a kind of racially signifying hieroglyph. Regnault also wrote about the need to establish an archive or museum of films and phonographic recordings of so-called vanishing peoples. Regnault's positivist legacy—his belief in film as a scientific instrument, an improved eye much like that of a microscope, and his promotion of the ethnographic film archive for anthropological research—was inherited by anthropologists such as Marcel Griaule, Franz Boas, Margaret Mead, Gregory Bateson, and even Alan Lomax, in his choreometric dance project of the 1970s.

I use Robert Flaherty's *Nanook of the North* as the paradigm of romantic, lyrical ethnography, the film of art, which hinges upon a nostalgic reconstruction of a more authentic humanity. In the second part of the triptych, I begin by describing travel films made before 1922, including Edward Sheriff Curtis's *In the Land of the Headhunters* (1914). I then offer an in-depth study of *Nanook of the North*. In 1922, the anthropologist Sir James G. Fraser observed that the ethnography of the younger Bronislaw Malinowski sees the native "in the round and not in the flat," praising his *The Argonauts of the Western Pacific* as "one of the completest and most scientific accounts ever given of a savage people."[29] Fraser's comment applies equally to Flaherty: if Regnault had portrayed natives in the flat, almost as ciphers, Flaherty portrayed natives in the round, in the mode of *taxidermy*. As Stephen Bann points out in his study of French and British historiography, the taxidermist uses artifice and reconstruction in order to make the dead look alive. Similarly, Flaherty himself emphasized that *Nanook* was made more authentic by the use of simulation: the Inuit actors were dressed in costume, the igloo was a set, etc. The "ethnographic" is reconstructed to appear real to the anticipated audience, and the fiction sustained is that film does not alter anything. This ideology undergirds the use of cinema in the salvage ethnography of "vanishing races." Later film theorists like André Bazin, Edgar Morin, and Luc de Heusch have exalted Flaherty as a poet who presented in *Nanook* not the reality of science, but the reality of "a higher truth," that of art. The strategies for encoding authenticity and the Primitive in *Nanook* inspired other kinds of documentary cinema, but *Nanook's* most immediate legacy is the scripted films of the period including Flaherty's *Moana: A Romance of the Golden Age* (1926), and F. W. Murnau and Flaherty's *Tabu: A Story of the South Seas* (1931), as well as later ethnographic film like Robert Gardner's *Dead Birds* (1962).

As Bann points out, the taxidermic specimen, created when the boundaries of the real are transgressed by repainting the dead as lifelike, is closely related to the monster, "the composite, incongruous beast which . . . simulated the seamless integrity of organic life."[30] The final part of my triptych includes a study of the "racial films" made before 1933, and culminates with a close analysis of *King Kong*. I have chosen to analyze *King Kong* for several reasons. *King Kong* is the ironic moment in ethnographic cinema. On first sight, the film appears to be a pure fantasy. As I hope to establish, however, this film is one more manifestation of fascinating cannibalism: it explicitly recalls the historical practice of exhibiting humans at ethnographic expositions, and partakes of many of the defining traits of the "racial film" genre which flourished in the wake of *Nanook of the North*. Unlike Regnault's chronophotography and *Nanook*, which are represented in the histories of ethnographic film as points of origin, *King Kong* is part of a long line of films representing the person of African, Asian, or Pacific Islander descent as an ape-monster. In its construction of the *ethnographiable* monster, *King Kong* draws on discourses which equate the native with the pathological, as well as on discourses—mainly nativist—on the fear of the hybrid as monster. *King Kong* summons a notion of time that feeds into ideologies of survival of the fittest, and of the indigenous body as the site of a collision between past and present, Ethnographic and Historical, Primitive and Modern. Cooper and Schoedsack had previously made films now considered "ethnographic" like *Grass* (1925), *Chang* (1927), and *Rango* (1931), but *King Kong* is a pastiche film about the making of an ethnographic film and hence offers a meta-commentary on "seeing anthropology," one which, I will argue, foreshadows the fear of the postcolonial Other as monster.

Regnault's *chronophotographie* of 1895, *Nanook of the North* (1922), and

King Kong (1933) may seem to reveal a developmentary sequence, especially since Regnault's films are really "proto-cinema," meant to be seen without projection, *Nanook* is a silent film, and *King Kong* is a sound film. Pierre Leprohon in his book *L'exotisme et cinéma* and André Bazin in his essay "The Cinema of Exploration" have already suggested that ethnographic cinema emerged in 1922 with *Nanook*, only to be replaced in the 1930s by pastiche exotic films like *King Kong*. Although I will try to show the development of each paradigm, I do not mean to suggest that they represent three modalities which evolved over time, one leading to the other. Rather, each work has been chosen for close analysis in order to shed light on three distinct themes of ethnographic cinema. Although the focus of this book will be the three bodies of work just described, a discussion of each film's relationship to other films, and its historical, political, cultural, and anthropological context, will inform the analysis. I could have chosen one paradigm and provided a survey of a subgenre within ethnographic film, but I wanted to show how "ethnographic film" moves across genres, how it is defined by an incessant movement between science and art, reality and fantasy. Although Regnault's films are intrascientific, meant to be studied by anthropologists, Regnault filmed people in popular ethnographic exhibitions which can accurately be described as human zoos; although faulted as a film which uses costumes and props, *Nanook* has been represented as an authentic ethnographic film about Inuit culture and is used in classes of cultural anthropology; and although *King Kong* is a film completely within the realm of popular culture, it was made by filmmakers whose previous works are considered ethnographic. I will thus attempt to show how these films explode the seemingly mutually exclusive boundaries of science, art, and entertainment.

The Third Eye

Sealed into that crushing objecthood, I turned beseechingly to others.
Their attention was a liberation, running over my body suddenly
abraded into nonbeing, endowing me once more with an agility that I
had thought lost, and by taking me out of the world, restoring me to it.
But just as I reached the other side, I stumbled, and the movements,
the attitudes, the glances of the other fixed me there, in the sense in
which a chemical solution is fixed by a dye. I was indignant; I de-
manded an explanation. Nothing happened. I burst apart. Now the
fragments have been put together again by another self.[31]
—Frantz Fanon, *Black Skin, White Masks* (1967)

With another eye I see how I am pictured as a landscape, a museum display, an ethnographic spectacle, an exotic. Across geographies and across histories, plunged in the darkness of watching *King Kong*, I wasn't the only one witnessing the encounter between the white Explorer and the islander Savage. In a film clamoring with the din of roaring monsters, screaming females, and howling Sumatran Islanders, there is one person who remains observantly silent. The Bride of Kong sits in her grass skirt staring mutely at the spectacle of the white filmmakers trying to talk to her people. I would like to imagine that with another eye she scrutinized this encounter between the Island Chief/Medicine Man and the white Filmmaker/Ship Captain, and read how they had made her into a spectacle. If only she had looked straight into the camera, and thus at me, a far-flung Sumatran. I wanted to cover the Bride of Kong, to unravel the weaving of this narrative, this screen—to pierce through the veil of the imagination of whiteness.

But the problem lies in hearing what the Bride was saying, and what all the other Brides, displayed for ethnographic spectacle, were saying: Saartje Baartmann, the Khoi-San woman, known as the Hottentot Venus, whose body in the 1700s was exhibited in London and Paris, only to end up dissected by the scientist Georges Cuvier who was fascinated by her genitalia; or the countless unnamed performers in nineteenth- and twentieth-century "native villages" in world's fairs and zoos who later died from flu or other illnesses—Minik Wallace, Ishi, Ota Benga.

How stories are told and whether to tell them is related to how history is told. Throughout the book I look at gaps and disturbances in the narrative of evolutionary imaging, particularly within the realm of performance, as manifested in such performance strategies as open resistance, recontextualization, parody, and even simple restraint. In addition, I draw upon the works of artists and writers like Lorna Simpson, Ousmane Sembène, Zacharias Kunuk, Elizabeth Alexander, Frantz Fanon, and James Baldwin, who implicitly and explicitly comment on and unveil the language of racialization in ethnographic cinema in complex ways. In my conclusion I return to the predicament described by Frantz Fanon of the viewer who, recognizing that he or she is racially aligned with the ethnographic Other yet unable to identify fully with the image, is left in uncomfortable suspension. I discuss early examples of ethnographic cinema that, although informed by or situated within the ethnographic context I have just described, incorporate elements of "third eye" perception: the ethnographic spectacle of Josephine Baker's filmed performances, and the films and work of Zora Neale Hurston. The boundaries blur as those with a third eye attempt to put together all the dispersed fragments of identity into other—never seamless—selves.

I INSCRIPTION

3. Charles Comte and Félix-Louis Regnault, "Negress walking with a light weight on her head" (1895). (Modern print from original glass plate chronophotographic negative, cat. no. Hn47, courtesy of the Collection of the Cinémathèque française)

anthropologists catalog as "savages"—instead of getting mere descriptions of their movements from written accounts, photography, and art.[3] You are convinced that these chronophotographic documents will elevate the new discipline of anthropology to the realm of science.

In the scenario just described, the divide between observer and observed appears clearly marked. The exchange of looks in the chronophotography produced by Regnault, however, belies any simple polarity of subject and object. There is, for example, a Frenchman, dressed in a city suit and hat, who accompanies the woman as she walks, never taking his eyes off her. His walk, meant to represent the urban walk, is there as comparative point of reference to what Regnault terms the woman's "savage locomotion."[4] In addition, he acts as an in-frame surrogate for the Western male gaze of the scientist. There are also two other performers visible at frame left, watching the Frenchman watch the woman. Finally, a little girl, also West African, stares alternately at the group being filmed and the scientist and his camera. She appears to break a cinematic code already established in fin-de-siècle time motion studies: she looks at the camera. In this scenario of comparative racial physiology, the little girl has not learned how properly to see or be seen. At the nexus of this exchange of looks is the Wolof woman. She, however, is not the agent of a look. Rendered nameless and faceless, it is her body which is deemed the most significant datum: she is doubly marginalized as both female and African.

This description of the chain of looks is taken from chronophotography by the physician Félix-Louis Regnault. I will refer to the chronophotography of Regnault as "film," even though they were not meant to be projected.[5] Invented by Etienne-Jules Marey in 1882, chronophotography was a form of proto-cinema which used cameras with oscillating shutters, so that precise intervals of movement could be distributed over one fixed plate. Although Regnault's images have been largely ignored by film historians, visual anthropologists eager to establish a lineage for their endeavors now claim Regnault's work as a precursor. Moreover, in the historiography of ethnographic film, Regnault is significant not only for his proto-cinema, but also for his body of theory on film as ethnographic tool.[6] His conception of ethnographic film as positivist record to be stored in archives and examined repeatedly, frame by frame, forms the basis for dominant conceptions of the anthropological research film.

There are two principal reasons why I wanted to show the chain of looks in this series of images. The first reason I begin with the idea of a chain of looks—or who's viewing who—is that I would like to begin to pose the question of what it means to *see* ethnographic film as performer, filmmaker, and audience. In *The Invention of Africa*, V. Y. Mudimbe describes a fundamental paradigm of the type of knowledge—his term is *gnosis*— determined and made possible by anthropological, colonial, and historical discourses on Africa as one which opposes tradition and modernity, a binary opposition also manifested as savagery versus civilization, and pathology versus normality. Mudimbe shows that the categories used to classify "natives" in the 1600s such as physical description, trade, arts, morals, customs, language, government, and religion continued to be used in the twentieth century: what changed was not the sophistication of the tools of knowledge but the system of values concerning otherness.[7] The fundamental paradigm opposing tradition and modernity remained. Thus explorers— and one should include in that category many anthropologists—do not reveal otherness, they comment upon "anthropology."

The second reason for the chain of looks is to underline the point that the West Africans and Malagasy filmed were performers, and not just bodies. These performers were people who returned gazes and who spoke, people who in many ways also were seeing anthropology. Of course, since we have no written record of the thoughts of these particular individuals, and of many of the other indigenous peoples who were made the object of written and filmic forms of ethnography, I agree with Gayatri Chakravorty Spivak that there is no simple way of recovering their subjectivity, of hearing them speak.[8] Yet, at the same time an exclusive focus which critiques the white anthropologist, writer, or artist all too often leaves in place the process by which indigenous people continue to be reified as specimens, metonyms for an entire culture, race, or monolithic condition known as "Primitiveness." The problem is compounded by the renewed reproduction of images which feed "fascinating cannibalism."[9] The chain of looks shows that more than one subjectivity surveyed the scene.

In order to show how the emergence of cinema is critically linked to the emergence of anthropology and its visualizing discourse of evolution, and equally importantly, to describe the historical conditions under which indigenous peoples increasingly confronted the image-hungry West, this chapter focuses on the historical and intellectual context in which Regnault worked. As I hope to show, the imbricated networks of science, spectacle, and seeing in popular culture, early anthropology and film brought into view by this examination underlie all of "ethnographic cinema." In chapter 2 I move from an analysis of the historical and intellectual context to a detailed visual analysis of Regnault's films themselves. I examine Regnault's conception of film as the ideal positivist scientific tool for recording movement. In Regnault's films, as in ethnographic film generally, the viewer is confronted with images of people who are not meant to be seen as individuals, but as specimens of race and culture, specimens which provide the viewer with a visualization of the evolutionary past. Like much of what is now termed early "ethnographic" cinema, Regnault's films appear to have no narrative. I contend, however, that there is a narrative implicit in these films, a narrative implicit, in fact, in all ethnographic film. The narrative is that of evolution. Although the Wolof woman and the Frenchman walk within the same space in the above example, they are made distant from each other both spatially and temporally by science and by popular culture.

History as Race: Anthropology/Medicine/Imperialism

Who was Félix-Louis Regnault? Not a founding father of French anthropology like Paul Broca, nor an inventing pioneer of cinema and physiology like his teacher Marey, nor a flamboyant social hygienist like the Turin criminal anthropologist Cesare Lombroso, Regnault would seem to deserve his obscurity. Yet he is precisely the sort of historical figure about whom people like to say that if he had not existed, he would have been invented. For Regnault was an astonishing figure: his films from 1895 and his huge output of writings reveal most of the nineteenth-century scientific obsessions that focused on the body. Using medicine, anthropology, prehistory, sociology, history, zoology, and psychology, Regnault wrote about the human body within an evolutionary conception of history. Although there is little evidence that Regnault continued to make time motion studies after 1895, he made extensive use of museums, collections of skulls, photography, and art, and he lobbied for the creation of museums of films of "ethnographic interest."[10]

Born in 1863, Regnault came from a bourgeois family from the provinces where his father was a professor of mathematics.[11] As an adolescent, Regnault began what was to become a lifetime passion for prehistory. Later in life, from 1928 to 1938, he was the president of the Société préhistorique française. He finished a medical degree in 1888, but up to the time of his death in 1938, he was better known as avid amateur prehistorian, anthropologist, teacher, active medical journalist, and editor, than as physician. He also wrote several books on such varied topics as hypnotism, religion, prostitution, decadence, and, of course, human locomotion.[12]

As early as 1893, Regnault studied with Marey at the Station physiologique at Boulogne, France.[13] The work of Marey, who invented chronophotography, and studied the movement of humans and animals, together with that of Eadweard Muybridge, who produced the first serial photography, is often considered to mark the beginning of cinema. Marey's films of humans focused on the movements of male European athletes, highlighting muscles and tendons, often in situations with strong homoerotic overtones; Muybridge filmed Euro-American men and women performing simple gender-specific movements.[14] Regnault on the other hand was interested in filming the movements of peoples from areas in Africa which were recently colonized: West Africa and Madagascar. His films, of which there are some seventy-five existing examples, can be divided into those recording the movements of West Africans and Malagasy performers from *expositions ethnographiques* and those recording the locomotion of French soldiers.

Regnault's interest in the body clearly stemmed from his fascination with anthropology, an emerging discipline of the nineteenth century, a discipline which took race as its defining problem.[15] Just as the nation-state, to use Benedict Anderson's phrasing, is an "imagined political community," race was not only the guiding construct of early evolutionist thinking, it formed the basis of an imagined biological community.[16] The desire to demarcate difference and the quest to describe pure racial types coincided with the rise of imperialism and nationalism: the discourses of race, nation, and imperialism were intimately linked.[17] Indeed, the concept of "nation" became common at around the same time as the concepts "race" and "volk," and these terms in the beginning of the century were fluidly intertwined: in the late eighteenth century, the word "race" appears in the work of natural historians but is used interchangeably with "nation" and "people."[18] The present-day breakdown of anthropology into physical anthropology and cultural anthropology (ethnography being the principal tool of the latter) did not emerge until the mid–twentieth century: in the nineteenth century, racial heredity was believed to determine culture.[19]

In France, the most important anthropological organization was the Société d'anthropologie de Paris, of which Regnault was a member. Founded in 1859 by the biologist Paul Broca in the same year that Darwin's *The Origin of Species* was published, the Société promoted a form of Lamarckian evolutionism called *transformisme*, which emphasized the importance of milieu or environment and the inheritance of acquired characteristics. Darwin's conception that evolution was arboreal, involving chance, was not readily accepted by late-nineteenth-century anthropologists, many of whom conceived of human history as a linear evolution. *Transformisme* became the French alternative to Darwin: it allowed for both a linear evolutionary history and sudden leaps in the form of spontaneous generation. It accommodated French positivist ideas concerning progress as a process guided by natural laws.[20]

A positivist zeal for the physical description, measurement, and classification of racially defined bodies was the driving force of anthropology at
the Société. Since it was thought that brain weight correlated with intelligence, and since it was often impossible to study the human brain itself,
craniology, the study of cranial measurements, came to be considered the
most important tool of racial studies.[21] One racial category seen as scientific was the capacity of a race to become civilized, its "degree of perfectibility." Broca wrote, "What varies above all is the degree of activity of intellectual functions, the predominance of this or that group of faculties, the
development of the social state and perfectibility, that is to say the aptitude
to conceive or receive progress."[22] As George W. Stocking Jr. writes, physical
human variety was interpreted "in regular rectilinear terms as the result of
differential progress up a ladder of cultural stages (savagery, barbarism, civilization) accompanied by a parallel transformation of particular cultural
forms (polytheism/monotheism; polygamy/monogamy."[23] The polygenist
doctrine of Société anthropology conceived of the races as being almost
species-like, revealing a fear of mixture and hybridity: Broca, for example,
believed that interracial children were likely to be sterile.[24] The impulse to
characterize most non-European groups as having all the features that the
West found undesirable and morally reprehensible was clearly one means of
creating a broad Western subjectivity that reached beyond the nation. Anthropologists took Primitive (Savage) society as their special subject, but, as
Adam Kuper explains,

> In practice primitive society proved to be their own society (as they
> understood it) seen in a distorting mirror. For them modern society was
> defined above all by the territorial state, the monogamous family and
> private property. Primitive society therefore must have been nomadic,
> ordered by blood ties, sexually promiscuous and communist. There had
> also been a progression in mentality. Primitive man was illogical and
> given to magic. In time he had developed more sophisticated religious
> ideas. Modern man, however, had invented science. Like their most
> reflective contemporaries, in short, the pioneer anthropologists be-
> lieved that their own was an age of massive transition. They looked
> back in order to understand the nature of the present, on the assump-
> tion that modern society had evolved from its antithesis.[25]

The Primitive was the "pathological" counterpoint to the European. For
example, sub-Saharan Africans and Australian Aborigines were classified as
"missing links" between man and the animal kingdom, and were described
as oversexed, intellectually inferior, and childlike.[26] L. J. B. Bérenger-Féraud,

the chief medical officer of Senegal, wrote that it appeared to be more natural for Wolof women to walk on all fours due to the angle of their pelvic bones and spine. He also believed that the big toes of Africans were large and more capable of independent movement, as did Regnault.[27] If one relates such ideas about the "animality" of West African movement to Regnault's chronophotography, one can begin to place Regnault's work in the context of a knowledge system whose paradigm was relentlessly comparative. In 1880, Société d'anthropologie de Paris member Charles Letourneau wrote, "In spite of its imperfections, its weaknesses and vices, the white race, semitic and indo-european holds, certainly for the present the head in the 'steeplechase' (sic) of human groups."[28]

The "steeplechase" is an important metaphor. *History was a race:* those who did not vanquish would vanish. It is significant, therefore, that Regnault would use film to record the movements of the performers he observed at the ethnographic exposition: film would inscribe race through the body (human difference) and would be evidence of history (which was also a race). Time was thus conceived in evolutionary terms, with race as the key factor, and the body as the marker of racial and thus temporal difference.

The question of why anthropology had such a voracious appetite for the Primitive body may be answered in part by looking at anthropological discourse in relation to the construction of the Social and/or National body. The 1890s was a period of great concern with modern urban change: theories of degeneration, a belief that the overstimulated modern urban citizen had become nervous and weakened, were prevalent. Max Nordau's *Degeneration* (1893), for example, was a popular treatise. City life, Nordau believed, led to degeneration and to the effeminization of "man," understood to mean white man.[29] Consistent with this theme, early chronophotographers took hysteria and neurasthenia as subjects, as Charcot's *Nouvelle iconographie de la Salpetrière* attests, and Regnault centered his researches on the "ethnographic" body, seeking in part to gain insights for use in ameliorating the condition of the urban French body.[30] The "ethnographic" Other was thus not just "savage" and pathological, but was also physically closer to the genuine and authentic in man.

After Paul Broca died in 1880, the applied anthropology of the prehistorian Gabriel de Mortillet came to dominate the Société d'anthropologie de Paris. Some anthropologists, including Regnault, began to apply their methods on internal "others," such as women, criminals, and prehistoric remains. Applied anthropology and racial politics were conjoined, as evidenced most blatantly by the criminal anthropology of Cesare Lombroso, who saw the criminal as a biological degenerate; the antisemitic Montpellier school of George Vacher de Lapouge that decried interbreeding as leading to degeneracy; and the studies of Gustave le Bon, who used cranial measurements to prove the inferiority of the masses and of women.[31] As suggested above, Regnault was fascinated with applied anthropology, and wrote over one hundred articles and a number of books on the prehistoric, the criminal, the pathological, and the "savage," including studies on decadence, how to improve the training of nurses, venereal disease and prostitution, and geniuses and strongmen. In later years he wrote extensively on the overrefinement of the *affiné* (the urban European), whom he juxtaposed with the *rustique* (a category comprised of those he called Savages, together with rural folk and the working class).[32]

Anthropology legitimized imperialism through its "scientific" findings that indigenous non-European peoples were inferior and at the bottom of the evolutionary ladder of history.[33] The link between anthropology and imperialism was strengthened by anthropology's voraciousness for data. Until 1926, with the founding of the Institut d'anthropologie under Marcel Mauss, anthropologists were not required to have actually gone to the field and "been there." These "armchair anthropologists" depended upon the reports of missionaries, travelers, and colonial physicians, as well as museum and learned societies' collections of skulls, maps, and photographs. Eager to acquire more standardized data in order to legitimize itself as a true science, the Société d'anthropologie de Paris published a manual to be used by colonial officers and travelers for measuring crania and reporting anthropological descriptions.[34]

In this Société manual, Broca made an analogy between the anthropological subject and the sick patient: "Just as the best description of a malady is that which rests on a series of observations taken singly and written by the bed of a sick man, so the best description of a race rests on a series of individual descriptions, written at the time of meeting, in the presence of a subject whom one is observing without any preconception to investigate one particular fact."[35]

The lens which anthropology focused on colonial subjects was thus profoundly medical and purported to be objective. The average member of the Société d'anthropologie de Paris after all was, like Regnault, a physician. The irony is that those seeking to explain the "normal" needed the pathological.[36] There was thus an intimate connection between the object of the physician's scrutiny—the pathological—and the object of the anthropologist's scrutiny—race.

The concept of "race" was never scientifically validated. Even though Regnault and other anthropologists energetically sought out the perfect index to measure and classify race, prominent anthropologists James Prichard and Paul Broca both admitted to the constructed nature of race, as did their predecessor, Count Buffon. After thousands of skulls had been measured and endless statistical analyses performed, no one could agree on what race was or how to measure it. If "race" could not be scientifically proven, however, the narrative of racial difference with its evolutionary premise proved ideologically powerful. The narrative was repeated and consumed in a deluge of late-nineteenth-century visual technologies displaying the body of the "Primitive," in the form of museum collections of skulls, dioramas with wax or plaster figures, photography, expositions, and film. Both anthropology, infused with the taxonomic imagination of natural history, and popular culture, as I will show later, incessantly visualized race. In this regard, Regnault is exemplary: he saw evidence of race and the pathological in all visual data relating to the body, including skulls, art, photography, popular fairs, and finally film.[37] The visual emphasis in Regnault's work is not fortuitous. As Johannes Fabian has argued convincingly, anthropology is premised upon naturalized and evolutionary time; moreover, anthropology has an inherent visualist bias, categorizing indigenous peoples by way of taxonomic tableaus.[38] This obsession with visualism, the "cultural, ideological bias toward vision as the 'noblest sense,'" is at the core of the modernist project.[39] Not only does modernity involve the extension of human powers of observation through the agency of technologies such as photography and film, but also, as Jonathan Crary has pointed out, it involves the collapse of classical models of vision. Reification in the form of "seeing anthropology," in other words, is not only an aspect of the colonizing gaze but is part of the primacy given to the optical in the twentieth century.[40] It is Regnault's obsession with the visual history of humankind to which I now turn my attention.

Regnault and the Body: The Search for Unmediated Description in Craniology, the Freak Show, Art, and Photography

The primary object of Regnault's beginning research was the physical anatomy of the body. At first, Regnault embraced craniology as the supremely objective method to understand the body. In his thesis of 1888 on cranial deformations in rickets patients, Regnault praised Broca's method of craniology for its mathematical exactitude: "How much more accurate is it to measure, to express in figures having an absolute value, a simple visual

4. Printed illustration in Félix-Louis Regnault's "De la fonction préhensile du pied." (*La nature* no. 1058, 9 September 1893)

impression, one will thus eliminate a factor which it is necessary above all to find a means to eliminate in science: 'the personal factor.' "[41]

Regnault's stance is thus that of *observateur*, but one whose vision is profoundly medical. Throughout his career Regnault wrote about idiots, microcephalics, hydrocephalics, and rickets patients, and he often brought patients to Société meetings to illustrate his findings on pathology.[42] Regnault even speculated in his writings that some groups of people afflicted with pathologies constituted separate races: he makes this suggestion in his research on lepers in France, and in his studies of polydactilism (those with extra fingers or toes) and teratology (the study of human "monsters").[43]

The non-European was also represented as pathological. Writing for medical journals as well as popular science journals such as *La nature*, Regnault wrote reams of articles and books throughout his life on race, anatomy, and environment. He saw race as immutable, and measured it in terms of physical anatomy, studying race as an empirical category of classification for both human and animal species as well as prehistoric creatures.[44] Many articles by Regnault concerned the physical characteristics of the "savage" and include discussions of scarification, weak color perception, "monkey-like" teeth, steatopygy or large buttocks, and "prehensile" feet.[45] A strong promoter of *milieu* or environment as an important influence on race, he claimed in one 1895 article that blacks were born light-skinned but become dark on contact with light, heat, and humidity.[46] Just as he had studied crania as well as living patients for his studies of pathological anatomy, Regnault also studied skulls of non-Europeans in his pursuit of race: in a visit to India in 1891, he stole nineteen skulls from a Bengali cemetery in the name of the science of anthropology and presented them to the Société.[47]

Significantly, in his report on his visit to India, Regnault described gatherings of Indian pilgrims as "real museums of the pathological where lepers, those with elephantiasis, microcephalics, and the deformed of all kinds happen to find themselves assembled together."[48] The world was thus seen as a visual array of pathology, race, and evolution—that is, as a museum. Regnault's metaphor of a museum of pathology was not fortuitous: at the turn of the century, major hospitals had their own museums of pathology, as evidenced by the Salpetrière hospital in which Charcot was both director and curator of its collections of aberrant human specimens. The fascination and search for what the French Marxist philosopher Etienne Balibar brilliantly terms "bodily stigmata" was indeed essential to the project of early anthropology. Balibar writes,

> Theories of academic racism mimic scientific discursivity by basing themselves upon visible "evidence" (whence the essential importance of the stigmata of race and in particular of bodily stigmata), or, more exactly, they mimic the way in which scientific discursivity articulates "visible facts" to "hidden causes" and thus connect up with a spontaneous process of theorization inherent in the racism of the masses. I shall therefore venture the idea that the racist complex inextricably combines a crucial function of *misrecognition* (without which the violence would not be tolerable to the very people engaging in it) and a "will to know," a violent *desire for* immediate *knowledge* of social relations.[49]

The desire to see "difference," and to establish iconographies for recognizing difference instantaneously, was thus a defining feature of early anthropological science.

The assumption that the Primitive and the Pathological were linked was also manifested in popular culture displays. Regnault's writings show that he made frequent forays into mass entertainments like fairs in his search for bodies to study. As a scientist, however, Regnault could be disappointed with the show. At one popular fair, Regnault quotes the barker's invitation to passersby to look at celebrated specimens of science: "These are not the vulgar phenomenons that one sees in fairs. Ours have been admired by scholars all over the world. They have been taken to laboratories in the great capitals; they have been measured from all angles and photographed." But what Regnault saw when he entered the tent was "in fact these primitives were nothing more than unfortunate degenerates, microcephalics."[50] In general, however, as discussed in detail later in this chapter, Regnault was an enthusiastic fair and exposition visitor.

Regnault also conducted research in physiology and was especially interested in comparative racial locomotion studies. He turned to art, found in museums and other collections, for empirical data concerning the body. Art history, anthropology, and medicine intersected in a unique way in the work of Regnault and his older colleagues Paul Richer and Jean-Martin Charcot. All three doctors used art as historical evidence of medical pathologies, and practiced photography and chronophotography in their researches. Richer, for example, used his work on anatomy and photography to write manuals for artists. Both Charcot and Richer wrote about deformities in art, as did Regnault.[51] What is curious about Regnault's studies is his insistence on the indexical nature of art. According to Regnault, artists may exaggerate, but they always represent the body that they see. Therefore art, especially Indian, Greek, Japanese, Egyptian, and Italian sculpture, may be used as evidence that certain pathologies—such as cranial deformations, rickets, and even hysteria—existed in the past.[52]

Besides using works of art as documents for the historical study of pathology, Regnault used art as evidence of evolutionary mental development.[53] Indeed, Regnault's interest in art as record of body posture (in turn reflecting differences in class, race, and gender) is essential to comprehending his use of film.[54] His evolutionary scheme for the history of body posture, which he would later call anthropographie or physiologie ethniques comparées, traced mankind from the Savage who crouches and kneels, to the Civilized who sits in chairs.[55] Each race, he wrote, has a predominant and characteristic posture.[56] Regnault produced an evolutionary hypothesis to explain different modes of walking, running, and carrying loads, one he would later test in his chronophotography.[57]

Regnault also consulted photographs to study body posture and gesture. In Great Britain, the police began to use photographs for criminal identification as early as the 1840s; anthropologists like Cesare Lombroso used photography for their studies of prostitutes.[58] Photography was used in both anthropological and geographical learned societies, especially in constructing racial types, photographed in left and right profile and head-on. Many

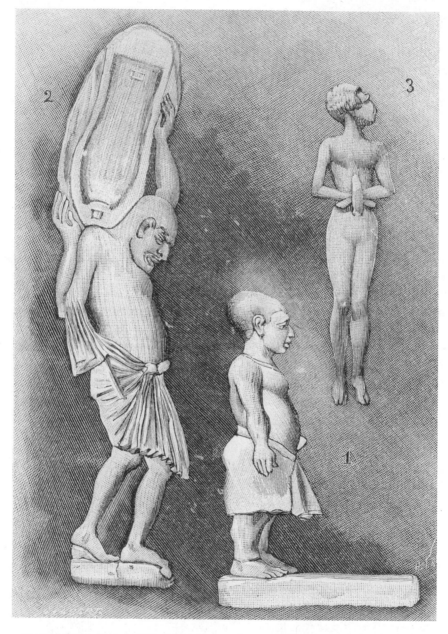

5. Printed illustration in Félix-Louis Regnault's "Les déformations crâniennes dans l'art antique." (*La nature* no. 1105, 4 August 1894)

attempts were made in the 1860s and 1870s to use photography anthropo-metrically: hence the grids and rulers one often sees in these kinds of pho-tographs.[59] Regnault certainly consulted photographs for evidence of the body, but he found that there was one essential ingredient missing, and that was movement. In one telling statement, Regnault wrote that a cadaver could not show unconscious movement:

> Surely it is true that the artistic anatomy, the dissection of the ca-daver, is not a sufficient reproduction, since it is necessary to see again the tendons and the muscles, flaccid when studied under the scalpel, flexing and releasing through action; not through an action that is by chance, or artificial, or studied, as in a model in a studio, but through an unconscious action, done by habit by a worker of a profession.[60]

The surgical eye could dissect the corpse but could not understand how the body had moved through space. Regnault's interest in film derived from his search for a medium which could capture movement. In searching for an index for race—the unfashioned clue—Regnault privileged movement, be-cause it is "in between" culture and nature, acting and being; movement is physical and objective, yet variable.

The medical eye of Regnault was forever searching for and diagnosing evidence in an attempt to establish the boundaries between truth and fraud, reality and fantasy.[61] For Regnault every referent had a meaning, every body its diagnosis. Carlo Ginzburg has explained that the disciplines in-volved in conjecturing about historical development—including anthropol-ogy with its desire to conjure up a history of mankind by making the Primi-tive the precursor to Civilized man—were intimately linked with a tight state power determined to find identity in physical traits which could not be manipulated by saboteurs.[62] Thus Ginzburg compares the invention of the fingerprint as a mechanism for criminal identification, one superior to that of the written signature, to the technique developed by Morelli, the well-known art connoisseur, of using the painted ear to distinguish the authentic work of the masters from works by their students or lesser art-ists.[63] Similarly, anthropology grew as the science of *reading* the human body. What distinguished anthropology from the other historical disci-plines, however, was that it included the study of people said to be without writing, without signature. The anthropologist was the seated observer of people who crouched. The unfashioned clue, the index for measuring race, was, in Regnault's eyes, movement and posture, the supreme and uncon-scious indicator of evolutionary development.

Spectacular Anthropology: The Ethnographic Exposition
and Popular Representations of Race

The public ends up ignoring written accounts of purely intuitive doc-
trines, they prefer studies which are well documented, even if these
studies do not end with a precise conclusion.—Félix-Louis Regnault,
L'évolution de la prostitution (1907)

In his search for ways to capture movement it is not surprising that Regnault, like other anthropologists, frequented popular entertainments such
as fairs, museums, and zoos where native peoples performed at the turn of
the century. These popular entertainments were not only sites of spectacle
but laboratories for anthropological investigation. In 1895 Regnault wrote
an ecstatic account of what he saw at the Exposition Ethnographique de
l'Afrique Occidentale located at the Champs de Mars, Paris:

> I am aware that I could not observe everything. A thousand details, a
> thousand particularities would require a volume.
>
> Yes, this is the true ethnographic exposition. No one has adorned
> savages with ridiculous costumes, and no one has taught them a role in
> advance. These negros live as they do in their country, and their cus-
> toms are faithfully respected, easy to see.
>
> May this exposition serve as a model for future expositions![64]

"A thousand details," Regnault exclaimed. And, indeed, the expositions
were full of details: at the 1895 exposition great lengths were made to re-
create the imagined environment of Senegal and the Sudan. There were 350
African performers living on a set made to look like a Sudanese village with
thick walls, dirt walled houses, and straw huts. People worked as tanners,
weavers, potters, and pipemakers; others were musicians; and families sitting in front of their houses cooked in the open air.[65] Events like religious
ritual performances, sheep sacrifices, and a human birth and a marriage
were advertised in the newspapers.[66]

A *horror vacui* was revealed at the exposition: every space was crammed
with costume, animals, vegetation, and architecture. At the same time that
the exposition was a site of excess, it was also a place of spectacle where
detail was ordered, classified, and rationalized. The ethnographic exposition framed the reading of race in what was above all a reconstruction: the
different ethnic groups at the fair were architecturally divided in an encyclopedic fashion, and there was a tendency to group the "villagers" in
nuclear family units, Noah's Ark–style.[67]

The "native village" was one of the many visual technologies—including

6. Printed illustration in Félix-Louis Regnault's "Exposition Ethnographique de l'Afrique Occidentale au Champs-de-Mars à Paris: Sénégal et Soudan français." (*La nature* 1159, 17 August 1895)

the natural history museum, the *carte de visite*, the colonial postcard, and even the zoo—that exhibited humans, reaffirming the reality of the Savage, even as it reassured the public that Western science had the Savage under control. According to Paul Greenhalgh, the genre of the French "native village" was invented by the anthropological community in the 1870s at the Jardin d'acclimation as a means of studying "ethnographic" bodies. The Exposition Universelle merely took the genre to a much larger scale.[68] In that positivist age, it was felt that bodies could teach the masses about empire, science, technology, and nation, as well as about family and racial hierarchies. It was no coincidence that the most popular of all the "native villages" in the 1880s and 1890s, the period of great imperial French expansion in Senegambia, western Sudan, and the west coast of Africa south from Senegal to Gabon, were the reconstructed villages of the Dahomeyans and Senegalese.[69] Part human zoo, part performance circus, part laboratory for physical anthropology, ethnographic expositions were meaning machines which helped define what it meant to be French as well as what it meant to be West African in the late nineteenth century.[70]

The word "ethnography" was first used in the 1820s in conjunction with geography and denoted the study of peoples and their relation to the environment, thus embodying the idea that one could map human groups just as one maps mountains and rivers.[71] Another early use of the word "ethnographic" was made by Edmé-François Jomard, the librarian of the Bibliothèque royale, who conceived the idea of an ethnographic museum. To Jomard, ethnography meant the collection of artifacts of "savage" peoples which would explain the history of race.[72] By the late nineteenth century, the word "ethnographic" had taken on the connotation of "exotic" and "picturesque." In art, the "ethnographic" manifested itself in a genre called "la peinture ethnographique," which referred to painting which was so detailed that it seemed close to science in its observation of "exotic" customs. Jean-Léon Gérôme, with his use of photographic-like detail—exemplified in his slave market and snake charmer scenes—was a master of this genre.[73] That Regnault should seize on the superabundant detail of the ethnographic exposition as its most salient feature is thus no accident. In both science and art, the "ethnographic" evoked the image of an encyclopedic *tableau vivant* depicting the life of indigenous peoples.

Ethnographic detail coalesced in the popular spectacle of the exposition. Detail is meant here in three senses. The first is detail as document: Regnault used the "detail" of the exposition as fodder for his scientific research. The second sense is detail as ornament. A good example of this use is evident in Adolf Loos's "Ornament as Crime": exotic, ornamental detail was aligned with decadence, femininity, the criminal element, and the Savage.[74] The third sense is detail as index: the anatomical and physiological details on which the visitor's eyes were trained were keyed to a classificatory index of race.

The "native village" or ethnographic exposition was popular in North American and European cosmopolitan cities other than Paris, but the Parisian expositions were especially praised for their emphasis on the display of ethnic groups in their purported habitats. As Paul Greenhalgh has explained, the encyclopedic dimensions of the fair encompassed geography and ethnography. At the Exposition Universelle of 1878, the fair in which the Palais de Trocadéro was built, there was a "rue des nations" along which all participating nations built representative architectural structures. There was an Algerian village and bazaar, a "rue de Caire," as well as an exhibit of French ethnic history.[75] The "rue de Caire," it should be noted, became an infamous prostitution venue, revealing that the labor of women of color featured at the fair entailed more than satisfying the scopic gratification of visitors to the "native village."[76] At the world's fair, people from all corners of the world lived and performed in reconstructed habitats. The "native village," however, was unique in that the focus was on the exotic and bizarre. Indeed, the impresarios who managed the "villages" were even known as *barnums*, a term which reveals the circus-like exploitation which the performers had to endure.

In his review of the 1895 ethnographic exposition, Regnault begins by painstakingly describing the different physical and cultural details of the various ethnic groups at the fair. At points he likens some of them to bronze statues, not surprising since he had previously analyzed race through art. Immediately following this lengthy description of ethnic differences, however, Regnault again invokes the idea of race: he calls all the performers "nègres." Difference is articulated, only to be erased by use of the flattening label "nègre." Just as he had claimed in an earlier review of an ethnographic fair that colonialism would be a benevolent force for the Dahomey because "the brain of the Negro is a wax upon which nothing is written," Regnault claimed that the performers in the 1895 fair were akin to big children.[77]

The way in which Regnault distances himself from the performers when he invokes the anthropological rhetoric of race indicates an extraordinary form of "us versus them" mentality. This mentality was reinforced at the exposition in the form of voyeurism, and sanctioned simultaneously by scientific knowledge, by the evolutionary paradigm of history, and by the imperialist imperative to civilize. The visitor was in a sense invited to act as a scientist and colonist, to acquire knowledge by looking at the body and its habitat. He was also invited to engage in sexual voyeurism: the exhibition was the site for what should ordinarily go unseen. Regnault, for example, described the Dahomeyan women at the 1893 exposition as seductive: "In their youth, they are sometimes seductive with their soft, timid, and laughing physiognomy."[78] Africa and other colonized lands were often portrayed as Woman in imperialist discourse, and, in his comment, Regnault unself-consciously betrays the links between eroticism, imperialism, and anthropology.[79]

If the boundary between science and popular culture was permeable at the fair, so too was the boundary between the observer and the observed, visitor and exposition performer. On the one hand, a railing separated the performers from the visitors, and this railing probably went around the "villages," allowing the crowds to gather for special performances. However, the exposition layout also included a mosque (where all Muslims, but only Muslims, could enter) and a brasserie (where visitors could mix freely with performers).[80] At these locations, the boundaries were permeable and interaction was allowed. The voyeurism of the exposition was thus imperfect: spectators could be made aware that the performers had eyes and voices too, and performers were made aware of the spectacle of the visitors ogling.

In his review of the 1895 exhibition, Regnault reveals that there was another form of interaction at the fair: spectators threw money to the performers. This was a common practice at the "native villages," and performers were known to demand such payment. Although some reports show that the performers were paid before the show, one assumes that the wages fell short of the performers' needs. But the very fact that the performers demanded money would seem to destroy the illusion of distance.[81] A revealing tension is revealed in Regnault's description of the "villagers":

> In the village animation and gaiety reigns. Everywhere the Negro character, the good child, is evident all over. He'll come shake your hand, make friends with you, and ask for some change with a laughing tone as if it's a natural thing. Only the marabout conserves a fierce and reserved disposition. One sees him surrounded by children whom he has recite verses of the Qur'an printed on large boards.[82]

Regnault predictably reads the laugh of the villager as evidence of the childlike "Negro character." But is it not possible that the laugh marked out a space of ironic resistance? Performance at the fair was not a simply visual objectification by a flattening male gaze. Performance also invites a composing of self for spectacle, a frank gaze returned, a mocking laugh, or a haughtiness such as in the case of the marabout who refused to return the visitors' curious looks.

A rare example of a recorded verbal interaction is found in a review of the 1893 Dahomeyan Ethnographic Exposition in which Regnault recalled asking a performer why there were different shades of skin color among the Dahomeyans. The answer he received was a question: "Why . . . are some of you brunettes, others blond, still others redheads?"[83] The answer Regnault received is like a reflection in a mirror, revealing that the purported objects of study—the Dahomeyan performers—were also observers of the French. Indeed, the idea that the French visitors might be a spectacle for the performers is commented on in an account which appeared in the journal *L'illustration*:

> A phrase that practically all know, men, women, and children, is "Give me some change!" The little ones, so funny with their shaved heads

that resemble bronze objects, suck happily on sticks of barley sugar that some ladies present to them. But what impression on their ignorant souls is produced of the curiosity of which they are the object? Does the spectacle of ourselves that we offer them amuse them just as we are amused by what they offer us? Perhaps they are delighted to be present for free at an exposition of Parisians.[84]

Visitors to the fair were meant to "see anthropology," but what they were seeing was not often comfortable: the gaze returned. Perhaps with a third eye, the performers at the fair were aware of being viewed as objects of ethnographic spectacle, and resisted this status by subverting the illusion of scientific voyeurism. The demand for money, rather than being "a natural thing," threatens to turn purportedly authentic daily activity into staged performance. The pointed mirroring back of a question at the brasserie threatens to upset the schema in which assertions of racially determined native ignorance led naturally to justifications of French colonial power.

The interactions available at the brasserie and the performers' practice of soliciting money suggest what I believe is a more general theme: part of the fascination that the public had for the fair was the play with boundaries that it facilitated. First, even as the exposition strived to construct and address clear subjectivities, and even as the "picturesque," the "ethnographic," and the "detail" reigned in the arena of spectacle, there were marginal spaces at the fair where one could "straddle the fence": the viewed could also remark upon the French body, there were places where the "specimens" could not be viewed at all (the mosques), and the very act of voyeurism was undermined by the constant haranguing by the performers for "un sou."[85] Second, since constructions of the Ethnographic or Savage embodied all that was taboo to Western society—nakedness, polygamy, fetishism, and cannibalism—white visitors could view at the fair all that was forbidden, flirting with the boundaries of the "historical" Self and the "ethnographic" Other while at the same time maintaining a distance. The fence at the fair provided physical reassurance; the structuring of racial visualization ensured cultural distance.

The narrative of evolution which slots humans in a hierarchy of color-coded categories and places the white race at the apex was scientifically illustrated through the live, dead, and skeletal bodies of indigenous non-Europeans displayed at fairs and museums. History is obfuscated in these displays: the native is shown as being without history, and is described in terms borrowed from zoology. The history of the circulation of African bodies as enslaved persons—and the histories of the entwinement of French and West African politics and economics—is erased, replaced by another form of circulation, that of anthropological spectacle.

Yet the fairs also manifested fear of degeneration, fear that the white man had reached the pinnacle and had nowhere to go but down. The native was perceived by science and by popular culture as authentic man, closer to nature. As I explain in the next chapter, Regnault made his films of West Africans, who were seen as hardier and more agile, not only to confirm notions of Western superiority, but in an effort to improve the French military march. The Ethnographic was both biological threat and example of authentic humanity: both aspects would be essential to cinema's form of visualizing anthropology.[86]

The remark made by the French journalist that the Parisian visitors might also be a source of entertainment for the African performers reveals the uneasy self-consciousness that resulted when the colonist found him- or herself the object of spectacle, an experience brilliantly illustrated by George Orwell in his essay "Shooting an Elephant." The narrator, a British colonial officer in Burma, is asked to shoot a ravaging elephant who has killed a coolie, an act he performs reluctantly and maladroitly under the gaze of a "sea of yellow faces." His reflections perfectly describe the politics of colonial performance:

> Here was I, the white man with his gun, standing in front of the un-armed native crowd—seemingly the leading actor of the piece; but in reality I was only an absurd puppet pushed to and fro by the will of those yellow faces behind. I perceived in this moment that when the white man turns tyrant it is his own freedom that he destroys. He becomes a sort of hollow, posing dummy, the conventionalized figure of a sahib. For it is the condition of his rule that he shall spend his life in trying to impress the "natives," and so in every crisis he has got to do what the "natives" expect of him. He wears a mask, and his face grows to fit it. I had got to shoot the elephant. . . . To come all that way, rifle in hand, with two thousand people marching at my heels, and then to trail feebly away, having done nothing—no, that was impossible. The crowd would laugh at me. And my whole life, every white man's life in the East, was one long struggle not to be laughed at.[87]

Orwell ends his essay by describing the many discussions centered around the shooting of the elephant. Among the Europeans, "the younger men said it was a damn shame to shoot an elephant for killing a coolie, because an elephant was worth more than any damn Coringhee coolie." The narrator reflects, "I often wondered whether any of the others grasped that I had done it solely to avoid looking a fool."[88]

It is the returned gaze of the colonized Native and the possibility of ridicule which so rattles the British officer. Likewise, the ethnographic spectacle of the fair mandated a circle of looks. The visitor to the exhibition, in his act of studiously looking, was also composing himself into a seemingly predestined "mask" or "conventionalized figure," into a colonial tableau, into the *flâneur* at the fair.

Cinema offers a potent way of vicariously circumscribing the threat of the return gaze. When the exhibiting of "native villages" was discontinued due to prohibitive cost, world wars, and the end of imperialism, cinema took over many of its ideological functions. Cinema, after all, is a much less expensive way of circulating non-Western bodies "in situ" than is circulating reconstructed "villages." Early cinema showed a fascination for the subject of indigenous, non-European peoples in its proliferation of travelogues, scientific research films, safari films, scripted narrative films, and colonial propaganda films. Like ethnography, cinema is also a topos for the meeting of science and fantasy. Cinema, however, eliminated the potentially threatening return look of the performer present in the exposition, thus offering more perfect scientific voyeurism. Films about the "customs and manners of the peoples of X" emphasized the family unit and habitat, as the fair did. The fence of the fair was now the movie screen, and the subject positioning of the European viewer was reaffirmed. Finally, cultures were presented as encapsulated "villages" on film, making ethnographic film, like the ethnographic fair, a superb time machine, inviting the viewer to travel spatially and temporally, back in evolutionary time to the "childhood" of modern white man, constructing the native body as hieroglyphs of a language of gesture or as frozen ethnographic tableaus.[89]

pology, a legacy that continues to inform prevalent assumptions about the evidentiary value of ethnographic film.

Regnault's Views on Anthropological Research Film

Walter Benjamin suggests that film is comparable to surgery, the instrument allowing the operator to penetrate the body of the subject while, paradoxically, maintaining his or her distance. Benjamin compared the filmmaker with the surgeon, and the painter with the magician: "Magician and surgeon compare to painter and cameraman. The painter maintains in his work a natural distance from reality, the cameraman penetrates deeply into its web."[3]

The anthropologist who looks to the camera as a superior recording device is proof of the appropriateness of Benjamin's association of filmmaker and surgeon: he or she delights in film's penetration of the human body and its dissection of human movement. This association, moreover, resonates with the themes discussed in the preceding chapter: anthropologists of Regnault's generation and beyond observed the indigenous person as a patient, often as pathological and near death (if not already dead). Anthropology was a science strewn with corpses, one obsessed with origins, death, and degeneration. It was a science in which scientists even dissected themselves: the Société d'autopsie mutuelle, part of the Société d'anthropologie de Paris, consisted of anthropologists who agreed to dissect each other after death.[4] No body was immune from the surgical gaze of science in the age of anthropometry.

The distance maintained by both cameraman and surgeon, alluded to by Benjamin, was reflected in Regnault's conception of the advantages of film technology. Regnault valued film because it enabled researchers to observe those he called "savages" without having to leave their laboratories. As such, Regnault was convinced that film was destined to become the ideal positivist, scientific medium for the study of race. If the fair was the site for regimenting proliferating ethnographic detail, film was the site where ethnographic detail could be recorded, magnified, dissected, and replayed for posterity. Regnault declared, "Cinema expands our vision in time as the microscope has expanded it in space. It permits us to see facts which escape our senses because they pass too quickly. It will become the instrument of the physiologist as the microscope has become that of the anatomist. Its importance is as great."[5]

For Regnault, film offered not only an improved means of getting to an index—he thought that the races reveal themselves in movement, and felt that film could assist him in the study of movement—but a medium which was also by its nature indexical: like a footprint, film is a document, testifying that the person filmed had passed in front of the camera lens. To quote Roland Barthes, film contains "an emanation of the referent."[6] Regnault proclaimed cinema the ultimate apparatus for positivist science:

> *It provides exact and permanent documents to those who study movements.* The film of a movement is better for research than the simple viewing of movement; it is superior, even if the movement is slow. Film decomposes movement in a series of images that one can examine at leisure while slowing the movement at will, while stopping it as necessary. Thus it eliminates the personal factor, whereas a movement, once it is finished, cannot be recalled except by memory, and this, even put in sequence, is not faithful. All in all, a film is superior to the best descriptions.[7]

It is astonishing how similar this description of film is to Regnault's 1888 description of craniology which I discussed in the first chapter. Both technologies are precise and scientific, and eliminate subjective factors. But film is superior even to craniology: it captures movement.[8] Regnault described two distinct kinds of cinema, the first being the *cinématographe*—the cinema of science—and the second the *cinématoscope*—the cinema of entertainment.[9] That scientific cinema involves *graphie* (writing and description) is significant: like Marey's early medical engineering inventions the sphygmograph and the kymograph, the chronophotograph was used to record and inscribe movement for the new science of physiology. Marey scholar Marta Braun explains the heralding of inscription devices by physiologists:

> The earliest attempts to construct machines that would convert motion into graphs and numbers were synonymous with attempts to forge a new science: physiology. It began in Germany where a group of young scientists, including Helmholtz, Ludwig, and Du Bois Reymond, set out at mid-century to create a kind of organic physics, a new physiology based on quantitative and experimental analyses. In their theoretical framework, organic functions were reducible to physics and chemistry, and as physics and chemistry they could be transformed into visual and mathematical data. Such a transformation required that a mechanical apparatus be substituted for the senses of the observer.[10]

Moreover, as demonstrated by the passage from Regnault quoted above, in which he emphasized the "decomposition" of movement made possible by the camera, Regnault believed that film's scientific nature also lay in its ability to capture rapid movements which the eye cannot see, like the beating of a bird's wing. The power of the anthropologist lies in his or her ability to thwart death and time: he or she can record vanishing ways of life and store them in his drawer until such time as he needs to study them. If history is a race, and if race reveals history, then the anthropologist can use film to control time:

> Only cinema provides objective documents in abundance; thanks to cinema, the anthropologist can, today, collect the life of all peoples; he will possess in his drawers all the special acts of different races. He will be able to thus have contact at the same time with a great number of peoples. He will study, when it pleases him, the series of movements that man executes for squatting, climbing trees, seizing and handling objects with his feet, etc. He will be present at fests, at battles, at religious and civil ceremonies, at different ways of trading, eating, relaxing.[11]

To Regnault, film was better than the referent.

Regnault was thus one of the first to envision an ever growing archive of ethnographic images: cinema would provide unmediated records of as much of the world as possible for present and future scientific consumption. Regnault's model for the archive, however, was not the all-encompassing, alphabetically organized encyclopedia, but the topically organized museum.[12] Like the ethnographic exhibition which presented peoples in orderly reconstructed village tableaus, Regnault conceived the ethnographic film archive as a visualizing technology for the taxonomic ranking of peoples.

Le langage par gestes: *Regnault's Chronophotography at the 1895 Exposition*

All savage peoples make recourse to gesture to express themselves; their language is so poor it does not suffice to make them understood.
—Félix-Louis Regnault, *"Le langage par gestes"* (1898)[13]

In 1895 Regnault, with his colleague Charles Comte, filmed West African and Malagasy men, women, and children from ethnographic expositions, usually alone and in profile, walking, running, jumping, pounding grain, cooking, carrying children on their backs, and climbing trees. The tableau of the fair and Regnault's own fascination with movement are inscribed into film, representing the kinds of scenes which would become a staple in later ethnographic film.

In Regnault's films, bodies are made abstract and mechanized. No detail, declared Regnault, is overlooked by film.[14] Yet detail must be ordered and rationalized, and the sense that one gets is of meticulous management of detail: performers enter the frame at right and exit at left, often with a chronometer in front and a white screen in the back. The fact that Regnault filmed movements from different perspectives—the subject is seen from the right, then left, and then back—reflects the codes of anthropometric photography that were already well established in the late nineteenth century. For films of walking and running, Regnault and his colleague Charles Comte often used a chronometer and a painted scale on the ground to measure the duration of the subject's step. Diagrams translating the movements into oscillating curves were used to test the efficacy of the *marche en flexion*, a gait in which the subject ran or walked with knees sharply bent, the body leaning forward in "la marche primitive de l'humanité."[15] The use of the chronometer, the painted scale at the bottom of the film, and the tightly controlled entrance and exit of each moving subject attests to Regnault's belief that chronophotography was a mathematical and scientific means of studying movement. The camera maintains a distance, and yet observes from all angles.

In his review of the ethnographic exposition, Regnault had revealed a fascination for all movements which involve interactions with objects, such as grain-pounding, child-carrying, tree-climbing, and dancing; these movements allowed Regnault to draw conclusions about those he classified as "savage." Even within the frames of single film sequences Regnault's interest in the comparative study of movement is often betrayed. For example, men of different ethnic groups are shown squatting for a comparative study—"Three Negros squat: a Wolof, a Peul, a Diola." Similarly, how the subject walked and moved in clothing clearly was of interest to the anthropologist: Regnault filmed Tijaan men dressed in *grand boubou*–style praying—"the salam"—as well as walking.[16]

Regnault wrote in detail about the West African technique for climbing trees, a form of climbing which interestingly was foregrounded in many later ethnographic films.[17] Like squatting, this manner of climbing was seen as monkey-like and deemed characteristic of those Regnault called Savage. In one sequence, a man, described by Regnault as "a Negro of the country of Rivières," is shown climbing from various points of view, without a chronometer or screen in the background.[18] Another film strip shows a white man climbing a tree as if attempting to climb in the West African way: we see him mugging for the camera as if to underline the ludicrous nature of a French man climbing as a West African does.[19]

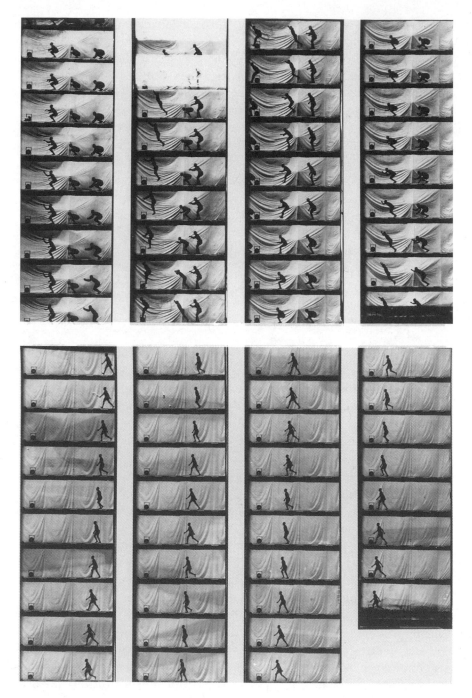

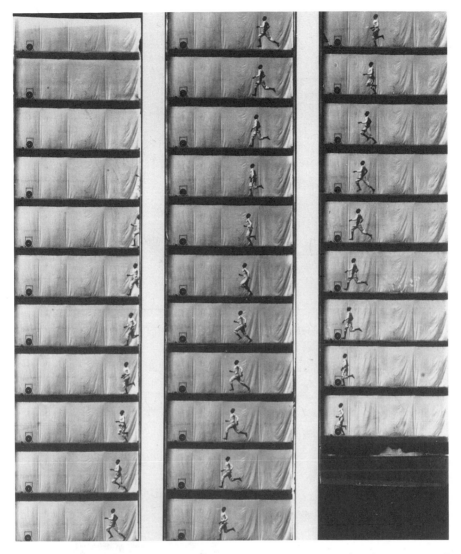

7. (*left top*) Charles Comte and Félix-Louis Regnault, "Jump by three Negroes" (1895). (Modern print from original glass plate chronophotographic negative, cat. no. Hn33, courtesy of the Collection of the Cinémathèque française) 8. (*bottom*) Charles Comte and Félix-Louis Regnault, "Walk" (1895). (Modern print from original glass plate chronophotographic negative, cat. no. Hn2, courtesy of the Collection of the Cinémathèque française) 9. (*above*) Charles Comte and Félix-Louis Regnault, "Run" (1895). (Modern print from original glass plate chronophotographic negative, cat. no. Hn21, courtesy of the Collection of the Cinémathèque française)

In Regnault's films, women are shown almost exclusively carrying loads or performing tasks at the fair. Indeed Regnault's first article on chronophotography is one concerning a film he made with Charles Comte of a Wolof woman making a pot at the Exposition Ethnographique in 1895. Filming the movements of a West African performing a task—such as making pottery— allowed the scientist, according to Regnault, to trace the evolutionary origin of pottery.[20] The trope of the woman pounding grain, and engaging in other "subsistence activities" (implicitly in opposition to the industrial activities of the West), would remain an essential part of ethnographic cinema.[21] Like the men and boys in Regnault's locomotion studies, the women do not usually look at the camera. Unlike the men, the women are always in full dress and are usually carrying babies on their backs or containers on their heads: woman is coded as nurturer, as mother, as sturdy laborer.[22] In one intriguing example that suggests the West African performers were directed to act in the films, we see a young woman looking directly at us, but then, after several frames, she looks down as if directed from someone off-screen not to look directly at the camera. In a sequence which presents her other profile, she never looks up at the camera, seemingly cowed.[23] In another film strip, a smiling woman is shown grinding grain, her hands clapping. She appears to be laughing: is her hilarity a reflection of her perception of the ridiculousness of the cameraman's attentions? a mask for feelings of anxiety? or a product of sheer joy? In the context of early anthropology, in which it is the actual motion that she performs and not her emotions or opinions which are considered, these questions remain unasked, unanswered. But the woman's laugh represents a possible site of subversion: she looks away but is not cowed, her laugh is strong. In the chronophotography of children, movement was less regulated: laughing, scampering children run in front of the camera helter-skelter, often curiously and brazenly returning the camera's gaze. Perhaps for this reason Regnault never reproduced stills from these sequences for his articles on ethnographic film.

In most of the films of West Africans, however, and in all of the ones which Regnault reproduced in articles, the bodies are rendered as *shadows*. Wearing tight long johns, French bathing shorts, Peul-type *pantalon bouffon* or just *ngebu* (shorts), these men do not look up and acknowledge the presence of the camera: they are often filmed in such a way that they are turned into ciphers, their faces indistinct. Although the performers walk in the foreground, they often appear to be behind a screen, like shadow puppets. If we compare these films of West Africans to one of a French man running, we see that the costume and mise-en-scène are different: the French

12. Charles Comte and Félix-Louis Regnault, "Negress walks" (1895). (Modern print from original glass plate chronophotographic negative, cat. no. Hn24, courtesy of the Collection of the Cinémathèque française)

subject is dressed in a suit and beret, and is shown running with large steps; his clothes, body, and face are clearly defined. His costume is more substantially rendered, and there is less of an emphasis on bare flesh or muscle tone.[24]

Racial identity is also signified by who gazes at whom. Performers do not look at the camera, but the gaze of the scientist is often acknowledged, if sometimes inadvertently. In two examples, a tall African man in French bathing shorts walks from right to left, but his body is so dark (probably due

13. Photographic reproduction, "Malagasy carrying a palanquin on their shoulders" (1895). The man seated in the palanquin is Regnault. (From "Le rôle du cinéma en ethnographie," Félix-Louis Regnault, *La nature* 2866, 1 October 1931)

to the fact that white flesh tones were a standard in cinema photochemistry) it becomes a silhouette.[25] On closer examination, however, one sees a man in a suit, possibly Regnault or an assistant, behind the screen which serves as the backdrop. The Western reader of the film is thus provided with a mirror image: he or she is also in the position of the scientist.[26]

In another example, Regnault himself waves at the camera as he is carried in a palanquin by four Malagasy men. The image of the French colonizer in a palanquin was a common one, especially in 1895 with the recent colonization of Madagascar by the French. Regnault the scientist tips his hat to the camera, and to the viewer: he tips his hat to his own power to record these movements of recently colonized people on film, while the men whose movements are filmed do not look into the camera. The filmmaker is both colonizer and researcher. Looming above the scene of the fair was the Eiffel Tower, the ultimate sign of French technology, progress, and power.

Regnault believed that those he called Savage had no language, and in-

14. Printed illustration of Colonel Gillon carried in a palanquin by four Malagasy men. (From *L'Illustration* 2732, 6 July 1895)

stead spoke through the body in what he called *le langage par gestes*. The language that film could inscribe was therefore the language of the body:

> It appears, moreover, unusual to affirm that there exists a science of gesture as interesting as that of language. However, all savage peoples make recourse to gesture to express themselves; their language is so poor it does not suffice to make them understood: plunged in darkness, two savages, as travelers who often witness this fact affirm, can communicate their thoughts, coarse and limited though they are.
>
> With primitive man, gesture precedes speech. . . .
>
> The gestures that savages make are in general the same everywhere, because these movements are natural reflexes rather than conventions like language.[27]

Gesture precedes speech. Thus humanity was divided into not only those who sit and those who squat, but those who have language and those who gesticulate. In many films, the subjects are rendered as mere silhouettes, pictographs of the *langage par gestes*. Their faces are unimportant: it is the body that provides the necessary data. And thus, Regnault writes, the "savage" has no real language: the scientist will inscribe his language—a *langage par gestes* common to all "savages"—into film. They become hieroglyphs for the language of science: race is written into film.

Improving the French Body: The marche en flexion

When the whites feel that they have become too mechanized, they
turn to the men of color and ask them for a little human sustenance.
—Frantz Fanon, *Black Skin, White Masks* (1967)[28]

As described in the last chapter, late-nineteenth-century French anthropologists were interested in applying their techniques not only to categorize non-Western peoples of color, but also to improve the European body. The obsession with evolutionary typologies was perversely double-edged: the Ethnographic Other was pathological, but in some ways more genuine; the Historical Same was normative, but possibly also decadent. Lurking behind the desire to classify the "savage" was the desire to ameliorate the "civilized." Indeed, in his later writings, Regnault wrote repeatedly of the danger that the urban European was becoming *suraffiné* (overrefined, overcivilized): too pale, too blond, too weak.[29] He and his colleague de Raoul complained that the European city dweller lacked grace when he walked: "In our day, the civilized man no longer knows how to walk well."[30] Looking for clues, Regnault compared his films of West Africans walking to films of French men walking.

There is an aspect of the turn-of-the-century *flâneur* in certain of Regnault's images. In the chronophotography with which I began the first chapter (see illustration 3) in which a West African woman is filmed walking with a Frenchman, only the French man is actively looking; her head is down, her look averted. Robert L. Herbert defines the *flâneur* as one with an active, naturalist gaze, one who, although engaged in "apparently idle strolling," is observing with the intensity of a police detective. Like the detective, the *flâneur* was a reader of details—both of the human subject and of location.[31] It is interesting that, as Walter Benjamin pointed out, the literature of the *flâneur* in the 1840s was called the *physiologie*, akin to the diorama. Benjamin writes,

> [The literature of the *physiologie*] investigated types that might be encountered by a person taking a look at the marketplace. From the itiner-

ant streetvendor of the boulevards to the dandy in the foyer of the opera-house, there was not a figure of Paris life that was not sketched by a *physiologue*. . . . After the types had been covered, the physiology of the city had its turn. . . . When this vein, too, was exhausted, a "physiologie" of the nations was attempted. Nor was the "physiologie" of the animals neglected. For animals have always been an innocuous subject. Innocuousness was of the essence.[32]

The observation of the Ethnographic and the spectacle of the ethnographic exposition was another instance of this marketplace of modernity. The innocuousness of Doctor Regnault waving at the camera and the urban glance which the French *citadin* aims at the West African woman reveals that the scientist also posed as *flâneur*, the distant nonchalant observer. The look of the *flâneur* was both part of urban spectacle (that is, meant to be *seen*) and a look in control: the anxiety of difference and of being seen, as I described in the last chapter, is smoothed over by the performance of the idle stroller.

The *flâneur*, however, was also viewed as a figure verging toward decadence, and the affinity noted here between scientific filmmaker and *flâneur* thus also suggests that the scientist's focus on the body was a focus on himself, betraying his fear of becoming *suraffiné*. The fear of overmechanization is expressed by Regnault's teacher Marey in his preface to Regnault and de Raoul's 1897 book, *Comment on marche*. Marey wrote that man (read: the urban European) had become a slave to aesthetic convention in how he walks.[33] He suggested that physiology and chronophotography, through researches such as that of Regnault on how humans walk, would contribute to perfecting the national body:

> Chronophotography . . . is, in this manner, the educator of our movements, it makes us aware of the ideal perfection that we must attain, and makes us observe the incorrectness of our movements or the progress we realize.
>
> Thanks to the progress of the graphic method, the mechanical acts of locomotion can be translated into geometric graphs in which all is measurable with a precision that observation alone could not achieve.[34]

Significantly, one of Regnault's principal reasons for filming the locomotion of West Africans and French soldiers was to prove his theory that the French military walk could be ameliorated through adoption of the *en flexion* gait, a highly flexed walk in which the knees were greatly bent and the torso bent forward, said to be the natural walk of "savages" as well as of prehistoric man. In 1896 Marey presented Regnault and Charles Comte's

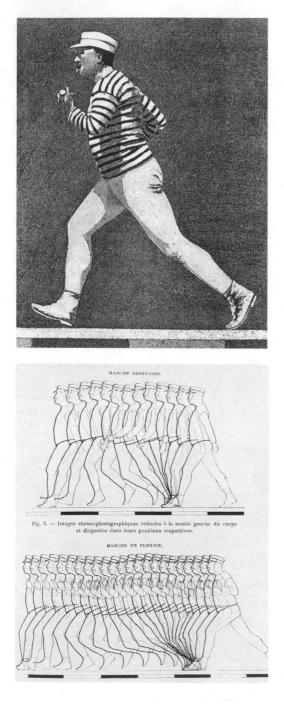

Fig. 3. — Images chronophotographiques réduites à la moitié gauche du corps et disposées dans leurs positions respectives.

findings on the *marche en flexion* to the Académie des sciences. Chrono-photography, they claimed, had proven that the *marche en flexion* was more efficient and less shocking to the body than the normal military walk.[35] As early as the 1870s, de Raoul, a French military commander, had promoted this type of gait for the French army, but it was Regnault who claimed to have scientifically proven its efficacy via film.[36] The Franco-Prussian War seems to have been an important impetus behind the promotion of this walk. Regnault asserted that the German goose step turned soldiers into automatons because it was too fatiguing: the *marche en flexion* was less tiring, and hence allowed the soldier to think clearly. This example again shows the relentlessly comparative nature of Regnault's work: here, the walk of the German soldier, France's military rival, serves as a counterpoint.[37]

In the film entitled "Docteur Regnault marche" (Doctor Regnault walks), however, we see a rather unassuming man, head down, wearing a body suit, whose features are as hard to identify as those of any of the West African subjects. Cinematically there is little difference between this example, and that of a West African man walking: the scientist himself has become a specimen. The ideological difference of course is that we know Regnault's name and biography; he is not rendered into a nameless specimen of some anthropological category known as the Negro or the Savage.[38] Thus the textual accompaniment of the film is absolutely essential to the interpretation (as were explanatory intertitles, and the authoritative voiceover in later ethnographic film). Although anthropology clearly involves vision—the anthropologist observes the cultures of indigenous peoples—it is above all a signifying practice accompanied by words and narrative strategies to convince the reader of its ethnographic authority. Images are slippery: although the image must contain visual signifiers of authenticity, captions are still often needed to explain, convince, and keep order.[39] Consequently, detail is not only tamed cinematically, but textually as well. It should not be surprising then that Regnault wrote at length about his films, reflecting the second aspect of Latour's insight into how inscription works as representation: the

15. (*left top*) Printed illustration of Commandant de Raoul walking *en flexion*. (From "Etude comparative entre la méthode de marche et de course dite de flexion et les allures ordinaires," *Archives de physiologie normale et pathologique*, April 1896) 16. (*left bottom*) Printed illustration of diagrams depicting Commandant de Raoul walking and running *en flexion*. (From "Etude comparative entre la méthode de marche et de course dite de flexion et les allures ordinaires," *Archives de physiologie normale et pathologique*, April 1896) 17. (*opposite right*) "Doctor Regnault walks," Institut de physiologie. (Courtesy of the Collection Jean Vivié)

scientist speaks *for* the actors in the text accompanying his inscriptions. The image is always possibly threatening, more so than other scientific inscriptions such as the graph: it has an iconic presence which must be regimented through verbal description. In the case of Regnault, this textual description portrayed the Ethnographic Body as a hieroglyph to be made sense of by scientists able to find the key to the *langage par gestes.*

Mary Ann Doane explains in her essay on the representation of femininity in cinema that the image of woman in film is akin to the hieroglyph, the most readable yet the most mysterious of signs. The hieroglyph is a component in an iconic system of representation in which the sign and the referent remain suffocatingly close, since the sign directly mimics the physical form of the referent. As a hieroglyph in Regnault's posited *langage par gestes,* the Ethnographic Body is always in a contradictory position, both "real" and sign.[40] While cinema makes the white woman into an image—Doane speaks of "a certain imbrication of the cinematic image and the representation of the woman"[41]—cinema makes the native person, man or woman, into unmediated referent. Whereas the female spectator, according to Doane, has difficulty establishing a distance from the image of the woman in cinema, the spectator of ethnographic cinema has no difficulty in establishing a distance, since the posited viewers are by definition not the filmed subjects themselves but a Euro-American public.

The Legacy of Regnault

As late as 1931 Regnault continued to trumpet the importance of ethnographic expositions and ethnographic films.[42] In an issue on colonialism for the journal *La nature,* Regnault exulted, "Thanks to the Colonial Exposition [of 1931], the ethnographer, who studies the behavior of peoples, is the man of the day. We are avid to know this science which reveals the multiple ways of human thinking."[43] Cinema and sound recording could unite the various disciplines which study humankind:

> Thanks to [films and phonographs], the psychologist, the ethnographer, the sociologist, the linguist, and the folklorist will collect in their laboratories all the manners of numerous ethnicities and will be able to call up life at their will. In analyzing, in measuring these objective documents, in comparing them, in organizing them, they will fix the methods which make up their science, and know the laws of human mentality. The ethnographic museum with its collections of objects, films, and phonographic records will become our laboratory and our center of teaching.[44]

Regnault's conception of a comprehensive archive of scientific research films is rarely considered. Regnault, however, was one of the first to articulate the desire for an archive of humanity, one later openly embraced by a number of other anthropologists and implicit in the work of nearly all who made and studied anthropological research film in the following decades. One need not posit a direct causal relationship between Regnault's theories on film and the anthropological research film which followed in order to use the figure of "Regnault" to draw attention to the central themes which were to constitute the ideological underpinnings of ethnographic film: (1) its intersecting discourse of science and spectacle, manifested, for example, in Regnault's enthusiasm for the ethnographic exposition; (2) its faith in cinema as an objective positivist recording tool; and (3) the ever present, if implicit, ideal of an archive of ethnographic film—what Regnault called a museum of film—which would allow for the cross-checking of detail and the preservation of "vanishing races" in cinematic form. Regnault, as we have seen, combined these elements in his belief that the ethnographic museum/archive could be elevated to the status of the scientific laboratory through the use of explanatory film and phonographs.

Until the 1920s, anthropology in Europe and the United States was still based in the museum. That is, anthropologists did not often go into "the field" and take down ethnographic observations, but relied on second-hand sources such as explorer, traveler, missionary, and colonial accounts. Indeed, anthropological books were coined as the "Amongtha" genre by the British anthropologist E. B. Tylor, due to the ubiquity of titles such as "Among the Watchandis of Australia . . ." or "Among the Esquimaux . . . ," and a similar "boxed-set" mentality also characterized early commercial travelogues (described in the next chapter).[45] Even those colleagues of Tylor and Regnault who did go into "the field" were often trained first in physiology and the natural sciences. (The use of the word "field" was borrowed from natural science terminology.) As historian of anthropology Martin Taureg writes, the anthropologists who followed Regnault's lead accepted his idea that film provides objective documents and his goal of building an archive of ethnographic film. Taureg states that the body of theory justifying ethnographic film developed from biases in physiology and the natural sciences remained unquestioned for a long time.[46] Hence the first anthropologists who used film "in the field" studied humans rather as zoological specimens.

Film technology during Regnault's time developed quickly. Contemporaries of Regnault went on to use motion picture cameras, and to actually do their filming in the "field": the British anthropologist Alfred Cort Haddon (trained in zoology) went to New Guinea and the Torres Strait Islands in 1898–99 on the Cambridge Anthropological Expeditions, and the Anglo-Australian anthropologist Walter Baldwin Spencer made films in 1901 in Central and Northern Australia. Rudolf Pöch, an Austrian, made films in New Guinea in 1904–6, and a number of other German-speaking anthropologists went to South America and Africa with cameras before 1915. All these anthropologists used their cameras much as Regnault used his: the camera is static, the subject entering and leaving the field of vision of the camera. The people portrayed in these films, like the West Africans in Regnault's films, are treated as specimens both textually and cinematographically.

Ethnographic footage purportedly obtained for research purposes was often used as entertainment (with an educational veneer) for mass audiences: the authoritative lecturer, the use of intertitles, and, later, the voice-over were different means used to control the interpretation of the films. Indeed, the figure of the anthropologist often appeared within the film, attesting to its legitimacy and serving as an intended entertaining contrast. Early film by anthropologists did not always announce itself as intended for science or for popular spectacle; the two domains were intertwined. Just as Regnault made his films for science at a popular fair, scientists and natural history museum curators often used ethnographic film both for research purposes and for commercial spectacle. Turn-of-the-century anthropologist Baldwin Spencer, for example, renowned for his books on cultural anthropology, used film in popular lectures in a sensationalist fashion. One of the first ethnographies to depart from the "Amongtha" mode was Spencer's *The Native Tribes of Central Australia* (1912), a work which attempted an ambitious, far-reaching analysis of Australian cultures.[47] In the same year that the book was published, however, Spencer cautioned a popular audience against the power of words to mask the true "savage" nature of the Australian aborigine:

> It is extremely difficult to convey in words a true idea of many of the native ceremonies. Any such description is apt to give the impression of a much higher degree of civilization, or, at least, of greater elaborateness than is really the case. It must always be remembered that though the native ceremonies reveal, to a certain extent, what has been described as an "elaborate ritual," they are eminently crude and savage. They are performed by naked, howling savages.[48]

It is no wonder then that Spencer (1860–1929), chair of biology at the University of Melbourne, director of the Victoria National Museum, and

Special Commissioner for Aborigines,[49] used film as well as lantern slides and phonographic records for his very popular public lectures.[50] Visual media presented to the public could turn aboriginal culture into Savage spectacle. In his lectures on aboriginal rituals, Spencer called the Arunta "children of darkness," and described the Arunta as "weird," "savage," and "disgusting." He said of the people in his films: "They were in a condition in which our ancestors were in past ages, and through them we learned something of the original conditions in which our ancestors lived."[51]

The anthropologist's frequent inclusion of scenes of indigenous dance, a feature already present in the films of Spencer and Haddon, contributed to the spectacle. Spencer's Austrian colleague Rudolf Pöch explained, "Dances are the simplest and most effective subjects for cinematography and the best means for practising the medium since they enable one to record what is most visual and effective when reproduced."[52] Dance was almost always represented as spectacle: to be watched at a distance. The public as well as scientists were fascinated by the bodies of indigenous peoples, and dance film showed how those bodies moved, how masks were worn. Moreover, an iconography is formed: the native—as we have seen in Regnault's conception of the *langage par gestes*—is identified with the body. Dances by indigenous peoples were projected as wild, "savage," frenzied movements by people lacking rationality: an image which became a popular stereotype in commercial film.

Although museum expeditions almost always brought along cameramen proficient in photography and film, the actual use of films for research was rare; far more often, the footage was used for public entertainment, or in some cases, to help construct museum dioramas. Anthropologists like Regnault, Pöch, and Spencer, to name only a few early ethnographic filmmakers, believed in the necessity of ethnographic film archives, but film was not a favored medium of presentation within the academy. Film was seen as a tool for inscription, much in the way that the photograph, phonograph, and calipers were, rather than as a medium for "writing" ethnography. Cinema, intended for scientific research purposes, was instead used for public spectacle, as a sensational means for attracting viewers and thus profit. The boundaries between the cinema of science (*cinématographe*) and cinema of entertainment (*cinématoscope*) were never clearly drawn.

Cinematographic Notes

Modern anthropology, Rudolf Pöch observed, would no longer be conducted with just a notebook, a pen, and measuring instruments, but would require use of a motion picture camera and a phonograph. For Pöch, the advantage of film is that it allows for true voyeurism because images could be captured for future study without the native's awareness. Pöch advocated setting up the camera in a public place and just letting the film roll, complaining only that the camera could not capture all of a scene because it can point in only one direction at a time.[53] Working in 1904–6 in German, British, and Dutch New Guinea and in New South Wales, Pöch filmed activities including dance, women carrying water, and a man being shaved.[54] His assertion that indigenous people were ignorant of the technology and that his own films were not choreographed, however, is belied by his own photography and films. In many films, the figure of Pöch is painfully conspicuous. In one scene, wearing a white pith helmet on his head, a rifle in one hand, and what appears to be a pole in the other, he stands among a group of Melanesian people (in New Guinea?) who pose for the camera.[55] The film footage is not candid but is staged, and the performers appear to recognize that they are part of a performance. Still, the notion of voyeurism, that the presence of the filmmaker did not disturb the scene, endured in ethnographic film until well after World War II.[56]

It is striking how much early ethnographic film borrowed from the iconography of anthropological photography and the construction of "anthropological types." Filming natives as "types" in profile and frontal shots and walking or standing in formation were important staples of the genre. In one sequence filmed by Haddon in the Torres Straits, the camera, which is stationary, films several men who, in dancing, pass the camera one by one in a line, only to disappear briefly offscreen before entering the camera's field of vision again from the other side.[57] In a sequence by Pöch, women walk one behind the other in profile, turn around, and then walk bare-breasted with their hands up in the air.[58] In this last image, anthropometric imagery combines with the clear tendency in both research and entertainment film to portray the indigenous female body in titillating voyeuristic ways.

Significantly, even those who felt that film could not achieve true voyeurism believed that film could serve as a faithful record of dances and ceremonies. In the 1960s, anthropologist André Leroi-Gourhan stated that the function of film was to act as "cinematographic notes," as a medium for recording movements, dances, and ceremonies, even if staged, that would subsequently serve as records for verification.[59]

Franz Boas, the most prominent anthropologist in the United States in the early twentieth century and the founder of the school of American culturalism, wrote about the importance of film in providing objective records. In 1930, Boas even shot some film himself of dances, craft-making, and games of the Kwakiutl (Kwakwaka'wakw) of the Northwest Coast. Ira Jacknis argues that Boas was interested in "relatively discrete behavioral sequences of a 'traditional' nature, especially motor patterns and material culture."[60] He writes,

> For Boas, a culture was imprinted on the very movements of a person, which would be expressed apart from his or her surroundings. Thus, in spite of his belief in cultural wholes, Boas tended to think of culture as embedded in isolable actions, so that one could, at least for the purposes of documentation, record only this behavior fragment, apart from the complex social matrix of which it was usually a part.[61]

Thus, like Regnault, Boas's interest in film stemmed from a concern with the body, and with the ability of the camera to record "isolable actions." Many of Boas's students went on to use film to aid their research: Melville Herskovits, who later encouraged Katherine Dunham to make films, filmed in Dahomey (now Benin) in 1931 and in Haiti in 1934; Zora Neale Hurston filmed in Florida in 1928–29; and Margaret Mead and Gregory Bateson filmed in Bali in 1936–39.[62] Mead, Boas's most famous student and probably the most enthusiastic and well-known U.S. anthropologist/filmmaker, argued well into the 1970s that film would eliminate much of the ambiguity of the written ethnography. She believed that long takes and an immobile camera could study nonverbal behavior objectively. Like Regnault, Mead thought that film could provide an important record of the ways of life of vanishing races; she also endorsed the idea that by collecting and examining an enormous amount of film material, the anthropologist could make anthropology a science.[63] This shift from an interest in the body as inscription to the body inscribed in a pictorial "whole" will be discussed in the following chapter.

The Ideology of the Archive

Thanks to cinema, the anthropologist can, today, collect the life of all peoples; he will possess in his drawers all the special acts of different races. He will be able to thus have contact at the same time with a great number of peoples.—Félix-Louis Regnault, "Films and Ethnographic Museums" (1923)[64]

Johannes Fabian notes that anthropological databanks are not just innocent depositories, but "are institutions which make possible the [politically charged] circulation of information."[65] In other words, while the ethnographic film archive purports to be nothing more than a collection of visual documents from a diverse array of cultures—the anthropologist-filmmaker merely goes out into the world, objectively captures life on celluloid, and brings it home for storage—the world is not being structured in a value-free manner. On the contrary, the circulation of images presupposed by the archive implicates social, historical, and political relations of dominance. James Clifford's statement that collecting in the West "has long been a strategy for the deployment of a possessive self, culture, and authenticity" casts a revealing light on the proliferation in the late nineteenth century of new forms of public collections such as the zoo, the museum, and the ethnographic exposition. The ordered plurality of forms itself suggests a desire to stem or otherwise control the inevitable march of historical time by preserving objects, artifacts, animals, and cultures. Clifford goes on to explain that with the emergence of modern classic anthropology, "cultures" came to be represented in collections as the embodiment of that which is pure and authentic. Even today, these collected "cultures" are nearly always represented in the "ethnographic present": they are explained in the present tense but conceived as remnants of the human past, and thus are represented as timeless, without history. Clifford explains that "both collector and salvage ethnographer would claim to be the last to rescue 'the real thing.' Authenticity . . . is produced by removing objects and customs from their current historical situation—a present-becoming-future."[66] Ethnographic cinema takes this process one step further; it takes you "there." In film, the time travel is immediate: you "enter" the ethnographic present of Bali, or Samoa, or the Northern Quebec Arctic.

The ethnographic archive necessitated the production of visual records.[67] Many anthropologists, however, considered film technology too difficult and bothersome to learn. To maximize time and energy, cameramen were often hired to accompany ethnographic expeditions. One of the earliest mentions of using film for collecting anthropological records is the Bureau of American Ethnology report of 1902. In this report, a certain O. P. Phillips is mentioned, a filmmaker employed to make films "representing the industries, amusements, and ceremonies of the Pueblo Indians and other tribes in New Mexico and Arizona. The object of the work was to obtain absolutely trustworthy records of aboriginal activities for the use of future students, as well as for the verification of current notes on fiducial dances and other ceremonies."[68]

Albert Kahn, the first to make a sustained effort to construct an archive of research film, also hired camera operators, and sent them around the world to film the "daily lives" of people and to capture the historical forces of evolution at work. I will discuss Kahn's archive in the next chapter; what is important at present is to recognize that the archive of ethnographic film was a shared ideal. Margaret Mead explained Boas's conception of the archive as follows: "[Boas] wanted a real corpus of materials to work on, large bodies of materials which would make possible the cross-checking of each detail and would provide a basis for making certain kinds of negative statements."[69] Both Regnault and Boas thus believed that an archive of ethnographic film should be created as a repository for permanent documents which would enable the scientist to examine detail, verify hypotheses, and jog his or her memory.[70]

Different national anthropological traditions had different theories about the use of ethnographic film, and yet the basic tenets which Regnault set forth underpinned popular and scientific notions of the genre across national boundaries. In France, anthropologist Marcel Mauss, in his essay "Les techniques du corps" (1934), took up questions that Regnault had raised and declared the body to be the first instrument of man. Mauss saw film as a privileged means of obtaining records of the use of that instrument.[71] Mauss's best-known student, Marcel Griaule, used film to document his study of Dogon ritual.[72]

It was German-speaking anthropology, however, that most fully embraced Regnault's ideal of a scientific archive of ethnographic film. In 1950 the Encyclopaedia Cinematographica at the Institut für den wissenschaftlichen Film (IWF) was established for the collection of research films. The IWF specifically invokes Regnault, and views its task as collecting visual ethnographic records, to facilitate future cross-cultural comparison by trained anthropologists. Like Regnault's films, the films of the Encyclopaedia Cinematographica emphasize movement and indigenous technology.[73] As IWF director Günther Spannaus declared, film was a "non-corruptible document" which allowed for "direct and unbiased observation."[74]

The German emphasis on "material culture" may explain why ethnographic film has been so relatively important to German anthropology and why British social anthropology, lacking the material cultural emphasis, has never had much interest in film.[75] Film, however, also appealed to those who believed culture could be classified through study of the body, through physiognomy and physiology, and German anthropology was a leader in physical anthropology (a body of research exploited by the Nazi regime to legitimize racial extermination and imperialism).[76] These contrasts do not tell the whole story, however. In Great Britain, although the "tradition" of ethnographic film as research tool for anthropology is comparatively weak, ethnographic film remains a popular staple of television programming, as evidenced, for example, by the success of the *Disappearing World* series.[77]

If "scientific" ethnographic film has had a wide, if disparate, impact among anthropologists, it has clearly failed to live up to the expectations of visionaries like Regnault and Pöch. One often overlooked explanation may be that people do not readily perform their "daily lives" on cue for the camera. Anthropologists M. W. Hilton-Simpson and J. A. Haeseler sought to film "only what the natives do for themselves," but there is the problem of the camera's conspicuousness, as Haeseler explains, "No matter where in the world one sets up a cinema camera, one becomes a centre of interest and attracts a crowd that soon runs into scores. Managing these is a task for two or three vociferous native assistants, and on market days or during cere-monies the conditions are particularly trying."[78]

Anthony Michaelis's enthusiastic explanation of how to film "native" peoples also establishes the need to hire "native police":

> Before departure, the anthropologist can easily obtain a few feet of 35-mm film from a commercial production company; for this purpose unwanted cuts from newsreels should prove highly suitable. They could show Europeans whose film images made them important-looking per-sonages, and they could be shown to natives as proof that the recording of images does not produce any harm; in case of continued distrust these cuts might be given as hostages. . . . The unwanted cuts, might also be offered to natives as reward for letting themselves be filmed. Instead of a reluctance to be filmed, precisely the opposite may occur, and an all-too-eager crowd of natives may cluster around and prevent the working of the cinematographer. The only solution is to engage some reliable na-tives as a "police" force to perform the same duties as their white colleagues have to undertake in a similar situation at home.[79]

Michaelis's recommendations for how to "capture" the native on film reveal that Regnault's ideal of the unfettered anthropologist filmmaker was far from reality. In the U.S. Southwest, for example, Native Americans were known to jump in front of the camera, throw sand or rocks, and even break cameras to prevent filming. Acts of resistance were not always so obvious: rituals could be performed in a false manner, without the anthropologist even knowing. Famed photographer Edward Sheriff Curtis made a film in 1904 of a Navajo Yeibichai ceremony; some have argued that the Navajo performing the ceremony did it intentionally backwards.[80] The world was not a perfect laboratory; film was rarely perfect voyeurism.

Although some of the footage from the thousands of feet of film made by

Margaret Mead and Gregory Bateson have been edited to produce ethno-graphic films now often used in undergraduate anthropology classes, the as yet unviewed boxes of their film sitting in museums and libraries attest to the fact that the use and study of film never became a central method of academic anthropology.[81] As anthropology shifted its domain from the mu-seum to the university, writing ethnography rather than filming ethnogra-phy remained the medium for advancement in the social sciences. Despite Pöch's turn-of-the-century prediction that the tools of modern anthropol-ogy would no longer be the notebook and pen, but the film camera, anthro-pology in the United States and Europe has remained a "writing" discourse. The profilmic—what occurs in front of the film camera—is not as easily managed as writing, as Anthony Michaelis's and M. W. Hilton-Simpson and J. A. Haeseler's telling descriptions of the problems of anthropological film-making attest. Photographs and films were thus used as evidence of having "been there," rather than as media to be studied in themselves.

But what is a more powerful legacy of Regnault and the conception of film as an ethnographic tool is how it teaches spectators to see native peoples in film and television as the Ethnographic. The iconography of race in films used for popular audiences will be discussed in the following chapters. Moreover, the anthropologist himself or herself often became a popular authoritative figure such as we have seen in the case of Baldwin Spencer or Margaret Mead.

The Language of Racialization

I began by showing how the "ethnographic" in film works to deny the voice and individuality of the indigenous subject. The performers in Regnault's films are meant to represent not only a typical West African body, but a body typical of what anthropology called Primitive. Their names and his-tory are not given: the fact that they are performers from a fair, the colonial nature of France's relation to West Africa, etc. Emptied of history, their bodies are *racialized*. The racialized body in cinema is a construction deny-ing people of color historical agency and psychological complexity. Individ-uals are read as metonyms for an entire category of people, whether it be ethnic group, race, or Savage/Primitive/Third World. Regnault is both in-formed by and informs the scientific and popular circulation of the image of the "ethnographic." Thus scientific cinema teaches us how to read bodies: the "ethnographic" squats, climbs trees differently, carries the colonialist in a palanquin, performs animal sacrifices, and goes about her affairs bare-breasted. A similar iconography of race is at work in the construction

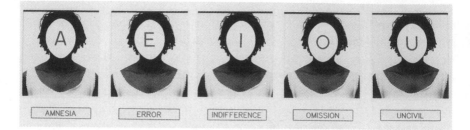

18. Lorna Simpson, *Easy for Who to Say* (1989).
(Courtesy of Sean Kelly Gallery)

of Hollywood cinema stereotypes like the black Mammy or the Chinese dragon lady, but the racialization which occurs in ethnographic film is particularly pernicious because it is "scientifically" legitimized, and the subjects of the film are tied to the evolutionary past.

But racialization is not necessarily the product of contempt. Notions of the native as pathological and savage often coexist with images of the "noble savage": Regnault himself believed Europeans to be in danger of becoming *suraffiné*, too refined, and he used his films of West Africans to support his theory that the *marche en flexion* was more natural, a healthier way to walk. Whether portrayed as savage, noble, or simply authentic, however, the "ethnographic" is a product of the taxonomic imagination of both anthropology and cinema. It is to the legacy of this kind of media cannibalism that Lorna Simpson's recent work, *Easy for Who to Say* (1989), answers directly. In Simpson's piece, faces are emptied and filled with the letters of vowels, and the resonating words underneath the faces speak to the denial of history so many people of color have faced: Amnesia, Error, Indifference, Omission, Uncivil.[82]

What lends ethnographic film its aura of truth is thus the Ethnographic body, coded since Regnault's time as authentic. Moreover, these films could not only be used for research into race and evolution, but also to improve the productive body of the capitalist and imperialist European world. As described above, Regnault used films of West Africans to improve the French military walk. One use-value of Regnault's work was thus war. In an ironic twist, beginning in World War I, many West African men were recruited into the French army to serve as the now-famous *tirailleurs*, their bodies used, this time as infantry for French battles. Accordingly, I would like to conclude by going from one camp—the 1895 Exposition Ethnographique where Regnault made his films—to another camp—the transit camp for Senegalese *tirailleurs* returning home to Africa depicted in Sembène Ousmane's film *Camp de Thiaroye* (1987). In *Camp de Thiaroye*, as in Regnault's films, almost all the principal characters are West African. Unlike the performers in Regnault's films, however, they are given names, history, psychological complexity, and agency. These soldiers, like colonized peoples in other parts of the world, return from World War II battles and concentration camps having learned one very important lesson: how small France is. Their profound consciousness that "a white corpse, a black corpse, it's all the same" leads to their explosion against their oppression as colonial subjects. It is clear therefore that what distinguishes the genre of the "ethnographic film" from a film like *Camp de Thiaroye* is not the color of the people filmed, but how they are racialized—how, in other words, the viewer is made to see "anthropology" rather than history.

When Regnault died in 1938 none of his obituaries mentioned his interest in film. His writings on cinema were discovered only later by ethnographic filmmakers like Jean Rouch eager to establish their ethnographic film lineage.[83] If film did not prove to be the positivist tool of science Regnault claimed it was, perhaps this is because, though people may want to inscribe others as Ethnographic, those others are not easily constrained in the position of objects of scrutiny. The chain of looks was and is never entirely one-sided.

II TAXIDERMY

3 GESTURES OF SELF-PROTECTION

The Picturesque and the Travelogue

They did not like me, but with the magical rifle in my hands I was momentarily worth watching.—George Orwell, "Shooting an Elephant" (1931)[1]

In 1922 the anthropologist Félix-Louis Regnault described seeing a beautiful film in Paris on the life of the Eskimo. One would surmise that he was referring to *Nanook of the North*, Robert Flaherty's popular film about a Northern Quebec Inuit hunter's struggle for survival in the Arctic. What is intriguing is that Regnault's comments are not about the film's aesthetic qualities or its realism, but about how the film illustrated Regnault's own theory that the "Savage" walked *en flexion:* "[The Inuit people in the film] walked and ran on the ice with a very accentuated flexed gait. This fact demonstrates how exact is the documentation furnished by the film."[2] For Regnault, the body in motion verifies the authenticity of the film. Regnault's reading of the film is still within the realm of the body as hieroglyph, an inscription of race, a document for scientists who study evolution.

Nanook of the North, made not by an anthropologist but by a mining prospector, was not intended as a scientific research film. However, even anthropologist Franz Boas praised *Nanook*. Often referred to as the founder of cultural anthropology in the United States and a proponent of the use of film for recording "isolable actions" of the body, Boas tried to encourage film collaborations between anthropologists and Hollywood on "the primitive races," a collaboration made all but imperative in his view in light of reports of "the complete breakdown, from a pictorial point of view,"[3] of native cultures. Footage could be used and recycled for films intended for scientific and educational as well as entertainment purposes. In a letter to Will Hays, president of the Motion Picture Producers and Distributers of America, Boas explained that commercial films like *Nanook* would have been better if a trained anthropologist had been on site to give expert advice:

Assuming . . . that a man who knows Eskimo life in and out, had been at hand to direct a film like NANOOK, many exceedingly picturesque and interesting features of native life might have been brought in which would not only have improved the quality of the film but would have also made it more attractive to the general audiences. . . . Most of the material of this kind has to be collected *now* because each year sees native cultures breaking down and disappearing under the onslaught of White civilization.[4]

At first glance, Regnault's anthropology with its stress on the physical gait and language of gesture of indigenous peoples appears to be the antithesis to the anthropology of Boas, a scholar who set out to disprove evolutionary theories of the inherent inferiority of the non-European brain in his 1911 study *The Mind of the Primitive Man*. Unlike Regnault, who was obsessed with the body of the Inuit in *Nanook*, and who conceived of the body as a character in a *langage par gestes*, Boas was concerned with the insufficient quantity of views of the *picturesque* in the film, and argued for the representation of indigenous cultures in the mode of salvage ethnography, that is to say, as he thought native peoples looked before they met the white man. If he feared the "pictorial breakdown" of the Ethnographic, he chose to defy its "death" through recording and reconstructing it in its diverse cultural forms.[5] And yet the complexity of Boas's relation to the production of visual images of native peoples is exceedingly complex: the powerful ideology of evolution is inherent in Boas's conception that it was the anthropologist's task to record native cultures who were vanishing "from a pictorial point of view," and in his desire to capture the "picturesque" ways of "primitive peoples"—those scenes of rituals, dance, food preparation, indigenous technology (pottery-making, for example), and so on, all that is replete with "authentic" detail and without the influence of European culture.

Boas's notion of the picturesque went hand in hand with what George W. Stocking Jr. has described as the dehistoricization or "ethnographicization" of anthropology, in which the empiricism and epistemological underpinnings of anthropological notions of evolutionary time were overlaid with an increasingly romantic Rousseauesque study of "surviving primitive peoples" and historical analysis was elided.[6] During this "classic period" of modern anthropology, which Stocking claims lasted up until the 1960s in the United States, the rising influence of Boas and the school of American culturalism made ethnographic film and other visual media an increasingly important tool for assembling data for description. Boas, considered by many to be the father of visual anthropology, was involved with many different kinds of visual representation of indigenous peoples: for example, he made anthropological exhibits for the World's Columbian Exhibition in Chicago in 1893, asked explorer Robert Peary to bring back "an Eskimo" to be studied at the American Museum of Natural History (see chapter 4), and worked at the same museum making life groups (models) and dioramas and curating collections.

The first and second chapters described how the colonial encounter at the ethnographic exposition with non-European peoples of color took the form of detailed tableaus of performers photographed by anthropologists like Regnault who believed they were inscribing the racial body onto films in the interests of evolutionary science. This chapter examines how these tableaus fused into a cinematic picturesque, creating a conceptual bridge between racial "inscription" and what I will be calling the "taxidermic" mode of ethnographic cinema. In early cinema, the picturesque is found in abundance in the film archive of Albert Kahn, in commercial travelogue films, and in Edward Sheriff Curtis's "Art/Science" archive of "vanishing Indians." The history of the appearance of the picturesque deserves a volume in itself; here I will only sketch its primary characteristics.

The Picturesque and the Archive

Even though Regnault's ideal of the scientific film archive never came to fruition, the archive continued to be, to paraphrase V. Y. Mudimbe again, a powerful means of "seeing anthropology," an implicit ideological context within which films of indigenous people were viewed. Commercial films shared the politics of visual domination from a distance inherent in the archive, and gave expression to a passion for the picturesque. These two impulses created a genre in which the world becomes a body landscaped.

Emerging originally from a British upper-class appreciation for landscaped scenery, the picturesque in poetry, painting, architecture, and the art of travel was conceptualized in the late eighteenth century as roughness, sudden variation, and irregularity in form, color, lighting, and even sound; the picturesque thus was defined in opposition to the sublime, the ideal, and the beautiful. Christopher Hussey explains that the picturesque was conceived as a way to inspire the imagination "to form the habit of feeling through the eyes."[7] Hussey describes the picturesque from the point of view of the dilettante British squire, Richard Payne Knight:

> Yet the very relation to painting, expressed by the word Picturesque, implied an association of ideas on the part of all subsequent observers.

> For nobody could see picturesquely who had no recollection of pictures, besides the power of abstract vision, to associate with objects perceived. Apart from such colouring and lighting as gave abstract pleasure, the enjoyment derived from, for instance, ruins, lanes, hovels, and gipsies consisted entirely in their association with pictures in the memory of the observer.[8]

The picturesque was thus powerfully associated with emotion and the subjective, with memory and death. It evoked the passing of time and distance—taking as its subjects the remote and marginal. Sara Suleri has discussed the picturesque in relation to Anglo-Indian narrative, but Suleri's discussion sheds light on early travelogue film as well. Suleri writes, "The picturesque becomes synonymous with a desire to transfix a dynamic cultural confrontation into a still life, converting a pictorial imperative into a gesture of self-protection that allows the colonial gaze a license to convert its ability not to see into studiously visual representations."[9]

From an accumulation of practices for imaging the exotic—from *la peinture ethnographique*, travel literature, the ethnographic exposition, travel photography; from street scenes, panoramic landscapes, scenes of dance and ritual—a genre is established. The picturesque is a shielding gesture: relations of dominance are preserved in ideologies of death (the "vanishing races"), in the entertainment of relentless binarisms ("we do this, they do that"), and in the use of text or intertitles to wrest a narrative out of potentially disturbing images, mechanisms already present in the works of Regnault and other scientific filmmakers. The disturbing gaze of the Native described by Orwell, as I explained in chapter 1, is tamed by visualizing the picturesque. The *langage par gestes* is actually a gesture of protection.

The archive provides the perfect framework for the collection and display of the picturesque. One of the first archives of moving picture images was the Archives de la planète, an archive of autochromes, photographs, and films collected by Albert Kahn, the French financier and patron of the social sciences.[10] This archive, begun in 1909 and directed by Jean Brunhes, the first Chair in Human Geography at the Collège de France, was intended to arrest history as it happened and preserve on film customs and manners before they disappeared. Unlike early films by Edison and others, the Archives were not intended for the general public. Instead, films were screened for selected meetings of intellectuals like Rabindranath Tagore, Henri Bergson, and Auguste Rodin. Kahn's camera operators filmed not only in Europe, but also in many of the French colonies in Africa, Asia, and the Middle East, as well as in China and Japan. Believing that cinema and photography could

19. Léon Busy, "Village performers—Ha-noi—Tonkin" (1916). (Original document: Autochrome, courtesy of the Musée Albert Kahn-Département des Hauts-de-Seine)

record ways of life that were vanishing quickly, Kahn felt that the forces of evolution could be captured by the camera. Another motivation for the archive was to provide both scholars and administrators photographic and cinematic records of directly observed ways of life. The resulting archival material includes many exceedingly lovely autochromes whose pale colors lend the images a ghostly, precious air. The tinted quality of the atmosphere in the photographs is heavy, almost gauzelike: in his autochromes, Kahn made the planet into a series of snapshot jewels.

In comparison to the autochromes, the films in Kahn's archive—unedited, intended for use in lectures or for research—are less arresting. Life in front of the camera passes quickly; the films do not allow for meditation or contemplation. They represent scenes similar to those portrayed in commercial travelogues: mostly market and street scenes, views from a train or a railroad, and scenes of dances and rituals. Like the commercial travelogues which I discuss below, the Kahn archive footage almost always includes panoramic views of the landscape, often from the point of view of an arriving traveler on an incoming ship or train. These views helped ground the representation of travel as penetration and discovery. Mary Louise Pratt's analysis of the landscape in the written travelogue is applicable to the panoramic landscape of early cinema. Pratt explains that such landscape views suggest

> the fantasy of dominance that is commonly built into this stance. The eye "commands" what falls within its gaze; the mountains "show themselves" or "present themselves"; the country "opens up" before the European newcomer, as does the unclothed indigenous bodyscape. At the same time, this eye seems powerless to act or interact with this landscape. Unheroic, unparticularized, without ego, interest, or desire of its own, it seems able to do nothing but gaze from a periphery of its own creation, like the self-effaced, noninterventionist eye that scans the Other's body.[11]

Within the context of imperialism and entrepreneurial prospecting, panoramic views condition viewers to see other lands precisely as places to be explored and inhabited by Europeans.

That the body landscaped was not only racialized but gendered may be seen in an Archives de la planète film of a village festival in Tonkin (now northern Vietnam) in which a young woman undresses and then dresses for the camera. It is clear that the absolute voyeurism and scopic possession of the native female body was palatable to a white audience; if conducted on the white female body, the same technique would have been declared pornographic.[12] The fact that the female native body is incessantly veiled and unveiled, however, reveals the simultaneous attraction and repulsion felt by the filmmaker for the perceived physicality of the native woman.

The desire to capture "vanishing" ways of life links the Kahn footage to the commercial travel genre, a genre which developed in step with the burgeoning commerce of tourism.[13] If the concept of the archive frames the Kahn footage, editing and intertitles frame the commercial travelogue. Many short actuality films of the travel genre were made with titles such as "Among the X," and "Customs and Manners of Y," popular counterpoints to what E. B. Tylor had earlier caricatured as the "Amongtha" literature in anthropology.[14] As the Lumières camera operator Félix Mesguich explained, "My own ambition was to enclose the world in my cameras."[15] Early commercial cinema of the Lumières, Pathé Frères, Thomas Edison, and others modeled itself on photographic travelogues and travel literature: the goal was to go "Around the World in X Days" with a camera, and many film camera operators were former still photographers. The "archive" thus manifested itself in popular cinema as the desire to prospect the world as tourist-explorer. As the travelogue filmmaker Burton Holmes's motto put it: "To travel is to possess the world."[16] Edison's series of travelogues in the teens was even called Conquest Pictures.

Although so many travelogues were made between 1898 and 1922 that it is difficult to generalize, most travelogues contained certain elements in common. They were short films, usually beginning and ending with panoramic views of landscape, or of a harbor or town from the point of view of a ship or train. The opening of the film with a map quickly became standard, locating the spectator and what he or she will see in a network of longitudinal and latitudinal grid lines. The sense of travel and exploration is highlighted, the point of view often that of a bourgeois tourist. Finally, there is rarely any attempt to construct the camera as a hidden voyeur: in early travelogues, people in markets and in the street openly stare at the camera.

Like the early scientific research films of Pöch, Spencer, and Haddon, these actualities focused on the body moving through "cultural activities": dances and rituals seen as sacred and taboo were especially popular. In Edison's *Circle Dance* (1898), an unidentified group of Plains Indians performs a round dance, probably intended to be danced at night.[17] Films about indigenous peoples often focused on scenes right out of a "native village" from a world's fair exposition. The 1910 Gaumont film *Sitten und Gebrauchen am Senegal* (Customs and Manners in Senegal) shows sequences of people dancing, playing musical instruments, engaged in various handicrafts, and cooking: scenes reminiscent of the visual tableaus that Regnault described in his reviews of ethnographic exhibitions. The camera is more often than not a fourth wall, establishing a distant relationship between the spectator and the subject filmed.

The "entertaining" narrative of evolution was emphasized by juxtaposing the white tourist with the peoples filmed: the Native versus the Civilized, the Ethnographic versus the Historical, the Colonized versus the Colonialist. Unlike most films made by anthropologists, however, the presence of whites in travelogues was an explicitly central focus of the genre. As film historian Charles Musser explains, the audience that views the travel film identifies with what it sees on three levels: it identifies with the traveler represented in the film, with the cameraman, and with the showman who lectures on stage.[18] In many travel films, the audience is presented with a fourth potential locus of identification—the colonialist. For example, in *Madagascar: Manners and Customs of the Sakalava* (Pathé Frères, 1910), there are two sequences which foreground colonial power and influence. One of the sequences, entitled "A Feast Day. The Natives Bring Presents to the White Man," shows whites in suits and hats distributing alcohol to

Malagasy men and women. The second sequence reminds one of the scenes Regnault described at the fair and is entitled "The Natives rush to pick up coppers." From a distance, the camera films Malagasy rushing in en masse to pick up money thrown at them by Europeans.[19]

Burton Holmes's travelogues were among the longest-running of the genre, and, like many other travel films, promoted tourism as a natural form of upper-middle-class enjoyment. As a travel lecturer, Holmes began by projecting lantern slides; as a filmmaker, he coined the word "travelogue" which he defined as "the gist of a journey ground fine by discrimination, leavened with information seasoned with humor, fashioned in literary form and embellished by pictures that delight the eye, while the spoken story charms the ear."[20] The style of Holmes's films was that of a bemused wealthy traveler, and his travelogues retained the didactic style of a worldly lecturer. Like the early films of the Lumières brothers and Edison, the subjects, especially crowds in the street or at the market, often gaze directly into the camera. *Beautiful Bermuda* (1921) is a cinematic postcard collection: it portrays Bermuda as, in effect, the ideal honeymoon site.

Jokes at the expense of the dignity of people of color are prominent in another Holmes travelogue, *Sights of Suva* (1918).[21] The focus is on native "types": "Fijians" are shown in both western and native dress, and "Chinese" storeowners and "Indian" workers are also represented, often artificially posed next to portly British colonials in white hats. Racial contrast was intended to startle and amuse, as in the spectacle of an English-educated Fijian judge, or of a Fijian woman in native dress whose cigarette is lighted by a plump European man in a white suit—an entertainment of binarisms similar in effect to that produced by Regnault's chronophotography of the Parisian *flâneur* walking with the West African woman (see illustration 3) or of the nonchalant scientist waving at the camera as he is carried by four Malagasy men in a palanquin (see illustration 13). In their relentless colonial contrasts, and their pejorative highlighting of the quaint and the remote, Holmes's films represented another form of the colonial picturesque; unlike Boas, however, whose vision of the picturesque was one without any trace of Western culture, Holmes presented the panoramic landscape in order to suggest the possibility of colonizing and peopling a distant land. At the end of *Sights of Suva,* there is a view of a river and an empty landscape from the point of view of a moving boat. It is a shot of Fiji without Fijians. The title reads "No further fear of cannibals—Even the fat and appetizing tourist may wander freely anywhere in Fiji . . ." The joke about cannibals again reveals the gesture of self-protection underlying the picturesque: despite the possible nervous laughter, the audience is meant to identify with the "fat tourist," whose imperialism and "civilization" has eliminated cannibals.[22]

The travel film offered up the world as an "archive" of human variation, and allowed the viewer a way to travel without leaving home, just as the research film enabled the anthropologist to remain in his armchair. It was also useful as colonial propaganda. All imperialist countries projected films of their colonies to an eager public at home: countries like Holland and Germany actually had government bureaus controlling and directing the output and distribution of colonial propaganda films.[23]

Entertaining binarisms pervade another popular form which emerged from the early travel film: the so-called *documentaires romancés* (coined by the anthropologist Patrick O'Reilly), which featured scripted fictionalized travelogues with white actors and indigenous extras.[24] Many critics have identified an early precursor of Flaherty in Gaston Méliès, who in 1912–13 brought a cast and crew on location to Tahiti, New Zealand, Australia, Java, Cambodia, and Japan, making sixty-four films under the name of "Round the World Films." Whereas the films of Gaston Méliès's more famous brother Georges are said to represent the magical fantasy side of cinema,[25] Gaston's films are curious hybrids of documentary and fantasy, shot on location using nonprofessional native actors. For example, in "The Misfortunes of Mr. and Mrs. Mott on Their Trip to Tahiti," the Motts, a newly rich American couple, encounter the god Neptune on their way from San Francisco to Papeete. Mr. Mott's flirtation with Tahitian women provides picturesque "humor."[26]

Méliès's humor is indicative of this genre: as in Holmes's films, "savages" are made to seem silly and not really dangerous. In *Captured by Aborigines* (1913), another Méliès film, a Chief rescues an English explorer in Queensland from being eaten by "savages." The Chief, who has secretly lived with white men and knows English, explains that he does not reveal his sophistication to his villagers because he is unwilling to destroy their "primitive happiness," an interesting comment given that Méliès himself complained that the indigenous peoples he encountered on his "Round the World" tour were not "savage" enough.[27] He created on film what he failed to find in reality.

Indigenous peoples were often the target of humor in another form which developed out of the travelogue genre: the expedition and/or safari film. The binarism that was a force in Holmes's films—colonial gentleman juxtaposed with native "type"—is exploited to even more dramatic effect in these films as the big game hunter stomps his way across foreign continents. Museums often used expedition films for public education programs and were

20. Still from Burton Holmes's *Sights of Suva* (1918). (Reproduced from the Collections of the Library of Congress)

led by the American Museum of Natural History which funded several filmed expeditions featuring big game hunters. Teddy Roosevelt was perhaps the most famous of the museum's star hunters. In Cherry Kearton's *Roosevelt in Africa* (1910), the camera focuses on Roosevelt as the great explorer, hunter, discoverer, and leader.[28] African workers are his foils, either as dangerous obstacles, trusty servants, or part of the picturesque scenery. In one scene, Roosevelt is filmed being carried, as Regnault had himself filmed, on the shoulders of African men. The Great Hunt is represented as an amusing party for whites in safari suits. Shots of Zulu dancers are intercut with shots of Roosevelt watching the dances while admiring and aiming with a large rifle: white superiority is established, as is the gun/camera parallel, a ubiquitous reference linking film spectacle with death.[29] There is nothing to distinguish some of the dance sequences of Kearton's films from those in a scientific film, but the subtitles are more jokingly denigrating. In one sequence, for example, the camera first pans a circle of barebreasted women and young girls with the intertitle "Zulu Belles," and then returns to offer a shot of the women with their backs to the camera.[30]

Another common image in the exploration/safari film was the comparison of the native to the animal, with the associated implicit comparison of

21. Still from Gaston Méliès's *Captured by Aborigines* (1913).
(Reproduced by permission from Mme. Madeleine Malthète-Méliès)

hunting a big game animal and shooting a "native," an association I discussed in chapter 1 using the example of George Orwell's "Shooting an
Elephant." The opinion of the younger European colonialists in Orwell's
essay that an elephant's life is worth more than a native's is reflected in this
genre in which the hunt for the big game animal is celebrated, and indigenous peoples are no more than menial assistants. (This fascination with
big game hunting and murder is displayed in extreme form in Cooper and
Schoedsack's *The Most Dangerous Game* [1932], a film discussed in chapter
6.) Carl E. Akeley, taxidermist and photographer at the American Museum
of Natural History, was the screenwriter of a film directed by Paul J. Rainey,
Military Drills of Kikuyu Tribe and Other Ceremonies (1914). The film,
which includes many dances filmed in extreme long shot, feeding the Western fascination with the dancing native body, also includes big game hunting scenes, with footage of the white hunters in their safari suits sitting
proudly on their horses, African porters bringing up the rear. In one sequence a leopard is filmed as he waits in a tree. The leopard jumps down and
is shot, but then the film jump cuts to an African sitting in the same position in a tree drawing the obvious parallel. In Rainey's film, moreover, film
footage is intercut with photographs, including one of a camera man accom-

22. Osa Johnson and unidentified actors on location in Osa and Martin Johnson's
Cannibals of the South Seas (1917). (Courtesy of the Museum of Modern Art)

panying a rifle-bearing hunter and several of the white hunters holding their
guns, posing with their hunting dogs. Rainey's film is a striking hybrid
of photography and film. Upon seeing the photographs in Rainey's film—
photographs of hunters who look the camera straight on, or of a dead leopard stuffed in a hanging sack—the viewer is forced to contemplate a sense of
loss, a stopping of time, a death, Barthes's "that-has-been."[31] The frozen
images of the photographs are akin to cinematic taxidermy: the camera and
the hunt are again literally linked.

Death becomes cartoonish in the jungle films of Osa and Martin Johnson,
whose *Simba* (1928) was produced and distributed by the American Museum of Natural History.[32] Part of the humor they employed was the juxtaposition of native people (especially men) with Martin Johnson's wife Osa,
who, like the German actress Meg Gehrts in Hans Schomburgk's films, was
portrayed alternately as intrepid hunter, scolding housewife, and beautiful
object of desire, a trope later used in 1930s jungle films like *King Kong* and
Trader Horn.[33]

When he was hired by the writer Jack London in 1908 as a still photographer for an expedition to the Solomon Islands, Martin Johnson met a group
of Pathé filmmakers who showed him how to use a film camera, and he
embarked on a career filming in the Pacific Islands, Indonesia, and Africa.

23. Still from Osa and Martin Johnson's *Simba* (1928).
(Courtesy of the Museum of Modern Art)

One of the Johnsons' early films, *Cannibals of the South Seas* (1917), said to have been filmed in Malekula, reveals how the Ethnographic picturesque could be almost entirely textual. The Malekulan actors hardly move for the camera, but instead appear to be constantly posing, as if for a photograph. Much in the way that a lecturer would concoct a lurid story out of a few anthropological photographs,[34] however, the Johnsons use overly long intertitles to establish that they have been chased by cannibals. A man stares at the camera in *plan américain* with only his genitals covered; this repeated shot, reminiscent of anthropological photographs of a "native type," is the pretense for the narrative. Titles explain that he is Chief Nagapate, Cannibal King. Interspersed with shots of this man staring at the camera are titles like "By this time we were literally scared stiff, and Nagapate's sarcastic laugh nearly paralyzed Mrs Johnson with fright," and "We packed our cameras and prepared to leave when Nagapate signalled his men. Each of us was seized, Nagapate himself holding Mrs. Johnson, dislocating a wrist bone as she struggled." In this film, a sensational narrative of cannibalism and rape is spun out of a rather innocuous image of a man staring at the camera. There is nothing in the man's face or actions to suggest that he is a cannibal: the spectacle is constructed entirely out of text. The Johnsons speak for the natives' desire, but what is revealed is their own fear, their own fascinating cannibalism, and consequently the audience's fearful delight in confronting the gaze of the "cannibal."

The Johnsons' image of indigenous peoples as stereotyped protagonists in "the age-old story of Man emerging from savagery" was unremittant.[35] In the Johnsons' *Simba, The King of Beasts, A Saga of the African Veldt* (1928)—"a dramatic record of sheer reality" filmed in East Africa—much of the action and adventure is in the very act of shooting with the camera. The big game hunting film was a natural outlet for *braggadoccio*; the film itself was proof of the filmmakers' expertise and courage. Through intertitles, the Johnsons describe the Africans they encounter as monstrous and ridiculous; the women are alternately labeled sexually desirable and ugly, foils for Osa's plump white "showgirl" looks. The climax of *Simba* is a scene in which Lumbwa men spear lions, but, even here, the focus is the daring of the Johnsons: at one point the lion is shown charging the camera, followed by a reaction shot of Osa shooting it. Rosen's notion of the ability of cinema to control meaning finds a perfect example in the cinema of the Johnsons. Osa is sexualized, but never entirely in control at least in relation to the real hero established, her filmmaker/hunter husband Martin. *Simba* ends with an aproned Osa smugly baking a pie.

The Archive of Salvage Ethnography: Edward Sheriff Curtis

The Johnsons were able to conjure ethnographic spectacle out of the gaze of a Malekulan man staring at the camera. Commercial cinema like that of showman Burton Holmes presented a travelogue collection from the point of view of the fat colonialist tourist; expedition films, like those of Cherry Kearton, were made from the point of view of the Great White Hunter. In the photographic "archive" of Edward Sheriff Curtis, author of the twenty-volume book of photography *The North American Indian*, the point of view is markedly different. Curtis's films mythologize the "vanishing native," spectral yet proud.

As suggested above, the picturesque tableau was aligned with authenticity through detail, conventionalized ethnographic detail serving to impose a unity on the inherent multiplicity of the "exotic." As a mask to hide colonial anxieties, the picturesque was a means to catalog the distant, in a discourse which Suleri describes as "an unhinged aestheticism that veils and sequesters questions of colonial culpability, but in so doing, becomes a casualty of its own abstracted guilt."[36] In the "picturesque" cataloging of peoples in Melanesia, the Americas, and so on, anthropology provided the justification for what was in many cases genocide: a central premise of much of anthropology was that the native was always already vanishing, and the anthropologist could do nothing but record and reconstruct, racing against the evolutionary clock. Often accompanying this premise, however, was "abstracted" guilt, as a nostalgia for lost origins, and as fear—contemplation of death in the abstract leading to contemplation of one's own death.

Colonialism in the Americas, Asia, Africa, Melanesia, Micronesia, and Polynesia did not, of course, destroy all indigenous peoples and their ways of life. Disease brought by the colonizers wiped out many populations— some have suggested as much as half of the colonized world—and native peoples were murdered, enslaved, and brutally exploited. Yet indigenous cultures responded and survived. The representation of the "vanishing native," however, which denied the coexistence of indigenous peoples and turned a blind eye to how they were able to resist and survive European encroachment and dispossession, was an extremely potent and popular image.

Curtis, like Regnault and Flaherty, is often cited as an early ethnographic filmmaker. In his photographs and film, Curtis did much to promote the myth of the timeless "authenticity" of the Native American. In the mythological archetype of the horse-riding Plains Indian warrior with feather headdress, essential to the ideology of U.S. westward expansion, the Native American was represented as dying, yet noble, a "last of the . . ." phenomenon. The complex ways that Native Americans have negotiated the presence of whites in the Americas were never part of Curtis's mythology of the Indian.

The cinema of Curtis represents the beginnings of a genre of ethnographic cinema which emerged from the early travel film, and which offered a qualitatively different point of view on the "ethnographic." Curtis aimed for the elegiac and aesthetically beautiful: his object was to produce images of the noble, vanishing "savage," and, together with filmmakers like Flaherty, he became the poetic and artistic accomplice of the academic purveyors of salvage ethnography. Salvage ethnography took as its central tenet that certain peoples would soon be extinct, and influenced representations of indigenous peoples both in the museum and in ethnographic film, whether "scientific" or popular: cultural reconstruction eclipsed bodily inscription in importance. Jacob W. Gruber explains how salvage ethnography necessarily produced a collection of data—an ad hoc accumulation of detail—and he argues that it was motivated by a value system which conceived of the collections as evidence of inherently *pathological* cultures:

> Such an approach could lead only to a collection of data rather than a
> body of data. The very operation of the collection itself infused the data

with a sense of separateness, a notion of item discontinuity that encouraged the use of an acontextual comparative method. . . . Moreover, the sense of salvage with its concern with loss and extinction, stressed the disorganization in a social system at the expense of the sense of community; it stressed the pathology of cultural loss in the absence of any real experience with the normally operating small community. The recognition of the pathology of that state provided the basis and rationale for the useful concept of the ethnographic present as the ideal of organization—but it was an ideal whose reality, stability, and order were to be the source of a continuing skepticism. The fact was that the very notion of salvage insisted on the investigation of those sociocultural systems already in a advanced state of destruction; as with the development of medicine itself it was the abnormal that set the norm of investigation.[37]

The strange doubleness of the politics of authenticity meant that the "vanishing native" was imagined as simultaneously pathological and genuine. If salvage ethnography was a race against the perceived destruction of native life "from a pictorial point of view,"[38] it was also a race backwards, to a less cluttered, simpler past. Joseph K. Dixon, whose photographs of the noble Plains Indian warrior, like those of Curtis, would become the image of native authenticity for white Americans, succinctly summed up the aesthetic of salvage ethnography in his own photography: "Every effort was exhausted to eliminate any hint of the white man's foot—the spirit of the native environment dominated."[39]

Impelled by similar motivations, Curtis became more famous than Dixon, mainly because of the popularity of the photographs in his twenty-volume set *The North American Indian*. Funded by some of the very people who were exploiting the land and thus changing Indian ways of life—northeastern merchants and industrialists like Teddy Roosevelt and J. P. Morgan—Curtis's collection of photographs was perhaps the largest visual contribution to salvage ethnography by a non-anthropologist. Curtis himself labeled his work "Art Science," conceiving of it as both art and ethnography.[40]

In his lectures, Curtis capitalized on the public's hunger for images—using lantern slides and film—of sacred Indian dances, including the popular Hopi Snake dance at Walpi, Arizona. With the opening of the Atchison, Topeka and the Santa Fe RR in 1880, the Southwest in the following decades had become a mecca for white Kodak-toting tourists attending dances. Besides the Hopi Snake Dance, Curtis made a film in 1904 of a Navajo ritual. Because the ritual itself took place during the ninth night of the Nightway

(Yeibichai) ceremony, it had to be staged for daylight filming: it was apparently legitimate to "stage" the visual representation of authenticity.[41]

Curtis, like Dixon, was determined to eliminate all signs of white culture from his films and photographs of Indians. As Christopher Lyman has documented, heads, torsos, and full-length bodies of Native Americans are shot in a dreamy pictorialist style, foregrounding the corporeal presence of the sitters while denying their contemporary presence. The smoky ghostlike backgrounds and the use of costumes which iconographically were seen as more "authentic," but which were worn exclusively during the photography sessions, were major aspects of Curtis's oeuvre. The Indian is portrayed as the romantic hero of a "vanishing race." The image that Curtis created for himself was of an explorer/photographer with a mission: to document Native Americans who he claimed had adopted him and initiated him into secret societies. Curtis even boasted that he had become a Hopi priest and that he participated in the Snake dance.[42]

Particularly significant among the earliest feature-length works of ethnographic cinema is Edward Sheriff Curtis's film *In the Land of the Head-hunters* (1914), a film which, like *Nanook of the North,* involves reconstruction and salvage ethnography—the desire to "re-create" what native life was like before European contact.[43] A melodrama filmed in the Vancouver Island area about a young Kwakwaka'wakw (Kwakiutl) man, the woman he falls in love with, and an evil sorcerer, the film also includes many scenes of war and ceremonial dances.[44] In a brochure for the film, Curtis wrote that because of the "historical and ethnological importance" of images of Indians, films like his would only increase in value, and could be used by students, scientists, and the masses.[45] *In the Land of the Head-hunters* was promoted as a authentic record of Kwakwaka'wakw life at the time, but it was clearly based on cultural reconstruction. The Kwak-waka'wakw actors wore cedar bark costumes and wigs and were made to shave off moustaches; building fronts were constructed and totem poles carved for the film. All traces of "the white man's foot," as Dixon put it, were painstakingly erased.

Ira Jacknis has outlined some of the similarities between the salvage ethnography of Curtis and Boas. As Jacknis writes, "Given the popular insistence for a 'picturesque savage,' Boas and other photographers (Curtis even more so) were encouraged to arrange the 'reality' before the lens to depict as much of the traditional culture as possible." Although Boas disapproved of Curtis's mode of representation and even attacked Curtis for manipulating photographic style in a letter to Curtis's patron Theodore Roosevelt in 1907, Boas did not hesitate himself to manipulate photographs to remove signs of white presence.[46] Both men were obsessed with the idea of vanishing races and recording the "authentic"; both men made films of the Kwak-waka'wakw and collaborated with George Hunt, an ethnographer of British and Tlingit descent.[47] Although their styles of reconstruction differed, both Boas and Curtis were satisfied that the representations they created were authentic.

Boas was actively engaged in reconstruction not only in his photography but in his design of museum exhibits as well. At the American Museum of Natural History, Boas reconstructed scenes for his life groups and used photographs based on reconstructions in museum dioramas (although he carefully labeled them as such). He spent much time collecting old artifacts and eliciting memories of elderly informants on the ways that certain items had been used. As Jacknis points out, however, photography and reconstruction were problematic for Boas—he felt they could deceive, and were thus a risky means of recording culture. For Boas, such media could never usurp the place of the written ethnography.[48]

Just as writing allowed Boas more control over the possible readings of his ethnographic description, the intertitles of *In the Land of the Headhunters* were extremely important in guiding interpretation of Curtis's film. In the film, the young warrior hero is embodied in the character of Motana. Motana marries the maiden Naida, angering the jealous Sorcerer. The Sorcerer performs black magic against Motana, and Motana and his fellow villagers respond by beheading the Sorcerer and several others. The Sorcerer's brother Yaklus takes revenge by going on a headhunting raid himself: Yaklus kidnaps Naida, but Motana eventually rescues her, and Yaklus and his men drown in a gorge when their boat capsizes.

The narrative is labored: Curtis's film is really an excuse to string together footage purporting to offer a view of the Kwakwaka'wakw way of life before the nineteenth century. The dreamy quality of Curtis's photographs is present in the film in his use of smoke, an element of the vision quest. Smoke and fire are associated not just with dreams and spirituality, but also with evil, magic, and power.[49] The figure of the Sorcerer is a popular stereotype in white films about American Indians: the Indian "Medicine Man" was deceitful, jealous, conniving, and a sham (in implied opposition to the white Physician or Scientist), and Curtis's characterization was no exception. The Sorcerer is portrayed as lowly: the viewer first sees him on all fours spying on the courtship of Motana and Naida, and later sitting with his troll-like cronies by a fire in a forest, a scene shot from a high camera angle so that the viewer looks down at him. Through the Sorcerer and his brother Yaklus, who uses fire to smoke out the villagers in the raid scene, the audience learns that, although necessary for the vision quest, the power of fire and smoke can be misused, put to evil purposes.

The paradox of Curtis's image-making was its complicity with the industrialization and colonization processes that were radically altering Indian ways of life, even as it celebrated the eternal authentic. Perhaps it is more than coincidental that fire and smoke, like photography and cinema, were both vision-makers and weapons of destruction.

The strength of *In the Land of the Headhunters* lies in its spectacular dance sequences. In one scene, three great war canoes are first seen from a distance, then much closer: we see the magnificent figures of the Thunderbird, the Wasp, and the Grizzly Bear dancing at the prows of the canoes. George Hunt, who grew up among the Kwakwaka'wakw, helped Curtis organize these scenes: they literally take the large, beautiful, striking masks of these Northwest Coast Indians, so beloved by Boas and Lévi-Strauss, off the museum wall and put them in their natural settings. Curtis was praised for making the pictorial scenes found in museums come to life:

> It was thought to be a great educational advance when the American Museum of Natural History and the Smithsonian set up groups of Indians modeled in wax and clothed in their everyday or gala costumes. But now a further step of equal importance has been taken by Edward S. Curtis. . . . The masks and costumes of the eagle and the bear which seemed merely grotesque when we saw them hung up in rows in the showcase at the museum become effective, even awe-inspiring, when seen on giant forms on the plow of a canoe filled with victorious warriors.[50]

Curtis's camera for the most part keeps its distance, much as a visitor to an exposition performance or a viewer of a museum display must stand back to take in the spectacle. The function of the ceremonies is left unexplained. With swirling black hair, women dance alongside dancers with wonderful masks. In one scene, described as a Winter Ceremonial, a man dances in the foreground while in the back a sheet is pulled down. The space is immediately covered with moving, whirling masked dancers, and the camera then cuts to an eagle dancer in a completely different, empty space, as if Curtis were attempting to isolate one movement from the whole. Continuity is not important: picturesque detail is. Vachel Lindsay wrote in 1915 that the Kwakiutl in Curtis's film looked like bronzes.[51] Thus Curtis brought to life the type of scenes that might be found in a museum display by Boas; he captured the motion which Boas had complained was lacking in the museum life group, while still managing to create timeless "bronzes."[52]

24. Edward Sheriff Curtis, "Bridal group" (1914).
(*North American Indian* vol. 10, courtesy of the Library of Congress)

Curtis's tale is convoluted and melodramatic, and only the intertitles carry forward the narrative. Curtis even allowed several different actors to play the same parts. Visually, however, the audience at times does see from the point of view of the actors, as when the shore is filmed from the point of view of Yaklus and his men as they move in to attack Motana's village, or when the seals are filmed from Motana's point of view as he stalks them. True to the salvage ethnography mode, there are no tourists, no hunters, and no scientists in the film—no trace of the "white foot."

Two aspects of the film were criticized by contemporary scientific reviewers as highly inaccurate, not true to Kwakwaka'wakw life in 1914: the vision quest and headhunting.[53] But these two themes, essential to the narrative, also carry an important allegorical impact. The vision quest parallels Curtis's quest, and, while headhunting was seen by Western viewers as pathological and "savage," Curtis's own profession as a photographer/filmmaker made him a hunter of Indian "heads." In several striking scenes, warriors stand at the prow of oncoming canoes, shaking the heads they have captured up and down as they approach shore. Motana himself dances with

25. Edward Sheriff Curtis, "Masked dancers in canoes" (1914).
(*North American Indian* vol. 10, courtesy of the Library of Congress)

skulls and is seen laying his head to sleep on them. The beheadings themselves, like Motana's hunting successes, are not portrayed.

Although the Kwakwaka'wakw performers in some scenes stand on
shore highlighted by the sun, appearing shadow-like, on the whole they are
not rendered hieroglyphs as were the West African performers in the Paris
Ethnographic Exposition filmed by Regnault. Instead, they are clearly actors, playing roles in a dramatized narrative of Noble Savagery. If the goal of
Curtis was truth, however, he clearly failed: the superimposed melodrama,
and the film's sensationalized version of salvage ethnography, predominate.
The actual historical and political situation of the Kwakwaka'wakw, whose
potlatch ceremonies, for example, had been forbidden by the Canadian government, is nowhere addressed.

In the Land of the Head Hunters leaves one strangely untouched: Curtis's
photography, with its topographic obsession with the surfaces of faces, is
more powerful and has more presence. Indeed, the film was not a great
success despite good reviews. The stillness of Curtis's photographs eerily
suggests death in a manner that his stilted feature film does not; Barthes's

suggestion that photography can be mad whereas cinema is perhaps only oneiric describes the difference between Curtis's photography at its best and his film.[54] Flaherty and his wife Frances, however, saw and appreciated Curtis's film: they would go on to make films of salvage ethnography which were not only more compelling, but which would come to define an entire genre of ethnographic cinema.[55]

Recontextualizing the Picturesque

The 1992 exhibition at the American Museum of Natural History "Chiefly Feasts: The Enduring Kwakiutl Potlatch," organized with the collaboration of Kwakwaka'wakw curators including Gloria Cranmer Webster, was a moving tribute to the fact that the Kwakwaka'wakw, one of the most popularly filmed native peoples, did not indeed vanish. Two community museums, the U'mista Cultural Centre (Alert Bay on Cormorant Island) and the Quadra Island Kwagiulth Museum (off the east coast of Vancouver Island), attest to the importance of community representation and the repatriation of sacred objects forcibly appropriated by the white government in the past. Significantly, although many Kwakwaka'wakw historians and activists describe *In the Land of the Head Hunters* (1914) as a white man's myth about vanishing races, footage of the sequence on war canoes was used in the "Chiefly Feasts" exhibition, as a testament to the magnificence of Kwakwaka'wakw culture. In the exhibition, the images are recovered by descendants of the people represented in the film: the Kwakwaka'wakw use of the war canoe footage thus can be thought of as the inverse of the cannibal-mongering overtextualization of the Johnsons.

   The way in which photographic and filmic images are inscribed and contextualized conditions the ways in which they are understood. Even as the anthropological museum and early travelogue films were embronzing what they perceived as dead cultures into picturesque tableaus intended for white spectators, Native American cultures like that of the Kwakwaka'wakw remained very much alive, adapting to the pressures of colonialization, and fighting to preserve their own cultures and histories. The gesture of the picturesque is unshielded; the Ethnographic detail is reclaimed and reconfigured.

4 TAXIDERMY AND ROMANTIC ETHNOGRAPHY

Robert Flaherty's Nanook of the North

Nanook of the North (1922), a film which focuses on the daily activities of a family of Itivimuit, a group of Quebec Inuit, is considered by many to be one of the great works of art of independent cinema. It is seen as a point of origin: it has been called the first documentary film, the first ethnographic film, as well as the first art film. The writings about *Nanook* are inextricably wound up with the image of its director, Robert J. Flaherty. There is an aura around the Flaherty name: he is praised as the father of documentary and ethnographic cinema, as a great storyteller and humanitarian, and as the first maverick independent artist uncorrupted by Hollywood. Unlike other white filmmakers of indigenous peoples, it is claimed that he never exploited his subjects. Flaherty embronzed his own myth when he declared: "First I was an explorer; then I was an artist."[1]

Nanook is also an artifact of popular culture. When it was released and distributed by Pathé in 1922 in both the United States and Europe, it fed upon an already established craze in those countries for the Inuit as a kind of cuddly "primitive" man. The writer Joseph E. Senungetuk, an Innupiat from Northwest Alaska, summarized this stereotype: "a people without technology, without a culture, lacking intelligence, living in igloos, and at best, a sort of simplistic 'native boy' type of subhuman arctic being."[2] *Nanook* was extremely popular when it was released worldwide, and spawned what ethnographic filmmaker Asen Balikci has called "Nanookmania."[3] Many writers consider *Nanook* as the high point of the *age d'or* of silent ethnographic cinema, the period from 1922 to 1932 which also saw the release of Flaherty's *Moana* (1926) and his collaboration with F. W. Murnau, *Tabu* (1931).[4] Revived on numerous occasions, *Nanook* remains a staple for high school and university courses in anthropology and ethnographic film.

The academic discourse on *Nanook of the North* centers on questions of authenticity. Some have argued that because the scenes of everyday Quebec Inuit life were reconstructed to enhance the film's visual and narrative impact, it cannot be considered true science. Other anthropologists contend that cinematic representation can never fully be objective—thus both Flaherty's innovative "flow of life" style, as Siegfried Kracauer termed it, and the purported participation of the Inuit people filmed are hailed as markers of Flaherty's pioneering genius. Still others add that the documentary value of the film lies in its portrayal of essential humanity. Ethnographic filmmaker Luc de Heusch is representative of this last school of thought. De Heusch exclaimed that *Nanook* was "a family portrait . . . the epic of a man, of a society frantically struggling to survive. . . . Family life, the human condition, are conquests from which animals are excluded. Such, in essence, is the theme of the film. Nanook, the hero of the first ethnographic film, is also the symbol of all civilization."[5]

The focus of this chapter will be on an overlooked aspect of the film: what the film and the discourse surrounding it can tell us about the nature of anthropological knowledge and the role of visual media in legitimating that knowledge and other regimes of truth. *Nanook* was praised as a film of universal human reality, and Flaherty was held up to be a "real" filmmaker, untainted by commercial concerns. Conversely the Oedipal slaying of this great father figure in recent criticism has focused on Flaherty as forger of the reality of the Quebec Inuit. In both cases, what is ignored is how *Nanook* emerges from a web of discourses which constructed the Inuit as Primitive man, and which considered cinema, and particularly Flaherty's form of cinema, to be a mode of representation which could only be truthful. The concern here will not be with whether or not Flaherty was an artist or a liar, but with ethnographic "taxidermy," and how the discourse of authenticity has created the film.

I take inspiration from the subtitle of Leprohon's fine book on the ethnographic cinema of travel and exploration, *L'exotisme et le cinéma: les "chasseurs d'images" à la conquête du monde* (1945), and examine *Nanook of the North* as the product of a hunt for images, as a kind of taxidermic display. First, I examine the discourse around the Inuit, a discourse which has been largely ignored: Nanookmania was preceded by a historical fascination for Inuit performers in exhibitions, zoos, fairs, museums, and early cinema. Second, I look closely at the film and show how the film represents a paradigm for a mode of representing indigenous peoples which parallels the romantic primitivism of modern anthropology. Finally, I examine the discourse on Flaherty as explorer/artist, a discourse which has painted him as either the great artist, or, like the Wizard of Oz, the Great Humbug or falsifier of reality. There are thus three hunts (and therefore three acts of taxidermy): the history of the hunt for representations of the Inuit for science and popular culture, the hunt for cinematic images of the Inuit for the film *Nanook*, and cinema's hunt for Flaherty as great artist and/or great liar.

Taxidermy, Salvage Ethnography, and Slight Narrative

Nanook of the North is often seen as a film without a scripted narrative. As Flaherty himself explained, he did not want to show the Inuit as they were at the time of the making of the film, but as (he thought) they *had been*. Filmed on location at Inukjuak (formerly Port Harrison), at the Inukjuak River in Quebec, Canada, the family of Quebec Inuit represented in the film consists of the hunter Nanook the Bear (played by Allakariallak), the wife and mother of his children Nyla (played by Alice (?) Nuvalinga) who is always shown caring for and carrying the baby Rainbow, another woman Cunayoo, and various children including Nanook's son Allegoo (played by Phillipoosie).[6] The narrative of Flaherty's film seems to ramble: it begins with the introduction of the family, the repair of kayaks and making of fuel; the family then trades furs at the trading post of the fur company; Nanook fishes and hunts walrus; the family builds an igloo and goes to sleep; they then wake up and go off in their dogsleds, a scene culminating in the famous seal-hunting scene so beloved by film theorist André Bazin.[7] The film ends with the arrival of a storm and the family taking shelter in an abandoned igloo.

I call the mode of representation of the "ethnographic" which emerged from this impulse *taxidermy*. Taxidermy seeks to make that which is dead look as if it were still living. In his study of the impact of the taxidermic impulse on the writing of history in the nineteenth century, Stephen Bann quotes British taxidermist Charles Waterton who complained that the unadorned dead beast was "a mere dried specimen, shrunk too much in this part, or too bloated in that; a mummy, a distortion, an hideous spectacle." Waterton explained that in order to reconstruct life, one must accept the fact of death, and use art as well as artifice: "It now depends upon the skill and anatomical knowledge of the operator (perhaps I ought to call him artist at this stage of the process), to do such complete justice to the skin before him, that, when a visitor shall gaze upon it afterwards, he will exclaim, 'That animal is alive!' "[8] As Bann comments, "The restoration of the lifelike is itself postulated as a response to a sense of loss. In other words, the Utopia of life-like reproduction depends upon, and reacts to, the fact of death. It is a strenuous attempt to recover, by means which must exceed those of convention, a state which is (and must be) recognized as lost."[9]

By loss, Bann was referring to the sense of loss or lack of wholeness that brought about a crisis in the nineteenth century: the realization that instead of one history there were many histories. Donna Haraway, in her marvelous article on Carl Akeley's early-twentieth-century dioramas, taxidermy, photography, and film at the American Museum of Natural History, likewise speaks of taxidermy as a means to protect against loss, in order that the body may be transcended: "Taxidermy fulfills the fatal desire to represent, to be whole; it is a politics of reproduction."[10] Thus in order to make a visual representation of indigenous peoples, one must believe that they are dying, as well as use artifice to make a picture which appears more true, more pure. Since indigenous peoples were assumed to be already dying if not dead, the ethnographic "taxidermist" turned to artifice, seeking an image more true to the posited original. When Flaherty stated, "One often has to distort a thing to catch its true spirit," he was not just referring to his own artistry but to the preconditions for the effective, "true" representation of so-called vanishing culture.[11]

It is a paradox of this cinema of romantic preservationism that the reaction—"That person is alive!"—is most easily elicited if the subjects filmed are represented as existing in a former epoch. As Johannes Fabian has pointed out, the specificity of anthropology is that the subjects of its inquiry are represented as existing in an earlier age. Fabian explains the significance of the use in modern anthropology of the "ethnographic present," the practice of writing in the present tense about the people whom the anthropologist studied. The dominant pronoun/verb form is "They are (do, have, etc.)" This form of rhetoric presupposes that the people studied are timeless, and establishes the anthropologist as hidden observer, akin to the natural historian in that he or she stands at the peephole into the distant past.[12] The ethnographic present obfuscates the dialogue and the encounters that took place between the anthropologist and the people studied. In other words, as Fabian writes, "pronouns and verb forms in the third person mark an Other outside the dialogue."[13]

The cinema of Flaherty worked in the same way: Nanook and his family were represented in a cinematic "ethnographic present" in which intertitles establish the camera, and thus the filmmaker, as observer. Furthermore, if the indigenous man, Nanook, is constructed as a being without artifice, as referent, the indigenous woman is there to be uncovered, her body—and this is true of ethnographic cinema in general—to be scopically possessed by the camera/filmmaker and the audience as well. As intended, however, this form of ethnographic film, infused with the notion of death and the idea of vanishing races, is a cinema of archetypal moments endlessly repeated.[14] In

26. Still from *Nanook of the North* (1922), dir. Robert Flaherty.
(Courtesy of the Museum of Modern Art)

Nanook, the archetypal moment is that of a society ignorant of guns or gramophones: a society of man the hunter, man against nature, man the eater of raw flesh. *Nanook of the North* was a cinema of origins in many ways: its appeal was the myth of authentic first man.

What has been called Flaherty's "slight narrative"[15] thus fits perfectly with a racializing representation of the Inuit, which situates indigenous peoples outside modern history. *Nanook*, however, is structured as a film about the daily life of the Inuit, its novelty deriving from the fact that it was neither a scientific expedition film meant to serve as a positivist record, nor a travelogue of jokey tourism. As mentioned above, Siegfried Kracauer described Flaherty as a filmmaker of the "flow of life." Kracauer writes, "Flaherty's 'slight narratives' portray or resuscitate modes of existence that obtain among primitive peoples. . . . Most Flaherty films are expressive of his romantic desire to summon, and preserve for posterity, the purity and 'majesty' [Flaherty's word] of a way of life not yet spoiled by the advance of civilization."[16]

Flaherty explained this best when he described film as "a very simple form." For Flaherty, the medium made simple was well suited to the subject matter:

> [Films] are very well-suited to portraying the lives of primitive people whose lives are simply lived and who feel strongly, but whose activities are external and dramatic rather than internal and complicated. I don't think you can make a good film of the love affairs of the Eskimo . . . because they never show much feeling in their faces, but you can make a very good film of Eskimos spearing a walrus.[17]

The Ethnographic is without intellect: he or she is best represented as merely existing. It is the camera of the explorer/artist who will capture the reality of their "simply lived" lives. Hence the notion (and myth) that the actors in *Nanook* were "non-actors."

The desire of Euro-American audiences and critics to perceive Nanook as authentic Primitive man, as an unmediated *referent,* is evident in the fact that until the 1970s, no one bothered to ask members of the Inuit community in which the film was made for their opinions of the film. Only then was it learned that the name of the actor who played Nanook was Allakariallak. The same applies to all the other characters in the film. Although it was typical for explorers to "nickname" the Inuit they encountered, Flaherty's innovation was in giving the Inuit nicknames that sounded Inuit. Hence Nanook (the Bear) was a better and more easily marketable name than Allakariallak, because of its seeming genuineness and its dual connotations of cuddly like a teddy bear, and wild like a savage beast.

At the end of the film there is a haunting shot of Nanook sleeping, a close-up of his head. He appears to be asleep, but his absolute stillness reminds us of a waxwork or a corpse. Taxidermy is also deeply religious: when Bazin writes that the mummy complex is the impulse behind the evolution of technologies of realism—"To preserve, artificially, his bodily appearance is to snatch it from the flow of time, to stow it away neatly, so to speak, in the hold of life"—one is reminded of the image of the sleeping Nanook.[18] In ethnographic cinema, the narrative of the film hinges upon the body of the native—plugged into the narrative of evolution and the myth of vanishing races. It is this body, and not that of an Oedipal father or mother, which must be slain and upon which the narrative rests.[19] That Allakariallak died two years after the film was released, of either starvation or disease, only enhanced the film's status as a work of authenticity.

The Hunt for the Inuit and the Alaskan Eskimo:
Explorers, Museums, Fairs, and Films

The trail of contact between Arctic peoples and whites was already littered with corpses by the time of *Nanook*. The appetite for the Inuit—specifically for images of their *bodies*—by both scientists and the public began in 1577 when the explorer Martin Frobisher presented Queen Elizabeth I with a man, woman, and child from Baffinland.[20] The representation of the Inuit began with explorers' accounts: the belief that the word "Eskimo" means "eater of raw meat" reveals what the public found most interesting about them. Because of their diet of raw meat, they were described as animal-like, savage, and cannibalistic. They also would be repeatedly compared to their sled dogs, and this canine metaphor was used in *Nanook*.[21]

Arctic explorers brought back more than just maps, furs and ivory. It was common for explorers to bring back Inuit and Alaskan Eskimo. It was also a "tradition" that these Inuit rarely returned to their homelands: they frequently died from diseases for which they had no immunity. Like the West Africans and Malagasy whom Regnault filmed in exhibitions, the Inuit were extremely popular performers in exhibitions, zoos, and museums. They were treated as specimens and objects of curiosity.

Some of the Inuit left behind written records of their experiences as performers. One such account is that of a man named Abraham, one of eight Labrador Inuit brought over by J. Adrian Jacobsen to perform in the Hagenbeck Zoo in Berlin.[22] Abraham kept a diary in which he described how one member of the group was beaten with a dog whip and how they performed at the zoo in freezing conditions. Like the climax of *Nanook*, the climax of these performers' acts at the zoo was a seal hunt. Within three months, however, all had died from smallpox. Their bones immediately were used for anthropological research.

Explorers like Robert Peary were dependent on the good will and money of industrialists and museum philanthropists to fund their expeditions. To increase their own fame, and to make some profit, explorers brought back Inuit and Alaskan Eskimo to be exhibited. Peary was notorious for his cruelty and arrogance toward the Inuit who worked for him, often treating them no better than dogs.[23] When they died, often from diseases which his ships inadvertently brought, he would exhume their bodies and sell them to museums. Explorers also made most of their fortunes through the furs and ivory they received from the Inuit.[24]

In 1896, Franz Boas, who was then assistant curator of the American Museum of Natural History, pleaded with Peary to bring back an Inuit for

27. Elisha Kent Kane, Joe, and Hanna, Smithsonian Institution life group, 1873. (Smithsonian Institution photo no. 28321, used by permission of the Smithsonian Institution, National Anthropological Archives)

the museum. It is surprising that Boas, who in 1893 had worked on anthropological exhibits at the World's Columbian Exhibition in Chicago where many performers, including Inuit, had died (their bodies were later used in the Field Museum), apparently did not consider the danger of exposing the Inuit to disease as an obstacle.[25] Of the six Inuit from Smith Sound who were brought back by Peary and housed in the American Museum of Natural History, only one did not immediately die of pnemonia, a little boy known as Minik Wallace. Abandoned by Peary, Boas, and the museum scientists who had brought him to the United States, Wallace was adopted and grew up in New York, only to discover as a teenager that when his father had died the scientists had staged a fake burial, and that indeed his father's bones were at the museum. As Wallace explained in a letter to a friend:

> You can't know the sad feelings I have. . . . No one can know unless they have been taken from their home and had their father die and put on exhibition, and be left to starve in a strange land where the men insult you when you ask for your own dear father's body to bury or to be sent home.
>
> These are the civilized men who steal, and murder, and torture, and pray and say "Science."[26]

Not surprisingly, the Inuit were popular subjects for museum models in dioramas. For example, the first museum models at the Smithsonian Institution's United States National Museum (now the Museum of Natural History), made in 1873, represented two Inuit named "Joe" and "Hanna," flanking the figure of the explorer Dr. Elisha Kent Kane. Museum displays of life groups—depicting cultures in nuclear family units performing rituals or subsistence activities—are another characteristic form of the "taxidermic" mode of salvage ethnography.[27]

In the nineteenth century, the image of the Inuit and the Alaskan Eskimo acquired nuances in addition to that of "wild Savage." As Ann Fienup-Riordan explains, the Eskimo were made into the mirror image of the explorers. Like the explorers, the Eskimo were represented as noble, brave, independent, persevering, and incorruptible. But ideas about the relatively lofty status of the Eskimo did not mean that the Eskimo were perceived as able to undergo their own "independent progress" without white intervention.[28] In a sense, the Eskimo were seen as Primitive success stories of an Arctic "survival of the fittest." Fienup-Riordan explains:

> The publicity these arctic representatives received marked the progressive transformation of the image of Eskimos from subhuman to superhuman. Displayed along with their sophisticated hunting tools and wearing polar bear skins, these living specimens came to represent the ultimate survivors, intrepid and courageous individualists who through sheer cunning were able to best their rivals in the free marketplace of the arctic world. Happy, peaceful, hardworking, independent, and adaptable—these were the images most often used to clothe Eskimos in the twentieth century. The nuances of Eskimo reality dimmed in comparison to this dramatically staged representation, an image increasingly acceptable because of its incorporation of traits Westerners valued in themselves.[29]

This notion of the Eskimo as an uncorrupt example of all the values of the West—independence, perseverance, and patriarchy—reached its epitome in the cinematic character of Nanook.[30] In both the United States and Europe, the 1920s were characterized by a pervasive fear of racial mixing: the white was constructed as the Nordic—pale, blond, blue-eyed, from the North. The term "Nordic" was used in popular culture to refer to whites of Northern European descent. The fear was that the Nordic was being annihilated by racial mixing. At best, the Inuit or Alaskan Eskimo was the primitive Nordic, or as Asen Balikci termed it, a "primitive Protestant."[31] I would like to suggest that the character Nanook was thus something of a mirror for the white audience: he too was from the North, and, as Balikci's comment suggests, like the Nordic, was seen as embodying the Protestant values of patriarchy, industriousness, independence, and courage. But the character Nanook is still the subject of voyeuristic observation, not acknowledged as coequal of the adventurer/anthropologist.

As I have argued in chapter 1, cinema took over from the world's fair many of the functions of the native village exhibition. Indeed, one of the earliest cinematic depictions of the Inuit is a body of film by Thomas Edison in 1901 of the "Esquimaux Village" at the Pan-American Exposition in Buffalo. Edison produced footage of the Inuit as happy gamesters in dogsleds amid papier-mâché igloo environments with painted backdrops of snowy mountains and fake ice floes.[32] Edison was not alone: numerous films about Arctic exploration that include footage of or relating to the Inuit and Alaskan Eskimo were made before *Nanook*. In almost all these films, the narrative centers on a whaling expedition or an arctic exploration. Footage of Inuit and Alaskan Eskimo hunting polar bears and paddling in kayaks were "picturesque" details which, as in other films of the period, lent an air of authenticity to the representations.[33]

The use of film to enhance lectures on expeditions and Arctic peoples was also common. In this genre as well, the indigenous people served as "picturesque" elements of the landscape, marking the exotic and primitive past through which the modern white explorers were passing. In William Van Valin's films of Point Barrow, Alaska (1912–18), for example, there is a noteworthy seal-hunting scene, apparently already a staple of films about the Inuit or Alaskan Eskimo.[34] In an empty landscape, a lone Alaskan Eskimo hunts patiently, the intertitles explaining that "Thought of hungry wife and kiddies urges weary hunter on." Because this title is followed by a pan of the landscape, it allows the viewer for a moment to see with the hunter's eyes. Like other expedition filmmaker/lecturers, Van Valin uses catchy, kitschy titles like "Dog eat dog" for a scene in which a dog eats raw meat. In Van Valin's films the Alaskan Eskimo are portrayed as carefree, playful, dancing, and instinctive: "Old Eskimo smell whale through twelve feet of ice." The Alaskan Eskimo filmed tend to line up and stare, laughing at the camera. Even in Van Valin's film, however, death is lurking: the camera pans the bones of Alaskan Eskimo, skeletons scattered everywhere in an empty landscape, with the accompanying intertitle: "Where solitude now reigns supreme, except when the wind whistles through the eye orbits and nasal cavities of these empties."[35]

Nanook shares several aspects with arctic expedition film predecessors such as the films of van Valin. In both, there is an emphasis on hunting and the eating of raw meat by people and dogs. As I have suggested, the seal hunt scene is all but obligatory. To the extent that Western contact is portrayed, it is as benign, even amusing, trade—the Inuit get novelties and the Euro-Americans get fur. In both *Nanook* and the expedition film, moreover, the Inuit and Alaskan Eskimo are portrayed as playful, and are given nicknames, but in both death is always lurking.[36] The close ups in *Nanook* also borrow from the expedition genre: the laughing Inuit holds up the fish for the camera; other portraits in Flaherty's film are infused with the dreamlike Pictorialist style characteristic of Edward Sheriff Curtis.[37]

Despite these many similarities, Flaherty's film stands out. As I argue in the next section, the innovation lies not only in Flaherty's distinctive film style, but also in the creation of the myth that Flaherty had produced for the first time a form of cinema paralleling participant observation.

The Historical Setting of Nanook of the North

The image of the Inuit was not always one of a simple, incessantly smiling people struggling heroically against the arctic cold. In the 1880s, Quebec Inuit murdered shipwrecked crews of white men, and were consequently not allowed access to the posts of the Hudson's Bay Company. Ironically, descendants of these men were among the Inuit who welcomed the firm that sponsored *Nanook*, the French company Revillon Frères (in 1910 Revillon Frères established several posts and became a fierce competitor of the Hudson's Bay Company), and were also among those Flaherty filmed in 1914.[38]

Because fur prices were at their height in the 1920s, the Inuit in Quebec were introduced to a cash economy, and the Inuit portrayed in *Nanook* thus were using guns, knew about gramophones, wore Western clothing, and, although many had died from Western diseases, certainly were not vanishing. Financial stability proved precarious, however: the fact that the actor Allakariallak, who played Nanook, died of starvation or disease two years after *Nanook* was made is not surprising. According to Bernard Saladin d'Anglure, the Canadian government during the early part of the twentieth century virtually ignored the Inuit and gave no social aid. D'Anglure writes that Quebec Inuit were dependent on the "good will of the few Euro-Canadian residents (traders, missionaries, and meteorological station employees) or to passing ships whose crews too often exchanged gifts for women's sexual favors."[39]

If Flaherty had not banished history from *Nanook of the North*, he would have had to acknowledge his own role as an agent of change in the lives of the Inuit. Ironically, Flaherty made several expeditions in the Hudson Bay region of northern Canada on behalf of Canadian industrialists. He thus followed in the footsteps of his father, a mining engineer who prospected Canadian areas for minerals for U.S. Steel and other corporations.[40] In 1910, Robert Flaherty went to work for the Canadian Railroad builder and financier Sir William Mackenzie as a prospector and mapmaker looking for mineral deposits, particularly iron ore. Mackenzie was also hoping to establish shipping from Hudson Bay to countries outside of Canada.

As Jo-Anne Birnie Danzker explains, during the period from 1900 to 1910, the territorial boundaries of the possessions of the United States and Canada were still in dispute, and photography became an important tool for establishing claims of possession.[41] In 1913 Mackenzie asked Flaherty to bring a film camera on his explorations. Flaherty brought along a Bell and Howell camera as well as equipment for developing and printing. These early films of 1914 and 1916 are said to have been destroyed in a fire.[42] It is clear that both Robert Flaherty and his wife Frances began to think that their careers might be in cinema, and they hoped to profit from their films, going to various organizations like the Explorer's Club, museums, and movie companies asking for financial backing. (Apparently both Boas and Curtis were consulted for financial advice and were shown the films.) The career of the explorer/artist was already in the mind of Frances Flaherty in 1914 when she wrote that she hoped the films "will attract a great deal of attention, be widely shown and gain recognition for R. [Robert] as an explorer, as an artist and interpreter of the Eskimo people, and consequently bring him greater opportunity."[43]

According to Danzker, the representation of the Eskimo as a type, and the idea of following the daily life of an Eskimo man and his family, was present even in these early films. Peter Pitseolak, an Inuit photographer from Seekooseelak (Cape Dorset, Baffin Island), remembers Flaherty coming one winter to film, giving out guns as well as other items. Pitseolak refers to

Flaherty as "the moving picture boss" as well as Koodjuk (swan) because of his white skin; he explains that his close relative Noogooshoweetok made many drawings for Flaherty, work which Noogooshoweetok found tiring.[44] It was these drawings which Flaherty drew on for inspiration for one part of his 1914 film (a segment about the making of a film from an Inuit drawing). Characteristic of these drawings was an emphasis on the snowy white vastness of the landscape suggested by the white of the page, in which Inuit individuals and dogsleds are rendered small in the overall scheme. Thanks to the vision of the Arctic environment of the artist Noogooshoweetok, and of later Inuit camera operators who worked for Flaherty, *Nanook* has some of the most beautiful landscape scenes ever filmed.[45]

The Film Nanook of the North

The images and the scenes in *Nanook* which have been most written about are the hunting scenes, especially the walrus and the seal-hunting scene. Ethnographic cinema is above all a cinema of the body: the focus is on the anatomy and gestures of the indigenous person, and on the body of the land they inhabit. *Nanook of the North* thus begins by introducing the two main landscapes of the film: the land of Inuit Quebec, and the face of Nanook. The shot which will be the defining image of the film—Nanook at the top of the hill, harpoon in hand—showcases both elements. When he faces the camera, the actor Allakariallak smiles, interpreted by critics to mean that he was childlike, not complex, feeding Flaherty's conception of "primitive Eskimos" as simple people. Until the 1930s, it was unseemly in the United States and Europe to face the camera smiling: smiling was considered to make the subject look foolish and childlike.[46] Recent research has shown that the Inuit found Flaherty and the filmmaking a source of great amusement,[47] and this amusement may well account for Nanook's smile. The enigma of Nanook's smile allows the audience to project its own cultural presuppositions: from the point of view of an outsider he is childlike, from the Inuit point of view he may be seen as laughing at the camera.

Nanook's subsequent arrival at the edge of a lake or sea by kayak, after which one-by-one various members of his family appear from within the seemingly diminutive vessel, perhaps appeals to an unconscious association of the Inuit with fairs and circuses. As Barsam has noted, this comic device is similar to the one with which one introduces clowns.[48] The last "member" of Nanook's family to emerge from the kayak is the puppy Comock. Later in the film, puppies will be compared to Inuit babies, and sled dogs to Inuit.

28. Still from *Nanook of the North* (1922), dir. Robert Flaherty.
(Courtesy of the Museum of Modern Art)

Like a museum display in which sculpted models of family groups perform "traditional activities," Nanook's family adopts a variety of poses for the camera. These scenes of the picturesque always represent a particular view of family or community, usually with the father as hunter and the mother as nurturer, paralleling Western views of the nuclear family.

In the following trading post sequence, Nanook is shown to be ignorant of Western technology. Against a wall of the white fur pelts, Nyla sits in the background rocking her body, with her baby, and Nanook, crouched in the left foreground with the trader at the right in a higher position, gazes at the gramophone in the center. Nanook touches the gramophone; intertitles explain that he does not understand where or how the sound is made. He then is shown biting the record three times while laughing at the camera. This conceit of the indigenous person who does not understand Western technology allows for voyeuristic pleasure and reassures the viewer of the contrast between the Primitive and the Modern: it ingrains the notion that the people are not really acting. Their naïveté—they do not understand this foreign technology—is another sign of authenticity. This conceit, of course, obscures the Inuit's own appropriation of the new technology, their participation in the production of the film.

In the next scene, intertitles first explain that Nanook's children "are banqueted by the trader—sea biscuit and lard?" The viewer sees two little children laughing contentedly, licking their lips. But Allegoo, the son, "indulged to excess," is given castor oil by the trader, a medicament which immediately cures him. Licking his lips as well, Allegoo smiles at the camera, while Nanook looks on delightedly. The trader is depicted as superior in both technology and medicine, in a message covered over by all the furs. It is also a scene of eroticism. Nyla sits on the fur-covered ground, her baby and the puppies playing affectionately, licking and touching. It is a space of pleasure, with music from a gramophone and gorging on biscuits. The eroticism continues in other ways throughout the film, especially in its emphasis on oral contact: Nyla licks her baby clean, Nanook licks his knife, the family lick their lips while eating raw meat. The bottle from which the trader pours cod liver oil to Allegoo, however, also looks like a liquor bottle; the encroachment of whites brought not only influenza, smallpox, and tuberculosis, but alcoholism as well. Eroticism, a lust for the Native body, is here conjoined with an image foreshadowing impending death and destruction: the myth of the vanishing race could be used to make genocide erotic.[49]

And the bodies must be uncovered: in a later scene where the camera serves as a fourth wall, the viewer sees the family getting dressed and undressed. The women are shown half-naked, their breasts displayed for the viewer. (It is difficult to imagine a film by Flaherty about his own life in which his wife Frances would be shown undressing for the camera before she goes to bed.) Because they are not actually in a closed igloo, but in an open igloo set, their bodies are shivering as they dress. Although the intertitle erroneously claims that the igloo has to be below freezing, the family is literally left out in the cold, and their cold is palpable.

The trading sequence, which includes the scenes described above, serves as a nexus for discourses of colonialism, race, and gender. It must be remembered that Nanook was sponsored by the French fur company Revillon Frères. The trading scene serves as propaganda for Revillon, who, as I have explained, was a staunch competitor with the Hudson's Bay Company at the time. The complexity of the Inuit/white trader relationship is glossed over by Flaherty's representation of the trading post as a joyful place.

The next sequence begins with Nanook "already on the thin edge of starvation," a surprising turn of events considering that the family has been "banqueted." Despite the grave intertitle, what follows are lovely outdoor fishing, hunting, and igloo-building scenes. The dramatic tension in many of the scenes is conveyed by intertitles which do not reveal too much too soon, and by the use of long takes and great depth of field. In the walrus scene, Nanook rushes out with the other men in kayaks, they stalk the walrus, and pull it in. Making this particular scene, Flaherty said, was a difficult struggle requiring subterfuge: the men were afraid that they would be pulled out to sea and kept on calling Flaherty to shoot the walrus with his rifle, but Flaherty pretended not to hear them.[50] Flaherty shows a close-up shot of the head of the dead walrus, a common shot in travelogues, and the film explains that the men "cannot restrain the pangs of hunger" as they immediately begin to eat ravenously. The scene in which Nanook and his family build an igloo is built on suspense: the viewer only realizes that Nanook is making a window for the igloo, for example, after he is almost finished installing it. In a subsequent scene, Nanook teaches his little son how to shoot a bow and arrow, while Nyla performs duties which show she is a devoted mother and cook. The Western ideal of the independent father struggling to make a living for his family is implied to be universal. As Richard Barsam points out, "In Nanook, [Flaherty] showed primitive man's realization that his destiny lay in his own hands, that it was his obligation to improve his lot on earth by working, and that the members of his family were probably his first and most important helpers."[51]

The climax of the film is the seal hunt, pitting Nanook against a wild animal. The seal hunt was always a big attraction at Inuit performances, and, as described above, was all but obligatory in travelogues which included scenes of Inuit life. This scene, so beloved by Bazin for its use of real time and the stark drama of the solitary struggling Nanook against a bleak landscape, was actually staged: the line at which Nanook pulls strenuously, apparently in a fierce struggle with a seal that has been harpooned beneath the surface of the ice, in fact did not lead to a seal at all but to a group of men, off-camera, who would periodically tug at the line, creating the impression of a great physical struggle.

After this scene, there is constant intercutting between shots of dogs and shots of the family. The beginning of these sequences starts with an intertitle, shown immediately after the seal is pulled out of the water:

> From the smell of flesh
> and blood comes the
> blood lust of the wolf
> —his forebear.

This last line is ambiguous, implying that the wolf is the forebear of Nanook. The intertitle is followed, however, by a close-up of a snarling dog. The subsequent intercuts of the dogs barking and the family eating raw seal, Nanook licking his knife and the dogs fighting, reinforce the parallel, visually associating Nanook and his family more closely with dogs than to the trader with his Western technology and medicine. Van Valin depicted the idea more bluntly with the intertitle "Dog eat dog"; Flaherty's use of intercutting shots of dogs is metaphorical and more ambiguous.

At the end of the film, there are extremely beautiful, long takes of the snowy landscape. Indeed, the land takes over as a protagonist, the sky becoming as heavy as the snow. The filmed landscape against which the figures of the actors appear small and remote takes on the spare, suggestive aesthetic of the Inuit drawings that Flaherty collected. Since a number of Inuit served as camera operators, one has to attribute much of the beauty of the way the landscape is filmed—great expanses of sky and ground—to an Inuit sensibility.[52] These haunting images of the landscape, moreover, are not present in films about the Arctic made before *Nanook*.

Just as the shots of the dogs show the dogs becoming increasingly sleepy, gradually blanketed by snow, so too the camera shots of the landscape appear to bob in a drowsy manner near the end of the film. The final image is of Nanook sleeping. Italian critic Ricciotto Canudo wrote that the tragedy at the end of the film is that Nanook does not choose to leave: "[Nanook] is Man, in all his truth. His tragedy, in its absolute simplicity, is that of Man, under any climate, despite all the possible complications of that many-shaped, changing outer dress known as civilization. . . . But fate made him master here, in this huge and solitary whiteness, in which his children, like him are destined to live and die.[53]

History is abolished when archetypal moments are repeated. In the end, *Nanook* is a film about hunting and killing, about the desire for death and the desire to defy death. The head of Nanook at the end of the film is shot in a similar fashion to the head of the walrus that we see at the end of the hunt: the walrus is hunted by Nanook, but Nanook is hunted by the explorer Flaherty. The film begins with a close-up of Nanook's face; throughout the film the camera surveys Nanook's face and it becomes a landscape; at the end of the film it is this landscape which is also penetrated. The sleeping body of Nanook, like a corpse, represents the triumph of salvage ethnography: he is captured forever on film, both alive and dead, his death and life to be replayed every time the film is screened.

To show how Allakariallak really dressed, to show his poverty or his sophistication with a gun or with a motion picture camera, would have been too brutal, too heavy. It would not have brought about the necessary Samuel Waterton response that taxidermy must evoke—"That man is Alive!" The irony is that in order to look most alive, the "native" must be perceived as always already dead.

Nanook of the North *and Participant Observation*

Those who have praised Flaherty see him as a great artist and observer, or as Calder-Marshall called him, "an innocent eye," a man who filmed out of love not greed. As Richard Corliss said, Flaherty "simply saw the truth and brought it home."[54] Many have complained, however, that *Nanook of the North* did not present a true depiction of Inuit life. Only seven years after *Nanook* was released, the explorer Vilhjalmur Stefannson claimed that *Nanook* was as authentic as Santa Claus.[55] But there were many rebuttals to the critics' denunciations of *Nanook* as staged. Flaherty's statement, "One often has to distort a thing to catch its true spirit," was seen to prove that Flaherty was an artist who portrayed "felt experience," not a mere mechanical recorder.[56]

Forty years after *Nanook*, ethnographic filmmakers Luc de Heusch and Jean Rouch as well as Asen Balikci praised *Nanook* as the first example of participatory cinema. Unlike early ethnographic filmmakers such as Baldwin Spencer and Rudolf Pöch, or later filmmakers such as Boas and Mead, de Heusch and Rouch did not put much stock in the value of using ethnographic film for mere empirical documentation. De Heusch in particular pointed out that films of everyday life in real time are usually quite boring and, at most, of interest only to the anthropologist. The irony—and this irony is at the heart of taxidermy—is that "reality" filmed does not appear real. The filmmaker must use artifice to convey truth. One way he or she can do this is by inviting the indigenous people who are the subjects of the film to act out their lives.[57] De Heusch explained that the Inuit actors in Flaherty's film willingly play-acted for the camera, a technique which he characterized as ethnographically sound, using French anthropologist Marcel Griaule's use of role-play as an example. De Heusch wrote,

> The authenticity of this sort of "documentary" ultimately depends entirely on the honesty of the director, who, through his work, asserts that "This is what I saw." In fact he has not seen exactly this or that aspect of what he shows, he has not always seen these things in the way he shows them, since that way is a language which he invents in coop-

eration with actors whose rôles are authentic. The documentary is a work of art imbued with rationality and truth.[58]

De Heusch states later,

> Flaherty, more than anyone, had the gift of entering into conversation, *on our behalf*, with the Stranger. Through "Nanook" we "grasp" to the fullest extent, that is emotionally and rationally, the essential condition of Eskimo man left to himself: he is no longer a phantasmal shadow moving across the snow, an anonymous creature whose body and real presence can only be imperfectly imagined from the reading of learned treatises.[59]

In a sense, then, what Flaherty was doing was opposing mere inscription (the objective of early ethnographic footage) to what I term taxidermy, and which Bazin praised as ontological realism. Flaherty's use of long takes, reframing, and depth-of-field cinematography using deep-focus lenses thus constituted a new style, one which Bazin describes as more moving, more realistic than what had gone before:

> The camera cannot see everything at once but it makes sure not to lose any part of what it chooses to see. What matters to Flaherty, confronted with Nanook hunting the seal, is the relation between Nanook and the animal; the actual length of the waiting period. Montage could suggest the time involved. Flaherty however confines himself to showing the actual waiting period; the length of the hunt is the very substance of the image, its true object.[60]

I do not contest the great influence of Flaherty's approach on subsequent documentary and realist forms of filmmaking, but would merely emphasize that Flaherty's reputation as "ontological realist" stems as much from the status of the Ethnographic Other as inherently "authentic," and from Flaherty's self-fashioned image as explorer/artist, as it does from his style.

In the same year that *Nanook* was released, the anthropologist Bronislaw Malinowski wrote his pioneering ethnography *Argonauts of the Western Pacific* (1922) about the inhabitants of the Trobriand Islands, off the coast of what is now Papua New Guinea. If *Nanook* is the archetypal documentary/ ethnographic/art film, *Argonauts* is without a doubt the archetypal written ethnography. The many common aspects of Malinowski's new conception of the anthropologist as fieldworker and Flaherty's notion of the filmmaker as "explorer/artist" show that the film and the book were made and received in a similar climate of ideas about indigenous peoples and truthful representation. Malinowski wrote, "The final goal, of which an Ethnographer should never lose sight . . . is, briefly, to grasp the natives' point of view, his relation to life, to realize *his* vision of *his* world."[61] The product of this ideal of the anthropologist entering the "field" as a solitary observer was to be a written ethnography, a cultural description of "a people," rather than a historical account of an encounter, a description meant to convince the reader that the anthropologist "had been there" as both all-knowing insider and as scrupulously objective observer.

Such "participant observation," notes Fabian, "was not canonized to promote participation but to improve observation." Like the time machine of cinema, anthropology as participant observation involved an oscillation between the positions of distance and closeness, subject and object. Anthropology's visualism, its "ideological bias toward vision," meant that knowledge was "based upon, and validated by, *observation*."[62]

Part of the appeal of participant observation is that it purportedly enables the Ethnographer to show not how the anthropologist sees the native, but how the native sees himself. Flaherty encouraged the belief that he was doing just that. He explained, "I wanted to show the Innuit [*sic*]. And I wanted to show them, not from the civilized point of view, but as they saw themselves, as 'we the people.' "[63] *Nanook* is perhaps the first example in film of a mode of representation which incorporates the participant observation ideal. Flaherty claimed to be a long-time explorer in the area, and his admirers even said that he had been adopted by Nanook and his family (this was never proved). Because Flaherty showed rushes to his Inuit crew, and because Inuit contributed to all aspects of filmmaking (from acting, to the repair of his cameras, to the printing and developing of the film, to the suggestion of scenes to film), critics from the art world as well as anthropology have claimed that *Nanook* represents true collaboration, the native acting out his or her own self-conception.

As James Clifford and Clifford Geertz have pointed out, the myth of "participant observation" was fashioned out of rhetorical devices creating the impression of "Being There." Although Flaherty wanted to create the impression that his film grew out of his intimate knowledge of Inuit culture, however, it would be hasty to take his account at face value (his writings boast of an intimacy which Inuit eyewitnesses do not seem to recall). Thus although Inuit undoubtedly assisted in the filmmaking, there are no existing Inuit accounts of the process, suggesting the film was not as "collaborative" as Flaherty would have one believe. Similarly, because we do not know whether Flaherty asked people to play themselves, and because we do not have an indigenous point of view against which to compare the film, it

29. Original drawing on paper, most likely by Wetalltok, from the Belcher Islands, 1916, of Flaherty and Inuit camera crew. (Courtesy of the Museum of Modern Art)

is more fruitful to view the claims of collaboration as evidence of the "romantic" ideal of the ethnographer/artist than as an essential aspect of the film.[64]

In *Nanook of the North*, as in the work of Dixon and Curtis, participant observation is achieved by the erasure of almost all signs of white contact. Thus the spectator views the landscape with Nanook; but he also views Nanook. The spectator becomes both participant (seeing with the eyes of Nanook) and observer (an omnipotent eye viewing Nanook). The viewers of *Nanook* thus become participant observers themselves: the audience participates in the hunt for the seal and the walrus along with Nanook. A white viewer may identify with the Nordic qualities of Nanook, but still participate in the "hunt" for the body of Nanook, as vanishing race, as First Man. The issue then is not "whether Flaherty was a legitimate anthropologist," but how the public was led to believe that they were *seeing anthropology* in a manner that allowed them to play with the boundary between viewer and viewed as vicarious participant observers, while reaffirming the boundaries between representation and reality. Intrinsic to this coding of *Nanook* as a work of Truth, a work of great art, was the construction of the image of Flaherty as Explorer/Artist, an image which Flaherty himself helped to construct through his various writings.

Flaherty as Explorer: Heart of Whiteness

Ethnographic filmmaker Asen Balikci has summed up the image of the explorer/ethnographic filmmaker from the time of *Nanook:*

> The ethnographer from Paris, London or New York, had usually gone to an extremely remote and exotic place where he studied the people and wrote books about them. The literature of exploration in exotic regions had further contributed to the popular perception of the ethnographer as hero. Building upon this reputation, the ethnocinematographer had the added advantage of showing to a large audience a film about strange and fascinating peoples—this was a demonstration that he was actually there, that the strange people liked him and that he liked them, otherwise how could the film have been made? His was a lonely and daring adventure, an exploration into the unknown, and so on.[65]

Because of the idea that the ethnographic filmmaker must have been friends with the natives—the film being the proof of the relationship—Flaherty's image as authentic communicator of the life of the natives remained intact even as critics complained of inaccuracies in the film.

Like Malinowski, who constructed "the Ethnographer" through rhetorical devices such as the ethnographic present, Flaherty contributed to the notion that his film was authentic through his own writings. In his autobiographical *My Eskimo Friends: "Nanook of the North"* (1924), the treasures Flaherty describes include his mineral discoveries and maps, as well as the film and photographs he took.[66] *My Eskimo Friends* is an account of Flaherty's career as explorer and filmmaker in the Arctic. Like all great explorers, he attributes the "discovery" of an island archipelago to himself. The Inuit he meets are depicted as grateful natives, although foul-smelling, and often "primitive looking"; he, on the other hand, a kind of explorer Santa Claus, gives them tobacco, needles, and candy at Christmas. Tellingly, he claims the Inuit call him Angarooka, "the white master,"[67] and at times he uses animal metaphors to describe them.[68]

The story constitutive of the relationship between Nanook (never referred to by his real name) and Flaherty is that of Nanook's devotion to the "aggie" (film). In *My Eskimo Friends*, Flaherty explains that he had asked Nanook if he understood that in filming the walrus hunt, the film was more important than the hunt. Nanook replied, " 'Yes, yes, the aggie will come first. . . . Not a man will stir, not a harpoon will be thrown until you give the sign. It is my word.' We shook hands and agreed to start the next day."[69] It is this anecdote that is so treasured by the critics, for it meant the film was a *real* ethnographic film, without voyeurism, the product of complete collaboration. The image of the devoted native is underlined by another anecdote in which Flaherty explains that the Inuit who worked for him gave up food so that he could eat. This prepares us for Flaherty's final words of reminiscence on Nanook's death. According to Flaherty, on his departure from Inukjuak, Nanook was sad to see him go and begged him to stay: "The kablunak's [white man's] movie igloo, into which thousands came, was utterly beyond his comprehension. They were many, I used to say, like the little stones along the shore. 'And will all these kablunaks see our "big aggie"?' he would ask. There was never need to answer, for incredulity was written large upon his face."[70]

My Eskimo Friends was a celebration of Flaherty as great humanist Explorer, beloved by the natives, privy to the essence of native life. The book is dedicated to Flaherty's father, also an explorer. Flaherty's later novel *The Captain's Chair* (1938) provides further evidence of what being an explorer meant to him. Told in the first person, it is the story of a young man who, like Flaherty, goes to look for minerals in the Hudson Bay area of Canada, but who throughout his years of travels in Northern Canada is searching above all for the great explorer and trader Captain Grant, the first man to trade with the Inuit. The narrator explains that it is a story of a captain and a ship penetrating into the heart of the Hudson's Bay Company's domain on Hudson Bay. It is also a search for a "father" hero by a young explorer.[71] During his expeditions the narrator learns of the "terrible disaster that had befallen Grant. He had left England on top of the world. The Company had given him all the means in their power to let him go ahead and open up the north . . . rich not only in furs but perhaps in gold, silver, copper, and who knew what other ores? They had given him also this wonderful new ship."[72]

The book is thus an Arctic *Heart of Darkness*—or perhaps *Heart of Whiteness* is the better term. For where Joseph Conrad revealed the dark and evil side of colonialism, Flaherty writes only about its good side. Like Marlow in *Heart of Darkness* who hears stories of Kurtz's exploits, the narrator in Flaherty's novel hears stories of Grant's hardships, his noble sacrifices, how he had to lash himself to the ship's crow's nest to fight storms. Like Kurtz in *Heart of Darkness*, Grant has confronted "the horror." The narrator muses, "I thought of the hardship, the horror, the strain of it."[73] The horror here, however, is not the heart of darkness within, but the horror of Nature's tide rips, blinding squalls, and burning cold.

Much has been written about how the anthropologist Malinowski identified with Kurtz, the mad company officer in *Heart of Darkness*, who the narrator Marlow sets out to find. In one section of his diary, Malinowski explicitly invokes Kurtz when he describes his anger at the people he is studying—the Trobrianders—for not posing long enough for adequate time exposures for his photographs, even after his bribe of tobacco: "On the whole my feelings toward the natives are decidedly tending to '*Exterminate the brutes.*' "[74] When Malinowski's diary was published, it unsettled cherished conceptions of the empathetic, value-neutral anthropologist.[75] In *The Captain's Chair*, by contrast, Grant remains a hero explorer who "penetrates" and opens up the North for the good of the company. Both the Inuit, faithful guides, and Indians of the region, crafty interlopers, are in awe of the great Explorer: "To the Indians . . . Captain Grant was a fabulous figure—chief of the biggest canoe that surely was ever in the world. Among the Eskimos in the north, too, he was a legend, he with his monster omiak [boat] with its long black tail and a voice that re-echoed among the hills."[76]

Like Kurtz, Grant's nerves are frayed after his harrowing experience aboard his ship (named the "Eskimo"), but he is no Kurtz, for the novel ends when the narrator finally meets Grant in person and discovers that he "looked more like a scholar than a seaman."[77] As Frances Flaherty commented, those who decry Flaherty's films as being overly romantic do not realize how much Flaherty was interested in the emergence of the machine.[78] In *The Captain's Chair*, the young explorer is not really looking for adventure and material treasure but for a mirror of his own masculine self in Grant, the Great White Explorer, his father surrogate. In similar fashion, ethnographic filmmakers like Rouch and de Heusch would find the mirror of their own selves in the myth of the father figure Flaherty. In the history of documentary and ethnographic film, Flaherty is kept reverently alive, the mode of taxidermy here serving the filmmaker, through the aura preserved around his name.

Nanook Revisited

In Claude Massot's documentary film *Nanook Revisited* (1988), a few of the Inuit residents of Inukjuak and of the Belcher Islands—including descendants of one of the Inuit sons fathered and left behind by Flaherty—are interviewed about their memories of Flaherty and the making of *Nanook*.[79] The interviews reveal a remarkable tension between the Western reception of the film as a great work of art, and the desire of the local Inuit to see records of their ancestors and their land, and their recognition of the fictional quality of many of the scenes, a number of which they find ludicrous. At a screening of *Nanook*, members of the Inukjuak community are shown convulsed with laughter over the famous seal-hunting scene so beloved by Bazin and usually received with solemnity by Western audiences.

The inaccuracies in the film are pointed out by Moses Nowkawalk, the manager of the local television station, and Charles Nayoumealuk, whose father was a friend of Allakariallak's. Flaherty, explained Nowkawalk, "doctored" scenes, including costuming the Inuit actors in polar bear skins, using an igloo set, and falsifying to a ridiculous extent (in the locals' eyes) the seal hunt, "so that the image would fit the Southern [i.e., non-Inuit or white] imagination." The scene with the gramophone was staged. As Nowkawalk succinctly phrases his reaction as he watches the gramophone scene, "This scene here is sort of . . . I'm not so crazy about this scene."

Explaining that Nanook's real name was Allakariallak, Nayoumealuk comments, "Nanook seemed to suit the whites better." He also points out that the two women in Nanook—Nyla (Alice (?) Nuvalinga) and Cunayoo (whose real name we do not know)—were not Allakariallak's wives, but were in fact common-law wives of Flaherty. The intended audience, as Nayoumealuk explains, was meant to be white. Nayoumealuk declares, "It was a film for white people, Inuit customs alone were to be shown. It was forbidden to see white men's tools. Flaherty wanted only Inuit objects."

The reception of a film as "authentic" is dependent upon the preconceptions of the audience. The smile of Allakariallak/Nanook is almost an icon of ethnographic cinema, and it is frequently described as unforgettable, yet Nayoumealuk explains that part of the reason for the smile is that Allakariallak simply found what he was told to do in front of the camera funny: "Each time a scene was shot, as soon as the camera was starting to shoot, he would burst out laughing. He couldn't help it. Flaherty would tell him—'Be serious.' He couldn't do it. He laughed each time."

If the Inuit who Flaherty encountered were interested in and soon became adept at filmmaking, so too their descendants have a passion and a command of visual media. Like other indigenous peoples in Australia, the Pacific Islands, and the Americas,[80] contemporary Inuit have embraced video, realizing that the power of white media can only be combatted with Native-produced media. Robert Flaherty's own grandson, Charlie Adams, took over Nowkawalk's position as manager of the local Inukjuak television station, Taqramiut Nipingat, Incorporated (Voices of the North). Adams is, as he puts it, "a one-man crew," as producer, director, cameraperson, and editor: his programs include coverage of local weekly events as well as shows about hunting with elders.[81] In 1981, a group of Inuit began the Inuit Broadcasting Corporation, the first indigenous broadcasting corporation in North America.[82] Inuit media producers believe that knowing the history of how they were represented by whites and understanding the image-making processes themselves will serve to empower their own communities. As the Inukjuak television station manager, Nowkawalk, said about *Nanook*, "Despite all the faults that I pointed out about this film this movie is a very important movie and the photographs that Robert [Flaherty] took, because they're . . . these pictures and the still shots are the only pictures of that time in this region. . . . 'Cause it's everybody else proclaiming it as a great film." Both Nowkawalk's and Nayoumealuk's comments reveal how early ethnographic cinema is not always received by the indigenous audience in the same manner as it is received by a Western audience. Neither art, nor empirical document, it is nevertheless of value because it evokes history and memory.

Starting Fire with Gunpowder (1991), a film about the Inuit Broadcasting Corporation made by the Inuit filmmaker David Poisey and the British filmmaker William Hansen, opens with a shot of a young Inuit woman who states, "This is not me. This is my picture." Then we see a longer shot of the woman in front of the previous image of herself on a television screen, saying "And here it's not me. It's my picture." The *mise-en-abyme* continues, and we realize that Hansen and Poisey are deconstructing the notion of the Inuit on film as "real." By using a female narrator, Poisey and Hansen also move away from the image of the Inuit typified by the male hunter Nanook. In the film, the narrator Ann Mikijuk Hansen, a producer at IBC, speaks of the lack of written Inuit history, and explains that Inuit video can help ameliorate the problem of documenting history. Furthermore, she clarifies that Inuit television is necessary to counteract the hegemony of white television, to preserve Inuit culture, and to promote Inuktiput language. Several television shows on IBC are adaptations of American shows such as Super Shamou (Superman), but there are also specials on specific Inuit problems such as PCB pollution, substance abuse, the need for midwifery, and Inuit politics.

Video, as Canadian Inuit videomaker Zacharias Kunuk has pointed out, is closer to Inuit culture which remembers history orally.[83] Although on the surface similar to Flaherty's, Kunuk uses reconstruction practices which are not used to further the kind of redemptive narrative, or taxidermic impulse present in the work of Flaherty.[84] In *Nunaqpa/Going Inland* (1991), Kunuk and his actors—all part of the community of Igloolik—collaborated to make a video reconstruction of Inuit life before World War II. Kunuk shot on location, with the actors wearing traditional seal-skin clothes. However, unlike Allakariallak in *Nanook of the North*, these Inuit actors are shown

30. Still from *Qaggiq/The Gathering Place* (1989), dir. Zacharias Kunuk.
(Courtesy of Zacharias Kunuk and Norman Cohn)

hunting with guns and using teakettles. It is clear that *Nunaqpa* is about remembering a recent past: older actors recount the games they used to play, and chide younger actors on their clumsiness in performing tasks. *Nunaqpa* depicts a hunt, which culminates when the younger hunters, wives, and children return to a tent where the older people are waiting. The Inuit actors return to the past, but in order to share it with the future, with the children, and with those who in the future will view the video.

Nunaqpa is a collaboration, made from an insider's point of view, without the conceit of any "ethnographic present": there is no subtitle, no voice-over narrative, just the voices of the people themselves, and their laughter at their own rustiness in trying to use old equipment. Outsiders to the culture are given no taxonomic devices such as a map with which to situate the events portrayed in the video: many culturally specific details are only comprehensible to members of the community themselves. Instead of introducing the viewer to the characters, the viewer is plunged immediately into the scene.

In *Qaggiq/The Gathering Place* (1989), Kunuk again uses historical reconstruction techniques. *Qaggiq* is a video about the communal quality of Igloolik life: the story centers on the building of a *qaggiq* or community gathering place, with a side story about the courting of a young woman by a young man. *Qaggiq* stresses the importance of communal activities such as joint hunting ventures and communal rituals and dances in Inuit life. As one woman sings at the end of *Qaggiq*, "Let's help one another. White people are coming." As in *Nunaqpa*, the importance of language is emphasized in the use of Inuktiput. Kunuk allows his actors to act out scenes from the recent past of their own culture, demonstrating that he views film and video as a means of expressing history and exploring memory. For Kunuk, as for many contemporary Inuit, a film about the community should be made in the same spirit that one builds a *qaggiq*. As Kunuk declared, "We are saying that we are recording history because it has never been recorded. It's been recorded by southern film makers from Toronto, but we want our input, to show history from our point of view. We know it best because we live it."[85]

The Inuit live history, according to Kunuk. Flaherty removed signs of history, such as the Inuit encounter with whites, in order to sustain the signs of the Ethnographic: the myth of the Inuit as archetypal Primitive man. My purpose has not been to prove whether or not *Nanook* was a truthful document of Quebec Inuit life in the 1920s, or whether Flaherty staged scenes. Instead, my goal has been to excavate the levels of discourse around the notion of authenticity, salvage ethnography, the history of the media cannibalism of the Inuit, the film's historical and intellectual context, and the style and content of the film. I have also attempted to show how a reading of the film is inextricably connected with the cult of the Ethnographic Filmmaker in ways that other film genres are not. Flaherty's awe for the figure of the great explorer, and his own similar self-fashioning, reveals the underlying narrative around his persona: Flaherty is the father of a men's club of explorer/artists. Like his fictional character Grant, Flaherty was the first to "penetrate" and open up ethnographic cinema for other *chasseurs d'images*, those many independent U.S. and European filmmakers like Jean Rouch and Richard Leacock who admire him. The awe that he is granted emerges from the myth of his relationship with Nanook: it is an ideal perfect relationship between ethnographer and his faithful, loyal, simple subject. Unlike the Trobrianders who were resistant at times to Malinowski's image-making, the Inuit who worked for Flaherty did so out of love, so the myth goes.

This is why *Nanook of the North* is seen as a point of origin for art film, documentary film, and ethnographic film: it represents the Garden of Eden, the perfect relationship between filmmaker and subject, the "innocent eye," a search for realism that was not just inscription, but which made the dead look alive and the living look dead.

III TERATOLOGY

5 TIME AND REDEMPTION IN THE

"RACIAL FILM" OF THE 1920S AND 1930S

The role of chaos is to summon up, to provoke its interruption and to become an order. Inversely, the order of the golden age cannot last because wild regularity is mediocrity . . .—Georges Canguilhem[1]

In 1895, H. G. Wells's *The Time Machine* was published, a novel foregrounding a fin-de-siècle disquietude about science and the control of time. A former student of zoology, Wells describes the experience of a scientist—the Time Traveller—who builds a machine that takes him to the year 802701. Wells's story is an obsessive fantasy of evolution and progress—it is science fiction—and the Time Machine is a fascinating metaphor for the technologies for manipulating time which became possible at the turn of the century. The museum was one such time machine: not fortuitously, Wells has his Time Traveller come across mummied heads, dessicated plants, and an array of idols in a long-deserted museum; in an act of territorialism, the Time Traveller even writes his name upon the nose of a "steatite monster from South America."[2] Photography was yet another time technology: at the end of the book, the scientist, whose claims of time travel are discredited by his colleagues, returns to the year 802701 in order to obtain photographs as documentary evidence, as proof of having been there.

Time travel is defined in racial and spatial terms. Wells's scientist likens his shock in going to the future—which he discovers is no Golden Age of Progress but rather an era of decline—to that which an African coming to London for the first time must feel:

> Conceive the tale of London which a negro, fresh from Central Africa, would take back to his tribe! What would he know of railway companies, of social movements, of telephone and telegraph wires, of the Parcels Delivery Company, and postal orders and the like? Yet we, at least, should be willing enough to explain these things to him! And

even of what he knew, how much could he make his untravelled friend either apprehend or believe? Then, think how narrow the gap between a negro and a white man of our own times, and how wide the interval between myself and these of the Golden Age![3]

The African in London is a symbol of incongruous time travel as Africans were situated by early anthropology as beings from an evolutionary past. Indeed, the roots of anthropology have been traced to the "philosophical travel" of the eighteenth century, which explicitly portrayed voyages of spatial distance as travel in time.[4] In the 1850s, with the archeological discoveries at Brixham Cave in Great Britain and the publication of Charles Darwin's *The Origin of the Species* (1859), the span of humankind's existence on earth could no longer be calculated using the Bible; time was secularized. This new sense of time was, according to Johannes Fabian, conceived of as natural and as having a spatial dimension, implying a taxonomic ranking of geographically dispersed peoples in terms borrowed from natural history. Fabian writes, "It is not the dispersal of human cultures in space that leads anthropology to 'temporalize' (something that is maintained in the image of the 'philosophical traveler' whose roaming in space leads to the discovery of 'ages'); it is naturalized-spatialized Time which gives meaning (in fact a variety of specific meanings) to the distribution of humanity in space."[5]

Two prominent arenas for "naturalized-spatialized Time," as we have seen, were the ethnographic exposition, and the anthropological museum, where artifacts extracted from a distant place and past, placed within the context of the museum, embodied an evolutionary "real." Yet perhaps the consummate time machine of the sort dreamt of by H. G. Wells was cinema, invented in the same year in which *The Time Machine* was first published. Cinema could launch the viewer into the future with science fiction, and, as we saw with *Nanook of the North*, into the timeless past.

In contrast to the historical film genre in which history is reconstructed through the use of actors who are recognized as such, the ethnographic reconstruction genre makes the indigenous subject into a document, the image of the body seen as "real," sufficient in itself to establish the truth of the implicit evolutionary narrative. The viewer in both cases is transported back in time, but with ethnographic reconstruction, the underlying fictional context is elided, a result justified by the notion that the Ethnographic, although living (we see the "actual" Ethnographic body, not an actor), is a survival of something long since dead. As suggested above, this notion of the vanquished/vanishing races gives *Nanook* and many other films of ethnographic reconstruction a deeply religious aspect. Significantly, this very religiosity resonates with the ontology manifest in leading film theorists' conceptions of cinema, and helps explain the attraction for many such theorists of ethnographic taxidermy. As Fredric Jameson has pointed out, both André Bazin's notion of the mummy complex in cinema and Siegfried Kracauer's belief in film as the *redemption* of physical reality take black and white photography as their ideal.[6] The black and white photograph, imbued with a sense of loss, is taken to be the embodiment of the cinematic potential to seize and preserve a moment of the "real." Thus Curtis's photographs were always more potent than his films: Curtis's use of melodrama, as opposed to Flaherty's "slight narrative," and his stilted editing in *In the Land of the Headhunters* worked against the quality of "the living dead" which his own black and white photographs of "vanishing Indians" and Flaherty's taxidermic cinema possessed. The implicit conception that Flaherty's film is holding onto death—witness the sleeping, Christ-like Nanook at the end of Flaherty's film—gives the film redemptive potential.[7]

The notion of redemption provides another link between cinema and anthropology. Both cinema and anthropology were interested not only in visualizing indigenous peoples for the future, prompted by the politics of salvage ethnography, but also in finding redemption for the West. The perceived sins of the West were manifested not only in a disillusionment with "civilization" after World War I, but also in colonial guilt over the genocide through massacre, disease, and the sheer brutality of slavery and colonialism inflicted on subject peoples, whether Native Americans, Tanzanians, Tahitians, West Africans, or Balinese. As Claude Lévi-Strauss emphasizes in his own Time Machine, *Tristes Tropiques* (1955), anthropology is impelled forward by remorse over the West's failure to fulfill the promise of scientific progress, the promise of eradicating brutality, evil, disease, and ignorance. The anthropologist (and I would add, the ethnographic filmmaker) is thus, says Lévi-Strauss, "the symbol of atonement."[8]

Redemption infuses many of the "racial films" of the 1920s and 1930s, a genre which played on the notion of time, race, and progress. The term "racial film" was first used by an unidentified film reviewer to describe Flaherty's *Moana* (1926), set in Samoa, and Karl Brown's film about Appalachia, *Stark Love* (1927). In a 1928 unsigned review the critic commented, "[These two films are] interesting because they present the daily life of out-of-the-way minorities. Secondly they are natural pictures with a minimum of posed and directed action. They are photographically excellent and both show indications of cinematography, which is not carried to the extent to which we have become accustomed in later films."[9]

The redemptive theme in *Moana* is implicit. The film is one of tropical simplicity, portraying a lost Golden Age, a garden of Eden implicitly set in opposition to the troubled world of "civilization." Although *Stark Love* is a film about poor rural Appalachians who yearn to become modern city-dwellers, like *Moana*, this film is "racial" in the sense that history is represented as a race: here, the distant Primitive is set explicitly in uncomfortable proximity to emerging modern industrialism, providing the context for a rumination on loss and the passing of time. The crucial difference between the two films is that whereas *Stark Love* ends with confidence that certain Appalachian "primitives" can make a successful transition to modernity, *Moana* ends where it begins: in a land without history.

It is no wonder that if Bazin loved Flaherty's *Nanook*, he also loved *Moana:* their mode of realism, what he describes as their respect for time and space, their narratives which take the viewer "back in time" to a Primitive age, and their use of location and indigenous actors provide a meditation on the mythical transition from the Primitive to the Modern. As will be discussed below, *Moana* differs from *Nanook* in that its image of tropical Primitivism heightens the contrast, and contradiction, between Primitive and Modern (Balikci's neatly labeled "primitive Protestant" strain—the struggle of the nuclear family against adversity—in *Nanook* allows for dramatic identification of viewer and subject). In the narrative of scripted ethnographic films subsequent to *Moana* (many of which are also set in the "South Seas") the contradiction becomes explicit, most often with tragic consequences for the indigenous protagonists. According to this narrative, the Primitive does not belong, and simply cannot exist, in association with the Modern. In these later films, contact with the West is conceded, but the result is seen to be racial pollution. Redemption takes the form of nostalgia for the pure, unadulterated Ethnographic, and contact leads not to complex cross-cultural adaptation, but to monstrous hybridity. This chapter examines how these themes developed in ethnographic cinema in the wake of *Nanook of the North*.

The "Racial Film" as Expedition

In Europe, the "racial film" accompanied what Pierre Leprohon has called "a violent upsurge of exoticism" during the years 1920–25, a phenomenon also reflected in literature, in the triumph of Gauguin, and in jazz music (labeled in France "la musique nègre").[10] Probably the most famous French "racial cruise" film was Léon Poirier's *La croisière noire* (The Black Cruise; 1926), a long travelogue which followed a Citroën motorcar expedition traversing Africa from the north to as far south as Madagascar. An explicitly colonial film, *La croisière noire* was a grand motorcar adventure designed to give witness to France's "civilizing action."[11]

In the United States the "racial film" vogue followed directly upon the success of *Nanook of the North:* Hollywood was willing to invest in films of ethnographic romanticism, time machines into a faraway present which represented a simpler, "savage" past. Critics who have discussed early ethnographic cinema, including anthropologist Franz Boas, frequently mention Cooper and Schoedsack's *Grass* (1925) and *Chang* (1927) as archetypes of the genre.[12] Merian C. Cooper was an airplane pilot in World War I and World War II, a man so opposed to Bolshevism that he volunteered to fight Russian Communists for Poland in 1919–21. He met Ernest B. Schoedsack, a freelance war photographer, in Europe during World War I. David H. Mould and Gerry Veeder explain that Cooper and Schoedsack were typical "photographer-adventurer" culture heroes, who, like other filmmakers in the period from 1895 to the 1930s, portrayed themselves as mavericks who had rebelled against the constraints of society, iconoclasts seeking adventure in the photographing and filming of peoples in foreign lands.[13] As Mould and Veeder put it, "The mission of the photographer-adventurer was to bring back the film, whatever the danger or cost."[14] Whether it was the "frontier" of world wars or remote places, Cooper and Schoedsack took on the macho, individualist personae of modern Davy Crocketts who risked their lives in order to film distant places, an image spectacularized in the jungle filmmaker character in their 1933 film *King Kong.*

Grass (1925), their first feature-length film, made with journalist Marguerite E. Harrison, took as its subject matter the Baktiari migration in southwest Iran across the snowy Zardeh Kuh pass in search of grass to feed the Baktiari's herds. Like other expedition films, *Grass* focuses on the filmmaker as intrepid Great White Hunter, flagrantly equating the camera with a gun and using ballistic point-of-view identification to create the thrill of "being there."[15] Visual anthropologist Asen Balikci asserts that *Grass* is markedly different from the humanist films of Flaherty in that it lacks a strong focus on a man and his family struggling for survival: "The basic theme of *Grass* emerges somewhat behind the screen; it lies in the grandiose conception of the filmmaker as the new explorer, the daring traveler and discoverer of exotic land, and this is the myth of the ethnographic filmmaker as a hero!"[16]

The expedition is a voyage through time to a remote locale in search of

31. Still from *Grass* (1925), dir. Merian C. Cooper and Ernest B. Schoedsack.
(Courtesy of the Museum of Modern Art)

a human unknown. The Baktiari of southwestern Iran are referred to as the "Forgotten People" living the life of "three thousand years ago." *Grass* begins:

> The way of the world is west.
> Long the sages have told us how our forefathers, the Aryans of old, rose remote in Asia and began conquest of earth, moving ever in the path of the sun.

After a panoramic shot of camels walking in profile on the horizon, the intertitles continue:

> Back in the East behind us are the secrets of our own past, and a tradition of our brothers still living in the cradle of the race—a long since Forgotten People.

The heroes of the film are introduced: pipe-smoking Cooper, rugged-looking Schoedsack, and female journalist Harrison. Titles explain that Cooper and Schoedsack will not be pictured *in* the film, because they are behind the camera. Subsequently, Harrison, portrayed as a genteel lady traveler fully dependent on her male traveler companions, is the only non-Baktiari person filmed. Although providing a white point of reference for an

American audience, her point of view is never established in the scenes or intertitles, and she almost fades into the mise-en-scène of the expedition. The film comments:

> But going ahead, we were turning the pages backwards—on and on further back into the centuries.
> Till we reached the first Chapter, arrived at the very beginning—

A voyage back in time to the origins of the "Aryan race" (and thus to the origins of the purported white viewer), *Grass* has no central native protagonist: even Haidar Khan, the chief of the tribe of Baktiari, portrayed as a leader of this trek, is not developed as a character.[17] Instead, what is fore grounded is epic endurance and spectacular nature: wide-angle shots of thousands of dark figures making a zigzagging line as they climb mountains of ice and rock. This epic theme, however, is adorned with cuteness. As the reviewer in the *New York Times* commented, "It is an unusual and remarkable film offering, one that is instructive and compelling but in no way a story. Yet in this picture, there is drama interspersed with captivating comedy, and the audience last night applauded some of the wonderful photographic sequences and at other times they were moved to laughter by the antics of the animals."[18] Thus picturesque details such as the blowing up of goat skins for floating across rapids are accompanied by jokey intertitles. The *Times* reviewer accurately noted that the intertitles appear to have been written for Barnum and Bailey's circus.

Grass ends with the triumph of the filmmakers as contemporary Aryan heroes who followed the Baktiari on their dangerous trek in order to make their film. The film thus betrays a curious anxiety with producing sufficient evidence, reminiscent of the Time Traveller in H. G. Wells's novel who goes back into the future with a camera in order to take photographs which will convince others of the veracity of his trip. The final film sequence in *Grass* even includes a close-up of a document signed by officials claiming that the filmmakers were the first foreigners to make the dangerous trek across the Zardeh Kuh pass. Despite the obvious effort to make the film succeed as Hollywood entertainment, the filmmakers were concerned with establishing the film's status as truthful document.

Cooper and Schoedsack's next film, *Chang* (1927), filmed in Thailand as if in the "ethnographic present," is about a family living in the jungle who must contend with wild animals, especially tigers and elephants.[19] The most feared beast is "chang" (elephant), a word that the audience repeatedly sees in intertitles but does not learn the meaning of until midway through the film. The voyage of discovery in *Chang* is one leading to the revela-

32. Still from *Chang* (1927), dir. Merian C. Cooper and Ernest B. Schoedsack. (Courtesy of the Museum of Modern Art)

tion of the identity of the beast, a discovery made all the more impressive when the film opened at the Rivoli theater in New York City, through the use of magnoscope technology for the climactic scene of the stampeding elephants.[20]

The stars of *Chang* are not the human characters Kru and his wife and children, but the animals and the filmmakers who capture them on film. Schoedsack wrote that, with *Chang*, they were pursuing the same theme as they pursued in *Grass*, "the theme of man's struggle against nature, only this time nature was represented by the jungle and its animals."[21] The film begins with the opening statement common in ethnographic cinema that Kru's family, these "natives of the wild," have never seen a motion picture. The family is represented as archaic Primitive Jungle people who must tame or kill wild animals in order to survive. In *Chang*, there is some attempt at depicting nuclear family life in the jungle (it is man and his family against nature), but again there is little character development and no sense of any broader social interaction. The real stars of the film, the animals, are both wild (hungry tigers, rampaging elephants) and domestic (especially Bimbo the pet monkey and a bear cub), with the intertitles even attributing dialogue to them. In his book *L'exotisme et le cinéma*, Pierre Leprohon explains that the success of *Chang* derived from its ability to evoke the shock of childhood: "It is here that cinema brought us back again to the most beautiful moment of our childhood. We suddenly found again our desire for discoveries, our nostalgia for these 'elsewheres' where we would never be able to set foot."[22]

As the product of "photographer-adventurers," the filmed scenes with wild animals were considered risky, thrilling, and dangerous, and *Chang* cnds with the spectacle of the elephants entering a corral, the intertitles underlining the lesson that "Brawn surrenders to the brain," man conquers nature. A glowing review in the *New York Times* called *Chang* "an unusual piece of work, beside which all big game hunting films pale into insignificance, and through the clever arrangement of its sequences, excellent comedy follows closely on the exciting episodes."[23] Slapstick comedy, especially evident in *Chang* in the scenes between the children and the pet animals, as well as patronizing and corny intertitles, are again present. In the expedition variant of the "racial film" genre in general, the filmmakers make "inside" jokes with the audience about the "ignorance" of the subjects through intertitles or with montage, the use of slapstick only serving to heighten the physicality of the characters. Much of the patronizing quality of the films derives from the use of the ape metaphor. In *Chang*, shots of a wizened old villager are intercut with that of a monkey, intended to lead the viewer to laugh at the parallel. This simian motif continues in Schoedsack's later *Rango* (1931), a film about a family in Aceh, a region of Sumatra, Indonesia, that takes as its premise a comparison between the orangutang and the Acehnese protagonist. Finally, of course, the anthropoid ape becomes the star in *King Kong*.

Moana, The Silent Enemy, *and Primitivist Romanticism*

Although there appear to have been two distinct categories of "racial film" in the 1920s and 1930s—one which glorified the Great White Hunt, and one which painted a picture of romantic primitivism—the two categories overlap and merge. *Grass*, for example, appears to be an expedition film, but it romanticizes the Baktiari as Aryan ancestors of the West; *Chang*, a film with only Thai actors, might be thought an exercise in romantic primitivism, but an underlying theme of the film is the courage and skill of Cooper and Schoedsack.

As George W. Stocking Jr. explains, the period after World War I in both Europe and North America was a period in which the cultural status quo was being questioned, a period of sexual experimentation and intellectual bohemianism. This "ethnographic sensibility" coalesced in the search for "genuine culture," and certain geographical places became the focal points of the search: Greenwich Village, the center of white bohemian life; the Southwest, where anthropologist Ruth Benedict found Pueblo culture exemplifying the Apollonian balance; Tepoztlán Mexico, romanticized by anthropologist Robert Redfield; and Samoa, pictured on the dust jacket of Mead's *Coming of Age in Samoa* as a barebreasted young woman running off hand-in-hand with a naked man for a moonlit encounter. In European and U.S. avant-garde movements in art, the application of aesthetic forms borrowed from African, Asian, Pre-Columbian, and Oceanic art burgeoned into the movement known as Primitivism, an art movement characterized, among other things, by the use of non-Western aesthetics as a means to rattle the "rational" status quo. As Stocking rightly points out, however, there was another side to this use of the "primitive" to criticize Western culture. Referring to the subtitle of Mead's *Coming of Age in Samoa,* Stocking writes,

> The presentation of cultural relativism in an evolutionary package ("A Study of Primitive Youth for Western Civilisation") made it possible to appeal simultaneously to motives of romantic primitivism and ethnocentric progressivism. On the one hand, Mead insisted that "our own ways are not humanly inevitable or God-ordained" . . . and that we "pay heavily for our heterogeneous, rapidly changing civilisation." . . . But in return, we gained "the possibility of choice," the recognition of "many possible ways of life, where other civilisations have recognized only one."[24]

This same duality, of course, was present in *Nanook of the North.* In Flaherty's film of 1922, the Inuit are shown as true hunters in an epochal struggle with nature, but they are also represented as tragically vanishing. While the West implicitly is portrayed as a civilization that can learn from other peoples, indigenous peoples implicitly are seen as threatened with imminent extinction. The anthropologist, like the ethnographic filmmaker, is thus the agent of redemption, but he or she can only really save the West.

As described in the last chapter, Frances Flaherty claimed that her husband was interested in "primitive" peoples precisely because he was interested in the emergence of the machine; we find that dual movement of romantic primitivism in his second film, *Moana: A Romance of the Golden*

33. Still from *Moana* (1926), dir. Robert Flaherty.
(Courtesy of the Museum of Modern Art)

Age (1926). After the success of *Nanook*, Paramount eagerly gave Flaherty a blank check to make *Moana*. Although purporting to be a film about the daily life of the island Savaii in British Samoa, *Moana*, like *Nanook of the North*, is a reconstruction of a projected idyllic past.[25] The film tells the story of the daily life of a young, handsome Samoan, Moana, who hunts for tortoises with the young boy Pe'a, and flirts with his girlfriend Fa'angase. As in the films of Regnault there is a fascination with native tree climbing. At the "climax" of the film, however, Moana undergoes a painful ritual tattooing process, a practice already prohibited in 1926. If the character Nanook embodied First Man, Man the Hunter, the young Moana embodies Primitive Man as Carefree Adolescent, whose only pain is culturally imposed. British documentary filmmaker John Grierson, who coined the term "documentary" film in his 1926 review of *Moana*, wrote, "The golden beauty of primitive beings, of a South Sea Island that is an earthly paradise, is caught and imprisoned in Robert J. Flaherty's *Moana*."[26]

   Moana begins by visually inviting the viewer to fall back into Paradise. The camera tilts from the top of tall palm trees down through foliage into a hidden tropical sanctuary: the viewer is thus welcomed into a mythical golden age without colonialism, without missionaries, where the most dangerous animal is the wild boar, and food and smiles are plentiful. The camera often adopts an observational perspective, placing the viewer above it all. The village, for example, shot from very high overhead, appears small, like a display in a glass museum case. Shots alternate between high camera angles and close-ups of hands, backs, and buttocks as the Savaii villagers wring coconut, prepare bark cloth, and tattoo each other. Frances Flaherty declared, "Simply in the beautiful movement of a hand the whole story of the race can be revealed," a statement with which Regnault probably would have agreed.[27] Although *Moana* lacks the drama of man versus nature present in *Nanook of the North*, Flaherty creates suspense by not revealing immediately the purpose of human action—as in a scene where the boy Pe'a is shown poking rocks with a stick. Only later does the viewer discover that Pe'a is smoking out a crab. Grierson complained of the film's chasteness, but sensuality is present in the way Moana pours water from a bamboo tube into Fa'angase's throat, and in the way she rubs his body with coconut oil. Desire is also manifest in the nocturnal dance of Moana and Fa'angase, described by intertitles as "The art, the worship, the courtship of the race." The viewer is meant to view the couple as the archetypal Samoan adolescent pair.

As in *Nanook*, the body of the native woman is revealed to the viewer. In one scene, Fa'angase is barebreasted facing the camera, her knees deep in water and her arms raised above her head to pick leaves. Unlike Paul Gauguin's *Where do we come from? What are we? Where are we going?* (1897–98), which represents Polynesian women in a similar pose, there are no enigmatic figures lurking in the background as devils in Flaherty's paradise. The Samoans are seen living in a timeless Eden, in "traditional" garb: there is no place in paradise for Christianity and British colonialism.

The visual effect of *Moana* depends in large part on Flaherty's use of a long lens and panchromatic film. According to Flaherty, this technology allowed for better voyeurism, since the Samoan actors were less self-conscious with a more distant camera presence;[28] it also lent "a roundness, a stereoscopic quality that gave to the picture a startling reality and beauty. . . . The figures were alive and real, the shadows softer, and the breadfruit seemed like living things rather than a flat background."[29] As with *Nanook*, it was this roundness, this three-dimensional quality in the representation of indigenous peoples—in contrast to the hieroglyphs of Regnault, or the exotic decor of early travelogues such as those by Gaston Méliès—which anthropologists were to praise.[30] Portrayed as without complexity or historical specificity, the Samoans are given a poetic and idealized form, reminiscent of the idealized representational manner used by artists to depict Renaissance angels. At times the images are quite effective: the faces of the elders as they sit around Moana as he is tattooed, shadows flickering across the lines and crevices of their solemn faces, are particularly moving. Again, as in *Nanook*, the landscape and the face are the film's foci. One intertitle explains:

> Through this pattern of the flesh, to you perhaps no more than cruel, useless ornament, the Samoan wins the dignity, the character and fibre which keep his race alive.

The irony was that tattooing was no longer practiced, having been banned after mass conversions to Christianity, but it remained an attractive trope for a Western audience eager to see and visualize a golden adolescence where the most threatening moment in life is a ritual ordeal.

In many ways, *Moana* is of a piece with *Nanook*, and both are premised on self-conscious reconstruction, thus manifesting the vanishing races theme. If both are works of Ethnographic taxidermy, however, *Moana*, with its implicit mourning of a lost Golden Age, more starkly sets a paradisical Primitive against the Modern. The character of Nanook, with his disciplined hard work and industriousness, is simultaneously an embodiment of the "living dead" and a dramatically heroic evolutionary "ancestor" for the Western viewer to identify with (as suggested by Balikci, he is a "primitive Protestant"). In *Moana*, by contrast, the lush tropical setting and utter absence of Western presence take the viewer to a Garden of Eden. Critic Grierson thus described *Moana* a welcome experience for those suffering from the "grime of modern civilization" and longing "for a South Sea island on the leafy shores of which to fritter away a life in what 'civilized' people would consider childish pursuits."[31] In catering to this longing, *Moana* reassures the viewer that all is well in the Ethnographic world (no colonialism, no war, etc.), and also holds out to the viewer the promise that earthly salvation might still be possible.

Salvation is given explicit Christian overtones in *The Silent Enemy* (1930), a "racial film" directed by H. P. Carver which was not a product of Hollywood but of the museum.[32] A wealthy young amateur and American Museum of Natural History trustee W. Douglas Burden produced the film, which purported to show the life of the Ojibwa (Chippewa) Indians before the coming of Jesuit priests. Carver used a natural history approach, with attention to material culture. The cast was advertised to be all-Indian and authentic: the characters included the Chief Chetoga (Chauncy Yellow

34. Still from *The Silent Enemy* (1930), dir. H. P. Carver.
(Courtesy of the Museum of Modern Art)

Robe); the Beautiful Maiden Neewa (Molly Spotted Elk), the Heroic Hunter
Baluk (Long Lance), and the evil Medicine Man Dagwan (Akawanush). The
Chippewa Indians are represented as always precariously involved in a
struggle with nature for adequate food.

Like several of the "racial films" of the late 1920s and early 1930s, *The
Silent Enemy*'s implicit theme of transition in its depictions of indigenous
peoples as innocent Primitives parallels the transition of film technology
occurring at the same time from silent film to sound. In many of these
films, the language of gesture of the silent film and accompanying intertitles coexist with sound sequences. *The Silent Enemy* begins with sound,
with Chauncy Yellow Robe declaring that the film is "the story of my people," thanking "the white man who helped us make this picture," and explaining that very few of the Native American actors had ever before seen a
motion picture. This conventional declaration of the natives' ignorance of

film technology sets the stage for the film as truth. A hybrid film, the rest of *The Silent Enemy* is without sound and uses intertitles.

The film, despite being set in a period before white contact, has a powerful Christian framework, as Elizabeth Weatherford has pointed out.[33] The shaman Dagwan is portrayed as evil in traditional Jesuit terms: he becomes the greedy capitalist. The Great Spirit is made into an Indian version of God. Baluk, who has led the tribe on a seemingly futile trek to find caribou, is unjustly sentenced to die by Dagwan. He is led to the pyre, his Christ-like body set momentarily aflame like a cross on fire, and he is only saved at the last minute when caribou are spotted. Given that the Chippewa did not practice immolation, the narrative apparently was intended to appeal to Euro-American notions of Christian sacrifice. In the expansionist ideology of the vanishing Indian found in the United States, this image may be taken as an indigenous Christ dying for the sins of the West, assuaging the guilt of genocide and dispossession that Anglo colonialism had inflicted on the native peoples of the Americas.

Like *Moana*, *The Silent Enemy* contains scientific pretensions to salvage ethnography and reconstruction for the purposes of redemption. The ideology of how *The Silent Enemy* reflects the Western pastime of picturing Native Americans as Noble Savages struggling to survive in the wild is belied by the biographies of the main actors of the film. Chauncy Yellow Robe was not a Chippewa, but a Lakota from Montana, one of the thousands of Indians who as a small child was taken from his parents and sent to the Carlyle School in Pennsylvania, forced to forget his native language. He later lived in New York and was married to an Euro-American woman. The handsome star Long Lance was also a Carlyle graduate, but had embellished a whole Indian biography for himself. Although he claimed he was a chief and a war hero, historians have discovered that he was listed as a "colored" soldier in World War I rosters. Both he and Yellow Robe were part of the New York social life: they could eat at the Explorer's Club, a wealthy elite men's club in New York, a privilege which, as an African American man, Long Lance would never have been granted. Molly Spotted Elk, a Penobscot from Maine, was known as an exotic dancer in New York and Paris. She performed in speakeasies in the 1920s, wearing for her act an Indian warbonnet, but was also a Native American historian and an assistant of anthropologist Frank Speck. In 1931, she was invited to go to Paris as part of the Indian Ballet Corps for the Paris Colonial Exposition, and she settled in Paris for several years.[34] Thus the lead actors in *The Silent Enemy*, "reel" Indians, participated in the popular culture of their day.

Political Physics

The treatment of time in anthropology turns on what Fabian calls "political physics," the cultural equivalent of the scientific principle that two bodies may not occupy the same space at the same time.[35] The "racial film" genre serves implicitly to reenact the logic of political physics: in the films discussed above, the Primitive is sacrificed like Christ, or otherwise as a figure of redemption; in other films of the genre, however, the Primitive is directly juxtaposed to the Modern and enters the same time and space as the posited audience. Either way, when the Primitive meets the Modern, the only possible outcomes, as Fabian put it, are the annihilation of the Primitive, or apartheid,[36] the Primitive trapped forever in the "imprisoning" image, to paraphrase Grierson, of the Ethnographic. This result, even in the guise of tragedy, reinforces the Historical/Ethnographic dichotomy. Primitivist films like W. S. van Dyke's *White Shadows in the South Seas* (1929), André Roosevelt and Armand Denis's *Goona Goona* (1932), and F. W. Murnau's *Tabu* (1931) all highlight the inevitably ruinous effects of modernity on the Ethnographic.

The colonial guilt which Lévi-Strauss speaks of in *Tristes Tropiques* is personified in the white protagonist Dr. Matthew Lloyd of W. S. van Dyke's *White Shadows in the South Seas* (1929).[37] One of the first films to use sound technology, *White Shadows in the South Seas* portrays Tahiti as in transition from paradiasical isle to adulterated colonial island. Tahiti in the 1920s was already seen by anthropologists as syphilis-infested, no longer genuine, corrupted from the French colonial presence and too much tourism.[38] In the film, the story of degeneration is presented from Lloyd's (Monte Blue) point of view. Shipwrecked on an "untouched" island, Lloyd saves the life of the chief's child and marries his wide-eyed daughter Faya-way (Rachel Torres). Lloyd's voyage back in time is suggested by one early scene in which he is washed up on the island. The first people he sees are the beautiful young women of the island bathing and sleeping by a waterfall, flowers in their hair. The lens of the camera is in soft focus, and slowly penetrates the foliage to give the viewer a closer look at this primeval scene. When Lloyd learns of the damage that the "white race" has inflicted on the Tahitians through disease and exploitation of male divers, he is ashamed: the "white shadows" of the title are the evil white capitalists. However, as a white man, Lloyd cannot eliminate the instinctive greed in his blood: he realizes that he can be rich when he notices the size of the pearls found in the waters near the island. He inadvertently triggers the demise of the island society, and, in the end, is himself shot by white capitalists. Time

35. Still from *White Shadows in the South Seas* (1929), dir. W. S. van Dyke. (Courtesy of the Museum of Modern Art)

travel inevitably brings contamination. The camera pans the beach with the mournful title "White shadows . . . White shadows": a boy is dressed in Western clothes, an alienated woman smokes a cigarette, and there is a long shot of a white man lounging and a glimpse of a native woman dancing in a bar for white men. The film ends with a close-up of Fayaway's sorrowful face, as veil upon veil of black gauze darkens the screen.

Like *White Shadows in the South Seas*, André Roosevelt and Armand Denis's love melodrama set in Bali, Indonesia, *Goona Goona: An Authentic Melodrama of the Isle of Bali* (1932) is a film in which political physics takes prominence. Since Bali was also the site of early research and films by anthropologists Mead and Bateson, it is useful to survey the historical setting of the film. In the 1930s, Bali replaced Tahiti and Samoa as the new dreamland topos for uninhibited desire: anthropologists, artists, and tourists came to Bali with ideas of romance, barebreasted dancing women, and handsome men. According to Tessel Pollman, Bali was a favorite tourist spot and a fashionable artists' colony in the mid-1930s: Mead and Bateson could thus enjoy a kind of café society existence whenever they wanted to take a vacation from the site of their fieldwork, the village Bajung Gde.[39] Pollman's article—written, perhaps subversively, in the "ethnographic present"—describes the machinations of this circle of white intellectuals in Bali. Like Derek Freeman, who went back to Samoa and interviewed Mead's informants, discovering evidence that Mead's research methodology and conclusions were faulty, Pollman concludes that Mead's work was suspect. Pollman, however, more pertinently emphasizes Mead's blindness to the political infighting in Bali and the brutalities being worked by Dutch colonialism at the time of her research. Mead's anthropology, Pollman explains, was in this way complicit with the Dutch policy of "Balinization," a set of colonial policies designed to maintain Bali as a static, folk culture. As the Balinese historian Prof. Dr. Ide Gde Ing. Bagus explains, "Balinization is this: the Dutch wanted us to be a living museum."[40] I Made Kaler, Mead and Bateson's main informant, explained that he did not dissuade Mead and Bateson from their belief that Bali was a "steady state." In other words, he did not explain to them that "rust en orde" (calm and order), the Dutch colonial slogan, was not an indigenous notion: "To Margaret Mead and Gregory Bateson I never talked about what was invisible, but very much alive in Bali. Talking was too dangerous, regarding the Dutch. Margaret Mead herself never broached a political discourse."[41] Mead's informants did not explain to her their fear of the Dutch police state and why they felt they had to comply with the demands of Westerners to pose nude. As I Made Kaler recalls, "The people don't want to sit nude and are angry when they were forced to do so, but yet agree. They are afraid to be arrested if they refuse."[42]

Like Regnault, who classified West African movement as Savage, and like Regnault's colleague Charcot, who used chronophotography to study hysteria in women, Mead and Bateson filmed Balinese in trance in the interest of medical pathology. Mead and Bateson's films of 1936–38 were financed by the Committee for the Research into Dementia Praecox (schizophrenia), and were motivated by a belief that the Balinese routinely entered into dissociated states of consciousness akin to those of the schizophrenic: pathology is still a part of the anthropologist's conception of the Ethnographic. In Mead and Bateson's film, *Trance and Dance in Bali* (1936), the camera is consistently always at a distance, always in control, a cool medical eye.[43] But, as Pollman points out, Mead did not really like Bali, and her works

36. Plate 56 from Margaret Mead's book *Balinese Character* (1942).
(Courtesy of the Institute for Intercultural Studies, Inc., New York)

imply that the Balinese are indeed schizoid. Mead and Bateson's use of a psychoanalytical approach, a methodology characteristic of the Culture and Personality school, and their personal discomfort with the Balinese are not as surprising as their eulogizing of Bali as a "last paradise."[44] In this last sense, "Balinization" picked up where representations of Tahiti left off, anthropologists, adventurers, and popular filmmakers alike adopting the lost Golden Age rhetoric characteristic of tourist promotion and colonial propaganda.

Mead and Bateson's view of Bali as a lost Eden is directly reflected in *Goona Goona*. A cinematic form of Balinization, *Goona Goona* indeed makes Bali a "living museum." In the film, Bali is allegorized as a lost paradise: colonialism and political infighting are erased. It begins by introducing the bespectacled André Roosevelt, notebook in hand just like the figure of the anthropologist, sitting under a tree with a few Balinese. Roosevelt, we are told, "reconstructed this Balinese story as it was told by the natives." Panoramic views of the landscape follow as a male voice-over declares, "Bali, the last paradise," and the viewer is then presented with population statistics, a map, and other postcard views. The story unfolds with intertitles carrying the narrative, and an authoritative male voice-over explaining the customs, for example, "In Bali, women only cover their body during ceremonial occasions," or "Rather commonly in primitive cultures marriage occurs after a prerequisite abduction." Roosevelt and Denis exploited the vogue for bare Balinese breasts in their film's title and representation of Balinese women: the slang term "goona-goona" was used in Hollywood trade magazines to refer to the use of shots of naked breasts of women of color in films (in Indonesian, the term actually means "black magic").[45] The breasts of women of color were not censored by the Motion Picture Producers and Distributors Association, especially in films marketed as "ethnographic."[46] Because Goona Goona was made during the transition of film from silent to sound technology, moreover, the film is a pastiche of many different styles: it is not just a museum of the Ethnographic but of cinematic styles. The film uses strategies of both silent and sound film, and straddles genres, combining elements of the travelogue, the melodrama, and anthropological film. This hybridity is apparent in its use of anthropological voice-over commentary; in its titillating "goona goona" (bare breasts); in the intertitles which explain the story; in its use of dialogue (in Indonesian, by someone with a European accent, rather than in Balinese); in travelogue scenes of the landscape, temples, outrigger canoes, and markets; in its use of Balinese court gamelan music; and in the sophisticated acting styles of the Balinese performers. Indeed, what allows Goona Goona to escape being merely a muddled pastiche of travelogue, melodrama, eroticism, and anthropology is the strong, expressive acting of the performers and the expertly performed dance sequences.

The essential drama lies in a question posed by the voice-over, the voice of the anthropologist: "Will Nonga, with the advantages of his European education, have the courage to protest or will he submit to his father's will?" Prince Nonga returns to Bali from his studies in Europe and falls in love with the young peasant woman Dasnee. She in turn elopes with her strikingly handsome boyfriend Wayan to escape the designs of the prince. Nevertheless, Prince Nonga manages to rape Dasnee. Wayan seeks revenge by surprising the prince as he is bathing, stabbing him with the ceremonial kris (dagger) in the water. In the final scene, Wayan is cornered at the temple. The king points a dagger at him, and we see Wayan's Christ-like body stretched out in the shape of a cross as the king withdraws. The body of Wayan slumps, and then we see a moving succession of close-ups of the faces of men—young, old, asymmetrical, handsome—who stare at Wayan. Instead of the contaminating white male interloper of White Shadows in the South Seas, it is Prince Nonga returning from Europe who spoils the

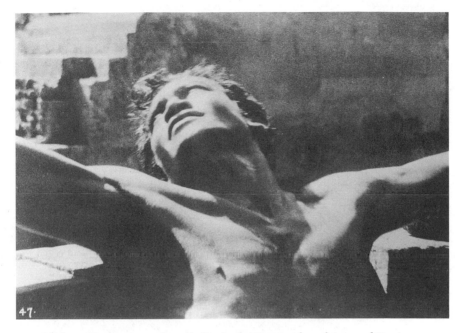

37. Still from *Goona Goona* (1932), dir. André Roosevelt and Armand Denis.
(Courtesy of the Museum of Modern Art)

harmony of the kingdom by falling in love with a peasant woman instead of
the woman of royal blood betrothed to him. His monstrousness—symbol-
ized by his European dress—is implicitly blamed on his Westernization.
Prince Nonga wreaks havoc by returning to his village, disrupting the integrity of Primitive space and time.

The native's inability to survive outside of his or her Garden of Eden is
again highlighted in one of the most famous films of the South Seas "racial
film" genre: F. W. Murnau's *Tabu: A Story of the South Seas* (1931). Although Flaherty worked on the film in the beginning stages, he disavowed
his own contribution and considered the film entirely the work of Murnau.
A meditation on loss and desire, Murnau's film is more sexually charged
than Flaherty's films, with more action, an expressionist use of mise-en-
scène, and melodramatic acting. The narrative of *Tabu* centers on two innocent lovers, Matahi and Reri, the latter a young girl declared *tabu* (forbidden), a sacrificial virgin for the gods. Bora-Bora is pictured as a society "still
untouched by the hand of civilization," a "land of enchantment." The film
begins when Matahi and his male friends discover several bathing women
under a waterfall, the pastoral Golden Age trope we saw in *White Shadows*

38. Still from *Tabu* (1931), dir. F. W. Murnau.
(Courtesy of the Museum of Modern Art)

in the South Seas. When the spectral elder Hitu declares that Reri must be brought to the chief of Fanuma as the new sacrificial virgin, the two lovers elope to another island, one under French rule. In his new house, Matahi makes a fortune as a pearl diver, but he is cheated by conniving merchants of Chinese descent and falls deeply in debt. Matahi and Reri then learn that Hitu has arrived (on the ship *Moana*), and when the young diver is forced to perform a dangerous dive at night in a *tabu* area, he returns to find that the grim-faced Hitu has taken Reri away on a small boat. Reri is at last resigned to her fate. Matahi swims after them, in the immense ocean lit only by the moon. This last scene is haunting: when he reaches the boat, Hitu cuts the rope which Matahi clings to, and the boat becomes progressively smaller as Matahi grows weaker, until finally he drowns, vanishing under the waves.

Unlike Flaherty with his observational high camera shots, and his emphasis on material culture and gesture, Murnau is much more concerned with allegorical spectacle and composition. Reri's village greets Hitu's ship by theatrically rushing on deck: the dance sequences are also well staged (such sequences, of course, include the obligatory "goona goona"). In one dance, when Reri dances, Matahi impulsively jumps in, their pleasure in being together quite palpable on their flushed, smiling faces, a pleasure that comes to an abrupt end with an angry silencing gesture from Hitu. Their actions have a choreographed, or preternaturally predetermined, air, as if they are figures who are moved by fate.

Reri is *tabu,* she is the mystery, the forbidden, and to touch her means death. The narrative centers on conflict concerning who may properly love Reri. Reri first chooses Matahi. As Charles Jameux writes, the film turns objects into characters: such as Reri's floral wreath, symbol of her beauty, fragility, and love, the black pearl (representative of the masculine), and the flower (the feminine) lying isolated on the sand.[47] Here, the "real," as Jameaux details, takes on the characteristics of the imaginary: the object is part of this world and of the imagination.

The central confrontation in *Tabu* is not man versus nature as in *Nanook,* but desire versus law. Reri and Matahi express their desire through dance, but are caught in a web spun out of writing and law. Hitu, the old man who is sent to bring Reri to the chief of Fanuma, is the figure of fate, and the agent of the archaic law of "primitive" society; but the other law is the greedy capitalist colonialism of the French. Polynesian law is manifested in the written decree that Hitu produces to prove that Reri is destined to become a sacrificial virgin for the gods. We are introduced to colonial law on the French-ruled island as soon as Reri and Matahi arrive: a colonial policeman records their arrival in his ledger. Later, a French policeman brings a letter from the colonial government showing that an award has been made available for the arrest leading to the return of Reri; Matahi bribes him with a pearl. Writing also circumscribes Reri and Matahi's ability to remain safe: the Chinese dry goods storekeeper fools the illiterate Matahi into signing for some fraudulent bills. Cornered on all sides by written decrees—the texts in the film are written in Tahitian, French, and Chinese, and are translated for the audience into English—the other islanders turn monstrous. In one compelling scene, set in a colonial bar, Reri and Matahi celebrate Matahi's discovery of a huge pearl. As the wine flows freely, the islanders dance, but it is no longer a dance of pleasure but of greed. Strikingly, Murnau focuses on the feet and calves of the dancers, some brown-skinned, some white, some barefoot, some in high heels. The incongruity—Primitive in proximity to Modern—is both a manifestation of desire gone awry and a device which foreshadows the impending disaster. The beaming faces of Reri and Matahi, by contrast, are ingenuous. Thus this Adam and Eve are trapped in a network of language, writing, and money, and the end result can only be annihilation or perversion.

39. Still from *Tabu* (1931), dir. F. W. Murnau.
(Courtesy of the Museum of Modern Art)

   In *Tabu* there is a shift in the relationship between word and image. In
early films like *Cannibals of the South Seas* or *In the Land of the Headhunters*, words are used to ascribe meaning to images in the twofold manner
of inscription described in chapters 2 and 3; in *Tabu*, words are mistrusted
as a form of colonial slavery.[48] Murnau emphasizes that writing is a societal
tool used to trap and control Matahi and Reri, whose mutual innocence is
represented in symbolic images rather than words. Interestingly, however,
it is precisely through the written word that Murnau has Reri express her
feelings, a rare attribute for the cinematic figure of the Native woman. Seeing the stone-faced Hitu in the moonlight, Reri knows that she must leave
to save Matahi, and she accepts her sacrificial fate. In order to explain
her actions, she writes Matahi a letter explaining why she must return
with Hitu. Yet although Reri is portrayed as a character with subjectivity
and emotions, she is still an allegorical figure for a bipolar universe. She
is ultimately the innocent human victim of both the rigid, despotic laws
of authentic Bora-Bora and of the mercenary greed of French colonialism.
Here the outcome is tragic: Reri and Matahi are stuck between the pa-

triarchy of the Primitive and the exploitation of the Modern. No less than in
Goona Goona, monstrosity is present where the Ethnographic meets the
Historical.

What would an inappropriate "racial film" be? In 1906 the Dutch conquer
the South of Bali, but the narrative of glorious colonialism, a narrative that
colludes with anthropology and cinema to picture Bali as a peaceful island
of dancing people and ancient preserved temples, is disrupted. The Raja of
Badung and his court, dressed in royal white finery and numbering in the
hundreds, greet the Dutch colonial soldiers by refusing to submit. The
scene turns red with their blood: in a *puputan* (finishing) these people kill
themselves, each other, or march forward toward the Dutch colonial army
to be gunned down.[49] The soldiers later loot the Raja's palace. A filmmaker
is there to produce documentation. The film of the *puputan* that he shoots
is placed in a drawer and never shown to the public. Only certain kinds of
ethnographic spectacle are acceptable in cinema, not those which expose
the repressive violence that undergirds the ideology of political physics.

From Taxidermy to the Monster

Films such as *Moana* and *Tabu* are characterized by critics as exemplary
products of a golden age of ethnographic cinema. André Bazin described the
films of the period as "tropical and equatorial," and as having "an authen-
tically poetic quality which does not age and is admirably exemplified in
Nanook." He asserts that the films actually mark the beginnings of a new
Western mythology: "But this poetry, especially in those films shot in the
South Seas, began to take on an exotic quality. From *Moana*, virtually an
ethnographic document, to *Tabu*, by way of *White Shadows*, we are aware
of the gradual formation of a mythology. We see the Western mind as it were
taking over a far-off civilization and interpreting it after its own fashion."[50]
But there was a problem with the "racial film": it soon became all too
predictable. Explaining the problem of the cinema of exoticism, of which
Nanook of the North was considered a masterpiece, Pierre Leprohon begins
by quoting Léon Poirier, the director of two *Croisière* films:

> "You see," Léon Poirier told me one day, "this is it, the real cinema. . . .
> Depart with a small crew, go far, and capture the brutal life, without
> make up, ignoring the studio, the decor, all the organization which
> paralyzes our enthusiasms."

But all filmmakers do not show such humble and noble ambitions.
Accompanied by a great publicity commotion, these productions in-

volve the voyage of a considerable crew and tons of material. They organize real expeditions to give some intrigue of an obvious impoverished nature a "sensational" frame. They accumulate impressive figures, dramatic episodes, with the desire to provoke the astonishment and the enthusiasm of the public. So much results that are not worth so much money dispensed, nor the dangers run. The film disappoints like vacation photos. Such a equatorial site takes on the look of a zoological garden and the natives have the air of figures deprived of their trade.[51]

Leprohon's use of the metaphor "zoological garden" is instructive: "racial films" more often than not rendered natives as specimens, and the inevitable ennui of the viewer soon approached that of a zoo visitor. At the zoo one sees what one already knows one will see: the interplay of wildness and domestication. With ethnographic cinema one also sees what one is already prepared to see, one "sees anthropology." The "roundness" of *Moana* soon became flat, at least to mass audiences.

To avoid this resemblance to the experience of the zoo, Leprohon writes, Hollywood turned to the use of sets as well as organized scenes of spectacle. As Bazin explains, the exotic film in the 1930s went into "a decline characterized by a shameless search after the spectacular and the sensational. It was not enough merely to hunt the lion, the lion must first gobble up the beasts."[52] This mannerist turn led to *King Kong,* one of the most outrageous "racial films" ever made. The genre of the "racial film" became increasingly baroque: if writers describe *Nanook* as epitomizing the Golden Age of such cinema, they describe *King Kong* as an example of how the genre degenerated.[53] André F. Liotard, Samivel, and Jean Thévenot explain the difference between *Chang* and *King Kong* as follows: "The travelers and the explorers themselves give in to the temptation of the 'spectacular.' Their works are less and less spontaneous, more and more premeditated, organized, and what they gain in coherence and formal qualities, they lose in authenticity and emotion."[54]

The time machine of ethnographic cinema attempts to maintain modernity, that is, to effectuate the complete separation of science from the subjective, the study of "nature" from the study of "society," through its polarization of the Ethnographic and Historical. The problem is that this polarization is effectuated by aligning the Ethnographic with Nature. In both *Chang* and *Moana,* as in *Nanook,* the filmmaker speaks for native peoples, raising the problem of the ethics of ventriloquism. In the "racial films" of the 1920s and early 1930s, the Ethnographic becomes emblem of the "vanishing races," an image which is the direct predecessor of the idea of

"endangered species." Ethnographic ventriloquism *assumes* the inarticu-
lateness of the Native, and it is the West's own narratives of evolution, loss,
and "political physics" which are expressed.

In trying to understand the shift in interest away from films constructed
on the model of *Moana,* to films like *King Kong,* Murnau's *Tabu* is a key
text. It embodies transition: it focuses on the drama of the clash between
the Modern and the Ethnographic, a clash typified by the image of Reri and
Matahi clapping their hands with innocent delight at the colonial bar,
caught up in the spectacle of the colonial dance, a transitional moment
which is further signified by the shot of feet—bare, brown, high-heeled,
white—of the faceless, dancing colonial subjects. The ideology of the inevitably destructive nature of this clash is present in *Tabu* but is given its
purest expression in the image of King Kong clinging to the Empire State
Building. This "entertaining contradiction," as Haraway succinctly puts it,
produces pleasure in its violation of boundaries, here between the "primitive" and the "modern."[55] *Tabu* contains a moral message which will reach
its fullest expression in *King Kong.* The indigenous person who does not
remain in his or her proper space is something abhorrent, and it is the
implicitly monstrous character of this hybridity which *King Kong* takes
literally.

6 KING KONG AND THE MONSTER
IN ETHNOGRAPHIC CINEMA

Qui dédaigne King Kong *n'entendra jamais rien au cinéma.*
—André Falk[1]

*If Poe were alive, he would not have to invent horror; horror would
invent him.* —Richard Wright

At the beginning of the century, a Chirichiri man named Ota Benga from the
Kasai region of what is now Zaire was exhibited at the Bronx Zoo. He and
other Batwa were brought to the United States by missionary anthropologist Samuel P. Verner at the request of William John McGee, director of the
Smithsonian Institution. After "exhibiting" Ota Benga and others at the
1904 St. Louis Exposition as anthropological specimens, Verner, unlike his
predecessors such as Arctic explorer Robert Peary (see chapter 4), ensured
their return back to their homeland.

One man, Ota Benga, chose to come back to the United States. It is unclear
why. Housed first at the American Museum of Natural History in New
York City, where Minik Wallace had also stayed, Ota Benga was one of several Africans "exhibited" at the St. Louis World's Fair. In one incident, Benga
and other African performers attacked a photographer who had taken their
photograph without asking first for their permission: they demanded that
he pay for the privilege. Benga was later put in a cage at the Monkey House
at the Bronx Zoo, rendered a zoological spectacle for the hungry public and
press. Contemporary press accounts reported that Ota Benga could not be
differentiated from the other monkeys. What Ota Benga thought about his
experience is unknown. The few documents that remain of his time in the
zoo include photographs of him looking seriously at the camera, posed in
characteristic anthropometric style: he is photographed frontally, from the
back, and in profile, holding props—a monkey in one arm and a club in
another—which reinforced his publicized "missing link" status.

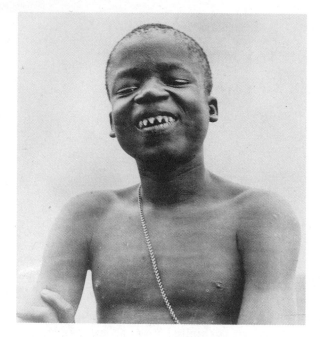

40. Photograph of Ota Benga (1904), St. Louis Exhibition. (Neg. No. 299134, photo by Jessie Tarbox Reals, courtesy Department of Library Services, American Museum of Natural History)

One may surmise from what happened later that the experience of being a zoological exhibit destroyed Ota Benga's mind if not his soul. Protests by African American ministers probably led to his release from the Monkey House, and he was allowed to walk freely about the grounds of the zoo. Ota Benga ended his time at the zoo when he brandished a knife at one of the zoo keepers. After this incident, Ota Benga left the zoo and in 1910 moved to Lynchburg, Virginia. Six years later, he committed suicide.[2]

King Kong *and Ethnographic Spectacle*

In Merian C. Cooper and Ernest B. Schoedsack's film *King Kong* (1933), the giant prehistoric gorilla Kong is captured and made into a lucrative Broadway attraction by the jungle picture filmmaker Carl Denham (Robert Montgomery). Kong then escapes, creating terror in the metropolis; he stalks the blonde heroine Ann Darrow (Fay Wray) and carries her off to the top of the Empire State Building where Kong is killed by an incessant barrage of bullets from fighter airplanes. The incredibly polysemous quality of *King Kong*, which has assured its continuing widespread popularity, has also led to a multitude of interpretations of the film—as dream, capitalist fairy tale, imperialist metaphor, allegory for the unconscious, and repressed spectacle for racial taboos. Its status as cinematic *fantasy*, as "a modern, movie-born myth" without historical antecedents, remains, however, largely unquestioned.[3] But *King Kong* is not merely a classic Hollywood film, it is a work which in significant respects builds on and redeploys themes borrowed from the scientific time machine of anthropology.

The lineage of *King Kong* should be obvious: the filming, capture, exhibition, photographing, and finally murder of Kong takes its cue from the historic exploitation of native peoples as freakish "ethnographic" specimens by science, cinema, and popular culture. Critics have consistently passed lightly over the fact that, in the 1920s, Cooper and Schoedsack were well-known ethnographic filmmakers, producing and directing both *Grass* (1925) and *Chang* (1927). *King Kong*, moreover, begins with an expedition, fully equipped with film camera, to a remote tropical island: *King Kong* is literally a film about the making of an ethnographic film. As exaggerated and baroque as *King Kong* may appear compared with Regnault's chronophotography or Robert Flaherty's *Nanook of the North*, the film makes reference to many of the themes that characterized the construction of the "ethnographic" in early cinema. If, as Cooper had complained, there were no longer any remote, genuinely alien cultures left to be discovered, monsters still lurked in the imagination of interwar ethnographic cinema. In the spectacular commercial cinema of this period, monstrosity was the mode of representation of the Ethnographic.

Pierre Leprohon writes that the cinema of exoticism—and under this rubric he includes both the research films of an anthropologist like Marcel Griaule and falsified documentaries like the film *Ingagi* (1933)—partakes at the same time of science and of dream: as scientific document, it furthers the pursuit of knowledge; as poetry, it is the food of dreams.[4] In this chapter, I will show how the monster is both the subject of scientific representation, as was the case with the Komodo dragon, the object of W. Douglas Burden's museum expedition in 1927, and of fantastic cinematic representation, as in Cooper and Schoedsack's *The Most Dangerous Game* (1932) and Erle C. Kenton's *The Island of Lost Souls* (1933), horror films which explore the notion of hybridity in teratological terms. Whether the monster was the object of science or fantasy, and whether shot with rifle or camera, it was a mode of representation inextricably linked with sex, power, and death.

Unlike most of the films of the "racial" genre which I described in the last chapter, *King Kong* was a sound film. With the advent of sound technology in the early 1930s, the "racial film" genre ironically lost one of the dimensions of its "realism." André F. Liotard, Samivel, and Jean Thévenot note, "Even if it doesn't have dialogue, the exotic sound film always risks being betrayed by its noises, and especially by its music and its voiceover."⁵ What propels *King Kong* forward is not the voice-over or intertitles of the scientific research film or lyrical ethnographic film, but sound of a different sort—the blonde heroine's screams, the giant gorilla Kong's roar, the lush Wagnerian score of Max Steiner—and *movement*—the longboat rushes to Skull Island to save Ann, the crew runs through the jungle in order to save her, and later the heroes run through Manhattan in an attempt to save Ann from Kong again. *King Kong* is not a film of poetic juxtaposition like *Nanook*, but of frenetic braggadocio, clunking the viewer over the head visually and aurally, a tone set by the very title of the film with its alliteration and rough-hewn rhythm. *King Kong* is the ultimate carnivalesque version of early ethnographic cinema.

Teratology and Fantasy: The Science Expedition and the Horror Film

My notion that the mode of representation of the "ethnographic" in spectacular commercial cinema takes the form of *teratology*—the study of monstrosity—derives once again from Stephen Bann's study of the rhetoric of history-writing in nineteenth-century France and Great Britain. Emphasizing the parallel between monstrosity and taxidermy, Bann points out that the monster is "the composite, incongruous beast which . . . simulated the seamless integrity of organic life."⁶ It is thus not surprising that *King Kong* emerges in large part out of the "racial film" genre initiated by *Nanook*. *Nanook* was a work of taxidermy, inspired by the politics and aesthetics of reconstruction, and *King Kong* is not only a film about a monster—the film itself is a monster, a hybrid of the scientific expedition and fantasy genres.

Bann states that the "very anxiety to establish [the] distinction between 'all' imagination and invention, on the one hand, and on the other the facts, is of course the evidence of a desire to repress the rhetorical status of historical writing."⁷ The desire to find true representation of the real, or true inscription, was characteristic of Regnault's work, and his writings and chronophotography betray a deep-seated anxiety with differentiating fact from imagination, the normal from the pathological. Teratology was an important aspect of early anthropology: the "monster," like the Primitive Other, was of keen interest because it could be used to study and define the normal. In *The Normal and the Pathological*, historian of science Georges Canguilhem describes how abnormality is necessary to constitute normality: "The abnormal, as ab-normal, comes after the definition of the normal, it is its logical negation. . . . The normal is the effect obtained by the execution of the normative project, it is the norm exhibited in the fact. . . . It is not paradoxical to say that the abnormal, while logically second, is existentially first."[8]

The Ethnographic, as we have seen, could be romanticized as authentic culture and/or as "pathological" culture, as in Margaret Mead's representation of the Balinese as schizoid. But one need not seek out extreme examples: the notion of the "ethnographic" as monster was only an exaggeration of the common propensity to see native peoples as strange, bizarre, and abhorrent. As I have already noted, it is significant that anthropologist Bronislaw Malinowski's infamous invocation of *Heart of Darkness*—"ex terminate the brutes"—comes out of his exasperation at the refusal of the Trobrianders to sit still long enough to be photographed. The Ethnographic becomes monstrous at the very moment of visual appropriation.[9]

Noël Carroll has explained that, in the horror film, the two essential characteristics of the monster are its impurity and its dangerousness. Borrowing from Mary Douglas's analysis in *Purity and Danger* (1966), he explains that monsters are impure in that, as hybrids, they are not easily categorized, and thus cross the boundaries of cultural schemas. Monsters are, Carroll emphasizes, interstitial. Kong, neither human nor ape, is impure in this sense. Thus the monster is not just physically threatening, but also cognitively threatening: its existence threatens cultural boundaries. As Carroll suggests, this cultural dangerousness explains why the geography of horror often involves lost continents and outer space.[10]

The Ethnographic is seen as monstrous because he or she is human and yet radically different. Early examples of the monstrosity of the Ethnographic include Regnault's association of race and cranial deformation; Spencer's description of "naked, howling savages"; the Johnsons' coding of Western Pacific peoples as lascivious cannibals; the obsessive filming of trance (a ubiquitous subject in ethnographic cinema); and the plethora of ways in which indigenous peoples were, through the use of cinematic spectacle, made into Savages, a term which still had credence in anthropology as late as 1930.[11] Monstrosity is essentially visual, an aspect of "seeing anthropology" that involves a search for visual evidence of the pathological, a theme made evident in both Paul Broca's and Franz Boas's recommendations that anthropologists observe the indigenous person as a patient.[12] Because the image in ethnographic film is taken as "real," footage of a person in trance frothing at the mouth and biting off a chicken head, or of a person slicing open a seal and eating raw meat, often is read by the intended viewer of ethnographic film, the Western viewer, as evidence of the essential savagery of the Ethnographic. As Wilson Martinez and Asen Balikci have explained and documented, cultures in ethnographic films are usually seen by students and other audiences as aberrant, bizarre, and even repulsive, unless the culture on display is similar to the culture of the audience.[13] Such audience studies raise questions about the ethics of filming acts which were never meant to be seen by outsiders, and showing the films in contexts in which—even with extensive commentary from anthropologists—abhorrence is aroused. Brazilian ethnographic filmmaker Jorge Preloran explains:

> After seeing dozens of films on ethnographic subjects, one thing stands out clearly for me: the majority of [the films] create a gulf between us and the "primitive" people they usually depict. This to me is a racist approach because unless we have a chance to listen firsthand to those people, letting them explain to us WHY they act as they do, WHY they have those extraordinary rituals, those fantastic, colorful, exotic, disgusting, fascinating—you label it—ceremonies that are shown to us, we will only think of them as savages.[14]

Several different tendencies converged to produce the image of the Ethnographic as monstrous. First, the great variety of indigenous societies continually destabilized the Modern/Primitive dichotomy. Second, the perception of indigenous peoples as a link between the ape and the white man, as in between animal and "human" (white), made the Ethnographic always already monstrous. Third, the image betrays anthropology's obsession with hybridity. The concern with hybridity manifested itself both through an abhorrence of interracial intercourse and "blood mixing," reflected in Paul Broca's influential research purportedly establishing that the offspring of blacks and whites were infertile,[15] and through notions of salvage ethnography, the belief that the "ethnographic" as embodiment of an earlier, purer humanity, would spoil upon contact with the West, a conceit which was played out in the "racial film" genre. This latter form of hybridity is best expressed cinematically in the scene of clashing styles of dancing in Murnau's *Tabu*, described in the last chapter.

Its literary counterpart to the spoils-upon-contact theme is exemplified in Lévi-Strauss's description of the society of Brazilian Indian rubber tappers in *Tristes Tropiques*. He explains that if the Nambikwara had taken him to the Stone Age, and the Tupi-Kawahib to the sixteenth century, then the society of the *seringal* (rubber plantation) in the Brazilian Amazon brought him to the eighteenth century. It is worth quoting his description of the Indian women at length:

Under a layer of rouge and powder they were hiding syphilis, tuberculosis and malaria. They came in high-heeled shoes from the *barracão*,
where they lived with "the man," their *seringueiro*, and, although
ragged and dishevelled all the rest of the year, for one evening they
appeared spick and span; yet they had had to walk two or three kilo-
metres in their evening dresses along muddy forest paths. And in order
to get ready, they had washed in darkness in filthy *igarapés* (streams),
and in the rain, since it had poured all day. There was a staggering
contrast between these flimsy appearances of civilization and the monstrous reality which lay just outside the door.[16]

Although with greater pathos, Lévi-Strauss, like Murnau, mourns the passage of time: acculturation brings disease and despair, and indigenous culture cannot withstand the onslaught. Mixture, whether it takes the form of
miscegenation or acculturation, produces monsters.
    Stephen Neale's description of the monster in the horror film reveals a
direct similarity between screen monsters and the Ethnographic rendered
as monster. In both cases, the focus is on bodily disruption:

The monster, and the disorder it initiates and concretises, is always
that which disrupts and challenges the definitions and categories of the
"human" and the "natural." Generally speaking, it is in the monster's
body which focuses the disruption. Either disfigured, or marked by a
heterogeneity of human and animal features, or marked only by a "non-
human" gaze, the body is always in some way signalled as "other,"
signalled, precisely, as monstrous.[17]

Not surprisingly, the archetypal narrative of many forms of ethnographic
cinema, but especially of the expedition film, mirrors that of the horror
film. Carroll points out that the horror film uses variations on the "complex
discovery" plot: the monster first appears or is created (onset); it is then
noticed by the human protagonists (discovery); its horrible existence is acknowledged (confirmation); and the film ends with a fight to the death
between human and monster (confrontation).[18] As Neale explains, the narrative process in the horror film is "marked by a search for that specialized
form of knowledge which will enable human characters to comprehend and
control that which simultaneously embodies and causes its 'trouble.' "[19]
Similarly, the plot of expedition films like *Grass* and *Moana* is structured
around the discovery and confirmation of a being (whether zoological rarity
or group of people) with incongruous features or habits.
    The expedition film did not have to take native peoples as its subject

matter in order for it to be informed by the obsession with race and fears of hybridity characteristic of ethnographic cinema. Perhaps the best example of an expedition film that contains "ethnographic" elements without being explicitly about indigenous peoples is a film by W. Douglas Burden, on the 1927 American Museum of Natural History expedition to study the Komodo dragon lizard. Komodo, an island in what is now Indonesia, is the home of *Varanus komodensis*, the Komodo dragon lizard, described as the largest lizard in the world and the closest living relative of the dinosaur.[20] Cooper would later claim that Burden's expedition was a direct inspiration for his film *King Kong*.

Burden's short film begins with a view of the American Museum of Natural History, followed by a map detailing the itinerary of the Burden voyage, and then scenes of the arrival of the expedition on Komodo Island, the hunting of animals for use as bait, the hunting and shooting of the lizard, and the capture of other live lizards. Although Carroll is discussing the plot of the horror film here, he might as well be discussing the Burden expedition film: "An initial, contested discovery calls forth a project or expedition for the purpose of corroborating it, and closure is secured when the confirmation can be made to stick."[21] *King Kong*, labeled a fantasy horror film, was successfully modeled on the narrative of an expedition film. The fantasy of the movie draws its sustenance from the science of the museum expedition.

The title of Burden's book on his expedition even sounds like a horror film title: *Dragon Lizards of Komodo: The Expedition to the Lost World of the Dutch East Indies.* Burden, like Carl Denham, the fictional expedition filmmaker in *King Kong*, stressed the importance of maintaining secrecy in order to be assured of being the first white man to lay claim to the exotic beast.[22] In Burden's book, Komodo Island is represented much as *King Kong*'s Skull Island will be represented by Cooper and Schoedsack: Burden writes of the sound of "tomtoms beating across the water; incessant, monotonous, rhythmic beats, thrilling and barbarous," evidence that the natives are "child-like and superstitious."[23] Burden's portrayal of the expedition's Chinese servant Chu as an amusing lackey prefigures *King Kong*'s portrayal of the Chinese cook Charlie.[24]

Similarly, just as Kong and the dinosaurs of Skull Island are portrayed as riveting, prehistoric monsters, the Komodo dragon according to Burden is "a perfectly marvelous sight,—a primeval monster in a primeval setting."[25] Cooper later explained that the character of Ann Darrow was inspired by Burden's wife, Katherine Burden, a photographer on the museum expedition.[26] Burden himself extolled the spectacle of a monster attracted to a beautiful white woman, a theme repeated frequently in *King Kong* in Carl Denham's oft-repeated reference to Ann's relationship with Kong as "Beauty and the Beast." Burden comments, "A fiery dragon in itself is a fascinating idea—so, also, is the thought of a beautiful white-skinned maiden. Link these two ideas together, in some way or other, and you have a story which by its very nature would survive through untold ages."[27] Thus the narrative of the expedition was propelled forward by the figure of the white woman, a kind of lure for the monster-like beast.

Cooper, the creative mind behind Kong, was struck by Burden's account of the immediate death of the two Komodo dragons which Burden brought back and displayed at the Bronx Zoo. In a letter to Burden dated 22 June 1964, Cooper wrote,

> When you told me that the two Komodo Dragons you brought back to the Bronx Zoo, where they drew great crowds, were eventually killed by civilization, I immediately thought of doing the same thing with my Giant Gorilla. I had already established him in my mind on a prehistoric island with prehistoric monsters, and I now thought of having him destroyed by the most sophisticated thing I could think of in civilization, and in the most fantastic way. My very original concept was to place him on the top of the Empire State Building and have him killed by airplanes. I made considerable investigation on how this could be done technically with a live gorilla.[28]

In the expedition film, Burden himself does the shooting. At one point, there is a shot of Katherine Burden cranking the camera juxtaposed to a shot of Douglas Burden shooting with his rifle. The positioning of the two makes it appear as if he is in fact shooting Katherine.[29] This scene is followed by one in which a Komodo dragon is shot and killed. Shooting with a camera and shooting with a rifle are conjoined: the product will be the display of the stuffed dragon lizards together with film footage at the American Museum of Natural History. But the woman is also shot and captured on Burden's film: sex and the hunt are implicitly made parallel.

In *King Kong*, the monster Kong's attraction to Ann is transgressive: Kong, a hybrid figure, a manlike beast, threatens the taboo on interracial sex. Burden's obsession with racial difference—the Javanese are "unfathomable," the "cannibals" of Wetar are "Oceanic Negroids"[30]—is exposed in his disgust for the Dutch colonials who do not enforce a caste system or color line:

> Where is this getting the world, this intermarriage between race and race, this breaking down of the barriers of race consciousness? In the

long run, as intermarriage becomes more and more frequent, does it not lead inevitably to one grand hodge podge, one loathsome mixture of all races into a pigsty breed? An unattractive thought, perhaps, but sure of fulfillment, as long as racial intermarriage continues.[31]

It is the body of the racially mixed hybrid which Burden finds loathsome, the hybrid body which defies the idealized polarization by science and modernity of the Ethnographic Other and Historical Same, nature and science, archaic and modern.

Islands of Fantasy: King Kong and the Horror Film

King Kong borrowed not only from the scientific expedition film, but also from the Hollywood horror film. The Most Dangerous Game (1932), directed by Irving Pichel and Schoedsack and produced by Cooper, was started before but made concurrently with King Kong, with some of the same sets and actors (Robert Armstrong, Fay Wray, Noble Johnson, and Steve Clemente). As in King Kong, the hunt in The Most Dangerous Game is a means of playing out the survival of the fittest. Count Zaroff (Leslie Banks), the bored, effete big game hunter, lures Rainsford (Joel McCrea) and Eve Trowridge (a brunette Fay Wray) onto his island and then forces them to become game for his hunting pleasure. The plot again follows Carroll's model—onset/discovery/confirmation/confrontation. Here, however, the monster is the Count, a man who embodies Regnault's nightmare of the suraffiné (overrefined, overcivilized).

The Most Dangerous Game also reveals that where taxidermy lurks, teratology is sure to follow. Zaroff violates cultural boundaries, but he also pushes certain notions to their logical limits, such as the link between sex and the hunt: "We barbarians know that it is after the chase, and then only, that man revels. You know the saying of the Ogandi chieftains: 'Hunt first the enemy, then the woman.' It is the natural instinct. The blood is quickened by the kill. One passion builds upon another. Kill, then love! When you have known that, you have known ecstasy!"

The monster is thus the Count himself who crosses the boundary between Civilization and Savagery, and tellingly invokes the "Ogandi chieftains." Rainsford is the hunter who remains within "proper" bounds: he hunts only animals and recognizes the value of expedition photography as evidence of "having been there." As Rainsford says to the Doctor, "You didn't turn out so hot as a hunter, Doc, but oh what a photographer! Say, if we'd had you to take pictures on the Sumatran trip, they might have believed my book." The Count, by contrast, takes the visual logic of the Great White Hunter to its logical extreme: his own desire to *see*, to visualize the hunted, is revealed in his collections of pickled human heads (he even has one taxidermic group depicting the hunt of an unfortunate victim). His pathological vision, embodied in his bulging, piercing eyes, in one scene fixes Eve, in the manner of a scientist gleefully pinning down a butterfly specimen.

According to film critic Claude Beylie, the very dry, nearly scientific style of the film mixes elements of the documentary with a touch of de Sade: *The Most Dangerous Game* utilizes "the words of science, or of teratology, because it was about a prehistoric animal, or a phenomenon of a fair." Thus the very tenor of the film betrays a fascination with teratology. Watching the film, Beylie asserts, is like watching animals at a zoological preserve.[32] In his intriguing analysis of *The Most Dangerous Game*, Thierry Kuntzel sees the film as revealing a relationship between dreams and cinema, because the viewer must believe a little, but not too much; he or she is drawn into viewing not only from the point of view of normality, that is, of the hunter hero, Rainsford, but also from the point of view of abnormality, that is, that of Zaroff.[33] The horror film thus makes the viewer complicit not only with the protagonists, but with the monster as well.

The Most Dangerous Game is an exploration of the relationship between the hunted and the hunter, between Savagery and Civilization, a theme signified by the recurrent image of the centaur. The centaur, half-beast and half-man, emblazons the film as both mythical and fantastic. Kuntzel has pointed out that all the men in the film figure for the centaur, especially Ivan, the Cossack servant (Noble Johnson).[34] The same fascination with hybridity betrayed in Burden's account of his expedition is made explicit in this fantasy horror film in the image of the centaur.

If *The Most Dangerous Game* is a meditation on Savagery and Progress, unlike the "racial film" which purported to offer a peephole into the past, the film also looks to the future, envisioning a "monster" of overcivilization. Another horror film that presents a vision of deviant evolution is Erle C. Kenton's *Island of Lost Souls* (1933) based on H. G. Wells's *The Island of Dr. Moreau* (1896).[35] The island of Dr. Moreau is described as "an experimental station for bioanthropological research." The narrative is again one of onset/discovery/confirmation/confrontation: the shipwrecked Edward Parker (Richard Arlen) is lured by the oily, odd-looking Moreau (Charles Laughton) to the latter's island station, where Moreau has caused evolution to be speeded up hundreds of thousands of years, producing not only giant plants, but also a new breed of "humans" from the sadistic vivi-

41. Still from *Island of Lost Souls* (1933), dir. Erle C. Kenton.
(Courtesy of the Museum of Modern Art)

section of live animals. The doctor hopes that Parker will mate with his most prized creation, the beautiful Lota, the Panther Woman (Kathleen Burke).

The monsters in the film, Moreau's creatures, are neither fully animal nor human. The racialist and imperialist underpinnings of the film are quite explicit, for the monsters are coded in racial terms. Ourlan, an ape-man, is coded as the lusty and bestial dark Savage. M'ling, Moreau's faithful dog-man, is coded as East Asian—servile and bestial—slightly higher in status than some of Moreau's other beasts who have become his slaves and perform hard physical labor. Lota passes as a Polynesian: with her heavily made-up eyes, rouged lips, long black curly hair, and skimpy bandeau and sarong, she is a typical "South Seas" screen siren. When they kiss, Parker discovers that her fingernails are really claws, and he confronts Moreau with his knowledge. Moreau is merely perturbed, because this fact is evidence that the animal nature of his "human" creatures reverts back and cannot be suppressed. Interbreeding fails (nineteenth-century anthropologist Paul Broca might have approved), and the monster is thus necessarily impure, no longer animal but not capable of becoming fully human.

The danger of miscegenation appears again when Parker's virtuous blonde fiancée, Ruth Thomas (Leila Hyams), comes to rescue Parker only to be nearly raped by Ourlan, the hairy ape-man, mirroring Ann Darrow in the paws of Kong. Parker saves her from this fate, but is warned not to do the same for Lota, the Panther Woman. Later, Ourlan pursues Lota: when he grabs her, they maul each other to death, as natural selection takes its toll on the unfit.

In the end of the film, Moreau's society of hybrid Savages rebels in a perfect enactment of the colonialist nightmare. Although forced to worship Moreau as a God, and as keeper of the Law, they revolt and torture Moreau with instruments from his own laboratory, called the House of Pain. In both films, the true monster is the insane white male who desires to manipulate nature and is willing to upset the boundaries separating man from beast.[36] In *Island of Lost Souls* as in *The Most Dangerous Game,* the viewer takes his or her cue as to how to react to what is happening from the human protagonists on the screen, but since the viewer at times sees the action from the point of view of Moreau or of the island's other "humans," the viewer is made into a monster as well. Like Moreau, a doctor obsessed with knowledge, with destroying the limits between the biological and the fantastic, the viewer is simultaneously fascinated and horrified by the transgression of boundaries. The revolt of Moreau's hybrid experimental subjects is signaled cinematographically by the reverse of a zoom: one by one, the beasts rush up to the camera lens, their hairy faces filling the lens as they peer up at the camera.

In his discussion of *King Kong,* J. P. Telotte has argued that an effective horror film draws the viewer into its world of excitement and terror through its manipulation of boundaries: "The horror film can play most effectively on its boundary position; monsterlike, it can simply reach into our world and make us part of its nightmarish realm, forcing us to complete horrific sequences."[37] Similarly, citing Tzvetan Todorov, Noël Carroll explains that the fantastic in cinema is produced by allowing for a vacillation between supernatural and naturalistic explanations. Many horror stories begin as narratives purporting to offer rational explanations for the fantastic, but then build up to a confrontation with the monster, a supernatural being that cannot be explained by science.[38] Above all, Carroll adds, the horror film demands proof, proof of the monster's existence and a clear explanation of why it exists. The horror film genre works because the audience is fascinated by the monster's impurity, its hybridity, and because it is curious to get at the heart of this unknowable: the audience follows the narrative until it discloses all the secrets of the monster.[39] This knowledge is arrived at only by observation. It is this desire for proof by observation that links the ethnographic film to the horror film: from its inception, the efficacy of ethnographic film was believed to derive from its status as pure observation, pure inscription, evidence for the archive. But this logic linking vision to knowledge, producing an incessant desire to see, is not without its attendant dangers.

King Kong: *A Close Analysis*

In a scene about two-thirds of the way through *King Kong*, a disheveled young couple—Ann Darrow, a pale blonde woman, and Jack Driscoll, her virile male lover—flee on foot from the giant ape-monster Kong through a jungle of enormous, primordial vegetation. As they run we see their wide-eyed but grimly set expressions as they frantically brush aside the leaves of the jungle that hang in their way, the young man pulling on the woman to run even faster as she becomes progressively weaker, until she is so exhausted that she has to be carried to safety in the man's arms. This scene of the two running, running, forever running, is full of suspense—Will Kong catch up? Will they make it? Moreover, will they make it back to Civilization? Their running is a literal embodiment of the race of history, a race which is a locus of ethnographic cinema. The outcome is known—the monster will be destroyed, and the heroic whites will triumph—but there is always a tension, an element of uncertainty, a possibility that the race may go either way.

1. At Dock: The White Male Elite—Hunters, Filmmakers, Voyagers, Heroes. King Kong begins and ends as a tribute to the Empire State Building, the triumph of modernity. After credits with graphics of the facade of the building, the film introduces the viewer to the humans whom anthropology had glorified as being at the "head of the steeplechase" of history: the white male, specifically the adventurous white male elite. We meet first the white male crew of the moving picture ship: the mastermind of the spectacle of the white beauty and the beast is a character named Carl Denham, labeled a jungle filmmaker, and his colleague Jack Driscoll, first mate of the ship and later the fiancé of the Fay Wray character, Ann Darrow. In addition to the model of Douglas Burden, Carl Denham was closely modeled on Cooper, Jack Driscoll on Schoedsack, and Ann Darrow on Schoedsack's wife, Ruth Rose, as well as Katherine Burden (Rose, in fact, was one of the screenwriters for *King Kong*).[40] Denham was apparently also modeled on the brash showman Frank Buck, who made films about capturing animals for zoos, such as *Bring 'Em Back Alive* (1932).

Noël Carroll writes, "No other film has ever been as self-congratulatory as *Kong*. It is a swaggering, arrogant film that spends much of its time telling us how great it is. . . . *Kong* is the quintessential American film—its self-image is so enormous."[41] The self-referential tenor of the film does not arise solely because of *King Kong*'s many references to film history, a point made by James Snead,[42] but also because, as shown in the last chapter through the discussion of *Grass* and *Chang*, self-referentiality is central to ethnographic cinema.

2. In Depression-era Manhattan: The White Woman—Criminal, Trouble, Object of Exchange. The second scene of the film takes us down one level in the evolutionary taxonomy of race and gender to the white woman—Ann Darrow—the forever fainting, screaming blonde heroine of *King Kong*. If necessary for the propagation of the "race" and the furtherance of Civilization, she is, as Jack says, always trouble. She is the object of the film spectacle, recognized as a necessary accessory because, as Denham explains wryly, "The public, Bless 'em! Must have a pretty face to look at." *King Kong* begins then as the hunt for an appropriate "pretty face" for the expedition—a white woman—just as it later becomes a hunt for Kong.

The film is set contemporaneously at the height of the Great Depression. Curiously, criticism of *King Kong* rarely mentions Ann's poverty and her implied criminal status. In the taxonomic classification system of early anthropology—and Regnault's conception of race as pathology provides an excellent illustration of this theme—the interest in indigenous peoples as Primitive was closely allied to the study of "sociological" types such as the prostitute, the criminal, the ethnic immigrant, laborers, homosexuals, and the Irish. All of these marginal groups were seen as deficient both morally and intellectually.[43]

Denham espies Ann Darrow when she is caught trying to steal an apple from a vendor; the heroine-to-be is an Eve who has already fallen. He takes Ann to a coffee shop to explain his intentions, and the audience as well as Denham gets to scrutinize her under the bright lights of the interior. In several close-ups from the chest up, Ann sits eagerly with her back against a wall lined like a Cartesian grid; she is posed in the manner of anthropological as well as criminal photographs. The lines of the wall imprison Ann as a type; it is Denham who has saved her from criminal punishment, but he will entrap her, even while elevating her, as object of trade and of spectacle. If, as a criminal in the darkened streets of Manhattan, Ann is first associated with darkness, she also represents lightness: as Cooper told Fay Wray, he wanted Ann to be a blonde beauty in order to highlight the contrast with Kong (Cooper referred to Kong as the darkest leading man she would ever have).[44] Throughout the film, Ann is compared implicitly to Kong. Cooper had his own notions about woman as beast:

> Woman has retained, fortunately, the fighting, dominant blood of the savage. . . . She would have perished as a distinctive individual long ago had it not been for her own rights. This quality can be found in the most fragile of women. For a long time I always thought that "the most dangerous" game naturally would be one in which a woman was involved.[45]

Cinema works as a time machine not only in the scientific research film, the romantic ethnographic reconstruction, or the Hollywood horror film: as this "racializing" of gender reveals, white women as well as people of color are "evolutionized." If the 1930s was the era of Frankenstein, Dracula, and King Kong, it was also the period which saw Lota the Panther Woman, Nina the Fetish in *Trader Horn* (1931), the gorilla-suited Helen Faraday (Marlene Dietrich) in Josef von Sternberg's *Blonde Venus* (1932), and the incessantly screaming characters played by Fay Wray.

The figure of the white woman is thus another object of knowledge needing to be explored, understood, and tamed. In *Trader Horn*, for example, a film by W. S. van Dyke (who also made *White Shadows in the South Seas* [1929] and *Tarzan the Ape Man* [1932]), the legendary Trader Horn and his sidekick Peru soon embark on a mission to save the young white woman Nina, who as a child had been abducted in an African raid and who has become a "fetish" for an African tribe. The characterization of Nina is ambiguous and strangely charged. Speaking no English, and with her wild, frizzy blond hair and skimpy feathered outfit, she is initially perceived as being "as great a savage" as the Africans with whom she lives. Like Lota the Panther Woman in *Island of Lost Souls*, Nina has the crackling long hair and the blazing, darting eyes of a creature who is half-animal, half-human. But while Lota is, in a sense, racially coded as a *mulatta*, Nina is coded as a true white woman capable of dominating the African men of her village,

42. Still from *Trader Horn* (1931), dir. W. S. van Dyke.
(Courtesy of the Museum of Modern Art)

through shouting at them and whipping them. At the film's end she and
Peru leave Africa to get married, effectively marking Nina's entry into Civi-
lization as a proper wife. Ranchero, Trader Horn's African assistant, be-
comes feminized and is made into the object of desire for the Great White
Hunter, as seen in the death scene where Trader Horn embraces the dying
Ranchero.[46]

Similarly in Josef von Sternberg's *Blonde Venus* (1932), it is unmistakably
the white woman who is the enticing object of inquiry. The film begins
when a group of students of science unexpectedly come across Helen and
her actress friends swimming nude in a secluded lake in Germany. Helen
later marries one of these men—Faraday, an American scientist—and they
have a son named Johnny. The image of Helen frolicking in the water is
reminiscent of the South Seas bathing beauties who represent a Golden Age
of Innocence in *Tabu* and *White Shadows in the South Seas*. Helen, a theater actress, is brought out of nature and thus "civilized." Because Faraday is
in need of money to pay for a medical operation, Helen returns to the theater. Her fall to a more "savage" state is indicated by her famous "Hot
Voodoo" number. In a fancy nightclub for an audience of rich white men,
the act begins with shots of the smiling gestures of the black orchestra
leader, while a conga line of white women wearing dark makeup and black

43. Still from *Blonde Venus* (1932), dir. Josef von Sternberg.
(Courtesy of the Museum of Modern Art)

Afro wigs weave their way on stage, swaying in their grass skirts, leading a squatting gorilla on a chain. Suddenly a pale blonde apparition with long white arms emerges from the black hairy gorilla suit: it is Helen, singing how "she wants to be bad," how she is "beginning to feel like an African queen." This "Hot Voodoo" number highlights how White Woman, as object of spectacle, was seen as savage, part of her appeal her inherent bestiality. But it is the myth of Africa which lends the image of Helen her "savagery": the image of Africa and blackness—the orchestra leader, the black stuttering man at the bar, the conga line, and Helen's gorilla/African queen stance—is exploited in order to spectacularize Helen's sexuality. The aristocratic society of the nightclub is seen as wickedly decadent, and Broadway becomes a present-day jungle.

The depiction of Ann Darrow, like that of her screen sisters Lota, Nina, and Helen, reveals a cinematic fascination with beautiful white women as unconscious source of disorder. The double-edged representation of the White Woman—as pillar of the white family, superior to non-white indigenous peoples, but also as a possibly Savage creature, inferior to white men—is expressed in the parallels drawn between Ann and Kong as objects of spectacle, and by Jack Driscoll's simultaneous fear of and lust for her.

Even as the White Woman is made into the visual object par excellence, her wildness is linked to her desire to know through seeing. As the object of the camera and of the viewer's gaze, Ann is punished for wanting to be an active viewer. It is Ann's curiosity to *see* that repeatedly gets her into trouble. Her own gaze must be continually frustrated, for the gaze has been established as allied with the camera, and thus with Carl Denham—the White Male.

3. On Deck at Sea: The Chinese Man—Barbaric, Comical, Feminized. The film crew together with Ann then embark on their voyage to a mysterious island. One scene aboard the ship magnificently coalesces into a racial tableau. On deck, Ann waits for her screen test to begin, while Charlie (Victor Wong)—the Chinese cook for the ship—peels potatoes. Ann laughs at Charlie's pidgin English. He is firmly established as a guest worker, not the agent of a cross-racial relationship. Charlie never really looks at Ann: he is a looking glass for Ann, a means to establish what Laura Mulvey has called her "to-be-looked-at-ness."[47] Moreover, Charlie is feminized by his position as cook and by his body language. Any possible hint of sexual tension between Ann and Charlie is diffused by the sudden appearance of Jack who looks actively at Ann's face, alternately telling her he approves of her looks, and complaining that she is trouble. Ann retorts, "Iggy's nice to me. Iggy likes me better than he likes anyone else on board," at which point the film cuts to reveal the identity of Iggy, a pet monkey on a string, a kind of miniature precursor to Kong. This scene establishes an evolutionary and thus anthropological hierarchy: Iggy the monkey jerks frantically on the ground, Charlie the Chinese man sits peeling potatoes in the background, Ann is standing and thus is higher than Charlie, and Jack stands over them all, looking intently at Ann.[48]

The character of Charlie, his lowered posture and pidgin English, draws attention to the place of Asia in the cinematic imagination. Films during this period shown in the bigger movie houses were often accompanied by acts labeled "exotic" such as a Siamese twins act. As evidenced by the fact that many early movie houses were built as faux Egyptian or Chinese palaces, East Asia, Egypt, and cinema were firmly intertwined: cinema could take the traveler/viewer either to the past and beyond to Savagery, or through the present to the future.[49] East Asia is seen as an intermediate point between the West and "the Rest," as midway between Savagery and Civilization. In a scene in *King Kong*, for example, the wall which prevents Kong from escaping from the jungle is described both as Egyptian and as akin to Angkor Wat. Asia is thus seen as an impenetrable wall, one side facing the future, one side opening onto prehistory. The prototypical Chinese in cinema—Chan, "the Yellow Man" of D. W. Griffith's film *Broken Blossoms* (1919), for example—was a liminal being, neither a real man nor a real woman, trapped in the role of looking glass, a reflecting surface.

After the racial tableau of the potato-peeling scene, Denham reveals to Jack and the Captain the destination of the voyage—a forgotten land called Skull Island off the coast of Sumatra. The next scene on deck emphatically locates Ann as spectacle for a sadistic white male gaze. Ann is implicitly compared to a charging rhino in Denham's explanation to her of why he shoots wild animals. Ann shivers and raises her hands as Denham's voice continues, "You're amazed!"

> You can't believe it! Your eyes open wider! It's horrible Ann but you can't look away. There's no chance for you Ann. No escape. You're helpless Ann. Helpless. There's just one chance. If you could scream, but your throat's paralyzed. Try to scream Ann. Try! Perhaps if you didn't see it you could scream. Throw your arms across your eyes and scream. Ann, scream for your life!

Ann is seen to be enjoying the attentions of the camera and the crew, and Fay Wray herself described the filming as "a kind of pleasurable torment."[50]

4. At the Village on Skull Island: Indigenous Islanders—Savage, Superstitious, Bestial, Childlike, Evil. Cutting through the water in dense blinding fog, the sound of drums beating in the distance, the moving picture ship arrives at Skull Island. When the fog clears, "seeing is believing," Denham exclaims, as he gloats to the Captain of how closely the island resembles the map of the island he had shown the Captain. Denham and the crew, including Ann, sneak on to the island, and see in the distance an enormous wall. Denham explains that the natives have "slipped back" and are inferior to the higher civilization that once inhabited the island and made the wall. The island is constructed as a feminine space with a wall which must be penetrated before male glory can be attained.[51]

The Skull Islanders—dark-skinned, fierce, lustful, and yet childlike, afraid of guns—are represented as the most Savage of men. Both David Rosen and James Snead have pointed out the racial politics played out in *King Kong* by way of the Skull Islanders, emphasizing that the portrayal of the Islanders built on racist fears of miscegenation by whites during the period of the great African American migration to the North.[52] James Snead also refers to Denham's voyage as "optical-colonialism" and sees Kong's capture as an ideological screen for the European-American slave trade.[53]

But the common interpretation that the natives are coded as black, merely derogatory stereotypes for African Americans, fails to take seriously the way that *King Kong* engages the racial discourse of ethnographic cinema. Just as Malinowski described the Trobriand Islanders using a racial slur for blacks in his diaries, the natives of Skull Island who are coded as black are also explicitly geographically situated off the coast of Sumatra, in what today is called Indonesia. Many Indonesians have been and are seen by the West as black or, to use the scientific category, "Oceanic Negroid."[54] Thus the use of African American extras to play the role of Indonesian islanders underlines how in the popular as well as scientific imagination dark skin was fully synonymous with Savagery. Anthropological accounts of Sumatran groups such as the Nias Islanders (whose dialect the Skull Islanders speak) and of the Dayak groups of Kalimantan and Sarawak (i.e., the Wild Man of Borneo) also painted the groups as dark-skinned Savages, Animists, Warlike Cannibals. *King Kong* is merely a baroque version of this image of the "ethnographic."

The arbitrariness of ethnic distinctions in Hollywood is reflected in the choice of the actor Noble P. Johnson to play the Chief of this Malayo-Polynesian island. Johnson, a light-skinned African American actor and a pioneer producer of black film (in 1916, he founded the Lincoln Motion Picture Company), also played Ivan, the Cossack servant in Cooper and Schoedsack's *The Most Dangerous Game*.[55] Similarly, the Yaqui actor Steve Clemente played the evil Mongolian servant in *The Most Dangerous Game*, and in *King Kong* he appears as the Medicine Man.

The representation of the native in *King Kong* is therefore extremely complex: it is true that, in the context of black/white relations in the United States, whites undoubtedly were intended to see the Islanders as black, but it is also true that the Islanders are clearly defined as being from the Indonesian archipelago. An African American viewer could thus locate the Skull Islanders as Sumatrans and still register them as Other. The curious obsession with authenticity in the use of the Nias language—the actors speak a few heavily American-accented phrases of the language—calls attention to the fact that these cinematic natives have a referent out in the real world, for Nias is an island off the coast of Sumatra.

One figure in the great island spectacle is practically erased. Ann is the Other to the white man, and the native man is the Other to Ann, but the native woman—the *bride* of Kong (when the film crew arrives on the island, the Islanders are preparing a ceremonial "bride" offering to Kong)—has no Other: timid, naked, docile, and mute, she is firmly established as less worthy of spectacle, a mere shadow next to Ann, and far less desirable as a commodity. Indeed, Kong's bride never speaks in the film, only looking up once at the moment that Denham and his crew are spotted. In the evolutionary schema of *King Kong* she hardly exists. As cultural critic Michele Wallace has pointed out, in racialized ideology there is no Other to the woman of color; she is denied a space of agency.[56] However, within the racial and gender economy of *King Kong*, it is impossible to imagine that a man be sacrificed in her place: the centerpiece of the spectacle must be female, to be visually possessed and violated by men.

Although we remember the name of Fay Wray and forget her character's name in *King Kong*, Ann Darrow, we remember the name Nanook, and never think of Allakariallak. Nobody deigned to ask if Nanook was the actor's real name in *Nanook of the North*, or to question the ethics of ventriloquism and taxidermy in romantic ethnography: the Native Man in ethnographic cinema is not even perceived as being an actor: his performance is always "real." At the other extreme is the White Woman. Fay Wray becomes, in the public's eye, the screaming heroine that she played; by identifying the heroine with the "real" name of the actress, the feminine is revealed as pure spectacle. The White Woman in ethnographic cinema cannot, like Allakariallak, be renamed, for she is the *star*, already a signifier, for beauty, glamour, the feminine, but also the unknown.

By contrast, the Native Woman almost always remains *unnamed*: she is typified by the compliant, silent, staring bride of Kong (see illustration 1). This is not to say that there are no exceptions—*Tabu*'s Reri, or *Goona Goona*'s Dasnee, for example—but she largely remains mute, a type. As exemplified by the character of Cunayou in *Nanook of the North*, the Native Woman is the silent, figure of maternity, and through the kind of "girlie" photos displayed by Burden, to take another example, she is the figure of eroticism, of *goona goona*. The Native Woman is silent because, as Michele Wallace has pointed out, there is no other for the other. If the White Woman is the other to the White Man, and the Native Man the other to the White Woman, the Native Woman is excluded from the space of production. Just as anthropology describes women as objects of exchange which enable kinship systems to function, cinema circulates the native woman as pure signifier, or as Wallace puts it, as a black hole, in a system that is largely one of male transaction.

Ann is kidnapped and replaces the bride of Kong, for the Skull Island Chief recognizes that she is six times more valuable than an indigenous woman (the Chief offers to purchase Ann from Denham at this price). Soon thereafter, however, Kong's arrival at the wall is announced with the striking of the gong, the three coups de théâtre announcing that the drama is to begin. A roar is heard, the natives silently watch, and Kong pushes the trees apart to get a better look at Ann.

5. The Jungle: King Kong—The Missing Link.   Kong is a cinematic fantasy of the Darwinian link between the anthropoid ape and man. As Donna Haraway explains in her brilliant analysis of the narratives implicit in Jane Goodall's primatological research project, the burden of the ideology of race after World War II was often placed on the anthropoid ape rather than on indigenous peoples.[57] Cooper's explanation for creating a monster Missing Link stemmed from his lament that there were no more places to discover. Perhaps even at the height of imperialism, the viability of representing native peoples as static Ethnographic beings was seen as impossible: there was always the problem that these colonial subjects spoke, and spoke quite vehemently. Apes, however, do not speak. And so the voyage of the moving picture ship culminates with an encounter with the prehistoric Kong.

As we have seen with the work of Regnault, the desire to rank the "races" and find the "missing link" between man and the ape was a defining obsession of nineteenth-century anthropology. This fascination manifested itself in popular culture in the portrayal of the ape as evil monster, a characterization which only gained currency in the latter half of the nineteenth century with the rise of Social Darwinism. Edgar Allan Poe's "The Murders in the Rue Morgue" (1841) is an early instance of this genre, in which the hideous murder of two Parisian women is ascribed to an escaped orangutan. A later example is H. G. Wells's *The Time Machine* (1896), in which power is held in the future by the Morlocks, evil, cannibalistic apes, the descendants of the modern-day working man. Cooper's own fascination with apes supposedly began with his childhood reading of Paul du Chaillu's *Explorations in Equatorial Africa* (1856). Du Chaillu, the first white man to shoot a gorilla, described the gorilla as "some hellish dream creature—a being of that hideous order, half-man half-beast," and already identified the gorilla as a creature notorious for abducting women.[58] Harold Hellenbrand explains that films like *King Kong* were representations which "cinematized, made larger than life, the conflict of white civilization with brute strength and consciousness in the guise of a prehistoric or backwards beast. Often enough the beast was an ape, and the ape black." This image, Hellenbrand explains, was a visualization of "the naturalist and Spencerian conceit of 'life as jungle.'"[59]

Like the centaur of *The Most Dangerous Game*, or the minotaur of the French surrealists, King Kong was half-man/half-beast. Many films before *King Kong* had depicted Africans and Asians as ape-men, lustful and savage.[60] Sometimes the films involved evil apelike creatures such as the evil ape in Edgar Rice Burroughs's novel *Tarzan of the Apes* (1912), which was first filmed in 1918, or the evil creatures featured in the film adaptation of Sir Arthur Conan Doyle's *The Lost World* (1921), produced by First National Studio. In the latter film, an expedition of scientists fights dinosaurs and evil apelike men in South America. The animator of *The Lost World*, Willis O'Brien, was also the animator of *King Kong*.[61]

But the ape-man did not merely lurk about in science fiction, ethnographic cinema, or jungle stories. The cinematic time machine was at work in the racial melodrama as well: D. W. Griffith's films were masterworks of racialist evolutionism. His early films often involved prehistoric tribes, and he made several racial melodramas.[62] In *The Birth of a Nation* (1915), Griffith's depiction of the African American character Gus is faithful to the book upon which the film was based, Thomas Dixon Jr.'s *The Clansman* (1905). Gus is represented in Dixon's book as a lascivious apelike beast who lusts after innocent white girls. This film, which many whites, including Robert and Frances Flaherty, found to be an extremely moving and profound masterpiece (and which many people of color found abominable), is not only a defining "monument" of the history of cinema, it also serves as a defining artifact of the nation: the nation is born through a demarcation of the African American as inferior Other against which white "superiority" is defined.[63]

Although Kong is monstrous—both in size and by virtue of his hybrid status as man/ape—Kong is a Noble Savage as well. Noble Savagery, as emphasized earlier, was important to the romantic ethnographic cinema of filmmakers like Flaherty and Murnau. There is a noble side to Kong: as in the ethnographic exposition, the boundaries between viewer and viewed were at times broken through, allowing the viewer of *King Kong* to see the world from Kong's eyes. This play with boundaries is made possible by the way that Kong is filmed. For example, in the scenes where Kong views Ann for the first time, there are shot/reaction shots of Kong and of what Kong sees. Similarly the viewer experiences Kong's view of the audience when he is later exhibited in the Broadway theater. As these shots suggest, Kong is decidedly anthropomorphized. He fights dinosaurs like a human prizefighter, is tender toward Ann, and is tragically defiant at the end of the film, his back arched like a diva just before he falls from the Empire State Building. On Skull Island, moreover, Kong is in control of the gaze; Ann, who "just wants to see," is identified only by her scream, and by her persistent inability to use her legs to stand up and run away whenever Kong is in the vicinity.

Both the desire to see and the dangers of seeing, essential to the horror film, are foregrounded in *King Kong*. The forbidden, what "no white man has seen," is above all the interracial, interspecies intercourse of Ann and Kong. This titillation propels the narrative forward. *King Kong* the film, like its eponymous character, is a monster, a hybrid of the ethnographic film and the science fiction film. As in the Komodo dragon expedition film, itself a hybrid, the white woman is a lure, an object to stimulate the beast's willingness to come out into the open and be seen. Kong sees Ann and immediately wants to possess her. Ann collapses: incapable of movement, she is an object to be possessed, an object of circulation; but it is Kong who must be captured.

6. The Jungle: Dinosaurs and the Prehistoric Age. Kong leaves the scene at the wall after taking possession of Ann, and the camera follows Kong beyond the wall to a "forgotten land": here the time voyage reaches its destination—a place where time has stopped and dinosaurs still roam, a prehistoric jungle of giant trees and plants. In his design for the opening shot of this scene, Willis O'Brien drew on nineteenth-century images of fantasy landscapes, inspired particularly by Arnold Böcklin's painting *The Isle of the Dead* (1880), and by Gustave Doré's illustrations of purgatories, hells, and wild landscapes.[64] O'Brien's animation is almost seamless, and its jarring sizes and spaces add up to a pastiche which is quite compelling. Using optical tricks such as projected backdrops and painted glass plates, Willis O'Brien created a hyperreal space.[65] As Denham, Jack, and the crew, Lilliputian in contrast to the giant vegetation, fire at a huge dinosaur in the background, the viewer has a sense that they are firing into a museum dinosaur display.

In one key scene, fantasy literally bumps up against reality. Kong places Ann on top of a tree in the foreground, and we see him dueling with a tyrannosaurus. Ann must sit and watch, rooted to the scene. The fighting beasts then literally bump into Ann's space, knocking down the tree on which she sits. Ann falls precipitously farther into the foreground: in a sense, she falls into our space, the space of the audience. Fantasy and reality are conjoined marvelously in O'Brien's animation. Praising the film's erotic, suffocatingly dreamlike power, Claude Ollier draws attention to this aspect of the animation:

> Even the minor flaws in the continuity of perspective or movement, far from destroying or enfeebling the credulity of the spectacle, are in accord rather with the presentation of a totally dreamlike state, a dream

created by means of spatial illusion, optical displacements, and disruptions between individual shots and the overall continuity. The "doubtful" space created by the depth montages of O'Brien and the necessity of filming in fragmented time results in a visual pattern altogether of a kind with the sort of "collage" manifest in all visions of nightmare worlds.[66]

As Noël Carroll has suggested, the dinosaur, though always used to invoke prehistory, was paradoxically a modern monster. The dinosaur, only made fashionable beginning in the mid–nineteenth century, soon became an object of study and of museum spectacle for those fascinated by the implications of time and evolution. Carroll explains why dinosaurs and warring tribes were key to the literature of such writers as Jules Verne and Edgar Rice Burroughs: "as symbols, dinosaurs and their fictional lost world are rather modern, i.e., as modern as our concept of prehistory."[67] Carroll argues that, from the turn of the century, the jungle metaphor referred to the necessarily savage character of economic competition, an economic survival of the fittest:

> The combination of dinosaurs with the biologically charged characterization of battling nation/tribes (in which the "humans" were aided by Europeans) is a recurring motif in prehistoric tales; it registers the application of intrinsically nondramatic biological concepts like "competition" and "survival" to social concepts where the biological concepts become particularized, dramatized, literalized. . . . This tendency to translate the terms of pure biological theory into vivid, combat-oriented metaphors for picturing society was rife at the turn of the century and prehistoric tales may, therefore, be seen in conjunction with the currency of Social Darwinism.[68]

In the jungle, Kong—the Missing Link—always wins in the eat-or-be-eaten world of ruthless competition for Ann.

7. *Broadway: The White Bourgeois Audience—Suraffiné, Consumerist, Cowed.* When Kong is finally subdued by Jack and Carl, felled by a gas bomb, and is brought to Manhattan, *King Kong* reverses itself and returns forward in time to the present. Although situated in the present, however, Manhattan is a city in which all is *not* in order (recall the early, dark scene of desperate women waiting in a soup line).[69] There is stylistic and narratival symmetry between Manhattan and Skull Island: it is not surprising then that the wall of Skull Island is mirrored in the theater wall in Manhattan

44. Still from *King Kong* (1933), dir. Merian C. Cooper and Ernest B. Schoedsack. (Courtesy of the Museum of Modern Art)

which Kong crushes down, or that the serpent-like body of the dinosaur foreshadows the snaking, elevated train, or that Kong should crunch a Skull Islander in his mouth in the same way that he does a New Yorker. Even the audience for the formal unveiling of Kong, made up of white theatergoers in formal evening dress, mirrors the Skull Islanders: both are hungry for the spectacle, and on Broadway, as on Skull Island, the spectacle is a subdued (placated or captive) Kong.

The fascinating cannibalism of the audience, its greedy desire to see Kong, is the subject matter of the next sequence. The desire of the audience is a mirror of our own desire to see. Depression Manhattan is portrayed as a harsh jungle in the beginning of *King Kong*, but for the bourgeois white theater audience awaiting the unveiling of Kong, the jungle must be brought closer, an example of what Haraway has called the entertainment of violated boundaries.[70] Like the nightclub crowd in *Blonde Venus*, or the members of the audience waiting for Kong, we, the viewers of the film, are also implicitly criticized for our voracious appetite to see the "real" thing, even though we already know that what we take for real is now only film, a simulacrum. As the theatergoers take their seats, one elderly, crotchety woman with spectacles complains, "I can't sit so near the screen. It hurts my eyes." To which the usher informs her, "This is not a moving picture, madam." She huffs, "Well! I never! I thought I was going to *see* something!" In this comic aside, the referent itself is secondary to the representation; the woman's comment, however, plays on the audience's desire to see the conflation of film and reality. Kong, of course, is an animated monster created through the use of eighteen-inch full-body models, and of separate models of his head and paws: the monster himself is not even whole, but made of pieces, already fetishized. Like Disneyland, Kong is presented as imaginary in order that we more firmly believe that the rest of the world is real.[71]

Denham tells the eager audience that he has "a story so strange that no one will believe it." He continues,

> But ladies and gentlemen, *seeing is believing.* And we, my partners and I, have brought back the living proof of our adventure. An adventure in which twelve of our party met horrible death. . . . I'm going to show you the greatest thing your eyes have ever beheld. He was a king and a god in the world he knew. But now he comes to civilization. Merely a captive. A show to gratify your curiosity.

Again the audience's desire to see is made visible. The curtain is pulled back and Kong appears, manacled as if crucified (Ann was also manacled on Skull Island). Next we see a reaction shot of the audience from Kong's (as well as Denham's) perspective. Denham then explains that he wants to allow the audience the privilege of witnessing the first photographs taken of Kong and his captors.

In ethnographic cinema the process of visualization is often brought to the fore through the use of maps, panoramic views, and scenes of the filmmaker as intrepid adventurer/photographer. *King Kong* reveals what happens when the processes of visualization break down. Infuriated at the photographers, whom he thinks are attacking Ann, Kong's huge body frees itself from the chains, and he penetrates the audience's space. Kong refuses to be "shot." He tears down the theater wall, grabs a sleeping woman through an open window in a nearby building, throws her down, and finally spots Ann in a hotel room with Jack.

Ann's cry that it is "like a terrible dream" makes explicit the oneiric character of the film, a perception shared by the surrealists when the film was released. *King Kong* was seen by some surrealists as a poetic film, the perfect cinematic version of a surrealist dream.[72] The strange horror of the film struck a chord in Jean Lévy. Writing for the surrealist art journal *Minotaure* in 1934, he recalled that as a child he had lost sleep from fear that gorilla-like monsters might appear at the window; *King Kong* was a visual-

45. Still from *King Kong* (1933), dir. Merian C. Cooper and Ernest B. Schoedsack. (Courtesy of the Museum of Modern Art)

ization of this fear. Lévy thus argued that the terror of being an unwilling viewer is what made the film work:

> I saw again trait by trait a remarkable detail of my familiar nightmares, with the anguish and the atrocious malaise which accompanies it. A spectator, not very reassured, would like to leave, but one makes him ashamed of his pusillanimity and he sits down again. This spectator, it's myself; one hundred times, in my dream.

He describes the film as akin to a Max Ernst fantasy of Maldoror: "It does not appear necessary to insist on the apocalyptic grandeur of certain tableaus, particularly the battle of King Kong in the grotto, with the monstrous serpent; the quality of the decors seems to me, in one hundred places, strictly Maldororien."[73] As Theodor W. Adorno pointed out, surrealism attempts to shock us with the experience of childhood, and thus makes frequent use of montage, a technique which leads the viewer to ask, "Where have I seen that before?"[74] The recognition of childhood experience, so much a part of surrealism, was made visceral in *King Kong*.[75]

Whether or not its form was exalted, however, *King Kong*'s subject matter was complicit with the avant-garde's love of Primitivism, its tendency to look at the Primitive as a figure of the unconscious, as a limit to the *ratio* of the West. Kong is a cinematic visualization of the male beast which the Surrealists so longed to unleash. In *King Kong*, visualization is a hunt which involves titillation, capture, spectacle, and death: *King Kong* is a mix of the surrealist ingredients of the erotic, the exotic, and the unconscious.[76] James Clifford suggests surrealism is in this sense a modern sensibility: "Reality is no longer a given, a natural, familiar environment. The self, cut loose from its attachments, must discover meaning where it may—a predicament, evoked at its most nihilistic, that underlies both surrealism and modern ethnography."[77] Clifford calls the object of this ethnographic/surrealist attitude—non-Western peoples, and women—the other.[78] If we take Lévy seriously and consider *King Kong* as, among other things, a surrealist text, the object of the ethnographic surrealist attitude of the film is thus the Ethnographic itself, King Kong as Other, and Woman—Ann—as Other.

8. At the Pinnacle of the Empire State Building: The White Male Military Progress, Technology, Imperialism, the Future. King Kong, which has taken us back in time and returned us to the present, now lurches forward and upwards—up to the future. Ann is seized by the rampaging Kong. The searchlights of the city keep Kong in sight, and all watch as he climbs to the top of the Empire State Building. Completed in 1932, the Empire State Building was, at the time of the film, the ultimate U.S. symbol of progress, technology, and Civilization. Like the Eiffel Tower at the turn of the century, perceived as embodying French greatness, and which provided the perfect contrast to the so-called "simple" cultures represented in the ethnographic expositions Regnault frequented, the Empire State Building provided the perfect contrast to the monster Kong. Ultimately only the most sophisticated technology can stop Kong—gas bombs subdue him on Skull Island, warplanes shoot him down in New York. Even as Kong meets his fate, the play with the boundaries between observer and observed continues: we see the action both from the point of view of Kong as the airplanes swoop toward him, and from the point of view of the planes as they gun him down. Ironically, two of the gunners were reportedly played by Cooper and Schoedsack themselves.[79]

This was the necessary conclusion to *King Kong*. As in *Tabu* and *Goona Goona*, the native must be crucified, murdered, or at least captured and made a wax figure, as suggested by the close-up of Allakariallak at the end of *Nanook of the North*. For, above all, in order for the myth of modernity to be

46. Still from *King Kong* (1933), dir. Merian C. Cooper and Ernest B. Schoedsack. (Courtesy of the Museum of Modern Art)

maintained, order must reign again, and everything must return to its place. As John Seeleye writes,

> King Kong is a movie inextricably tied by intertextual references to a long literary tradition in America, one that can be traced back via fairy stories to the Wild Man myth. It is a tradition, moreover, that promotes the majority opinion found in American literature, that wild things— whether whales, apes, or men—belong where the wild things are, that to attempt any interplay with civilized forces is to guarantee the destruction (not the assimilation) of wildness.[80]

This fear of mixing was explicit in Douglas Burden's loathing of the "pigsty breed,"[81] a fear that was also aroused by migration, whether it was the migration of African Americans from the rural South to Northern cities, or the immigration of non–Northern Europeans and inhabitants of formerly colonized nations to colonial metropolitan centers. The fear of interbreeding was manifest in the study of race and hybridity in early anthropology: it was a prominent strain in German anthropology and was, of course, later

embraced by Adolf Hitler. In the United States, the nativist Lothrop Stoddard was particularly influential in mobilizing fears of racial impurity. In
The Revolt against Civilization, he asserted,

> Usually highly prolific, often endowed with extraordinary physical
> vigor, and able to migrate easily, owing to modern facilities of transpor-
> tation, the more backwards people of the earth tend increasingly to
> seek the centres of civilization, attracted thither by the higher wage
> and easier living conditions which there prevail. The influx of such
> lower elements into civilised society is an unmitigated disaster. . . . The
> racial foundations of civilization are undermined.[82]

This again is the realm of "political physics": the Ethnographic is not coeval
with the Historical, and the two simply cannot exist in the same temporal
space. To preserve the separation, the Civilized man will resort to apartheid
and murder. To set evolution back on course in *King Kong,* the white man
seizes upon war technology. The film moves into the future with its depiction of fighter planes as cutting-edge technological achievements, but it
also anticipates the postcolonial future by anticipating the end of the age of
high imperialism. In this sense, the film may be taken as an unintended
advance metaphor for racial conflict within the United States, and the imperialist wars that the United States fought in Asian and Central American
countries after 1933.[83]

Kong is thus both prehistorical—the Ethnographic—and postcolonial—
the Postmodern, at the end of History. As a monster, he embodies the col-
lapsing of the future into the prehistorical, the "primitive" into the technological, the Ethnographic into the Historical. *King Kong* insists that the
public desires or hungers for authenticity: it is more spectacular to bring
back Kong, than to take pictures of him. *King Kong* is a meditation on
ethnographic realism, on the audience's desire to believe and disbelieve, to
travel backward and forwards in time, to embrace the Ethnographic, see the
world from his eyes, and then be rid of him, murder him. *King Kong* creates
both a monster object and a monster viewer. The audience can only be
monsters, since the image precedes the referent: *King Kong* becomes a spectacle, a monstrous parade of horrific images, and—to borrow Baudrillard's
expression—a "precession of simulacra."[84]

Donna Haraway, as indicated above, has argued insightfully that, in the
twentieth century, the narrative of race and evolution has come to be placed
increasingly upon the figure of the anthropoid ape: Cooper and Schoedsack
take this allegorical figure one step further, creating the perfect Ethnographic monster. Stuck in the past, doomed to die, Kong is pure simula-

crum, the raising of the Ethnographic to the level of horror. He is no longer a referent to anything, for the referent is cannibalized from within. When Kong stares into Ann's eyes, and Ann looks back at Kong, they are creating their own *mise-en-abyme*. The viewer, figured in this viewing process by the Skull Islanders and the Broadway theater audience, is within this endless precession of signifiers. *King Kong* celebrates its own technology: although the film glorifies the Empire State Building, its greatest boast is its own technology, the very ability of animator Willis O'Brien to create a cinematic monster like Kong, the monster of evolutionary nightmare. *King Kong* thus ultimately celebrates cinema's tendency to create monsters which mirror the anxieties of any given age. In so doing, it screens from our vision the historical cannibalisms which turned West Africans into hieroglyphs for medical science, stole the bones of Minik Wallace's father for a museum display, and led a Chirichiri man named Ota Benga to commit suicide.

Ethnographic Spectacle Revisited

Poet Elizabeth Alexander subverts the representation of the African as Ethnographic spectacle in her poem about Sarah Bartman (Saartjie Baartman), a Khoi-San woman who was exhibited in France in the nineteenth century, only to be dissected after death by the French biologist Georges Cuvier, her genitals put on display at the Musée de l'homme in a bell jar:

> Observe the wordless Odalisque.
> I have not forgotten my Xhosa
> clicks. My flexible tongue
> and healthy mouth bewilder
> this man with his rotting teeth.
> If he were to let me rise up
> from this table, I'd spirit
> his knives and cut out his black heart,
> seal it with science fluid inside
> a bell jar, place it on a low
> shelf in a white man's museum
> so the whole world could see
> it was shriveled and hard,
> geometric, deformed, unnatural.[85]

In her poem, Alexander slides from the voice of the observing anthropologist and scientist to Bartman's own voice, speaking her revenge in the pres-

47. Coco Fusco and Guillermo Gómez-Peña in "The Couple in the Cage" (1992).
(Photograph by Peter Barker, courtesy of Coco Fusco)

ent tense. Alexander's poem responds to the long-established tradition of ethnographic spectacle in which indigenous peoples are exhibited and dissected—both visually and literally—a tradition carried forward in cinematic pastiche in Cooper and Schoedsack's *King Kong*; but it also speaks to the possible forms of resistance. Poets and artists like Alexander upset the structure of fascinating cannibalism, by imagining (or perhaps listening to) the silenced displayed person, by destroying the shell of the ethnographic simulacrum which encases the historical person.[86]

A response to the racist politics of ethnographic display is literally embodied in the parodic performance of Coco Fusco and Guillermo Gómez-Peña who defy the silencing and murder of native peoples in ethnographic spectacle. In the quincentennial year of Columbus's arrival in North America, Fusco and Gómez-Peña commemorated the event by drawing attention to the West's practice of exhibiting humans, highlighting the fact that Columbus brought back several Arawak Indians to the court of Spain. In "The Year of the White Bear: Take One—Two Undiscovered Aborigines," presented at the University of California at Irvine, in Madrid's Columbus Plaza, and in London's Covent Garden, in 1992, Fusco and Gómez-Peña dressed in spectacular Hollywood "native" dress and lived in a cage. Their daily activities included watching television and working at computers, but they also performed "traditional" aboriginal activities. A plaque presented visitors with a map and a taxonomic description of Guatinau, an imaginary island in the Caribbean, and explained that the people there were only recently "discovered." Visitors could speak to them by telephone, but only in Spanish.[87] Gómez-Peña explained this parodic performance in the following terms:

> We want to bring back the ghosts and unleash the demons of history, but we want to do it in a way that the demons don't scare the Anglo-European others, but force them to begin a negotiation with these ghosts and demons that will lead to a pact of co-existence. The ghosts we are trying to unleash are extremely whimsical, irreverent, and grotesque, extremely crazy and picaresque.[88]

By rereading artifacts of ethnographic cinema like *King Kong,* and by creating works that reveal gaps in dominant discourse, these demons may also be unleashed to confront the monstrous imaging of indigenous peoples as Ethnographic.

CONCLUSION.

PASSION OF REMEMBRANCE[1]

Facing the Camera/Grabbing the Camera

Margaret Mead: No, you see, I do not accept that I have done things because I dreamt about them.
James Baldwin: But I had to accept that I was on a slave boat once.
Mead: No.
Baldwin: But I was.
Mead: Wait, you were not. Look, you don't believe in reincarnation?
Baldwin: But my whole life was defined by history. . . . My life was defined by the time I was five by the history written on my brow.[2]

In 1971 at the American Museum of Natural History, anthropologist Margaret Mead and the novelist and cultural critic James Baldwin conducted a fascinating public debate on—among other topics—definitions of history and time. As Baldwin declared, there is "this time and *time,*" that is, chronologically measurable time and a notion of time that collapses the past into the present and future.[3] He asserted to Mead's dismay, "I don't think history is the past. . . . History is the present."[4] Mead, on the other hand, saw history as a process of compiling facts about past momentous events, such as great battles like the Battle of Waterloo. The problems of racism in this country, she affirmed, would be ameliorated if one could establish the exact facts of the historical relationship between blacks and whites. Mead explained, "Now my definition of what did happen is that if there'd have been a camera there running on its own steam with no human being to press the button on or off what would have been on the film is what really happened."[5]

Mead's vision of history as the unfolding of events, as a linear temporal process that could be captured by a film camera running without any human intervention, is a vision rooted in the nineteenth-century Rankean notion of History: *wie es eigentlich gewesen.* Since Mead saw film as a positivist medium for recording data and events, "a camera running on its own steam" would be sufficient to capture history as it happened. In Jean

Rouch's film about her, *Portrait of a Friend* (1978), Mead proclaims confidently that she and other anthropologists have largely succeeded with their project of documenting all the "vanishing," "primitive" cultures left on the earth: the next project of the anthropologist, she said, was to build space colonies. Although Mead derided doctrines of racial determinism, she never discarded the evolutionary division of the world into "primitive" versus "modern" peoples: history was for Mead one of progress, expansion, exploration, and benign colonialization.

James Baldwin's "history" was vastly different. First of all, Baldwin claimed that history was "written in the color of my skin."[6] In a colonial or slave society, whose effects linger into the present day, the person of color could never escape the constructed difference placed on skin color. As Frantz Fanon elucidated, the "racial epidermal schema" located the person of color in three places: as a body, as a race, and as one's ancestors.[7] Baldwin, however, refused to place himself within the Eurocentric view of History; indeed, he saw it as impossible: "I am one of the dispossessed. According to the West I have no history. There is that difference. I have had to wrest my identity out of the jaws of the West."[8] With a third eye, Baldwin was not only rejecting a discourse which represented people of color as "savages," but also the Western notion of rational, linear History. Instead, for Baldwin, history was composed of histories: the history of racialization, the history of a people, the history of individuals, and the necessity to bear witness for the future.

Story-telling/History-telling

The telling of history is linked to the telling of stories, both textual and cinematic (as is often remarked, the Latin word *storia* contains both meanings). The epic story of human history told by the West, bounded by the evolutionary schema reflected in Mead's comments, has itself had a pernicious history. Early anthropology, cinema, and popular culture constructed indigenous peoples as Ethnographic: of an earlier time, without history, without archives. The construction of the Ethnographic, however, was always ambivalent, for the Ethnographic was not only viewed as Savage but also was seen as alternatively authentic, macho, pure, spiritual, and an antidote to the ills of modern, industrialized capitalism, a myth embodied in the image of the Noble Savage. No matter the particular variant of the story, however, the Native was portrayed as stuck in the evolutionary past, as living evidence of a biological progression. Whether the story was told in scientific research terms or imbued with romanticism, indigenous peoples were seen as embodying and conferring authenticity. Even today, the realism of ethnographic representation is less contested than is the realism of historical representation. At the center of the story, is the *body* of the Native, the essential index of authenticity, and thus visual media, capable of capturing the body and holding it for the viewer, have long played a lead role in transmitting the narrative of race and evolution.

In order to begin to come to terms with the continued hold of this narrative and the role of visual media in transmitting it, I have attempted in this book to identify and delineate what I believe are the three central modalities of Ethnographic representation in early cinema. I used Regnault's chronophotography of West African performers at the Paris Ethnographic Exposition of 1895, a body of work concerned exclusively with gesture and locomotion, to exemplify the first of the three modalities, termed here Ethnographic "inscription." In Regnault's film sequences, the indigenous body in motion, perceived as raw data, is literally written into film for the scientifically trained "reader"—the *langage par gestes*. Regnault believed that such images would serve as an index for race, much as subsequent anthropologists such as Boas and Mead believed that films of gesture and behavior would provide unimpeachable records for the classification of cultures. Regnault's work shares with later scientific research film the fate that all but a small fraction of the images are not viewed even by specialists. The narrative of evolution emerges only through the written text accompanying the images and the conceptual framing of the images as entries in a projected global "archive" for the scientific mapping and classification of race and culture. Direct echos of Regnault's conception are apparent not only in racially ordered university collections of research footage, but also in the Archives de la planète of Albert Kahn, the choreometrics dance project of Alan Lomax, and so on.

A second modality of Ethnographic representation is exemplified in Robert Flaherty's *Nanook of the North*. Flaherty's film, which hinges upon a nostalgic reconstruction of a more authentic humanity (the "unspoiled" Primitive) and is considered today a pioneering work of the romantic, lyrical ethnographic film, embodies what I term the "taxidermic" mode of Ethnographic representation. Flaherty's film was produced within the same evolutionary frame that gave rise to Regnault's "ciphers" of race, the indigenous body still serving as evidence of a time before history, but, with Flaherty (and before him, Curtis), the ideology of the "vanishing races" comes to the fore. The Ethnographic, although now portrayed "in the round," is set in a picturesque past innocent of, rather than in fierce, complex struggle with, the spread of Western capitalist society. Posited as already dead, long since passed by in the steeplechase of history, the "vanishing" Native is "redeemed" through taxidermic reconstruction: the dead is brought to life. The premise of the inevitable death of the Native, moreover, allows the physical and cultural destruction wrought by the West to appear ineluctable, and such films, albeit with pathos, implicitly provide ideological justification for the very colonial and economic conquests that brought filmmakers like Flaherty to the Arctic.

Finally, in *King Kong*, a sublime example of ironic Hollywood pastiche replaying many of the Ethnographic themes central to Regnault's chronophotography and Flaherty's *Nanook of the North*, Ethnographic spectacle takes the form of "monstrosity." Here the Ethnographic is made to enter the temporal and physical space of the white audience, the resulting "incongruous beast" generating fears of contamination and hybrid pathology. *King Kong* itself is a hybrid between museum diorama and horror film, teratology and the fantasy illustrations of Gustave Doré. Although baroque in expression, the film implicitly links anthropology, or at least the camera-wielding scientific expedition, with nationalism and imperialism: in order to bring back Kong for examination and spectacle, the Skull Islanders must be defeated, and, in order to subdue Kong, the latest war technology must be marshaled. The film, made by early ethnographic filmmakers Cooper and Schoedsack, explicitly recalls the historical practice of exhibiting humans at ethnographic expositions, and partakes of many of the aspects of the "racial film" which flourished in the wake of the commercial success of *Nanook of the North*. In its construction of the *ethnographiable* monster, *King Kong* summons a notion of time that feeds into ideologies of the indigenous body as the site of a collision between past and present, Ethnographic and Historical, Primitive and Modern. In the end, history yanks the monster from the past only to kill it.

Although the discipline of anthropology has undergone significant changes since the 1930s, it has continued to provide fodder for both popular and scientific conceptions of the Ethnographic. The conception of ethnographic film as a scientific tool for anthropologists studying the lives of "disappearing," "primitive," "uncontaminated" tribes survived after World War II. Films made from the 1950s to the 1970s, including works by filmmakers now considered major figures in ethnographic film—John Marshall, Robert Gardner, and Timothy Asch—were often labeled "observational cinema." This cinema, characterized by a restrained style—the use of long takes, slow pacing, seamless editing, and often synchronized sound—was, however, a troubling form of "observation." With the presence of the camera obscured, the viewer is meant to observe and experience the film as if he or she had been there, from a "fly on the wall" perspective.[9] The beginnings of a shift in academic ethnographic film to a more participatory cinema also occurred in the 1950s with the self-reflexive films of French ethnographic filmmaker Jean Rouch, but this shift did not have an appreciable impact on mainstream academic ethnographic film until very recently.

The "crisis" in anthropology which began in the late 1970s has introduced a more interpretive and questioning stance concerning the colonialist underpinnings of the discipline's representational practices. This growing self-reflexivity did not simply reflect changes in anthropological thought, but also resulted from post–World War II decolonization, a movement marked by independence struggles and demands for self-determination. Anthropology's temporal suppositions could no longer be sustained: indigenous peoples and other marginalized peoples of color were criticizing the history of their representation by Euro-Americans, and were attempting to counteract Western media exploitation by obtaining greater access to television and film production.[10] Today, the reform is being carried forward by a growing number of filmmakers/scholars including David and Judith MacDougall, Gary Kildea, and Faye Ginsburg. Another recent development in academic ethnographic film—initiated by filmmakers and videomakers such as Terry Turner, Timothy Asch, and Vincent Carelli—is to teach indigenous peoples how to use video and film technology.[11]

Despite these innovations and growing self-criticism within anthropology generally, however, the camera is still too often seen by ethnographic filmmakers as an unproblematic, innocent eye on indigenous peoples, a useful tool for science, many filmmakers turning to self-reflexive examination of the process of production to make ethnographic film more scientific.[12] Furthermore, even though many academic anthropologists are highly critical of the discipline's complicity with racializing stereotyping, the episteme of the Ethnographic is still alive and well, especially in popular media. Television specials like Harvard anthropologist David Maybury-Lewis's *Millenium: Tribal Wisdom and the Modern World* (1992), Hollywood films like Kevin Costner's *Dances With Wolves* (1990), Michael Mann's *The Last of the Mohicans* (1992), or Frank Marshall's *Congo* (1995)— a 1990s update of *King Kong*—and science fiction epics like George Lucas's *The Return of the Jedi* (1983), with its representation of the "Ewok" tribesmen as peaceful, brown creatures, continue to reinforce established conceptions of the Ethnographic.

Ward Churchill explains the differences and the similarities that a recent film like *Dances with Wolves* shares with earlier Hollywood representations of Native Americans:

> Stripped of its pretty pictures and progressive flourishes in directions and affirmative action hiring, *Dances With Wolves* is by no means a movie about Indians. Instead, it is at base an elaboration of movieland's Great White Hunter theme. . . .
>
> If Kevin Costner or anyone else in Hollywood held an honest inclination to make a movie which would alter public perceptions of Native America in some meaningful way, it would, first and foremost, be set in the present day, not in the mid–19th century. It would feature, front and center, the real struggles of living native people to liberate themselves from the oppression which has beset them in the contemporary era, not the adventures of some fictional non-Indian out to save the savage.[13]

What is at stake, asserts Churchill, is the obscuring of pressing Native American problems such as the expropriation of water rights and minerals, involuntary sterilization, and FBI repression of Indian activism, in favor of a romanticized and thus pernicious myth.[14] The continued proliferation of images of indigenous peoples as spatially and temporally distant, however, sustains a denial of the history of native peoples' struggles against colonialization and genocide, and their ongoing struggles for cultural identity against the forces of an image-hungry dominant culture which sees them as always already dead.

Before I conclude my book, I want to turn my attention to two contemporaries of Flaherty, Cooper, and Schoedsack who worked within dominant Western media and academic institutions and yet have been almost completely ignored in the history of cinema's relationship to anthropology. Josephine Baker was a popular performer whose stage and screen identity was based upon a spectacularization of the collapse of the Primitive into the Modern; Zora Neale Hurston was an anthropologist who studied her own community of origin—the African American South—and in so doing violated the boundaries between Observer/Observed. In their very positions as women of color moving in and out of white-dominated fields—in Josephine Baker's case, the entertainment business, and in Zora Neale Hurston's case, anthropology and folklore—Baker and Hurston embody the very precariousness of such dichotomies and reveal their limits. In their cultural productions, they upset the categories of Ethnographic/Historical, Primitive/Modern to the extent they mobilize the third eye in responding to the racialization processes of Ethnographic cinema.

Josephine Baker and the Stereotype of the
Ethnographic Primitive

Josephine Baker, the great music hall star of the 1920s and 1930s, is decried by some as an agent of minstrelsy and a toady to whites, by others as a black heroine and the first modern international black star.[15] Because of the hybridity of the stereotyped images she embodied, both spectacular Primitive and fashionable French star, the figure of Baker is susceptible to disparate interpretations. Born in 1906 in St. Louis, Missouri, to a poor family, Josephine Baker moved to Paris in 1925 and soon became a focal point for the French fascination for the black, colonial female body, jazz, and *l'art nègre*. When Baker debuted in Paris, she was portrayed as monstrous. In her autobiography, Baker cites an astonishing review of one of her performances:

> Woman or man? Her lips are painted black, her skin is the color of bananas, her cropped hair sticks to her head like caviar, her voice squeaks. She is in constant motion, her body writhing like a snake or more precisely like a dipping saxophone. Music seems to pour from her body. She grimaces, crosses her eyes, puffs out her cheeks, wiggles disjointedly, does a split and finally crawls off the stage stiff-legged, her rump higher than her head, like a young giraffe. . . . This is no woman, no dancer. It's something as exotic and elusive as music, the embodiment of all the sounds we know. . . . And now the finale, a wildly indecent dance which takes us back to primeval times . . . arms high, belly thrust forward, buttocks quivering, Josephine is stark naked except for a ring of blue and red feathers circling her hips and another around her neck.[16]

Baker was thus made by the media into an "ethnographic" spectacle, a monster, neither man nor woman, neither human nor animal.

Placed in a contradictory position, Baker believed that she was making strides for African Americans as a black star in a white entertainment world, even as she understood that Euro-American culture constructed her as "nothing but a body to be exhibited in various stages of undress."[17] The fascination in ethnographic cinema for the displayed body of the woman of color is rendered carnivalesque in Baker's shows. For Baker was not only the symbol of the "black woman," but of all colonized women, and she performed in acts which represented her as Inuit, Indochinese, African, Arab, and Caribbean:[18]

> Again and again we rehearsed a flamboyant number about the French colonies, which included Algerian drums, Indian bells, tom-toms from Madagascar, coconuts from the Congo, cha-chas from Guadeloupe, a

> number laid in Marinique during which I distributed sugar cane to the audience, Indochinese gongs, Arab dances, camels and finally my appearance as the Empress of Jazz.[19]

If Baker was trapped by Ethnographic spectacle, her fame never enabling her to escape the roles she was consigned to play in a story scripted by white society, she was acutely aware of her predicament and responded to it. As Baker commented, "Since I personified the savage on the stage, I tried to be as civilized as possible in daily life."[20]

Ironically, although Baker was admired not only for her "primitive" persona, but for her elegance of manner and hyperfeminine style, on a par with Mae West and Marlene Dietrich, these same characteristics led to what many saw as an intolerable hybridity. Reviewer Janet Flanner, for example, deplored Baker's transformation into "almost . . . a little lady":

> Her caramel-colored body, which overnight became a legend in Europe, is still magnificent, but it has become thinned, trained, almost civilized. Her voice, especially in the voo-deo-do's, is still a magic flute that hasn't yet heard of Mozart—though even that, one fears, will come in time. There is a rumor that she wants to sing refined ballads; one is surprised that she doesn't want to play Othello. On that lovely animal visage lies now a sad look, not of captivity, but of dawning intelligence.[21]

The figure of the Ethnographic is thus imposed again: Flanner reads Baker as an innocent Savage falling from grace to become a decadent half-Civilized monster, a sister to the "racial film" heroines Reri, Dasnee, Fayaway.

In Baker's first sound film, Marc Allegret's Zou Zou (1932), the camera pans a circus scene of performers and spectators, halting backstage to capture the sight of a few French boys spying through a window at a black girl powdering her face. The girl is Zou Zou, a circus act, whose stage brother is a white boy named Jean. From the outset, the spectacle of racial and sexual difference is highlighted, providing voyeuristic pleasure, and setting the stage for a version of Haraway's "entertainment of violated boundaries."

If Zou Zou is a sister to a white boy, she is also the object of aggressivity, for, as a black woman, she is a threat which must be controlled and tamed, a figure appropriate for the stage but not as marriage partner for the white French boy Jean. Although Zou Zou grows up to become a great music hall star, she falls secretly in love with Jean (played as an adult by Jean Gabin), only to discover that Jean has instead fallen for her blonde French friend, tellingly named Claire (Yvette Lebon). Zou Zou's proper place is the circus where we first saw her, where she can forever serve as the object of the white

48. Still from *Zou Zou* (1932), dir. Marc Allegret.
(Courtesy of the Museum of Modern Art)

male gaze, as the exotic, black, female performer. At the end of the film, heartbroken by Jean's choice of Claire, she sobs as she walks past poster images of herself as icon Zou Zou. At the film's end, there is a flashback of Zou Zou in a music hall performance as a feathered bird in a golden cage.

Drawing upon Frantz Fanon's analyses of the psychic economy of race in *Black Skin, White Masks*, Homi Bhabha has explored the stereotype as an ambivalent, indeed hybrid image. As Homi Bhabha argues,

Stereotyping is not the setting up of a false image which becomes the scapegoat of discriminatory practices. It is a much more ambivalent text of projection and introjection, metaphoric and metonymic strategies, displacement, overdetermination, guilt, aggressivity; the masking and splitting of "official" and fantasmatic knowledges to construct the positionalities and oppositionalities of racist discourse.[22]

The obvious fabrication of Zou Zou into a sign of the Primitive—the posters which render Zou Zou into a stereotyped symbol of black female sexuality, Zou Zou's theatrical presentation as both exotic bird and elegant star— underline Bhabha's assertion that

> the recognition and disavowal of "difference" is always disturbed by the question of its re-presentation or construction. The stereotype is, in fact, an impossible object. For that very reason, the exertions of the "official knowledges" of colonialism—pseudo-scientific, typological, legal-administrative, eugenicist—are imbricated at the point of their production of meaning and power with the fantasy that dramatizes the impossible desire for a pure, undifferentiated origin.[23]

The character Zou Zou is thus flattened into a sign, much as Baker was made into an icon for the French "primitive," an object of projection and repudiation. In one of her music hall acts, Zou Zou sings "Haiti," a song which denies Zou Zou's status as a postcolonial subject, as a U.S.-born woman of color living in Paris, for it is a song about her desire to return to see the blue skies of her distant "homeland." In other words, even as the viewer is meant to sympathize with the "caged" Zou Zou, she is being categorized and labeled according to Ethnographic convention. In the West, she can only serve as what Bhabha calls a visible fetish of racism—a marker in Fanon's color-coded epidermal schema of skin color. In this way, Baker's own hybrid status as a black star in white society is contained.

According to renowned theater director Max Reinhardt, a man central to the dazzling Berlin theater scene, Baker "personified Expressionism." The poet Erich Maria Remarque told Baker that she "brought a whiff of jungle air and an elemental strength and beauty to the tired showplace of Western Civilization."[24] This perception of Baker as antidote to the alienation of European society, together with the "Savage" connotations which, as Baker herself was aware, accompanied such praise, beautifully illustrates Bhabha's point that the colonial stereotype, which is necessarily visual, turns on both recognition ("they are just like us") and a disavowal of difference ("they are moral and biological degenerates").

Baker also embodied what critic Michele Wallace calls the postmodern "negative scene of instruction" between African American and Euro-American art. Wallace defines the negative scene of instruction as one in which "the exchange is disavowed and disallowed—no one admits to having learned anything from anyone else."[25] The reluctance of Euro-American critics to acknowledge the contribution to world culture and to Euro-American art itself of African American and other artistic traditions stemming from non-Western sources also betrays cultural anxiety. A desire to contain this anxiety manifests itself in the stereotype of the Primitive/Ethnographic as mute and inferior counterpoint to the Modern. According to the logic identified by Wallace, there can be no dialogue because, by definition, the Ethnographic is constructed as lacking fully developed subjectivity.

If Baker was not able to escape her predicament, her awareness of it and the finesse and exuberant parody of her theatrical performance allowed her at times to transcend the gilded cage of her situation. In Baker's filmed performance, there are gaps and disruptions. At times, like many great African American performers such as singer and actor Paul Robeson, Baker seems to rise above the stereotyped roles she was given, in her portrayal of Zou Zou, or Aouina the goat herder in *Princess Tam Tam* (1935). Although racialized as a sign of the Primitive, contained by a discourse which could only read her as Ethnographic spectacle, Baker in her extraordinary use of masquerade appears to be winking at the viewer.

Sis Cat's Perspective: Zora Neale Hurston

The Primitive was a stereotype consigned not only to black performers like Baker but also to scholars and artists of color. Born in Eatonville, Florida, around 1901, filmmaker, writer, and folklorist Zora Neale Hurston was one of the first African Americans to receive a B.A. from Barnard College. Hurston was encouraged by Franz Boas, then the department Head of Anthropology at Barnard, to collect folklore in the South. As part of her research, Hurston made films in 1928 and 1929 of children's games, dancing, a baptism, and activities in a logging camp, and in 1940 of activities in Beaufort, South Carolina, including road scenes, dock scenes, landscape, the activities of farm workers, prison laborers, and, most importantly, the activities of the Commandment Keeper Church, a local African American church. As described below, although part of Boas's attraction to Hurston was as a "native student"—an insider ethnographer who could provide data (Boas did not seriously encourage Hurston to consider a career as a professor), and although her films served as a form of vicarious cultural tourism for her patron Mrs. Charlotte Osgood Mason, Hurston's anthropology broke with Ethnographic convention in complex ways.

Hurston referred to Boas as "the greatest anthropologist alive" and praised his "insatiable hunger for knowledge." Boas, Hurston wrote, was a man characterized by "[a] genius for pure objectivity. He has no pet wishes to prove. His instructions are to go out and find what is there."[26] This stance of objectivity, the impetus to observe cultural practice as if from a distance, Hurston would later write, was what she had gained from her anthropological studies. In her book on African American southern folklore, *Mules and Men* (1935), Hurston explains how she became attracted to the discipline: "It was only when I was off in college, away from my native surroundings, that I could see myself like somebody else and stand off and look at my garment. Then I had to have the spy-glass of Anthropology to look through at that."[27] The "spy-glass of Anthropology," as Hurston so cogently put it, had traditionally been reserved for the white anthropologist, the white scholar who believed in the objective, descriptive recording of so-called "vanishing" peoples. Not surprisingly, Hurston herself was not innocent of objectifying the people she studied as Ethnographic. As Hazel V. Carby has observed, Hurston romanticized the "black folk," in order to preserve "an aesthetically purified version of blackness," a romanticization of black society that was seen by critics such as Richard Wright as a continuance of the stereotypes of minstrelsy.[28] Even as she was in part caught up in the Ethnographic romanticization of the period, however, Hurston also broke from that romanticization in significant ways.

In one sense, Hurston's short, unedited research films of 1928–29 of African Americans from the South indeed appear to be within the positivist scientific tradition begun by Regnault and carried on by Boas and Mead.[29] Much of her footage seems to have been conceived as scientific samplings for Boas. Boas's interests in "isolable actions" are reflected, for example, in Hurston's footage of children playing: they are made into "types," holding up pieces of paper with their ages, filing past the camera frontally and then in profile. Yet at one point there is a marked disruption from the normal iconography of Ethnographic inscription, a certain knowing playfulness. A young, barefoot African American woman emerges from a house onto the front porch and walks toward the camera. She smiles at the camera as she turns her head left, and then right. It is clear here that, despite the bit of play betrayed by the woman's smile, the woman is meant to be portrayed as a type: Hurston uses the poses typical of anthropometry. But then the next shots take on an experimental quality, the camera cutting from a shot of

49. Still from Zora Neale Hurston's films of 1928–29.
(Courtesy of Lucy Ann Hurston and the Library of Congress)

two women on the porch, to an extreme long shot of the garden with the houses in the background, followed by a shot of the young woman lying odalisque-style facing the camera on the porch, concluding with a low-angle shot of a woman's feet rocking on the porch next to the paws of a cat. In other shots, two women are seen on the porch, and the camera is obviously shooting from behind a tree, from the position of voyeur (or, perhaps, neighbor). Elaine Charnov has brilliantly explained how Hurston, in what seems a radical attempt to call attention to the fetishizing and the voyeuristic qualities of the camera, anticipates the self-reflexive, deconstruction technique of Maya Deren.[30]

Hurston's own use of the "spy-glass of Anthropology" was a constant process of negotiation. Hurston was perceived by Mason as a sweet, unspoiled Primitive: on Boas's advice, Hurston had sought Mason's financial assistance so that she could pursue a Ph.D. in anthropology at Columbia University, but Mason coldly refused, apparently believing that Hurston could be ruined by too much education. Sidestepping this obstacle, Hurston worked to create her own fieldwork methodology, borrowing from teachers like Boas, but refusing to confine herself to the dry observational mode that

Malinowski and Boas espoused. At one point during her 1928 research trip, for example, Hurston even posed as a Jacksonville bootlegger's woman on the run.[31] During her hoodoo research of 1928 in New Orleans she lay for sixty-nine hours nude without food or water in order to become a novitiate of Samuel Thompson, a Creole conjurer.[32] Unlike Mead, who approached her subjects from the outside and pursued what she saw as a rigorous scientific agenda, associating Balinese trance, for example, with schizophrenia, Hurston was not willing to scientifically analyze her own psychic experiences due to what her biographer Robert E. Hemenway describes as "Hurston's awareness of the spiritual possibilities in the hoodoo experience . . . her *belief* in the magic."[33] Instead of participant observation, Hurston's methods may be characterized as observing participation.

During the late 1920s, Hurston became interested in new forms of ethnographic cultural production. At the time that she made her 1928–29 film, she began to collaborate with Langston Hughes on a black opera, having seen first-hand the popularity of Hughes's poems with the people she studied in the South.[34] Hurston's goal, one that emerged from living with and participating in the culture of the people she studied, was to show the world the great originality of southern black culture, a culture which had its roots in African cultures. Instead of salvage ethnography, seeking to document and preserve evidence of an ostensibly dying culture, Hurston in her research, writings, theatrical productions, and films was portraying black culture as a living culture, one marked by continual, dynamic *transformation*. As she explained, "Negro folklore is *still* in the making. A new kind is crowding out the old."[35]

In 1935 Hurston told an interviewer: "I needed my Barnard education to help me see my people as they really are. But I found that it did not do to be too detached as I stepped aside to study them. I had to go back, dress as they did, talk as they did, live their life, so that I could get into my stories the world I knew as a child."[36] In April and May of 1940, Hurston made her second set of films of activities in Beaufort, South Carolina. This second set of footage includes road scenes, dock scenes, landscapes, the activities of farm workers, and prison laborers, and, most importantly, the activities of the Commandment Keeper Church. The church, a Seventh Day Church of God, was a local African American Baptist church with a congregation of sixteen. These 1940 films were financed by Jane Belo, an anthropologist who had studied trance in Bali during the time of Margaret Mead, but the films reveal a new direction away from the Ethnographic inscription of Hurston's films from the late 1920s.[37] Two camera operators and a sound person were hired by Belo to document the activities of the Commandment Keeper Church, whose African American congregation often fell into trance, "testifying" to their spiritual visions and speaking in tongues.[38] Hurston again saw these forms of religious ecstasy as stemming from African religions. She wrote:

> This church seems to be a protest against the stereotype form of Methodist and Baptist churches among Negroes. It is a revolt against the white man's view of religion which has been so generally accepted by the literate Negro, and is therefore a version [sic] to the more African form of expression.
>
> Its keynote is rhythm. In this church they have two guitars, three symbols [sic], two tambourines, one pair of rattle gourds, and two washboards. Every song is rhythmic as are their prayers and their sermons.[39]

What makes these films unlike any other ethnographic research film of its kind is that Hurston herself appears in them as a participating worshipper, either playing music or walking among the congregation. In one scene in the church, among the worshippers playing musical instruments is Hurston playing drums while a congregation member, Julia Jones, goes first into ecstasy, then into trance as she proclaims prophecies.[40] In another scene in which a religious service is held outdoors on a river bank, the congregation sings and plays various instruments, and the preacher eventually passes a hat to white male onlookers. Hurston is again among the worshippers, playing the drums. At one point she appears to push a woman singer closer to the microphone. Hurston is both directing the action and taking part in it. Moreover, this particular section of the footage reveals Hurston's great awareness of the politics of spectatorship: in the scenes of the service on the river, the Reverend George Washington is represented as being fully in command of an impassioned congregation, but when the footage cuts to the lounging white male onlookers he becomes merely a hand passing a hat. The entertainment value of black spirituality to white onlookers is foregrounded here in a manner that is unthinkable in Boas's or Mead's ethnographic films, revealing again Hurston's third eye sensibility to Subject and Object double consciousness.

Again the key theme here is that of living culture, of active *transformation*. Hurston used film not only to create a historical record, but also as a means to participate in and transmit to others the ongoing artistry of the highly visual world of black culture in which Hurston was involved. These films record transition and process, hence Hurston's great interest in trance. The metaphor that Hurston uses in her writings is the transformation from gaseous to solid. Hurston describes how white hymns sung by Blacks become "a sort of liquifying of words."[41] She explains the role of the preacher in these terms:

> The voice of the people is truly the voice of God, but it is necessary that some unusual man shall arise and pronounce the things strongly felt by his people but vaguely spoken. He acts as a sort of catalyser. From gaseous to solid. After this stage has been reached, the religion grows by accretion. Things come into it from various sources and become inseparably a part of it.[42]

As Hurston wrote, "the church is the visualizing of emotions."[43] And thus Hurston's filming of trance, the movement from consciousness to the speaking in tongues, the jerks and the spasms, is connected to her belief in black culture as not dying but as an ever-emerging and dynamic culture, a culture in which she readily took part.

In 1935, Hurston described to the folklorist Alan Lomax her technique of collecting songs. She states:

> I just get in the crowd with the people and if they sing it I listen as best I can and then I start to joinin' in with a phrase or two and then finally I get so I can sing a verse. And then I keep on until I learn all the verses and then I sing 'em back to the people until they tell me that I can sing 'em just like them. And then I take part and I try it out on different people who already know the song until they are quite satisfied that I know it. Then I carry it in my memory. . . . I learn the song myself and then I can take it with me wherever I go.[44]

Here again, it is clear that Hurston is engaged in much more than observation and documentation—she learns the song so that she "can take it with [her] wherever [she goes]." In a letter to Belo dated May 2, 1940, however, Hurston wrote that the congregation members of the church "are not taking to it any too kindly" that "white men" were to come in and make a film of them.[45] Sound person Norman Chalfin explained later that the Commandment Keeper Church resisted being filmed because of their religious prohibition against graven images: Hurston convinced the church that since film had no contour it was not graven.[46] One could speculate that by taking part in the film she was trying to make the congregation members feel more comfortable about the cameras. But Hurston's participation gives the film an intimacy missing from many ethnographic films. Once again, unlike in standard anthropological films of the period such as Mead's *Trance and Dance in Bali*, Hurston is not present in the film as the figure of the scribbling anthropologist, notebook in hand, but as both viewer and viewed.

Underlying it all, however, is Hurston's newfound embrace of black spirituality, one which could never be fully recorded or expressed in words. In writing about the Commandment Keeper Church, Hurston uses the image of the limbs of a tree to underline the mystery of the church's spirituality. She writes:

> The unanimous prayer is one in which every member of the church prays at the same time but prays his own prayer aloud, which consists of exotic sentences, liquefied by intermittent chanting so that the words are partly submerged in the flowing rising and falling chant. The form of prayer is like the limbs of a tree, glimpsed now and then through the smothered leaves. It is a thing of wondrous beauty, drenched in harmony and rhythm.[47]

In the 1940s footage, there is a beautiful shot of Spanish moss and tree leaves reflecting in the water. Hurston stands in three-quarter profile while at her left are the great twisting branches and wisteria for which the Beaufort landscape is so famous. She turns her head slightly, her eyebrows raised, smiling enigmatically: her glance among the trees is a third bemused eye acknowledging the spectacle of the camera.[48]

There is thus a tension in Hurston's work, one which I believe reveals an alternative space within which to begin to understand an important aspect of African American culture. Part of Hurston's dilemma was that she was forced to please many different audiences: the African American community of the Harlem Renaissance; the scientific audience of "Papa Franz" Boas who wanted anthropological, so-called "objective," data; her mercurial white financial patron, Mason; and the community that produced her— Eatonville, Florida—the site of much of her research. This multiplicity of audiences is evident in her writings, both literary and anthropological, and in her films. One of the strategies for establishing Ethnographic authenticity is to write in the "ethnographic present," describing the people studied in third person, present tense. Hurston begins the following excerpt from her study of southern African American folklore *Mules and Men* in the "ethnographic present," present tense, but then shifts and subverts the external vantage point by using the pronoun "we":

> Folk-lore is not as easy to collect as it sounds. The best source is where there are the least outside influences and these people, being usually underprivileged are the shyest. They are most reluctant at times to reveal that which the soul lives by. And the Negro, in spite of his open-faced laughter, his seeming acquiescence, is particularly evasive. You

see we are a polite people and we do not say to our questioner, "Get out of here!" We smile and tell him or her something that satisfies the white person, because, knowing so little about us, he doesn't know what he is missing.[49]

In this incredible shift from "they" to "we," Hurston dramatically switches from the voice of the anthropologist speaking to a white Western audience to the voice of her African American cultural identity: *You see we are a polite people and we do not say to our questioner, "Get out of here!"* Hurston is alternately insider and outsider, subject and object. As she explains, her book is about the recording of all those "big old lies" which she and the rest of the black community grew up listening to in Eatonville.

Hurston's work thus not only anticipates Deren, it is a direct precursor of the movement toward self-reflexivity that one begins to see in academic anthropology in the late 1970s. Hurston's work, moreover, is pioneering in another sense: Hurston created new forms of communicating what she learned from her experiences with the communities that she studied. She put her anthropological knowledge to work in a wide array of cultural productions, including novels, children's tales, essays, and theatrical productions. In this regard, Hurston is similar to Katherine Dunham, pioneering African American choreographer, teacher, and anthropologist (Dunham studied at the University of Chicago under Boas's student Melville Herskovits), who shot ethnographic film (Dunham's films were of Afro-Caribbean dance), but excelled by applying her knowledge in her dance and choreography.[50] Instead of upholding the tradition of Boas and Mead in which the ultimate objective of the anthropological encounter is the written ethnography, a book intended for academic discourse, Hurston and Dunham posed radical forms for ethnography, producing works which transgress the boundaries between academic objectivity and subjective insight.

These new forms are within the realm of what I call the third eye. Even as Hurston championed Boas's attempts at objectivity, she was extraordinarily aware of anthropology's powerful propensity to temporalize and make evolutionary specimens of the peoples being studied. In her essay "What White Publishers Won't Print," she decries the racialization processes at work in museums like the American Museum of Natural History:

The question naturally arises as to the why of this indifference, not to say scepticism, to the internal life of educated minorities.

The answer lies in what we may call THE AMERICAN MUSEUM OF UNNATURAL HISTORY. This is an intangible built on folk belief. It is assumed that all non-Anglo-Saxons are uncomplicated stereotypes. Everybody knows all about them. They are lay figures mounted in the museum where all may take them at a glance. They are made of bent wires without insides at all. So how could anybody write a book about the non-existent?[51]

From her perspective as both Viewer and Viewed, Subject and Object, attracted to yet aware of the perverse history of anthropological "objectivity," Hurston was able to use her training for novel and experimental ends. In the concluding paragraphs of *Mules and Men,* Hurston recounts the tale of Sis Cat and de Rat. Rat manages to escape Sis Cat a first time by chiding Sis Cat's lack of manners in not having washed her face and hands prior to eating, but is thwarted by the wily Sis Cat when he tries to use the trick a second time. Hurston narrates Sis Cat's response the second time around:

> "Oh, Ah got plenty manners," de cat told 'im. "But Ah eats mah dinner and washes mah face and uses mah manners afterwards." So she et right on 'im and washed her face and hands. And cat's been washin' after eatin' ever since.
>
> I'm sitting here like Sis Cat, washing my face and usin' my manners.[52]

Hurston's daring ending to her study, shifting from the position of anthropologist/folklorist to that of Sis Cat, a character who learns to get what she wants in a story told by one of her informants, is radical: like the camera shot in which the camera is right up next to the paws of the cat on a porch, Hurston breaks with both the anthropological and the ethnographic film tradition of being the cool, distanced, observing, scientific eye.

Grabbing the Camera/Facing the Camera:
Image Sovereignty

I am one of them, and I am their daughter.—Helen Nabasuta Mugambi, on her relationship to the Baganda women that she filmed[53]

In the late 1960s, Sol Worth and John Adair conducted an anthropological experiment: they gave film cameras to a few Navajo youths to see if what they filmed would reflect an animist sensibility. The assumption was that the Navajo had little knowledge of Hollywood film language, and an analysis of the kinds of film they chose to make and the ways they framed their images would reveal something of the cultural lens through which they perceived the world. Worth and Adair's entire project was premised on Western film conventions as the normal, a standard against which Navajo deviations could be measured. The book that Worth and Adair wrote, *Through Navajo*

Eyes, is fascinating for what it reveals about anthropological assumptions of "proper" ethnographic filmmaking. At one point in the project, as the book relates, Sol Worth became so irritated by the way that Maryjane Tsosie was filming her grandfather Sam Yazzie as he engaged in sand painting that Worth grabbed the camera away from her. She had not chosen to go in for a close-up.

That Tsosie had refused to use that essential form of classical film grammar—the close-up—reveals not only the great respect which she held for her grandfather as an elder and an important spiritual leader in her community, but perhaps also her discomfort imposed by a historical divide. As a child, Tsosie, like many other young Native Americans in the United States, had been sent to boarding schools in a measure promoted by the U.S. government in order that Native Americans would forget their own language and assimilate into white society.[54] The violence of the gesture—the anthropologist Worth seizing the camera from Maryjane Tsosie—is an apt metaphor for the control the West has long sought to exercise over the representation of indigenous peoples in the pursuit of "science."

Tsosie's reticence to enter too closely into her grandfather's "space" mirrors as well a restraint that many contemporary indigenous filmmakers feel toward revealing certain aspects of their culture. The definition of what is photographable is often in variance with the standards of the anthropologist and the filmmaker. Hopi filmmaker Victor Masayesva Jr. says it succinctly, "Refraining from photographing certain subjects has become a kind of worship."[55] Masayesva's statement would appear to tread dangerously close to censorship, violating one of the basic tenets of Western democracy: that the health of a state can be gauged by the degree to which it tolerates the free flow of information, both textual and visual. The conviction that all people should have the liberty to appropriate and disseminate information is widely viewed as pertaining as much to the right of academicians such as anthropologists and historians to publish data on the people and events that they study as it does to the media journalist's right to expose corrupt politicians. In stark contrast, the importance of *not* photographing certain subjects, whether profane or sacred, is a central theme in the works of many indigenous filmmakers.

Masayesva's new and often sly forms of film language in his work concerning the Hopi vividly demonstrate the complex potential of this theme. In one particularly fascinating section of his video *Itam Hakim, Hopiit* (1985), Masayesva scans turn-of-the-century photographs of Hopi dancers, sometimes settling briefly on certain sections of the sepia-toned photographs: the filmmaker refuses or is uninterested in revealing the whole body, defeating the expectations of the viewer accustomed to ethnographic film. The expected full-body shot never materializes. In another scene, a row of Hopi adults and children till the land in extreme long shot: we are not allowed to see their bodies up close. And in the final dance sequences by Hopis in Native costume as well as in jeans and platform sandals, we are introduced to the dancers by shots of their heads or their feet, a reticence which denies the audience the sense of visual power inherent in seeing and consuming everything. Thus the wholistic—cultural anthropology's traditional thirst for studying whole cultures—and the holistic—the New Age fascination with Native ceremonial rituals—are obfuscated in a clever and yet moving rendering of Hopi history.

Part of the history Masayesva is evoking here is the history of the representation of Hopi as racialized, ethnographic bodies. Masayesva, like other Native filmmakers and video-makers including Dean Curtis Bear Claw, Fidel Moreno, Diane Reyna, and Edward Ladd, does not so much repudiate as recontextualize archival photography, reclaiming his own histories from the museum's deep freeze of Native Americans as metonyms of a "timeless past."[56] Yet Masayesva does not deny the ability of photography to give testimony to the past. As he explained, "I wouldn't know my grandfather if not for photography, because I never met him and I saw him in [a photograph of] a Snake Dance. So that's how I've met him." Film is not just a positivist record of the world but a spiritual intervention with one's ancestors, what Masayesva describes as a Ghost Dance, a means to exorcise the demons of colonialism and communicate with the beloved dead and the yet to be born.[57]

The third eye turns on a recognition: the Other perceives the veil, the process of being visualized as an object, but returns the glance. The gesture of being frozen into a picturesque is deflected. In a circulating economy of seeing and representation, there are moments in early ethnographic cinema which halt the flow of the evolutionary narrative: the Historical collapses into the Ethnographic, the Savage parodies the Civilized.

The strategies that Masayesva calls into play—open resistance, recontextualization of archival images, parody, and even refraining from representing certain subjects—recall instances of the third eye that I have examined throughout this book. Open resistance, as we have seen, is one mode of the third eye. Sometimes resistance is direct, as in the testimony of the Inuit boy Minik Wallace who embarked on a publicity campaign to force the American Museum of Natural History (his former "home") to return his stolen father's bones. Or, to take another example, at the 1904 St. Louis Fair, Ota Benga and other African performers charged at a photographer for pho-

50. Still from *Itam Hakim, Hopiit* (1985), dir. Victor Masayesva Jr.
(Courtesy of Victor Masayesva Jr.)

tographing them without their permission: they demanded to be reim-
bursed for the privilege. In other instances, resistance shapes itself in a form
of great subtlety. Dances do not lose their sacredness if they are purpose-
fully performed backwards, a fact understood by the Navajo who performed
the Yeibichai dance in such manner, a detail of which Edward S. Curtis and
other gleeful camera-toting tourists were unaware.

Another mode of the third eye is in the recontextualization of ethnographic footage. The Kwakwaka'wakw who fought successfully for the repatriation of potlatch objects seized by the Canadian government ignore the
stiltedness of the melodrama of Curtis's *In the Land of the Headhunters* as
well as his sensationalizing of headhunting; instead, footage from the film
of the war canoes of the Thunderbird, the Wasp and the Grizzly Bear is used
to remember a great and enduring history in a collaborative museum exhibition. *Nanook of the North* becomes a valuable document to the Inukjuak community where it was filmed, not because of its truthfulness (the
"sacred" Bazinian scene of the seal hunt is the object of laughter in appreciation of its obviously staged quality), but because it contains images of
their land and their ancestors, a means of provoking contemplation of his-

tory and memory. Looking at early photography and film is to acknowledge the present in the past, a means, to paraphrase Masayesva, of "meeting" one's ancestors.

Sometimes the third eye winks at us. Parody is present in the spectacular performances of Josephine Baker, singing in her flimsy golden cage masquerade. See me as a Primitive, if you want to, but notice how ridiculous my cage and my image are, Baker seems to say as she pushes her Mae West–like mink stole over her shoulder. The carnivalesque is pushed to another level in the cage of Coco Fusco and Guillermo Gómez-Peña, who demand that the contemporary audience confront the history of "exhibiting" humans for Ethnographic titillation.

Although some artists and writers ignore Ethnographic conventions entirely, as James Baldwin's comments quoted at the beginning of this chapter powerfully demonstrate, the Ethnographic imagination is still pervasive, and thus many other people of color engage such conventions head-on or enter into indirect, but complex mediations with them. Finally, then, I have drawn from examples from contemporary film and art, examining the works of some of those who refuse (or pretend not) to listen to the admonishing anthropologist who grabs the camera from their hands. Photographer Lorna Simpson refuses to show the face—that which is seen as the most individual aspect of the body yet is precisely what is vulnerable to the kind of pillaging of the spirit that many cultures have found objectionable in photography. What is figured instead in Simpson's work like *Easy for Who to Say* is a whole language of racialization that turns people of color into bodies for a narrative of evolution (see illustration 18). The Ethnographic image presented by Regnault, in which the bodies of West African performers at the 1895 Ethnographic Exposition become exemplars of a Primitive *marche en flexion* suitable for war, is exploded in Ousmane Sembène's *Camp de Thiaroye* which concentrates instead on the individualities of the various soldiers whose lives are being shaped and exploited by French colonialists. In an Inuit village of Igloolik, a community uses video cameras to create a new form of oral history in order to reconstruct their recent past on video; their Inuit colleagues form the Inuit Broadcasting Corporation to combat the hegemonic effects of dominant television on their children and communities. An African American woman, Zora Neale Hurston, is instructed by her anthropologist mentor to film ethnographic types, but she is a trickster: she experiments with zooming back and forth between different points of view, Self and Other, Native and Scientist, shattering the voyeurism of the gaze in the late 1920s, long before such self-reflexivity is legitimated in anthropology. Hands, feet, but not the whole body: Masayesva, like the Hopi clown who remonstrates and educates, declines to film certain aspects of the entire dancing body, respectful of the belief that refraining from photographing certain things can also be a spiritual act.

Demanding sovereignty over one's image does mean that the filmmaker representing his or her own community can easily elide the multifarious problems of representation, as Masayesva, Sembène, and Hurston's work attests. Helen Nabasuta Mugambi, a U.S.-educated scholar, explains that within the colonial structure of hierarchy, she is posited as superior in status to the Baganda women of her village which she filmed, but culturally, Mugambi explains, she is subordinate, she is their "daughter." Her relationship to the women she is filming distorts the Western structure that views the Western-educated scholar as expert. The predicament of the media producer filming within his or her own community is indeed complex, requiring the negotiation of several cultures, media, languages, and notions of history.

WHO Took This Picture?

What is the task of the postcolonial scholar examining the history of media representation of native peoples and people of color? Pat Ward Williams asks the important question of how one can be a person of color and look at pictures—now collected as historical documents—that exploit the pain of one's own people. In *Accused/Blowtorch/Padlock* (1986), Williams accompanies framed photographs of a lynched African American man taken from the book *The Best of "Life" Magazine* with text, asking the question, "WHO took this picture? Oh, God, Life answers—Page 141—no credit." The identity of the viewer is crucial to the reception of photography and film: the Observer/Observed dichotomy implodes when the Observer realizes that he or she is the Observed. Moreover, the arrogance of Western culture which looks at a *Life* magazine photograph of a lynched man as merely an objective document of historical brutality is emphatically called into question by the Observer who knows that this is somebody's loved one, this could be my loved one, this could be me. How could this photo have been taken?

Williams's question reveals the inadequacy of Margaret Mead's tenet that a camera running on its own steam is an objective eye. In my example from chapter 5 of the inappropriate "racial film"—Balinese who respond to invading Dutch colonial soldiers by walking straight towards them, only to be gunned down—the violence of the guns is equal to the violence of the film camera. A filmmaker was there to record, but is complicit with the guns of the colonialists: the camera-person colludes by not doing anything. Hence the inappropriateness of the film: it shoves in the viewer's face the horror of colonialization, and, unlike the more soothing narrative of "vanishing races," does not conceal the annihilation and apartheid of political physics.

Yet to confine historical scholarship exclusively to the model of critiquing "negative images" presents the critic with the suffocating trap of fascinating cannibalism: the reproduction feeds the West's appetite for images of people of color as marvelous Savages. Like Fanon, Baldwin, and poet Elizabeth Alexander, I have tried to read images of indigenous peoples made into the Ethnographic for the spaces of resistance contained within them, cognizant of the danger of trying to recover voices that can never fully be represented. It is with this objective in mind that I have attempted throughout this book to reveal disturbances within the linear narrative of evolutionary imaging. Recovery is incomplete, always with gaps, cracks, and other evidence of reconstruction. In a work which is considered the "first ethnographic film," a West African woman walks with a calabash, and becomes the nexus of a gaze of male looks including the white Parisian *flâneur*; yet in the same frame, a little girl's look disturbs the neat Observer/Observed dichotomy. In her glance, I would like to imagine that she knows this: the Emperor has no clothes. Reading *performance* is thus one important space of resistance brought into view by the third eye in images from early ethnographic cinema. The comfortable distance of the Colonizer Voyeur from the Colonized Native necessary for the machine of spectacle to grind on collapses when a Wolof man harangues a Parisian visitor to the Fair to toss some coins over the fence separating him from the Parisian: this is not free, but for your entertainment, and you must pay. The laughing West African performer is read by the European as a childlike and authentic Primitive: he or she is not even seen as a performer, but is said to be "exhibited" and just "existing." But in that laugh, there may also be irony. The laugh back at the visitor exposes the fact that the latter is also wearing a mask, a mask imposed by the relations of dominance peculiar to a visualizing colonial system, as George Orwell's "Shooting an Elephant" so insightfully indicates. Those made into Ethnographic subjects stare back at the camera, at us, one hundred years later, and the directness of that gaze declares, "I am here, and so are you." The ghostliness of testimony and presence is made vivid in these fragments of early ethnographic film.

Whether throwing stones at the photographer, recontextualizing early footage, winking at the camera, refraining from representing certain subjects, or taking up the camera, the third eye is also us, the Others, the native informants who question, mock, disquiet, and inform, descendants of ethnographic spectacle, forced to build an identity from veiled selves. We at times have an extra eye in our encounter with a society that fails to acknowledge our humanness, that denies us our presence in the present. James Baldwin's statement that so puzzled Mead—"I had to accept that I was on a slave boat once"—reveals that the writing of history is a means of giving a present voice to the past, an affirmative act by dispossessed peoples in their struggles for physical and cultural survival, a means of bearing witness for the future. Who is photographing and what is being photographed are no longer innocuous questions. These are the extraordinarily multivalent problems of representation that must be addressed in contemporary photography, video, and film as practiced at the beginning of the second millennium.

This could be my mother, this could be my daughter, this could be me.

NOTES

Introduction

1 Félix Regnault, "Des attitudes du repos dans les race humaines," *Revue encyclopédique* (7 January 1896): 9–12.

2 Félix Regnault, "Le langage par gestes," *La nature* 1324 (15 October 1898): 315.

3 See chapter 1 for my discussion on chronophotography, and chapter 2 for more detailed discussion of Regnault's theories on film.

4 W. E. B. Dubois, *The Souls of Black Folk* (New York: Bantam Books, 1989; orig. publ. 1903), 3.

5 Ibid., 6.

6 Frantz Fanon, *Black Skin, White Masks: The Experiences of a Black Man in a White World*, trans. Charles Lam Markmann (New York: Grove Press, 1967), 140.

7 Ibid., 147.

8 Lévi-Strauss writes, "Nowadays, being an explorer is a trade, which consists not, as one might think, in discovering hitherto unknown facts after years of study, but in covering a great many miles and assembling lantern-slides or motion pictures, preferably in colour, so as to fill a hall with an audience for several days in succession. For this audience, platitudes and commonplaces seem to have been miraculously transmuted into revelations by the sole fact that their author, instead of doing his plagiarizing at home, has supposedly sanctified it by covering some twenty thousand miles" (Claude Lévi-Strauss, *Tristes Tropiques*, trans. John and Doreen Weightman [New York: Penguin Books, 1992], 17–18).

9 Ibid., 335.

10 "An Interview with Gayatri Spivak," ed. Judy Burns, *Women & Performance: A Journal of Feminist Theory* 5, no. 1.9 (1990): 82.

11 George W. Stocking Jr., *Victorian Anthropology* (New York: Free Press, 1987), 47, 239.

12 Jay Ruby, "Is Ethnographic Film a Filmic Ethnography?" *Studies in the Anthropology of Visual Communication* 2, no. 2 (fall 1975): 108.

13 Michèle Duchet, *Le partage des savoirs: discours historique et discours ethnologique* (Paris: Éditions la Découverte, 1985), 19.

14 Even standard references to early "ethnographic film," of course, are subject to the charge. Despite Margaret Mead and Gregory Bateson's extensive filmmaking in Bali

and New Guinea in the 1930s, ethnographic film began to be considered a distinct genre only in the 1950s: two important signs of its arrival were Harvard University's funding of anthropological films after the success of the Marshalls' *The Hunters* (1958) and, in France, the attention paid to the films of Jean Rouch in high art venues like *Cahiers du cinéma* and in educational organizations like UNESCO (Claudia Springer, "Ethnocentric Circles: A Short History of Ethnographic Film," *The Independent* [December 1984]: 16).

In 1952 the International Committee on Ethnographic Film (CIFE), headed by Rouch, was formed to promote the preservation, production, and distribution of ethnographic film (Emilie de Brigard, "The History of Ethnographic Film," in *Principles of Visual Anthropology*, ed. Paul Hockings [The Hague: Mouton, 1975], 28).

Films made before the 1950s which today qualify as ethnographic were only defined as such retroactively by visual anthropologists like Emilie de Brigard, Karl Heider, and Jean Rouch looking for historical precursors. See de Brigard; Martin Taureg, "The Development of Standards for Scientific Films in German Ethnography," *Studies in Visual Communication* 9, no. 1 (winter 1983): 19–29; Karl Heider, *Ethnographic Film* (Austin: University of Texas Press, 1976); and Jean Rouch, "Le film ethnographique," in *Ethnologie générale*, ed. Jean Poirier, *Encyclopédie de la Pleiade* (Paris: Éditions Gallimard, 1968), 24: 429–71.

15 Faye Ginsburg, "Indigenous Media: Faustian Contract or Global Village?" *Cultural Anthropology* 6, no. 1 (February 1991): 104.

16 Recent examples of what I term ethnographic cinema include David Maybury-Lewis's *Millenium: Tribal Wisdom and the Modern World* (PBS special, 1992), which, although self-reflexive about anthropology, continues to represent and romanticize indigenous peoples as exotic Others; the Ewoks in George Lucas's *Return of the Jedi* (1983) are veiled science fiction references to the "ethnographic" as simple, fuzzy, brown tribespeople.

17 Phil Rosen, "From Document to Diegesis: Historical Detail and Film Spectacle," early draft of a chapter from the forthcoming *Past, Present: Theory, Cinema, History.*

18 Walter Benjamin, "The Work of Art in the Age of Mechanical Reproduction," in *Illuminations: Essays and Reflections*, trans. Harry Zohn (New York: Schocken Books, 1969), 223.

19 Rosen, 20.

20 V. Y. Mudimbe, *The Invention of Africa: Gnosis, Philosophy, and the Order of Knowledge* (Bloomington: Indiana University Press, 1988), 15–16.

21 George W. Stocking Jr., "Bones, Bodies, Behavior," in *Bones, Bodies, Behavior: Essays on Biological Anthropology*, ed. George W. Stocking Jr., *History of Anthropology* (Madison: University of Wisconsin Press, 1988), 5:8. See also George W. Stocking Jr., *Race, Culture and Evolution: Essays in the History of Anthropology* (New York: Free Press, 1968).

22 Claude Lévi-Strauss explains in *Tristes Tropiques* how travel involves space, time, and status (85).

23 Johannes Fabian, *Time and the Other: How Anthropology Makes Its Object* (New York: Columbia University Press, 1983), 39.

24 The inspiration for the label, of course, comes from Susan Sontag's essay "Fascinat-

ing Fascism," which investigates the aesthetics of fascism and why fascism continues to fascinate even those born after the 1940s. See "Fascinating Fascism," in *Under the Sign of Saturn* (New York: Vintage Books, 1980), 73–105.

25 Similarly, D. W. Griffith's *Broken Blossoms* (1919), considered by many to be the first art film, portrays a Chinese male as a feminized Other thwarted in his desire for an innocent blonde girl. Again, an important cinematic "milestone" takes its sustenance from stereotyped views of gender and racial difference.

Richard Fung has pointed out that Asian men are stereotyped as undersexed ("Looking for My Penis: The Eroticised Asian in Gay Video Porn," in *How Do I Look? Queer Film and Video*, ed. Bad Object-Choices [Seattle: Bay Press, 1991], 146). In this light, the title of Wayne Wang's 1981 film *Chan Is Missing* can be taken as a brilliant pun on the cinematic construction of the Chinese American male: what Chan—the Chinese American character—is missing in Hollywood cinema is, in fact, his masculinity, his penis. Moreover Chan, i.e., an unstereotyped depiction of the East Asian American male, is literally missing from cinema. The Asian American, whether male or female, is consistently allied with Art: with costume, surface, design, detail, and artifice. The "Oriental" is thus made akin to the "Ornamental." But like other people of color, whether African American or Inuit, the Asian American is also pathologized, hence the use of "Yellow Peril" and other metaphors that portray Asian Americans as virulent. Frantz Fanon writes, "The terms the settler uses when he mentions the native are zoological terms. He speaks of the yellow man's reptilian motions, of the stink of the native quarter, of breeding swarms, of foulness, of spawn, of gesticulations" (*The Wretched of the Earth*, trans. Constance Farrington [New York: Grove Press, 1964], 42).

26 For an insightful article on the representation of race in *The Birth of the Nation* see Clyde Taylor, "The Re-birth of the Aesthetic in Cinema," *Wide Angle* 13, nos. 3–4 (July–October 1991): 12–13.

27 Jean Rouch applies the term self-consciously to Regnault, Flaherty, Mead, Gregory Bateson, Dziga Vertov, and others. See, e.g., Jean Rouch, "Our Totemic Ancestors and Crazed Masters," *Senri Ethnological Studies* 24 (1988): 225–38.

28 Lila Abu-Lughod, "Can There Be a Feminist Ethnography?" *Woman & Performance: A Journal of Feminist Theory* 5.1, no. 9 (1991): 24.

29 James G. Fraser, Foreword to *The Argonauts of the Western Pacific* by Bronislaw Malinowski (New York: E. P. Dutton, 1961; orig. publ. 1922), ix, xiv.

30 Stephen Bann, *The Clothing of Clio: A Study of the Representation of History in Nineteenth-century Britain and France* (Cambridge: Cambridge University Press, 1984), 22.

31 Fanon, 109.

I Seeing Anthropology

1 V. Y. Mudimbe, *The Invention of Africa: Gnosis, Philosophy and the Order of Knowledge* (Bloomington: Indiana University Press, 1988), 15 (citing R. I. Rotberg, *Africa and Its Explorers: Motives, Method and Impact* [Cambridge, Mass.: Harvard University Press, 1970]).

2   Marcel Mauss, "Les techniques du corps," in *Sociologie et anthropologie* (Paris: Presses Universitaires de France, 1934), 379.

3   Regnault, for example, used the word "savage" to describe the West African performers he filmed in 1895 in "L'histoire du cinéma: son rôle en anthropologie," *Bulletins et mémoires de la Société d'anthropologie de Paris* 3d tome, 7th ser. (6 July 1922): 64. According to George W. Stocking Jr., the word "savage" ceased to be a legitimate anthropological term for indigenous peoples only by the 1930s (George W. Stocking Jr., *Victorian Anthropology* [New York: Free Press, 1987], xv).

4   Félix Regnault and Cdt. de Raoul, *Comment on marche: des divers mode de progression de la supériorité du mode en flexion* (Paris: Henri Charles-Lavauzelle, Éditeur militaire, 1897). Illustration of man reproduced on p. 23.

5   See more detailed discussion of Regnault's chronophotography in chapter 2.

6   Martin Taureg, "The Development of Standards for Scientific Films in German Ethnography," *Studies in Visual Communication* 9, no. 1 (winter 1983): 22–23; Emilie de Brigard, "The History of Ethnographic Film," in *Principles of Visual Anthropology*, ed. Paul Hockings (The Hague: Mouton, 1975), 15–17. Ethnographic filmmaker Jean Rouch claims that the conceptions embodied in present-day museum displays are timid in comparison with Regnault's vision of a museum "of gesture and sound" (Jean Rouch, "L'itinéraire initiatique," in *CinémAction: la science à l'écran*, ed. Jean-Jacques Mensy [Paris: Les Editions du Cerf, 1986], 6).

7   Mudimbe, *Invention of Africa*, 191–92.

8   Gayatri Chakravorty Spivak, "Can the Subaltern Speak? Speculations on Widow-Sacrifice," *Wedge* 7–8 (winter–spring 1985): 271–313.

9   See my introduction.

10 In 1921, Regnault along with the director of the Institut de Marey, Pierre Noguès, filmed the boxer Johnny Coulon, a man who billed himself as "unliftable," in order to give scientific explanation behind Coulon's supposed supernatural powers. I have found no evidence that Regnault made any other films (Pierre Noguès and Félix Regnault, "Explication mécanique des trucs de l'homme insoulevable," *Revue de pathologie comparée* [10 May 1921]: 191–94).

11 According to Regnault's birth certificate at the Archives of the City of Rennes, his father was a professor of physics. In his dedication to his medical thesis, however, Regnault described his father as a professor of mathematics (correspondence with Mme. Catherine Laurent, archivist of the Archives of the City of Rennes).

12 Books which Regnault wrote include *Hypnotisme, religion* (1897), *Comment on marche* with Cdt. de Raoul (1897), *Les gardes-malades* (1901) with Dr. Mlle. Hamilton, *L'évolution de la prostitution* (1906), and *La genèse des miracles* (1910).

13 Félix Regnault, "Le rôle du cinéma en ethnographie," *La nature* 2866 (1 October 1931): 305.

14 For more on film and physiology, see Lisa Cartwright's excellent *Screening the Body: Tracing Medicine's Visual Culture* (Minneapolis: University of Minnesota Press, 1995), which makes explicit the ties between physiology, cinema, and the construction of gender. For an insightful analysis of how Muybridge's time motion studies construct gender, see Linda Williams, "Film Body: An Implantation of Perversions,"

in *Narrative, Apparatus, Ideology: A Film Theory Reader*, ed. Phil Rosen (New York: Columbia University Press, 1986), 507–34.

15 For studies of the history of French anthropology, see Elizabeth A. Williams, "The Science of Man: Anthropological Thought and Institutions in Nineteenth-century France" (Ph.D. diss., Indiana University, 1983); Joy Dorothy Harvey, "Races Specified, Evolution Transformed: The Social Context of Scientific Debates Originating in the Société d'anthropologie de Paris 1859–1902" (Ph.D. diss., Harvard University, 1983); Donald Bender, "The Development of French Anthropology," *Journal of the History of the Behavioral Sciences* 1, no. 2 (April 1965), 139–51; and Britta Rupp-Eisenreich, ed., *Histoires de l'anthropologie XVIe–XIXe siècles: colloque la pratique de l'anthropologie aujourd'hui 19–21 novembre 1981, Sèvres* (Paris: Klincksieck, 1984).

16 Benedict Anderson, *Imagined Communities: Reflections on the Origin and Spread of Nationalism* (London: Verso, 1983).

17 The first anthropologist to discuss race, William Frederic Edwards, applied the concept to French history in an attempt to justify French nationalism (see Claude Blanckaert, "On the Origins of French Ethnology: William Edwards and the Doctrine of Race," in *Bones, Bodies, Behavior: Essays on Biological Anthropology*, ed. George W. Stocking Jr., *History of Anthropology*, vol. 5 [Madison: University of Wisconsin Press, 1988], 18–55). Racial determinism also characterized the thought of probably the most famous French historian of the nineteenth century, Jules Michelet, who claimed that France's superiority was due to its unique mixture of the Celtic and Roman races (William B. Cohen, *The French Encounter with Africans: White Response to Blacks, 1530–1880* [Bloomington: Indiana University Press, 1980], 215–16).

18 George W. Stocking Jr., "Polygenist Thought in Post-Darwinian French Anthropology," in *Race, Culture and Evolution: Essays in the History of Anthropology* (New York: Free Press, 1968), 42–68.

19 In the later nineteenth century in France and Germany, "anthropology" was used to refer to what in the United States is described as physical anthropology, and "ethnology" was used for cultural anthropology. In the British tradition, anthropology was divided into social anthropology, physical anthropology, linguistics, and archeology.

20 See Harvey, 50–51, and Elizabeth Williams, 116–21, for more on *transformisme*. An important aspect of evolutionist anthropology was positivism. Positivism, with its concern with phenomenological description and the study of long historical development, as well as its emphasis on the physiological bases of psychology, the importance of technology and progress, and the environment as shaper of human behavior, informed much of anthropology during the nineteenth century (*Historical Dictionary of the Third French Republic*, ed. Patrick H. Hutton [Westport, Conn.: Greenwood Press, 1986], 796–98). For more on anthropology and Auguste Comte's notion of progress, see Stocking, *Victorian Anthropology*, 25–30.

21 Thomas S. Kuhn argues that measurement became an essential element of the physical science paradigm starting in 1840 ("The Function of Measurement in Physical Science," in *The Essential Tension: Selected Studies in Scientific Tradition and Change* [Chicago: University of Chicago Press, 1979], 220).

Use of comparative anatomical studies, especially comparative study of crania, began in the late eighteenth century and burgeoned in the nineteenth century. In the late eighteenth century Johannes Blumenbach used new anatomical techniques, including cranial measurement, to classify man into five races, and Peter Camper described a way to measure facial angles. In the early nineteenth century, U.S. physician Samuel Morton initiated what came to be called the "American School" of anthropology, a school which based its research on comparison of massive collections of skulls; the Viennese medical doctor Franz-Josef Gall popularized phrenology, a science in which the bumps of the head were read to determine character and intelligence; Belgian biostatistician Adolphe Quételet used statistics and physiognomy in an attempt to identify the "average" man, i.e., European man; and, in 1840, Anders Retzius invented the cephalic index, which was the ratio of head length to head breadth. Retzius divided humanity into two groups: the brachycephalics (broad-headed) and the dolichocephalic (long-headed). Regnault made extensive use of cephalic measurements in his studies of pathology.

22   Paul Broca, "Anthropologie," in *Dictionnaire des sciences médicales,* vol. 5 (1866), 280–300, quoted in Harvey, 42. That those who were considered "primitive" or "savage" were often politically despised groups is best seen in British characterizations of members of the Irish as low on the evolutionary scale: the Irish skull was said to be akin to that of the Australian Aborigine and the higher primate (Pitt Rivers, A.H.L.F., *Catalogue of the anthropological collection lent by Colonel Lane Fox for exhibition in the Bethnal Green Branch of the South Kensington Museum, June 1874, Parts I and II* (London), cited in William Ryan Chapman, "Arranging Ethnology: A.H.L.F. Pitt Rivers and the Typological Tradition," in *Objects and Others: Essays on Museums and Material Culture,* ed. George W. Stocking Jr., *History of Anthropology,* vol. 3 [Madison: University of Wisconsin Press, 1985], 28). Pitt Rivers established the first anthropological museum in Great Britain, the Pitt Rivers Museum, at Oxford University in 1884.

23   George W. Stocking Jr., "Bones, Bodies, Behavior," in *Bones, Bodies, Behavior: Essays on Biological Anthropology,* ed. George W. Stocking Jr., *History of Anthropology,* vol. 5 (Madison: University of Wisconsin Press, 1988), 7–8.

24   Cohen, 234.

25   Adam Kuper, *The Invention of Primitive Society: Transformations of an Illusion* (London: Routledge, 1988), 5.

26   French anthropologists Pierre Gratiolet and Carl Vogt, for example, believed that black skulls were similar to those of microcephalic idiots, and thus believed that blacks would always be mentally inferior to whites, a conclusion used by the proslavery movement (Harvey, 125).

27   L. J. B. Bérenger-Féraud, *Peuplades,* 2–4, cited in Cohen, 241, and Félix Regnault, "De la fonction préhensile du pied," *La nature* 1058 (9 September 1893): 229–31.

28   Charles Letourneau, *Sociologie d'après l'ethnographie* (Paris: Reinwald, 1880), 4, quoted in Harvey, 139.

29   Max Simon Nordau, *Degeneration* (New York: H. Fertig, 1895; repr. 1968).

30   For more on Charcot, see Debora Silverman, *Art Nouveau in Fin-de-siècle France: Politics, Psychology, and Style* (Berkeley: University of California Press, 1989), 75–106.

31 For more on Mortillet's applied anthropology and pseudo-sociological trends, see Harvey, 269–326. One of the most influential writers on racial hygiene was, of course, Count Joseph Arthur de Gobineau. In his now famous *Essay on the Inequality of Human Races* (1853–55), Gobineau asserted that race determines history, and that the intermixture of races will cause degeneration and ultimately death. His work, later often cited by Adolf Hitler, was not widely read during his own time, and predates the founding of the Société d'anthropologie de Paris.

32 On decadence see "De la dépopulation de la France," *La médecine moderne* (1893): 1256–57; and "The rôle of depopulation, deforestation and malaria in the decadence of certain nations," *Smithsonian Institution Annual Report* (trans. from *Revue scientifique* [Paris, 10 January 1914]: 46–48) (Washington, D.C., 1914), 593–97. On nursing, see Regnault and Dr. Mlle. Hamilton, *Les gardes-malades*; on prostitution, see *L'évolution de la prostitution*; on strong men, see Noguès and Regnault, "Explication mécanique des trucs de l'homme insoulevable," 191–94; and on geniuses, see "Conférence Lamarck: des infirmités des organes des sens dans la production des oeuvres de génie," *Bulletins et mémoires de la Société d'anthropologie de Paris* 9th tome, 7th ser. (1928): 79–81.

33 Harvey, 133–38.

34 Many colonial naval doctors learned anthropometry at Broca's laboratory. Louis Faidherbe, Governor-General of the Sudan, was a Société d'anthropologie de Paris member from 1865 to 1879, and served as president of the Société in 1874 (Harvey, 115, 133–34, and 155). Faidherbe claimed that African brains were of "relatively weak volume," explaining the "weak will" of the African. This, he wrote, accounted for why Africans could be enslaved (Louis Faidherbe, *Essai sur la langue peul* [Paris, 1875], 14, cited in Cohen, 230–31). Paul Bert, another Société member, was Governor-General of Indochina during the Ferry government (Harvey, 133, 159).

35 Paul Broca, "Instructions Générales pour les récherches et observations anthropologiques," *Mémoires de la Société d'anthropologie de Paris* II (Paris, 1865), 69–204, quoted and trans. in Harvey, 128.

36 See Georges Canguilhem, *The Normal and the Pathological*, trans. Carolyn R. Fawcett (New York: Zone Books, 1991).

37 The interest in visualizing hybridity was also present in the earlier colonial (Spanish and Portuguese) obsession with visual categorizing "castes" generated by particular "racial" mixtures. I thank Mary Miller for this insight.

38 Fabian, *Time and the Other.*

39 Ibid., 106. Fabian explains that visualism encourages quantification and diagrammatic representation "so that the ability to 'visualize' a culture or society almost becomes synonymous for understanding it."

40 Jonathan Crary, *Techniques of the Observer: On Vision and Modernity in the Nineteenth Century* (Cambridge, Mass.: MIT Press, 1988). I thank Esther da Costa Meyer for this insight.

41 Félix Regnault, *Des altérations crâniennes dans le rachitisme* (Paris: Steinheil, 1888), 12.

42 At the Museum d'histoire naturelle, the most important French scientific research institution of the time, skeletons of those afflicted with rickets, as well as skeletons

of microcephalics, hydrocephalics, and so on, were displayed as point of comparison to the "normal" skeleton. In the same museum one could view the Ethnographic Hall series classifying the races (G. Xert, "Les nouvelles galleries du muséum," *La nature* 1297 [9 April 1898]: 297–98). Anthropometry was also extensively used in the new field of criminology. In 1884, Alphonse Bertillon, the son of Société d'anthropologie de Paris member L. A. Bertillon, began work on criminal identification using anthropological measuring techniques. See Harvey, 305–6. Regnault himself was influenced by and wrote about the Italian criminologist Lombroso. See, e.g., "Des anomalies osseuses chez les arriérés criminels et les brigands," *Bulletins et mémoires de la Société d'anthropologie de Paris* 9th tome, 7th ser. (4 November 1926): 92–95.

43   Félix Regnault, "Les cagots et la lèpre en France," *La nature* 1022 (31 December 1892): 67–68; J. Lajard and Félix Regnault, *De l'existence de la lèpre atténuée chez les cagots des Pyrenées*, ed. Progrès médical (Paris: Lecrosnier et Babé, 1893); "Les mains polydactyles," *La nature* 1044 (3 June 1893): 5–6; Félix Regnault, "Les monstres dans l'ethnographie et dans l'art," *Bulletins et mémoires de la Société d'anthropologie de Paris* 4th tome, 6th ser. (3 July 1913): 400–411.

44   See, e.g., Félix Regnault, "Nouvelle race d'ours des cavernes," *La nature* 720 (19 March 1887): 255.

45   See, e.g., "De la perception des couleurs suivant les races humaines," *La médecine moderne* (1893): 1062–65; "Les scarifications," *La médecine moderne* (1895): 507; "De la fonction préhensile du pied." The French were fascinated with steatopygy, a trait thought to be characteristic of prehistoric French sculptures of women. One of the most tragic outcomes of this fascination was the treatment of Saartjie Baartman, a Khoi-San woman (then referred to as Hottentot) from South Africa who was brought to Europe and performed in an animal show in Paris, displaying her body. After her death from tuberculosis in Paris, anthropologist Georges Cuvier of the Muséum d'histoire naturelle dissected her body and her reproductive organs. See Cohen, 239–41, and "The Hottentot Venus," in Steven Jay Gould, *The Flamingo's Smile: Reflections in Natural History* (New York: W. W. Norton, 1985), 291–305.

   Sander L. Gilman's article "Black Bodies, White Bodies: Toward an Iconography of Female Sexuality in Late-nineteenth-century Art, Medicine, and Literature," in *"Race," Writing, and Difference,* ed. Henry Louis Gates Jr. (Chicago: University of Chicago Press, 1985), 223–61, is frequently cited by critics discussing the representation of Woman in the nineteenth and twentieth century. I agree with Gilman that there is a connection between the representation of women of color and of white prostitutes: as Etienne Balibar explains, racism and sexism function together (Etienne Balibar, "Racism and Nationalism," *Race, Nation, Class: Ambiguous Identities,* ed. Etienne Balibar and Immanuel Wallerstein [London: Verso, 1991], 42). I disagree, however, with the manner in which Gilman links the exploitative representation of Sarah Bartman to the representation of the *courtisane* Nana in Edouard Manet's painting *Nana* (1877). First, Gilman's own reproduction of images of Sarah Bartman and her genitals constitutes yet another exploitation of Bartman, and reveals that the critique of visualism may itself be visualist, with all of the associated imperialist and patriarchal connotations. Second, Gilman jumps to the conclusion that the French focus on the buttocks of white women's bodies in the nineteenth century reflects French perception of the pathology of the large rounded buttocks of some African women. Gilman himself thus pathologizes African women, and he forecloses the possibility that the cultural highlighting of this physical characteristic may instead reflect the borrowing of an aesthetic of beauty from other cultures, such as Brazil. For a work which addresses the problem of the silencing of the African woman's voice by science, see Elizabeth Alexander, *The Venus Hottentot*, in *Callaloo Poetry Series*, ed. Charles H. Rowell (Charlottesville: University Press of Virginia, 1990), and my discussion of her in chapter 5.

46 Félix Regnault, "Pourquoi les nègres sont-ils noirs? (Études sur les causes de la coloration de la peau)," *La médecine moderne* (2 October 1895): 606–7.

47 Félix Regnault, "Crânes d'Indiens du Bengale," *Bulletins de la Société d'anthropologie de Paris* 3d tome, 4th ser. (4 February 1892): 66–68. In later years, Regnault moved away from his strictly physical notion of race and developed the idea of *ethnie*—implicating both linguistic and cultural difference—as an additional index for classifying humanity. This idea put him at loggerheads with Georges Montandon, a well-known antisemitic anthropologist and supporter of the Vichy regime in the late 1930s. As early as 1902 Regnault defined *ethnie* as "une union psychique à opposer à la ressemblance anatomique donnée par le mot race" (a psychic unity as opposed to the anatomical look intended by the word race) (Discussion for Adolphe Bloch's "De la race qui précéde les sémiles en Chaldée et en Susiane," *Bulletins de la Société d'anthropologie de Paris* 3d tome, 5th ser. [3 July 1902]: 681. See also *Encyclopoedia universalis*, s.v. "Ethnie," by Jean-Loup Amselle, vol. 8 (Paris: Encyclopoedia Universalis France S.A., 1990), 971.

48 Regnault, *Hypnotisme, religion*, 161.

49 Etienne Balibar, "Is There a 'Neo-Racism'?" in *Race, Nation, Class: Ambiguous Identities*, 19.

50 "Exhibitions foraines," *La nature* 1297 (9 April 1898): 300–301. In "La caricature dans l'art antique (déformations crâniennes)," *La nature* 1123 (8 December 1894): 21–22, Regnault comments that circus microcephalics exhibited as the "last Aztecs" made P. T. Barnum a fortune.

51 J. M. Charcot and Paul Richer, *Les difformes et les malades dans l'art* (Paris: Lecrosnier et Babé, 1889). For an excellent description of Charcot's study of art and medicine see Silverman, 75–106.

52 Discussion for "À propos des déformations crâniennes dans l'art antique," *Bulletins de la Société d'anthropologie de Paris* 6th tome, 4th ser. (3 January 1895): 10.

53 Regnault wrote extensively on "primitive art." He claimed that art by those he termed Savages was originally realistic but had given way to ornamentation. ("Déformations crâniennes dans l'art sino-japonais," *Bulletins de la Société d'anthropologie de Paris* 6th tome, 4th ser. [6 June 1895]: 411). The Greeks, on the other hand, were "marvelous observers" who did not give way too much to the imagination ("La caricature dans l'art antique," 21). For Regnault, race thus was a key determinant of the artistic temperament. Regnault conceded that environment influences art as well. Still in his "savage" mode, Regnault commented, "Quand le sauvage chasseur habite un pays pauvre, son imagination ornementale est moins fertile" (When the

savage hunter lives in a non-fertile environment, his ornamental imagination is less fertile) ("Essai sur les débuts de l'art ornemental géometrique chez les peuples primitifs," *Bulletins de la Société d'anthropologie de Paris* 7th tome, 4th ser. [1 October 1896]: 539).

Regnault averred that the study of art helps one to understand both Primitive and Civilized man. The more advanced the civilization, the greater its imagination. The Primitive, Regnault explained, depicted real monsters, i.e., deformed people, whereas the ancients (for Regnault, the Greeks and the Egyptians) and Italian Renaissance artists depicted imaginary monsters (see "Les monstres dans l'ethnographie et dans l'art").

54 See, e.g., Regnault and Lajard, "La Venus accroupie dans l'art grec," *La nature* 1152 (29 June 1895): 69–70.

55 Félix Regnault, "Classifications des sciences anthropologiques," *Revue anthropologique* (1931): 122.

56 Félix Regnault, "Des attitudes du repos dans les races humaines," *Revue encyclopédique* (7 January 1896): 9.

57 See, e.g., Félix Regnault, "Les attitudes de repos dans l'art sino-Japonais," *La nature* 1154 (15 July 1895): 106; "Des attitudes du repos dans les races humaines"; "Présentation d'une hotte primitive," *Bulletins de la Société d'anthropologie de Paris* 3d tome, 4th ser. (21 July 1892): 471–79; and Regnault and Lajard, "La Venus accroupie dans l'art grec."

58 John Tagg, *The Burden of Representation: Essays on Photographies and Histories* (Amherst: University of Massachusetts Press, 1988), 74.

59 For more on anthropometric photography see *Visual Anthropology* 3, nos. 2–3 (1990), special issue, "Picturing Cultures: Historical Photographs in Anthropological Inquiry"; and Melissa Banta and Curtis M. Hinsley, *From Site to Sight: Anthropology, Photography, and the Power of Imagery* (Cambridge, Mass.: Peabody Museum Press, 1986).

60 "Dilation des joues: chez les souffleurs de verre et dans l'art," *La nature* 1030 (25 February 1893): 200.

61 Regnault believed that religion could be explained in medical and scientific terms. He suggested, for example, that Jesus was a hysteric (see *Hypnotisme, Religion*, 100).

62 Carlo Ginzburg, "Morelli, Freud, and Sherlock Holmes: Clues and Scientific Method," in *The Sign of Three: Dupin, Holmes, Peirce*, ed. Umberto Eco and Thomas Sebeok (Bloomington: Indiana University Press, 1983), 81–118.

63 Art historians trace their roots to connoisseurship studies by Johann Joachim Winckelmann, Bernard Berenson, and Giovanni Morelli, but the writings of Regnault, Richer, and Charcot on art remain overlooked.

64 Félix Regnault, "Exposition ethnographique de l'Afrique occidentale au Champs-de-Mars à Paris: Sénégal et Soudan français," *La nature* 1159 (17 August 1895): 186.

65 "Un village nègre au Champ de Mars," *L'illustration* 2729 (15 June 1895): 508.

66 *Petit journal* 5 June, 14 July, 26 July, and 15 August 1895, quoted in William H. Schneider, *An Empire For the Masses: The French Popular Image of Africa, 1870–1900* (Westport, Conn.: Greenwood Press, 1982), 169. The justification for such expositions included colonialism; in the 7 August 1893 *Petit journal*, one journalist

claimed that the Pai-Pi-Bris were brought to Paris "in the hope that the memories they take back will permit us to establish French trading stations more easily in their country" (Schneider, 171).

67 Paul Greenhalgh, *Ephemeral Vistas: The Expositions Universelles, Great Exhibitions and World's Fairs, 1851–1939* (Manchester, U.K.: Manchester University Press, 1988), 89; and Greenhalgh, "Education, Entertainment and Politics: Lessons from the Great International Exhibitions," in *The New Museology*, ed. Peter Vergo (London: Redaktion Books, 1989), 74–98.

68 Greenhalgh, *Ephemeral Vistas*, 87.

69 Cohen, 281.

70 The story of the display of indigenous ethnic peoples is incomplete: there is little written record of the thoughts of the performers, and little record of the biographies and aspirations of the promoters of the shows. Accounts of the mass illustrated press, however, shed some light on public response to the exhibitions, and accounts by visitors such as Regnault shed light on the scientific response.

71 Elizabeth Williams, "Science of Man," 139.

72 Ibid., 144. According to Williams, Jomard defined ethnography as "the science which studied the advance of civilization among primitive peoples." The short-lived Société d'ethnographie, founded by Léon de Rosny in 1859, was never as powerful as the Société d'anthropologie de Paris. Its stated goal was to promote ethnography as the science of progress, a science which would take as its object the societies of all peoples, particularly "savages."

73 Patricia Mainardi, *Art and Politics of the Second Empire: The Universal Expositions of 1855 and 1867* (New Haven: Yale University Press, 1987), 169. Another aspect of the artistic interest in the "ethnographic" is Primitivism, whose first proponent was arguably Postimpressionist Paul Gauguin. After painting peasants in Britanny, Gauguin began painting in the French colony of Tahiti in 1890.

74 See Adolf Loos, "Ornament as Crime," in *The Architecture of Adolf Loos*, ed. Yehuda Safran and Wilfried Wang (London: Arts Council of Great Britain and the Authors, 1908). On the detail, see Naomi Schor, *Reading in Detail: Aesthetics and the Feminine* (New York: Methuen, 1987). On the detail and historical film, see Phil Rosen, "From Document to Diegesis: Historical Detail and Film Spectacle," early draft of a chapter from the forthcoming *Past, Present: Theory, Cinema, History*.

75 Greenhalgh, *Ephemeral Vistas*, 89.

76 Théophile Gautier had already remarked on prostitution of the "rue du Caire" in 1889. See Leila Kinney and Zeynep Celik, "Ethnography and Exhibitionism at the Expositions Universelles," *Assemblage* 13 (December 1990): [34]–59.

77 Regnault described the performers in a Dahomeyan exhibition of 1893 as little civilized and lazy, a fact he derived from the study of their body postures. He also spoke of the performers as artworks, calling them "belles statues de bronzes" (beautiful bronze statues), a reference which would seem to reveal how little he saw them as people ("Les dahoméens," *La nature* 1041 [13 March 1893]: 371–74). In a later article on prehistoric sculptures, Regnault again mentioned the 1893 Dahomeyan exhibition when he wrote, "Rappelez-vous ces femmes à l'aspect bizarre que la Jardin d'Acclimation de Paris exhiba il y a quelques années: Hottentots aux seins pendants,

aux jambes faissant une énorme saillie" (Do you recall the bizarre looking women at the Jardin d'Acclimation de Paris exhibited some years ago: Hottentots with pendulous breasts, with legs curved to an enormous projection) (Félix Regnault, "Les artistes préhistoriques d'après les derniers découvertes," *La nature* 1167 [12 October 1895]: 306).

78 Regnault, "Les dahoméens," 372.

79 Ella Shohat gives a survey of cinema, gender, and colonialism in "Imaging Terra Incognita: The Disciplinary Gaze of Empire," *Public Culture* 3, no. 2 (spring 1991): 41–70.

80 Regnault, "Un village nègre," 508.

81 Regnault noted, however, that in "the black continent" the European practice of throwing money to African children was an established one (in this sense the visitor could play at being a French tourist in an African colony). He comments that money-throwing at the ethnographic exposition was merely an amusing practice (Regnault, "Exposition ethnographique," 186). Regnault fails to recount that in both the 1893 Dahomeyan exhibition and the 1895 Senegalese exhibition, one performer was assigned the job of policeman to make sure no one crossed the railing to get coins which had fallen short (Schneider, 148).

82 Regnault, "Exposition ethnographique," 184.

83 Regnault, "Les dahoméens," 372.

84 Regnault, "Un village nègre," 508.

85 The throwing of money to performers in native villages was popular. If one imagines a day at the 1895 ethnographic exhibition, one is likely to adopt the viewpoint of a Frenchman or an African: the fair addressed viewers as national and racial subjects. But what about visitors of mixed heritage, or performers who stayed on after the expositions and settled in Europe or North America? One wonders about the response of visitors who were the children of French colonialist fathers and West African mothers sent to be educated in France. I have no records, but one might suppose that if asked to choose, they would likely have identified with the French, with the Eiffel Tower technology. It is a sad fact that the exhibitions were so demeaning to Africans that a person of mixed blood would have had little choice but to identify himself or herself as a French subject.

Timothy Mitchell has written an insightful article in which he describes the written reactions of Middle Eastern visitors to various Universal Expositions in Paris. On the whole, Mitchell states, travelers from the Middle East were amazed at the use of spectacle, a reality effect in which the world was represented as though it were an exhibition (Timothy Mitchell, "The World as Exhibition," *Comparative Studies in Society and History* 31, no. 2 [April 1989]: 217–36).

86 The "ethnographic" body also represented biological danger, that which must be attacked in its very corporeality. Frantz Fanon explained the representation of people of African descent by white society in these terms (Frantz Fanon, *Black Skin White Masks: The Experiences of a Black Man in a White World*, trans. Charles Lam Markmann [New York: Grove Press, 1967], 163–65).

87 George Orwell, *Shooting an Elephant and Other Essays* (New York: Harcourt, Brace & World, 1950), 8.

88 Ibid., 11–12.

89 Many of the themes of the fair transferred to film: there are several early films, for example, showing young, non-European children in harbors diving for money. In addition, films of the world's fairs were made by almost all major commercial film companies, including Edison and Pathé.

2 The Writing of Race in Film

1 Walter Benjamin, "The Work of Art in the Age of Mechanical Reproduction," in *Illuminations: Essays and Reflections,* trans. Harry Zohn (New York: Schocken Books, 1969), 233.

2 Bruno Latour, *Science in Action* (Cambridge, Mass.: Harvard University Press, 1987), 68, 66, 71, 90.

3 Benjamin, "Work of Art," 233.

4 Michael Hammond, "Anthropology as a Weapon of Social Combat in Late Nineteenth-century France," *Journal of the History of the Behavioral Sciences* 16 (1980): 127.

5 Félix Regnault, "L'histoire du cinéma: son rôle en anthropologie," *Bulletins et mémoires de la Société d'anthropologie de Paris* 3d tome, 7th ser. (6 July 1922): 65.

6 Roland Barthes, *Camera Lucida: Reflections on Photography,* trans. Richard Howard (New York: Hill and Wang, 1981), 80.

7 Regnault, "L'histoire du cinéma," 64.

8 Ibid.

9 Regnault wrote, "The first, or cinematograph, takes successive movements and decomposes them in a series of photographic images: it is only important from a scientific point of view. The second, or cinematoscope, recomposes the movement and gives us an animated spectacle, it has a commercial interest" ("L'histoire du cinéma," 60–61). Throughout the early twentieth century, Regnault wrote about cinema and its history, a history he saw as an evolution originating from both science and popular entertainment, beginning with the concept of the persistence of the image on the retina, Plateau's phénakistiscope, and Reynaud's praxinoscope, and reaching its apex with the invention of cinema by Marey, whom Regnault referred to as *le père du cinéma* (Félix Regnault, "L'évolution du cinéma," *La revue scientifique* [1922]: 79–85).

10 Marta Braun, "The Photographic Work of E. J. Marey," *Studies in Visual Communication* 9, no. 4 (fall 1983): 2. See also her excellent *Picturing Time: The Work of Etienne-Jules Marey (1830–1904)* (Chicago: University of Chicago Press, 1992). For more on Marey see Michel Frizot, *E. J. Marey 1830/1904: la photographie du mouvement* (Paris: Centre national d'art et de culture Georges Pompidou, Musée national d'art moderne, 1977–78), and Frizot, *La chronophotographie: temps, photographie et mouvement autour de E. J. Marey,* exhibition catalog for La Chapelle de l'Oratoire, Beaune (Côte-d'Or) 27 May–3 September 1984 (Michel Frizot and Beaune: Association des amis de Marey, 1984).

11 Félix Regnault, "Films et musées d'ethnographie," *Comptes rendus de l'association française pour l'avancement des sciences* 2 (1923): 680–81.

12   "Les musées des films," *Biologica* 2, no. 16, supplement 20 (1912): XX, and "Un musée des films," *Bulletins et mémoires de la société d'anthropologie de Paris* 3d tome, 6th ser. (7 March 1912): 95–96.

13   Félix Regnault, "Le langage par gestes," *La nature* 1324 (15 October 1898): 315.

14   Félix Regnault, "Films et musées d'ethnographie," 681.

15   For a description of Regnault's methods of chronophotography, see Félix Regnault, "Des diverses méthodes de marche et de course," *L'illustration* 2765 (22 February 1896): 155.

16   "Le rôle du cinéma en ethnographie," *La nature* 2866 (1 October 1931): 305; and Félix Regnault and Cdt. de Raoul, *Comment on marche: des divers modes de progression de la supériorité du mode en flexion* (Paris: Henri Charles-Lavauzelle, Editeur militaire, 1897), 13–15. Regnault wrote an account of the evolution of fashion in "La mode," *La nature* 1088 (7 April 1894): 289–91. I am indebted to Samba Diop for providing information on the clothes and possible cultural identities of the people in Regnault's chronophotography.

17   "Le grimper," *Revue encyclopédique* (1897): 904–5.

18   "Un musée des films," 96.

19   Hd25 at the Cinémathèque française.

20   Lajard and Félix Regnault, "Poterie crue et origine du tour," *Bulletins de la Société d'anthropologie de Paris* 6th tome, 4th ser. (19 December 1895): 734–39.

21   Regnault described this film sequence in this way: "Une négresse pile dans un grand mortier. Elle lève le pilou, le lâche en battant des mains, le laisse retomber et le reprend dans sa chute" (A Negro woman grinds in a large mortar. She lifts the pestle, lets it go while clapping her hands, lets it fall again and then picks it up again) ("Un musée des films," 96). In some photographs of African women (unnamed) taken at world's fairs, the women often appear barebreasted. See, e.g., the photograph entitled "Rencontre insolite" of a Frenchman in a suit and an African woman lighting each other's cigarettes. This example was taken during the Exposition Universelle in Paris in 1889 (Exhibition catalog, *La tour Eiffel* [Paris: Musée d'Orsay, 1989], 117).

22   See Regnault and de Raoul, 171, for more on the evolution of carrying.

23   See cat. no. Hn13 (Cinémathèque française).

24   This example is "Course à grands pas" (1895), cat. no. Hn22 (Cinémathèque française).

25   See LPhot 194, "Nègre marche," and LPhot 198, "Nègre marche d'après 546277" which are available in the Eric Vivié collection at the Archives du film, not reproduced here. Lisa Cartwright describes the "China Girl" test image as follows: "A static medium close-up of an anonymous young white woman . . . holding a color scale test card. . . . The image sets in place a photochemical standard, establishing as a norm grades of filmstock that resolve light skin tones with the greatest range of subtlety and detail, responding to darker tones with a much more restricted range of tonal resolution." Cartwright explains that the China Girl image is an "absence," a "private laboratory fetish object . . . closely related to the establishment of physiognomical norms in nineteenth century science" (Lisa Cartwright, material from a chapter draft to *Screening the Body: Tracing Medicine's Visual Culture* [Minneapolis: University of Minnesota Press, 1995] which was not included in the final book).

26   These examples belong to the collection of Jean Vivié and are housed at the Archives du film, cat. nos. 193 and 197.

27   Regnault, "Le langage par gestes."

28   Frantz Fanon, *Black Skin White Masks: The Experiences of a Black Man in a White World*, trans. Charles Lam Markmann (New York: Grove Press, 1967), 129.

29   See especially Regnault's long article "Les tempéraments rustique et affiné," *Revue anthropologique* (1938): 18–40.

30   Regnault and de Raoul, 28.

31   Robert L. Herbert, *Impressionism: Art, Leisure, and Parisian Society* (New Haven: Yale University Press, 1988), 33–34.

32   Walter Benjamin, *Charles Baudelaire: A Lyric Poet in the Era of High Capitalism*, trans. Harry Zohn (London: Verso, 1985), 35–36. I thank Mary Miller for this insight.

33   Etienne-Jules Marey, Préface to Regnault and de Raoul, 6. *Comment on marche* promotes the *marche en flexion* and reveals Regnault's emphasis on body movements and what he believed they could tell the scientist about race, class, profession, education, costume, personality, and environment.

34   Ibid., 8.

35   Note by Charles Comte and Félix Regnault presented by Marey, *Comptes rendus hebdomadaires des séances de l'Académie des sciences* 122 (February 1896): 401–4.

36   See "Des différentes manières de marcher," *La médecine moderne* (1893): 596–97; "Ouvrages offerts," *Bulletins de la Société d'anthropologie de Paris* 4th tome (15 June 1893): 382; "La marche et le pas gymnastique militaires," *La nature* 1052 (29 July 1893): 129; "Des diverses méthodes de marche et de course," *L'illustration* 2765 (22 February 1896): 154–55; Regnault and de Raoul, *Comment on marche*.

   Regnault also made films of Commander de Raoul in a striped maillot shirt with hat, white leggings, and baton, demonstrating the *marche en flexion*. The Cinémathèque française collection includes films of de Raoul as well as of other soldiers performing the *marche en flexion*. Although the filmmaker is not attributed, and the titles for the films were reportedly provided by Lucien Bull, Marey's assistant and director of the Institut Marey (years after they were made), I believe that these films as well as all the Hn (*Homme nègre*) series were made by Regnault with the help of Charles Comte and Commander de Raoul. Other films by Regnault are in the Collection Eric Vivié, at the Archives du film, and at the Collège de France.

37   See Regnault, "Des diverses méthodes de marche et de course," 155; Regnault and de Raoul, *Comment on marche*; Félix Regnault, "La locomotion chez l'homme (Travail de l'Institut Marey)" *Journal de physiologie et de pathologie générale* 15th tome, no. 1 (1 January 1913): 46–61. Throughout Europe and North America the use of film to improve the efficacy of the Euro-American body must be seen in relation to burgeoning discourses around eugenics and Social Darwinism. Cinema and anthropology joined forces not only in Taylorism, Henry Ford's use of analyses of films of workers to make the assembly line more efficient, but also in the birth of the field of physical education, to which Regnault's colleague at the Institut de physiologie, Georges Demeney, contributed through the study of the body in chronophotography.

38   The extent to which such images are open to interpretation can be seen in the recent shredding of a cache of nude photographs of undergraduates at elite colleges that

were taken in the 1950s and 1960s. These photos, which had been stored at the National Anthropological Archives at the Smithsonian, featured full frontal and side poses, and were used by scientists to study the link between body shape and posture. Those photographed, including many individuals now in powerful positions such as Hillary Clinton and Diane Sawyer, had sufficient clout to lobby successfully for the destruction of such photos (Ron Rosenbaum, "The Great Ivy League Nude Posture Photo Scandal," *New York Times Magazine*, 15 January 1995, 26–31, 40, 46, 55–56; and "Museum Shreds Nude Photos of Former Students at Yale," *New York Times*, 29 January 1995, 14). Needless to say, nude photographs of indigenous peoples and other people of color from the same period are not greeted with comparable shock and disapproval by dominant society, nor are the people photographed likely to have sufficient clout to demand the destruction of the images.

39 In this sense, ethnography is also inscription, as Ira Jacknis explains: "An ethnography is the description of a single culture, usually foreign to the describer. . . . At the heart of ethnography, the initial act making all the rest possible is the act of *inscription*, the fixing in permanent form of selected aspects of the field of sociocultural meaning. The process moves in stages of revision and analysis, resulting in the final *presentation*, usually in the form of written ethnography." I have found Jacknis's explanation of inscription and presentation to be quite useful (Ira Jacknis, "Franz Boas and Photography," *Studies in Visual Communication* 10, no. 1 [1984]: 2–3).

40 Mary Ann Doane, "Film and the Masquerade: Theorizing the Female Spectator," in *Femmes Fatales: Feminism, Film Theory, Psychoanalysis* (New York: Routledge, 1991), 18–19.

41 Ibid., 19.

42 It is not my aim to survey all of anthropological research film in what follows. A good survey is found in Emilie de Brigard, "The History of Ethnographic Film," in *Principles of Visual Anthropology*, ed. Paul Hockings (The Hague: Mouton, 1975), 13–44, and Claudia Springer, "Ethnocentric Circles: A Short History of Ethnographic Film," *The Independent* (December 1984): 13–18.

43 Regnault, "Le rôle du cinéma en ethnographie," 304.

44 Ibid., 306.

45 E. B. Tylor, *Primitive Culture: Researches into the Development of Mythology, Philosophy, Religion, Language, Art and Custom* (London, 1871), 2:200–201, quoted in George W. Stocking Jr., "The Ethnographic Sensibility of the 1920s and the Dualism of the Anthropological Tradition," in *Romantic Motives: Essays on Anthropological Sensibility*, ed. George W. Stocking Jr., *History of Anthropology*, vol. 6 (Madison: University of Wisconsin Press, 1989), 209.

46 Martin Taureg, "The Development of Standards for Scientific Films in German Ethnography," *Studies in Visual Communication* 9, no. 1 (winter 1983): 22–23.

47 George W. Stocking Jr., "The Ethnographer's Magic: Fieldwork in British Anthropology from Tylor to Malinowski," in *Observers Observed: Essays on Ethnographic Fieldwork*, ed. George W. Stocking Jr., *History of Anthropology*, vol. 1 (Madison: University of Wisconsin Press, 1983), 79.

48 Walter Baldwin Spencer, *Across Australia* (1912), quoted in Arthur and Corinne

Cantrill, "The 1901 Cinematography of Walter Baldwin Spencer," *Cantrill's Film-notes* 37–38 (April 1982): 41.

49   Spencer placed Australian Aborigines in compounds in Darwin and implemented many racist laws directed against Aborigines and Asians. Most of the information on Spencer is taken from the excellent article by Arthur and Corinne Cantrill, ibid., 26–42, 56. I disagree, however, with their conclusion that permission from the Arunta Tribal Council should not be a precondition for viewing these films. They argue that "Film and photography are our 'objects,' and they transcend the 'pro-filmic' subjects" (56).

50   Spencer was encouraged to use film by British anthropologist Alfred Cort Haddon who had also used film on the 1898 Cambridge Anthropological Expedition to the Torres Strait Islands, and who called film not only "an indispensable piece of anthropological apparatus," but also an endeavor which could be profitable if footage was sold for use in commercial cinema (Ian Dunlop, "Ethnographic Filmmaking in Australia: The First Seventy Years [1898–1968]," *Studies in Visual Communication* 9, no. 1 [winter 1983]: 11).

51   Walter Baldwin Spencer, "The Argus" (1902), quoted in Cantrill and Cantrill, 38.

52   Rudolf Pöch, quoted in Paul Spindler, "New Guinea 1904–1906," *Science and Film* 8, no. 1 (March 1959): 11.

53   Rudolf Pöch, "Reisen in Neu-Guinea in den Jahren 1904–1906," *Zeitschrift für Ethnologie* (1907): 382–400.

54   Spindler, 10–14; and Pöch, 395.

55   Pöch footage has been edited to produce the film *Neu Guinea, 1904–1906*, available at the Institut für den wissenschaftlichen Film, Göttingen, Germany.

56   One example is Robert Gardner's *Dead Birds* (1961), a film which takes as its theme the life of the Dani, an ethnic group centered in highland New Guinea. An opening intertitle declares, "The people in the film merely did what they had done before we came and, for those who are not dead, as they do now that we have left."

57   This film may be seen at the National Film Archives in London, under the title [Torres Strait]. See Ian Dunlop, 11; Spindler; and de Brigard, "History of Ethnographic Film," 16–17.

58   *Neu-Guinea, 1904–1906* by Rudolf Pöch at the Institut für den wissenschaftlichen Film in Göttingen.

59   Cited in Luc de Heusch, *The Cinema and Social Science: A Survey of Ethnographic and Sociological Films*, Reports and Papers in the Social Sciences, vol. 16 (Paris: UNESCO, 1962), 18. De Heusch argued that although cinema was not a magic eye, it could be "a marvelous corrector of impressions." And when the subject is gesture, he suggested, film "rightly belongs to cinematographic *writing*" (25).

60   Ira Jacknis, "The Picturesque and the Scientific: Franz Boas's Plan for Anthropological Filmmaking," *Visual Anthropology* 1, no. 1 (1987): 63.

61   Jacknis, "Franz Boas and Photography," 42.

62   Jay Ruby, "Franz Boas and Early Camera Study of Behavior," *Kinesis* 3, no. 1 (fall 1980): 6–11. For more on Dunham and Hurston see the concluding chapter.

63   Unlike Regnault, however, her stated aim was the explanation of cultural totalities—

the whole culture—and she argued that an anthropologist must first conduct a cultural study before filming anything (Asen Balikci, "Visual Anthropology: The Legacy of Margaret Mead," unpublished paper presented at the annual meeting of the Commission on Visual Anthropology, 1985; Ira Jacknis, "Margaret Mead and Gregory Bateson in Bali: Their Use of Photography and Film," *Cultural Anthropology* 3, no. 2 [May 1988]: 160–77; Margaret Mead, "Visual Anthropology in a Discipline of Words," in *Principles of Visual Anthropology*, ed. Paul Hockings [The Hague: Mouton, 1974], 3–12).

In sound films, the voice of the authoritative anthropologist became crucial. Margaret Mead, for example, became a popular scientific icon herself. A leading figure in the popularization of cultural anthropology, Mead used footage shot by herself and Gregory Bateson for films and television shows dealing with comparative studies of personality. Prominent examples include *Trance and Dance in Bali* (1951), *Bathing Babies in Three Cultures* (1951), and *First Days in the Life of a New Guinea Baby* (1951). Although many of Mead's films, often staple films of undergraduate introductory anthropology courses, focus on themes like child-rearing which might be considered "women's" themes, her stance is decidedly that of the Scientist, the authority who expounds upon the timeless, stable essences of "primitive cultures." A proponent of what was called the Culture and Personality school within U.S. cultural anthropology, Mead classified cultures psychoanalytically, giving particular attention to child-rearing practices, and attitudes toward sex. I discuss Mead in more detail in chapter 5.

64   Félix Regnault, "Films et musées d'ethnographie."

65   Johannes Fabian, *Time and the Other: How Anthropology Makes Its Object* (New York: Columbia University Press, 1983), 92.

66   James Clifford, "On Collecting Art and Culture," in *The Predicament of Culture: Twentieth-century Ethnography, Literature, and Art* (Cambridge, Mass.: Harvard University Press, 1988), 228.

67   Even if ethnographic film has not triumphed in the academy, Regnault's vision of a museum or archive of film remains a powerful ideal. There are many contemporary projects which echo Regnault's aspiration: in his choreometrics project, the U.S. anthropologist Alan Lomax aspired to collect footage of all the dances of the world. Using the classification system developed by George P. Murdock, who worked on the Human Relations Area files at Yale University, Lomax outlined seven rules for making films to be included in archives of comparative movement (Paolo Chiozzi, "Reflections on Ethnographic Film with a General Bibliography," *Visual Anthropology* 2 [1989]: 15, 22–23). Similarly, the Institut für den wissenschaftlichen Film continues to collect and make films with an undying faith in film as objective document, and, in France, Jean-Dominique Lajoux at the Centre national de la recherche scientifique is working on an archive of movements, a collection of films of how people from around the world eat, sleep, sit, and perform other basic tasks.

68   J. W. Powell, "Twenty-Third Annual Report of the Bureau of American Ethnology," *Annual Report, Bureau of American Ethnology* 23 (1901–2): xvi. I thank Ira Jacknis for pointing out this article to me.

69   See Margaret Mead, *An Anthropologist at Work* (New York: Avon, 1959): 16, quoted in Balikci, "Visual Anthropology: The Legacy of Margaret Mead."

70   Chiozzi, 18. Since the 1980s, Native Americans and Inuit/Alaskan Eskimo in North America have been recontextualizing images from early ethnographic photography and film in their own film and video productions. See chapters 3 and 4 and the conclusion for discussion of media production by indigenous peoples.

71   Marcel Mauss, "Les techniques du corps," in *Sociologie et anthropologie* (Paris: Presses Universitaires de France, 1934), 362–86.

72   Griaule disapproved of the use of reconstructed scenes unless absolutely necessary; he also felt that anthropologists should make separate films specifically intended for the public, and did so himself in *Au pays Dogon* (1938) and *Sous les masques noirs* (1938). French ethnographic film is best known today, however, for the work of directors like Jean Rouch and Luc de Heusch who foreground the subjectivity of film, declaring that true ethnographic film must be participatory, collaborative cinema.

73   According to Alan Feldman, early German anthropology focused on the diffusionist theories of the Kulturkreis school and was less concerned with participant observation than with the collecting and categorizing of data concerning cultural traits, activities, and behaviors. Accordingly, German ethnographic films tend to hold the subject at a distance (the camera as a "fourth wall"), with long takes, clear foreground and background differentiation, and little or no intertitle commentary. The Kulturkreis emphasis on material aspects of culture and quantitative analysis of cultural artifacts may explain in part why German ethnographic film tends to frame dances and rituals much as dioramas in natural history museum displays do, rather than attempting to penetrate cultural life with the intrusive camera movement, close-ups, and point-of-view shots more characteristic of later British ethnographic film (Alan Feldman, Notes for the Asia Society film festival, "Germany in Asia," February 1989). Also see Luc de Heusch, *The Cinema and Social Science*, 21.

74   Günther Spannaus, "Vergleich ethnographischer Töpfereifilme als Beispiel für die wissenschaftliche Auswertung von enzyklopädischem Filmmaterial," *Research Film* 2, no. 5 (1957): 251–55, cited in Taureg, 25. For a list of strict guidelines for ethnographic filmmakers at the IWF, see Institut für den wissenschaftlichen Film, "Rules for Documentation in Ethnology and Folklore," *Research Film* 3, no. 4 (1959): 238–40.

75   Balikci, "Visual Anthropology," and Feldman.

76   Robert Proctor, "From *Anthropologie* to *Rassenkunde* in the German Anthropological Tradition," in *Bones, Bodies, Behavior: Essays on Biological Anthropology*, ed. George W. Stocking Jr., *History of Anthropology*, vol. 5 (Madison: University of Wisconsin Press, 1988), 138–79.

77   Asen Balikci, "Anthropology, Film and the Arctic Peoples," *Anthropology Today* 5, no. 2 (April 1989): 9; and Balikci, "Visual Anthropology." The emphasis on functionalist explanation in British social anthropology tended to make British anthropologists less interested in amassing so-called positivist records, including film, and relatively more interested in constructing analytic theories concerning social and political structures.

78   M. W. Hilton-Simpson and J. A. Haeseler, like Haddon, Spencer, and Boas, perceived
the commercial benefits of anthropological film, and specifically noted the profit
that could be made in selling footage to commercial interests. They discuss the
importance of using telephoto lenses in order to take in scenes without the natives'
awareness, and even describe filming a woman as she is sleeping (M. W. Hilton-
Simpson and J. A. Haeseler, "Cinema and Ethnology," *Discovery* 6 [1925]: 328).

79   Anthony R. Michaelis, *Research Films in Biology, Anthropology, Psychology, and
Medicine* (New York: Academic Press, 1955), 199.

80   Christopher M. Lyman, *The Vanishing Race and Other Illusions: Photographs of
Indians by Edward S. Curtis* (Washington, D.C.: Smithsonian Institution Press,
1982), 69. Luke Lyon writes that the footage reproduced in T. C. McLuhan's film on
Curtis, *The Shadow Catcher* (1975), is reproduced incorrectly as a mirror image
(Lyon, "History of the Prohibition of Photography of Southwestern Indian Cere-
monies," unpublished paper).

81   Most museums have film collections, but the general emphasis is on the use of film
for public education, rather than for research. In 1981, for example, Richard Sorenson
established the Human Studies Film Archives (a collection of travelogues and ethnographic cinema of all genres) at the Smithsonian Institution. Nevertheless, most
anthropologists do not choose to study films about the cultures of the peoples portrayed such as those at the HSFA; instead, such facilities are used more often by
scholars doing research on film history, or the history of visual anthropology.

82   For more on recent African American women's photography, see Fatimah Tobing
Rony, " 'We Must First See Ourselves': Documentary Subversions in Contemporary
African-American Women's Photography," in *Personal Narratives: Women Photographers of Color*, exhibition catalog (Winston-Salem: Southeastern Center for Contemporary Art, 1993), 11–15.

83   Regnault was one of the first to consider "les techniques du corps," or body techniques, as a subject in its own right, and his work paved the way for Marcel Mauss's
ideas on the body as the first instrument of culture. This association of a cinematic
interest in temporalizing the body and ethnography—the *langage par gestes*—continues today: when someone calls a scene in a commercial film "ethnographic," he or
she is likely referring to a scene in which ordinary gesture and physical detail are
highlighted, a tableau of the picturesque which is suggestive of a prior authenticity.

3   *Gestures of Self-Protection*

1   George Orwell, *Shooting an Elephant and Other Essays* (New York: Harcourt, Brace
& World, 1950), 8.

2   Félix Regnault, "L'histoire du cinéma: son rôle en anthropologie," *Bulletins et mémoires de la Société d'anthropologie de Paris* 3d tome 7th ser (6 July 1922): 65.

3   Ira Jacknis, "The Picturesque and the Scientific: Franz Boas's Plan for Anthropological Filmmaking," *Visual Anthropology* 1, no. 1 (1987): 61.

4   Ibid. For Boas's discussion of "isolable actions," see Ira Jacknis, "Franz Boas and
Photography," *Studies in Visual Communication* 10, no. 1 (1984): 42.

5   Jacknis, "The Picturesque and the Scientific."

6   George W. Stocking Jr., *Victorian Anthropology* (New York: Free Press, 1987), 289.

7   Christopher Hussey, *The Picturesque: Studies in a Point of View* (London: Archon Books, 1967; orig. publ. 1927), 4, 14.

8   Richard Payne Knight, *Analytical Inquiry into the Principles of Taste* (1805), cited in ibid., 79–80.

9   Sara Suleri, *The Rhetoric of English India* (Chicago: University of Chicago Press, 1992), 76.

10 I thank Jeanne Beausoleil and the excellent staff at the Archives for their generous assistance and for providing information on Albert Kahn. See also Jeanne Beausoleil, "Au service d'un idéal de compréhension internationale: les opérateurs d'Albert Kahn dans le monde," in *Le cinéma français muet dans le monde, influences réciproques: Symposium de la FIAF* (Paris: Cinémathèque de Toulouse–Institut Jean Vigo, 1988), 61–69; Jeanne Beausoleil and Catherine Fortassier, " 'Les archives de la planète' d'Albert Kahn," *Prestige de la photographie* 3 (December 1977): 40–65; and Jeanne Beausoleil, "La planète d'Albert Kahn," *Les nouvelles littéraires* 2658 (12–19 October 1978): 11.

11 Mary Louise Pratt, "Scratches on the Face of the Country; or, What Mr. Barrow Saw in the Land of the Bushmen," in *"Race," Writing, and Difference*, ed. Henry Louis Gates Jr. (Chicago: University of Chicago Press, 1985), 143.

12 Films in which white women were unclothed were also prevalent in medical and social science films of women classified as pathological, criminal, or homosexual. See Lisa Cartwright's *Screening the Body: Tracing Medicine's Visual Culture* (Minneapolis: University of Minnesota Press, 1995).

13 Charles Musser concludes that the travel film engenders a particular mode of perception which he calls "separation": just as the passenger on a train watches the landscape whiz by and experiences it as separation, so does the viewer experience a film. See Charles Musser, "The Travel Genre in 1903–1904: Moving towards Fictional Narrative," in *Early Cinema: Space, Frame, Narrative*, ed. Thomas Elsaesser (London: British Film Institute, 1992), 123–32.

14 E. B. Tylor, *Primitive culture: Researches into the development of mythology, philosophy, religion, language, art and custom* (London, 1871), 2:200–201, quoted in George W. Stocking Jr., "The Ethnographic Sensibility of the 1920s and the Dualism of the Anthropological Tradition," in *Romantic Motives: Essays on Anthropological Sensibility*, ed. George W. Stocking Jr., *History of Anthropology*, vol. 6 (Madison: University of Wisconsin Press, 1989), 209.

15 Félix Mesguich, quoted in André F. Liotard, Samivel, and Jean Thévenot, *Cinéma d'exploration: cinéma au long cours* (Paris: P.-A. Chavane, 1950), 28.

16 Holmes's logo of a white silhouette of a white man in a bush hat typified this style of tourist possession.

17 The most filmed dance in the United States was the Hopi Snake dance at Walpi, Arizona, in which the Antelope and Snake societies handled and danced with snakes. The first film of this dance was made in 1898, possibly by Thomas Edison (Luke Lyon, "History of the Prohibition of Photography of Southwestern Indian Cere-

monies," unpublished paper; and Emilie de Brigard, "The History of Ethnographic Film," in *Principles of Visual Anthropology*, ed. Paul Hockings [The Hague: Mouton, 1975], caption of plate 7).

According to Luke Lyon, authorities often clashed with the photographers. In 1913, for example, Indian agent Leo Crane chased Victor Miller of Pathe's Weekly (a pictorial news service) through the desert, knowing that Miller's film of Hopi dances would be used for commercial purposes, rather than "private or historical purposes." In 1921, Charles Burke, Commissioner of Indian Affairs, banned certain Indian dances, feeling that they encouraged "savagery." The Native Americans themselves chose to prohibit photographing of many of their dances, citing exploitation; they also feared that the pictures might be used as evidence against them. Many Native Americans of the Southwest would jump in front of the camera, throw sand or rocks, and even break cameras to prevent filming.

18   Musser, 127.

19   Both are at the National Film Archives in London.

20   Burton Holmes, *Burton Holmes: The Man Who Photographed the World*, ed. Genoa Caldwell (New York: Harry N. Abrams, 1977), 23.

21   This is in the collections of the Library of Congress.

22   One express aim of at least some of Holmes's films was explicitly to promote tourism. His film *The Melting Pot of the Pacific* (1923?), for example, was commissioned by the World Travel Department of the U.S. Shipping Board to promote tourism in Hawaii.

23   The Nederlands Filmmuseum in Amsterdam has four recently restored films from this period. The films include works for the Colonial Institute by a man named Lamster, and for Pathé Frères, and feature court dances in what is today Indonesia, the arrival of the Resident (local Dutch colonial officer) at his post, a colonial prison in Batavia (now Jakarta) with scenes of orderly prison life, and rice farming among the Karo Batak in North Sumatra. Lamster began to make colonial films in 1912, probably hiring a French camera operator. The films were used as visual aids at lectures given by the Colonial Institute in Amsterdam. I thank the archivists Rogier Schmeele and Marÿke von Kester for this information.

24   Patrick O'Reilly, "Le 'documentaire' ethnographique en Océanie," in *Premier catalogue sélectif international de films ethnographiques sur la région du Pacifique* (Paris: UNESCO, 1970), 289–90.

25   See Linda Williams, "Film Body: An Implantation of Perversions," in *Narrative, Apparatus, Ideology: A Film Theory Reader*, ed. Phil Rosen (New York: Columbia University Press, 1986), 507–34.

26   This joke—of the married man flirting with native girls only to be heckled by his spouse—occurs again and again in the films of this period. See, e.g., "Fatty and Mable at the San Diego Exposition" (Keystone, 1915), in which a white man in love with a "South Seas woman" at the fair is beaten by his wife.

27   See Gaston Méliès, *Le voyage autour du monde de la G. Méliès Manufacturing Company (July 1912–May 1913)* (Paris: Association "Les amis de Georges Méliès," 1988), and Patrick McInroy, "The American Méliès," *Sight and Sound International Film Quarterly* (autumn 1979): 250–54.

28   For a description of *Roosevelt in Africa* see *The Moving Picture World*, 6:528–29.

29 In *The River of Doubt* (1913–14, compiled 1928?), available at the Library of Congress, a film of an expedition sponsored by the American Museum of Natural History and the Brazilian government, the Indians are described as "wilder and more primitive than anyone we came across in Africa." The men who paddle for Roosevelt are compared to animals: "Men of the forest, lithe as panthers, brawny as bears. They swam like waterdogs." In contrast, Roosevelt is hailed as a great hunter, geographer, and discoverer of an unknown river.

Another example of the exploration genre is Carl Lumholtz's *In Borneo, Land of the Headhunters* (1916), available at the National Film Archives in London. The film focuses on the explorer as hero with scenes of the Dayak population in between. The first intertitle declares, "These are the first motion pictures ever taken in Borneo. They were secured by Dr. Lumholtz, scientist and explorer, during two years spent among the native tribes." Despite the serious opening, the film adopts a joking style when it comes to the interaction of Lumholtz and the Dayak. When Lumholtz goes to a village and views some natives dancing, for example, humor is meant to be evoked when he joins in the dancing, accompanying "the most beautiful maiden." Other intertitles joke that it may be difficult to see that "this Saputan swimmer is a man" and "Young Murung Dayaks display a monkey-like agility in climbing."

30 Herbert Tynes Cowling's *Some Tribes of Central Africa* (1922), another African film safari, features many exploitative close-ups of African women's bodies.

31 Roland Barthes, *Camera Lucida: Reflections on Photography*, trans. Richard Howard (New York: Hill and Wang, 1981), 77.

32 Nina J. Root, ed., *Catalog of the American Museum of Natural History Film Archives* (New York: American Museum of Natural History Department of Library Services, 1987), xv. Almost all of the anthropological museums in the United States sponsored lectures which used lantern slides and sometimes film: for example, the University of Archaelogy/Anthropology in Philadelphia showed lantern slides from the Dixon Wanamaker Expedition and sponsored van Valin's expedition.

33 Another Great White Hunter filmmaker who made both ethnographic and scripted films abroad was Hans Hermann Schomburgk, whose films made in Togo (1913) and Liberia (1922–23) are available at the Institut für den wissenschaftlichen Film in Göttingen, Germany. Schomburgk was part of a small group of white hunters who became famous as great explorers/filmmakers. In his film *The White Goddess of Wangora* (1913) starring Meg Gehrts, the story is of a white woman, worshipped by Africans, who later falls in love and runs off with a white big game hunter. The Togo locals were used as extras (Caroline Alexander, "The White Goddess of the Wangora," *New Yorker* [8 April 1991]: 43–76).

34 The anthropologist Baldwin Spencer himself had already done this in lectures; he found that film of the Arunta, humorous to white audiences, could be used to attract people to his talks (Arthur and Corinne Cantrill, "The 1901 Cinematography of Walter Baldwin Spencer," *Cantrill's Filmnotes* 37–38 [April 1982]: 26–42, 56). See Martin Johnson, *Cannibal-Land: Adventures with a Camera in the New Hebrides* (Boston: Houghton Mifflin, 1922), and Pascal James Imperato and Eleanor M. Imperato, *They Married Adventure: The Wandering Lives of Martin and Osa Johnson* (New Brunswick, N.J.: Rutgers University Press, 1992) for more on the Johnsons.

35 Intertitle in the film *Simba.*

36 Suleri, 108.

37 Jacob W. Gruber, "Ethnographic Salvage and the Shaping of Anthropology," *American Anthropologist* 172 (1970): 1297.

38 Ira Jacknis, "The Picturesque and the Scientific," 61.

39 Joseph K. Dixon in *Wanamaker Primer on the North American Indian* (Philadelphia: Wanamaker Originator, 1909), 44, quoted in Susan Applegate Krouse, "Filming the Vanishing Race," in *Visual Explorations of the World: Selected Papers from the International Conference on Visual Communication,* ed. Jay Ruby and Martin Taureg (Aachen: Edition Herodot im Rader-Verlag, 1987), 257. Curtis's contemporary Joseph Dixon actually wrote a book entitled *The Vanishing Race* (1913). Like Curtis, Dixon was a white photographer and filmmaker of Native Americans. See Susan Applegate Krouse, "Photographing the Vanishing Race," *Visual Anthropology* 3, nos. 2–3 (1990): 213–33.

40 Lois Flury, "A Magnificent Obsession," *Pacific Northwest* (January–February 1984): 24–43.

41 See chapter 2 for discussion of the film of the Yeibichai ceremony.

42 Mick Gidley, "From the Hopi Snake Dance to 'The Ten Commandments': Edward S. Curtis as Filmmaker," *Studies in Visual Communication* 8, no. 3 (summer 1982): 71–73. See chapter 2 for discussion on how the Yeibichai dance was performed backwards.

43 When rereleased in the 1980s, the film's title was changed to *In the Land of the War Canoes.*

44 Edward S. Curtis, *In the Land of the Headhunters: Indian Life and Indian Lore* (Yonkers-on-Hudson, N.Y.: World Book, 1915).

45 Cited in Bill Holm and George Irving Quimby, *Edward S. Curtis in the Land of the War Canoes: A Pioneer Cinematographer in the Pacific Northwest* (Seattle: University of Washington Press, 1980): 113.

46 Ira Jacknis, "Franz Boas and Photography," 12. See also Jacknis, "Franz Boas and Exhibits: On the Limitations of the Museum Method of Anthropology," in *Objects and Others,* ed. George W. Stocking Jr., *History of Anthropology,* vol. 3 (Madison: University of Wisconsin Press, 1985), 75–111.

47 For more on Hunt, see Ira Jacknis, "George Hunt, Collector of Indian Specimens," in *Chiefly Feasts: The Enduring Kwakiutl Potlach,* ed. Aldona Jonaitis (New York: American Museum of Natural History, 1991), 177–224.

48 Jacknis, "Franz Boas and Photography," 44–47.

49 I am not dismissing the fact that smoke was an important symbol and form of communication in Native American communities. However, the quest was apparently not a prevalent ritual among the Kwakwaka'wakw at the time, according to community members, and smoke was a fitting motif in Curtis's work which emphasized the picturesque to represent Native Americans as "vanishing peoples."

50 Anonymous, "Ethnology in Action," *The Independent* (11 January 1915): 72, as quoted in Gidley, 75.

51 Vachel Lindsay, *The Art of the Moving Picture,* rev. ed. (New York: Liveright, 1970 [1922]), 114, as quoted in Gidley, 70.

52 Regnault had used the same metaphor of the "bronze" to describe West Africans at

the ethnographic exhibition (see chapter 1). Franz Boas pioneered the display of artifacts by culture group instead of by evolutionary schemes, with an emphasis on the "life group," or set of figures in native costume engaged in some sort of work or art process. But the divide between science and art needed to be clearly drawn. Boas, for example, argued that mannequins should not look too realistic: "No figure, however well it may have been gotten up, will look like man himself. If nothing else, the lack of motion will show at once that there is an attempt at copying nature, not nature itself. When the figure is absolutely lifelike the lack of motion causes a ghastly impression such as we notice in wax-figures. For this reason the artistic effect will be better when we bear in mind this fact and do not attempt too close an approach to nature; that is to say, since there is a line of demarcation between nature and plastic art, it is better to draw the line consciously than to try to hide it" (Franz Boas, Frederic Ward Putnam Papers: Correspondence, 7 November 1896, quoted in Ira Jacknis, "Franz Boas and Exhibits," 102).

53 Holm and Quimby, 65.
54 Barthes, 115.
55 Jay Ruby, "A Reexamination of the Early Career of Robert J. Flaherty," *Quarterly Review of Film Studies* 5, no. 4 (fall 1980): 456.

4 Taxidermy and Romantic Ethnography

1 Arthur Calder-Marshall, *The Innocent Eye: The Life of Robert J. Flaherty* (New York: Harcourt, Brace & World, 1963), 72.

2 Joseph E. Senungetuk, *Give or Take a Century: An Eskimo Chronicle* (San Francisco: Indian Historian Press, 1971), 25.

3 Asen Balikci, "Anthropology, Film and the Arctic Peoples," *Anthropology Today* 5, no. 2 (April 1989): 7. Among the popular culture items *Nanook* spawned were ice cream bars (in Germany) and a song (Erik Barnouw, *Documentary: A History of the Non-Fiction Film* [Oxford: Oxford University Press, 1983], 43).

4 André F. Liotard, Samivel, and Jean Thévenot, *Cinéma d'exploration: cinéma au long cours* (Paris: P.-A. Chavane, 1950), 43, and André Bazin, "The Evolution of the Language of Cinema," in *What Is Cinema?* trans. and ed. Hugh Gray (Berkeley: University of California Press, 1967), 1:23–40.

5 Luc de Heusch, *The Cinema and Social Science: A Survey of Ethnographic and Sociological Films*, vol. 16, Reports and Papers in the Social Sciences (Paris: UNESCO, 1962), 37.

6 Jo-Anne Birnie Danzker writes, "Research with Inuit participants in *Nanook of the North* is in its initial stages. It would appear, however, that none of the leading characters were identified by their actual names; that Allakariallak's (Nanook's) clothing was not indigenous to the region; that the contrived sequences were highly amusing to the Inuit; that the seal hunt was contrived. It is also possible that the walrus-hunting sequence had been shot in 1914 or 1916 as part of Flaherty's earlier films, either in the Ottawa or Belcher Islands" (Jo-Anne Birnie Danzker, ed., *Robert Flaherty Photographer/Filmmaker: The Inuit 1910–1922* [Vancouver: Vancouver Art Gallery, 1980], 62). Names spelled with question marks are Danzker's spelling.

7   Bazin, 1:27.

8   Charles Waterton, *Essays on Natural History Chiefly Ornithology* (London, 1838), 300–304, quoted in Stephen Bann, *The Clothing of Clio: A Study of the Representation of History in Nineteenth-century Britain and France* (Cambridge: Cambridge University Press, 1984), 17.

9   Bann, 15.

10   Donna Haraway, "Teddy Bear Patriarchy: Taxidermy in the Garden of Eden, New York City, 1908–1936," *Social Text: Theory/Culture/Ideology* 11 (winter 1984–85): 25. The metaphor of taxidermy—a form of representation which is infused with an acknowledgement of death, but also a desire "to be whole"—describes a plethora of technologies popular at the turn of the century used to represent the human body, including photography, film, and wax figures. Vanessa R. Schwartz argues that wax models of crime victims at the morgue and at the Musée Grevin (such models were extremely popular in Paris) were important precursors to cinema (Vanessa R. Schwartz, "The Public's Taste for Reality: The Morgue, Wax Museums and Early Mass Culture in Fin-de-siècle Paris," paper presented at the Society for Cinema Studies Conference, New Orleans, La., 11–14 February 1993).

11   Robert Flaherty, quoted in Richard Corliss, "Robert Flaherty: The Man in the Iron Myth," in *Nonfiction Film Theory and Criticism,* ed. Richard Meran Barsam (New York: E. P. Dutton, 1973), 234.

12   Johannes Fabian, *Time and the Other: How Anthropology Makes Its Object* (New York: Columbia University Press, 1983), 84–87.

13   Ibid., 85.

14   I am borrowing here from Naomi Greene's insightful use of Mircea Eliade's description of the mythic for her analysis of Pier Paolo Pasolini's films of the 1960s. She quotes Eliade on the sacrifice: "[Every sacrifice] repeats the initial sacrifice and coincides with it. . . . And the same holds true for all repetitions, i.e., all imitations of archetypes; through such imitations, man is projected into the mythical epoch in which the archetypes were first revealed. Thus we perceive a second aspect of primitive ontology: insofar as an act (or an object) acquires a certain reality through the repetition of certain paradigmatic gestures, and acquires it through that alone, there is an implicit abolition of profane time, of duration, of 'history'; and he who reproduces the exemplary gesture thus finds himself transported into the mythical epoch in which its revelation took place" (*The Myth of the Eternal Return,* trans. Willard Trask [London: Routledge & Kegan Paul, 1955], 35, quoted in Naomi Greene, *Pier Paolo Pasolini: Cinema as Heresy* [Princeton: Princeton University Press, 1990], 167).

15   Siegfried Kracauer, *Theory of Film: The Redemption of Physical Reality* (New York: Oxford University Press, 1960), 273.

16   Ibid., 273–74.

17   Robert Flaherty, Recorded BBC Talks, London, 14 June, 25 July, 5 September 1949, quoted in Jay Ruby, "A Reexamination of the Early Career of Robert J. Flaherty," *Quarterly Review of Film Studies* 5, no. 4 (fall 1980): 448.

18   André Bazin, "The Ontology of the Photographic Image," in Bazin, 1:9.

19   I am referring here to Teresa de Lauretis's description of the Oedipal logic of narrative

in "Desire in Narrative," in *Alice Doesn't: Feminism, Semiotics, Cinema* (Bloomington: Indiana University Press, 1984), 103–57. De Lauretis writes that Freud's question of what is femininity "acts precisely as the impulse, the desire that will generate a narrative" (111). In the narratives I am considering, of course, it is not only the female body which must be slain, but that of the indigenous person, male or female.

20 For an excellent summary of the representation of the Inuit and Alaskan Eskimo by Euro-Americans, see Ann Fienup-Riordan, *Eskimo Essays: Yup'ik Lives and How We See Them* (New Brunswick, N.J.: Rutgers University Press, 1990), 11–23.

21 Richard Hakluyt, *The Principal Navigations, Voyages, Traffiques and Discoveries of the English Nation in Twelve Volumes*, vol. 7 (1589; repr., New York: Augustus M. Kelley, 1969), 305, quoted in ibid., 12. Another example was a newspaper account which explained that Minik Wallace who returned to Smith Sound after many years in the United States soon became a "full-fledged 'huskie' " (Kenn Harper, *Give Me My Father's Body: The Life of Minik the New York Eskimo* [Frobisher Bay, N.W.T.: Blacklead Books, 1986], 149).

22 J. Garth Taylor, "An Eskimo Abroad, 1880: His Diary and Death," *Canadian Geographic* 101, no. 5 (October–November 1981): 38–43. Jacobsen's collection of ethnographic artifacts would become the core of the collections at the Berlin Royal Ethnographic Museum, where Franz Boas later worked. In 1881, Jacobsen collected Kwakw̲a̲ka'wakw (Kwakiutl) artifacts in the same part of Canada where Boas studied. In 1883 Boas went to Baffinland himself to collect Inuit artifacts and exhume bones from graves surreptitiously. In 1886 Jacobsen brought a group of Bella Coola Indians to Berlin, an event which sparked Boas's own interest in Northwest Coast Indians. See Ira Jacknis, "Franz Boas and Exhibits: On the Limitations of the Museum Method of Anthropology," in *Objects and Others*, ed. George W. Stocking Jr., *History of Anthropology*, vol. 3 (Madison: University of Wisconsin Press, 1985), 75–111.

23 Peter Matthiessen, "Survival of the Hunter," *New Yorker* (24 April 1995): 75.

24 Harper, 4, 12–33. This book contains many of Minik's letters. Minik's family was also studied by anthropologist Alfred Kroeber who would later write papers on Ishi, a Yahi Indian forced to live in a museum. See Theodora Kroeber, *Ishi in Two Worlds: A Biography of the Last Wild Indian in North America* (Berkeley: University of California Press, 1961).

25 Harper, 99.

26 Minik Wallace, quoted in ibid., 132.

27 Thomas W. Kavanaugh, "A Brief Illustrated History of the Manikins, Statues, Lay-Figures, and Life-Groups Illustrating American Ethnology in the National Museum of Natural History," unpublished paper (16 June 1990). Kavanaugh points out that the same model was used by the Smithsonian for a Jivaro Indian and a Samoan youth.

28 Stocking points out that the anthropologist John Lubbock, in his *Origin of Civilisation* (1870), suggested that Eskimo did well for themselves considering their environment, but that they could not achieve progress without civilized intervention (Stocking, *Victorian Anthropology* [New York: Free Press, 1987], 154).

29 Fienup-Riordan, 16.

30 This characterization is present in anthropological literature as well. As recently as 1982, the French anthropologist Jean Malaurie described going to study the Inuit of

Thule, Greenland, as "a return to the Stone Age" (Jean Malaurie, *The Last Kings of Thule,* trans. Adrienne Foulke [Chicago: University of Chicago Press, 1982], 19, quoted in ibid., 21).

31 Balikci, "Anthropology, Film and the Arctic Peoples," 7.

32 These films, *Esquimaux Game of Snap-The-Whip, Esquimaux Leap Frog,* and *Esquimaux Village,* are at the Library of Congress. The camera operators were Edwin S. Porter and Arthur White. As an example of the representation of the Alaskan Eskimo at the exhibition, consider the 1909 Alaska-Yukon-Pacific Exposition in Seattle, the promotional blurb for which reads "These strange people, existing only on the products of the icy North, half civilized in their nature, knowing no god, having no laws, no government, unable to read or write, with no history of their antecedents, give continuous performances of skill, marksmanship, canoeing, dancing, singing and seal catching never before seen" ("The Alaska-Yukon-Pacific Exposition of 1909: Photographs by Frank Howell," *Alaska Journal* [summer 1984]: 14, quoted in Fienup-Riordan, 16–17).

33 Films of U.S., British, Italian, German, and French origin featuring Inuit include *Wellman Polar Expedition: The Nordpol Expedition* (Charles Urban Trading Co., 1906), *A Dash to the North Pole* (Kineto, 1909), *Fangen junger Eisbären* (Hunting for Young Polar Bears) (Imperium Film, 1914), *Eine Forschungsexpedition durch das Nördliche Eismeer nach Grönland* (Meßter, 1911), and *Islands of New Zembla* (Gaumont, 1913). These films are located at the National Film Archives in London.

34 This film is available at the Human Studies Film Archives at the National Museum of Natural History. For information on the film I consulted the correspondence file of the Human Studies Film Archives.

35 These bones, said to be those of prehistoric Eskimo, were taken to the Wistar Institute of Anatomy at the University of Pennsylvania, Philadelphia.

36 Flaherty was said to have admired *Jack London in the South Seas* by Martin Johnson (1912), also an expedition film (Richard Barsam, *The Vision of Robert Flaherty: The Artist as Myth and Filmmaker* [Bloomington: Indiana University Press, 1988], 16).

37 For more on Curtis and Flaherty, see Brian Winston, "Before Grierson, before Flaherty: The Documentary Film in 1914," *Sight and Sound* 57, no. 4 (autumn 1988): 277–79, and Bill Holm and George Irving Quimby, *Edward S. Curtis in the Land of the War Canoes: A Pioneer Cinematographer in the Pacific Northwest* (Seattle: University of Washington Press, 1980), 30. Both Holm and Quimby believe that Flaherty, who saw *In the Land of the Headhunters* and asked Curtis for advice, was influenced by Curtis in his decision to film only what appeared traditional, i.e., salvage ethnography. For the complete diary entry of Robert and Frances Flaherty's visit to Curtis see Jay Ruby, "A Reexamination of the Early Career of Robert J. Flaherty."

Two films of famous expeditions to the South Pole are Frank Hurley's film of Sir Ernest Shackleton's 1914–17 polar expedition, *South: Sir Ernest Shackleton's Glorious Epic of the Antarctic* (1919), a film which focuses on the expedition members and their camp life, as well as their rescue, and Herbert G. Ponting's *With Captain Scott to the South Pole* (1911–12, British Gaumont) released later as *The Great White Silence* (1924), a film of Captain Robert Falcon Scott's expedition to the South Pole. Both films are at the National Film Archives, London. For more on polar expeditions, see Lisa Bloom, *Gender on Ice: American Ideologies of Polar Expeditions* (Minneapolis: University of Minnesota Press, 1993).

38   Bernard Saladin d'Anglure, "Inuit of Quebec," in *Arctic*, ed. David Damas, vol. 5, *Handbook of North American Indians* (Washington, D.C.: Smithsonian Institution, 1984), 500.

39   Ibid., 505. This period was also marked by religious movements among the Quebec Inuit predicting the end of the world (neither missionary activities nor these syncretic, messianic religious movements were represented in *Nanook*).

40   Erik Barnouw, *Documentary: A History of the Non-Fiction Film* (Oxford: Oxford University Press, 1983), 33.

41   Jo-Anne Birnie Danzker, "Robert Flaherty/Photographer," *Studies in Visual Communication* 6, no. 2 (summer 1980): 9.

42   For an excellent description of Flaherty's activities during this period, see Jo-Anne Birnie Danzker, ed., *Robert Flaherty Photographer/Filmmaker: The Inuit 1910–1922* (Vancouver: Vancouver Art Gallery, 1980), 52–65, and Ruby, "A Reexamination of the Early Career of Robert J. Flaherty."

43   Frances Flaherty from her diary of 17 December 1914, quoted in Danzker, "Robert Flaherty/Photographer," 22.

44   Peter Pitseolak, *People from Our Side: An Inuit Record of Seekooseelak, the Land of the People of Cape Dorset, Baffin Land: A Life Story with Photographs* (Edmonton: Hurtig Press, 1975), 87–88.

45   Flaherty's use of drawings shows that he learned from the art of the Inuit. Flaherty also wrote that he made it a practice to show rushes to the actors; indeed, his own photographs show that the Inuit he hired performed all aspects of camera work (Danzker, *Robert Flaherty Photographer/Filmmaker*, 53–54).

46   Christraud Geary, "Photographs as Materials for African History: Some Methodological Considerations," *History in Africa* 13 (1986): 112.

47   Danzker, ed., *Robert Flaherty Photographer/Filmmaker*, 57.

48   Barsam, 20.

49   James R. Kincaid, "Who Gets to Tell Their Stories?" *New York Times Book Review*, 3 May 1992, 26–27.

50   Barnouw, 37.

51   Barsam, 19.

52   Barnouw writes that Flaherty's compositions reflect Inuit drawings (44).

53   Ricciotto Canudo, "Another View of *Nanook*," in *L'usine aux images* (Paris, 1927), trans. Harold J. Salemson, quoted in Lewis Jacobs, ed., *The Documentary Tradition* (New York: W. W. Norton, 1979), 20–21.

54   Corliss, 231. For a more recent study of Robert Flaherty's films see Barsam.

55   Vilhjalmur Stefansson argued that the Inuit used guns and did not hunt seals through the ice, and asserted that the seal in the film was obviously already dead. He also decried the fake igloo and the accompanying intertitle which explained that the igloo must be colder than freezing (Vilhjalmur Stefansson, *The Standardisation of Error* [London: Kegan Paul, Trench, Trubner, 1929], 86–92, quoted in Paul Rotha with the assistance of Basil Wright, "Nanook and the North," *Studies in Visual Communication* 6, no. 2 [summer 1980]: 50).

56   Robert Flaherty, quoted in Corliss, 234.

57   De Heusch, 16–28.

58   Ibid., 35.

59   Ibid., 64.

60   Bazin, 27.

61   Bronislaw Malinowski, *Argonauts of the Western Pacific* (New York: E. P. Dutton, 1961), 25.

62   Fabian, 95, 106–7.

63   Flaherty, quoted in Richard Griffith, *The World of Robert Flaherty* (New York: Duell, Sloan and Pearce, 1953), 36.

64   If Margaret Mead's image of Polynesian society in her ethnography *Coming of Age in Samoa* (1928) was offered as a counterpoint to U.S. society which she saw as puritan, repressive, and patriarchal, Flaherty's image of the Inuit was a foil for a romantic critique of technology and the machine. See George W. Stocking Jr., "The Ethnographic Sensibility of the 1920s and the Dualism of the Anthropological Tradition," in *Romantic Motives: Essays on Anthropological Sensibility*, ed. George W. Stocking Jr., *History of Anthropology*, vol. 6 (Madison: University of Wisconsin Press, 1989), 208–76.

65   Balikci, 6.

66   Robert J. Flaherty, in collaboration with Frances Hubbard Flaherty, *My Eskimo Friends: "Nanook of the North"* (Garden City, N.Y.: Doubleday, Page, 1924). For information on Flaherty's work as a prospector and cartographer, see Robert Flaherty, "The Belcher Islands of Hudson Bay: Their Discovery and Exploration," *Geographical Review* 5, no. 6 (1918): 433–58; and Flaherty, "Two Traverses across Ungava Peninsula, Labrador," *Geographical Review* 6, no. 2 (1918): 116–32.

67   Charlie Nayoumealuk (sp?) in the documentary *Nanook Revisited* (directed by Claude Massot, 1988) remembers the filming of *Nanook,* and that the Inuit called Flaherty an Inuit name meaning, "tall, left-handedman." In Frances Flaherty's account of the filming of *Elephant Boy,* she refers to Flaherty as Borah Sahib or "Great White Chief" (Barsam, 131).

68   Flaherty, in collaboration with Frances Hubbard Flaherty, 126.

69   Ibid., 134.

70   Ibid., 169. Danzker points out that another section of Flaherty's account in which he explains that Nanook protested the great bother of making a film about himself is almost identical to comments attributed to another man, "Old Atchaweek," in his discussion of his role in his 1914 film by Flaherty, *Early Account of the Film.* See "Filmography," ed. Danzker, 57.

71   Another book by Flaherty about a great explorer in the Arctic who is helped by the Inuit was conspicuously titled *White Master* (London: George Routledge & Sons, 1939).

72   Robert J. Flaherty, *The Captain's Chair: A Story of the North* (New York: Scribner's, 1938), 290.

73   Ibid., 291.

74   Bronislaw Malinowski, *A Diary in the Strict Sense of the Term* (Stanford: Stanford University Press, 1989; orig. publ. 1967), 69.

75 James Clifford, "On Ethnographic Self-Fashioning: Conrad and Malinowski," in *The Predicament of Culture: Twentieth-century Ethnography, Literature, and Art* (Cambridge, Mass.: Harvard University Press, 1988), 110.

76 Flaherty, *The Captain's Chair*, 15.

77 Ibid., 312.

78 Frances Flaherty, "Robert Flaherty: Explorer and Film Maker: The Film of Discovery and Revelation" (mimeographed c. 1958), 14–15, quoted in Jack C. Ellis, *The Documentary Idea: A Critical History of English-language Documentary Film and Video* (Englewood Cliffs, N.J.: Prentice-Hall, 1989).

79 *Nanook Revisited* contains interviews of Inuit from the areas in which Flaherty filmed and photographed, but it quickly becomes a film about a man portrayed as a kind of latter-day Flaherty, John Johnson, the white school principal. His voice, discussing the erosion of Inuit values, dominates the second half of the film. Unlike Mary, the wife of one of Flaherty's Inuit sons, who responds to the filmmakers' questions about Flaherty and *Nanook* with enigmatic nonanswers, Johnson is eager to explain Inuit culture to the camera. The other Inuit Johnson is shown interacting with in the course of the film—his Inuit hunting partner and an Inuit schoolteacher— are neither named nor interviewed. *Nanook Revisited* is aptly titled: it becomes a film dominated by a white point of view.

80 Intrinsic to political activism over land sovereignty is the issue of image sovereignty, in the eyes of many indigenous nations. In Hawaii, for example, native Hawaiian, or *kanaka maoli*, filmmakers are producing video with the support of such organizations as Pacific Islanders in Communication. See Haunani-Kay Trask, *From a Native Daughter: Colonialism and Sovereignty in Hawai'i* (Monroe, Maine: Common Courage Press, 1993), and Fatimah Tobing Rony, "Image Sovereignty," *Afterimage* 21, no. 7 (February 1994): 4–5; for information on Aboriginal Australian broadcasting, see Faye Ginsburg, "Indigenous Media: Faustian Contract or Global Village?" *Cultural Anthropology* 6 (February 1991): 92–112.

81 Interview with Charlie Adams, 9 February 1996, by the author.

82 Laura U. Marks, "Reconfigured Nationhood: A Partisan History of the Inuit Broadcasting Corporation," *Afterimage* 21, no. 8 (March 1994): 4–7.

83 See Nancy Baele, "Video Award Winners Make Compelling Series on Inuit Life," *Ottawa Citizen*, 25 May 1994.

84 See Stephen Hendrick and Kathleen Fleming, "Zacharias Kunuk: Video Maker and Inuit Historian," *Inuit Art Quarterly* (summer 1991): 25–28.

85 Ibid., 26.

5 Time and Redemption in the "Racial Film" of the 1920s and 1930s

1 Georges Canguilhem, *The Normal and the Pathological*, trans. Carolyn R. Fawcett (New York: Zone Books, 1991), 242.

2 H. G. Wells, *The Time Machine* (Great Britain, 1895; repr., New York: Random House, 1991), 65.

3 Ibid., 39.

4   Johannes Fabian, *Time and the Other: How Anthropology Makes Its Object* (New York: Columbia University Press, 1983), 7.

5   Ibid., 25.

6   Fredric Jameson, "The Existence of Italy," in *Signatures of the Visible* (New York: Routledge, 1992), 186.

7   André Bazin, "The Ontology of the Photographic Image," in *What Is Cinema?* ed. Hugh Gray (Berkeley: University of California Press, 1967), 1:9.

8   Claude Lévi-Strauss, *Tristes Tropiques*, trans. John and Doreen Weightman (New York: Penguin Books, 1992; orig. publ. Paris: Librairie Plon, 1955), 385, 389.

9   "*Stark Love* and *Moana*," unsigned review in *Movie Makers* (November 1928), in *The Documentary Tradition*, ed. Lewis Jacobs (New York: W. W. Norton, 1979), 27.

10 Pierre Leprohon, *L'exotisme et le cinéma* (Paris: J. Susse, 1945), 13. In France, a whole series of "cruise" films appeared with titles reflecting the color coding of the "race" or region of the people visited. One cruise, *La croisière blanche* (The White Cruise; 1923), was an expedition film of Captain Kleinschmidt and his wife in Alaska, Siberia, and other parts of the Arctic. In 1929, Léon Poirier's *La croisière jaune* (The Yellow Cruise) was released, a film of the Citroën-sponsored motor car expedition from Lebanon to Indochina.

11 Leprohon, 64. In *La croisière noire*, Africa is feminized (the camera fetishizes the breasts and buttocks of African women), portrayed as a body to be mapped and crossed over. The image of the uniformed expedition officers motorcading through the deserts, forests, and rivers of colonial Africa clearly was meant to make the heart of any young French child flutter with patriotic pride. The film, praised by Bazin as poetic, is a glorifying tribute to progress, imperialism, colonial expansion, and the motorcar: its stated purpose is to help Africa "evolve" toward "humanity, justice, and happiness." The automobile voyage quickly becomes a collection of stereotyped views: the audience is offered shots of pith-helmeted French officers behind the wheels of their cars; panoramic views of landscape, market, and village scenes; scenes of African dances, sacred rituals, and warriors; and scenes of Frenchmen collecting museum artifacts and hunting wild animals. The various ethnic groups encountered are persistently categorized temporally: the Pygmies of the Belgian Congo are said to be in "the most primitive state of human life," and African Muslims are described as evoking the Crusades and *A Thousand and One Nights*. *La croisière noire* is a tightly organized voyage through time and through Africa: if it is poetry, as Bazin claims, then it is a poetry which celebrates primarily the greatness of France's *mission civilisatrice*, and the exoticism of her colonial subjects as generalized cultural types (André Bazin, "Cinema and Exploration," in *What Is Cinema?* 1:154). Another French expedition film, Marc Allégret and André Gide's *Voyage au Congo: scènes de la vie indigène en Afrique equatoriale* (1926), also is a travelogue highlighting exoticism and the colonial imperative.

    One of the most famous French anthropological expeditions was the Mission Dakar-Djibouti, begun in 1931, in which Marcel Griaule and other anthropologists spent twenty-one months collecting materials and documents for the Trocadéro Ethnographic Museum. A discussion of Griaule's emphasis on documentation rather than on participant observation may be found in James Clifford, "Power and Dialogue in Ethnography: Marcel Griaule's Initiation," in *The Predicament of Culture: Twentieth-century Ethnography, Literature and Art* (Cambridge, Mass.: Harvard University Press, 1988), 55–91. Both of Griaule's films on the Dogon, *Sous les masques noirs* (1938) and *Au pays Dogon* (1938), are similar to other anthropological research films in their emphasis on dancing and other activities like cooking, and on the absence of a sense of the individuality of the peoples filmed. *Sous les masques noirs*, however, has a fascinating montage of Dogon masked dances edited with fast cuts, giving the scene a sense of frenzy.

12   See chapter 3 for more on Franz Boas.

13   David H. Mould and Gerry Veeder, "The 'Photographer-Adventurers': Forgotten Heroes of the Silent Screen," *Journal of Popular Film and Television* 16, no. 3 (1988): 124.

14   Ibid., 125. Mould and Veeder explain that when the popularity of these films began to decrease, they were relegated to "lecture halls, schools, libraries" (126).

15   In his book *Grass*, Cooper explained the importance of cinema to the study of Human Geography, in words reminiscent of Regnault: "In the study of Human Geography the motion picture can and will play an increasingly important part. With the flexible means of expression given by the film, it is possible to record the great natural geographical dramas which go on all over the world, wherever Man contends against Nature in the struggle for existence. . . . When man fights for his life, all the world looks on" (Merian C. Cooper, *Grass* [New York: G. P. Putnam's Sons, 1925], ix).

16   Asen Balikci, "Review of *Grass*," *American Anthropologist* 82, no. 1 (1980): 230.

17   Cooper wrote that Haidar Khan had "gorilla arms," anticipating the use of simian tropes in Cooper and Schoedsack's films (Cooper, 88).

18   Mordaunt Hall, review of *Grass*, *New York Times*, 31 March 1925, 17.

19   In an interview, Cooper explained that *Chang*, unlike *Grass*, was not a documentary but a staged film using natives as actors (John Stag Hanson, "The Man Who Killed King Kong," *Movies International* 1, no. 3 [1966]: 23).

20   Review of *Chang*, *New York Times*, 30 April 1927, 25.

21   Ernest B. Schoedsack, "The Making of an Epic," *American Cinematographer* 64 (February 1983): 113.

22   Leprohon, 116.

23   Review of *Chang*, *New York Times*, 30 April 1927, 25.

24   George W. Stocking Jr., "The Ethnographic Sensibility of the 1920s and the Dualism of the Anthropological Tradition," in *Romantic Motives: Essays on Anthropological Sensibility*, ed. George W. Stocking Jr., *History of Anthropology*, vol. 6 (Madison: University of Wisconsin Press, 1989), 245.

25   Erik Barnouw, *Documentary: A History of the Non-fiction Film* (Oxford: Oxford University Press, 1983), 47.

26   John Grierson, "Flaherty's Poetic *Moana*," in *The Documentary Tradition*, ed. Lewis Jacobs (New York: W. W. Norton, 1979), 25–26. It was not only films that were promoting this romantic image of the sexy South Seas, however, as Mead's work mythologizing the relatively sexually uninhibited Samoan to set in relief the problems of the repressed adolescent of the United States unmistakably attests.

27   Frances Hubbard Flaherty, "The Camera's Eye," in *Spellbound in Darkness: A His-*

tory of the Silent Film, ed. George C. Pratt (Rochester: University of Rochester Press, 1966; repr., Greenwich, Conn.: New York Graphic Society, 1973), 346.

28 Research anthropologists such as Hilton-Simpson and J. A. Haeseler also recommended using long lenses to allow for better voyeurism; see chapter 2.

29 Robert Flaherty, "Filming Real People," *Movie Makers* (December 1934), in *The Documentary Tradition*, ed. Lewis Jacobs (New York: W. W. Norton, 1979), 97–98.

30 *Nanook* and *Moana* were later hailed as "the classics of the ethnographic and sociological film" (Luc de Heusch, *The Cinema and Social Science: A Survey of Ethnographic and Sociological Films*, vol. 16, Reports and Papers in the Social Sciences [Paris: UNESCO, 1962], 39).

31 Grierson, 25.

32 Some of my discussion of *The Silent Enemy* is based on information presented at a panel discussion, "Early Cinema Imagines Native Americans," held at New York University, 31 January 1992. The panelists included Elizabeth Weatherford, Amy Heller, Dennis Doros, Clinton Elliott, and Rosebud Yellow Robe Frantz. See also Donald B. Smith, *Long Lance: The True Story of an Imposter* (Lincoln: University of Nebraska Press, 1982); Kevin Brownlow, *The War, The West, and the Wilderness* (New York: Alfred A. Knopf, 1979); and Elizabeth Weatherford with Emilia Seubert, *Native Americans on Film and Video* (New York: Museum of the American Indian/ Heye Foundation, 1981).

33 Weatherford put forth this insightful observation in the panel discussion mentioned in n. 32.

34 See Bunny McBride, "A Penobscot in Paris," *Down East: The Magazine of Maine* 36, no. 1 (1989): 62–64, 80–84.

35 Fabian, 29–30.

36 Ibid.

37 It was also a film which Flaherty worked on briefly on location in Tahiti in 1927–28 (Barsam, 47). For a survey of films set in the Pacific Islands, see Diane Mei Lin Mark, "The Reel Hawaii," in *Moving the Image: Independent Asian Pacific American Media Arts*, ed. Russell Leong (Los Angeles: UCLA Asian American Studies Center and Visual Communications, 1991), 109–17. See also Ingrid Heermann, *Mythos Tahiti: Südsee—Traum und Realität* (Berlin: Dietrich Reimer Verlag, 1987).

38 Tessel Pollman, "Margaret Mead's Balinese," *Indonesia* 49 (April 1990): 10.

39 Ibid., 1–35.

40 Prof. Dr. Ide Gde Ing. Bagus, quoted in ibid., 15.

41 I Made Kaler, quoted in ibid., 20.

42 I Made Kaler, quoted in ibid., 17.

43 Mead wrote, "One of our most successful films was made when we ordered a group to play in the daytime that ordinarily performed only late at night. . . . The man who made the arrangements decided to substitute young beautiful women for the withered old women who performed at night" (Margaret Mead, *Blackberry Winter: My Earlier Years* [New York: William Morrow, 1972], 252–53.

44 Pollman, 34. One of the best portraits of Mead is Jean Rouch's *Portrait of a Friend* (1978). We see the elderly Margaret Mead represented as intrepid explorer and great mother walking about the American Museum of Natural History as a sort of *emi-*

nence grise. In this film, many of the issues which Johannes Fabian discusses about how anthropology creates a Primitive Other are revealed. For example, the possessiveness of the anthropologists toward "his or her village" is explained by Mead. She describes to Rouch how she went to a congress of anthropologists in 1924, and how everyone there talked about "my people," and how she wanted "my people" too. Visually, this possessive past is displayed in the "Pacific Whole," the modular model villages that can be put on coasters for easy filming. Pointing to one she explains, "This is my village." Mead's comments underline Regnault's ideal, which was to solve the vanishing races problem through archives of film and artifacts. With her studies of personality and psychology, Mead went further, using anthropology to study "culture at a distance" and "national character," e.g., the Balinese are schizophrenic, etc. One particularly popular instance of this kind of anthropology was Ruth Benedict's study of the Japanese character in *The Chrysanthemum and the Sword* (1946).

45 In the United States, *Goona Goona* was not shown in first-run houses, but in theaters known as "arties," and other "subsequent run" houses. The film did well in Europe. See the review of *Goona Goona* by André Roosevelt and Armand Denis in *Variety* (17 September 1932). Another film on Bali as "the last escape from tired machine civilizations," as the *New York Times* reviewer put it, was *Isle of Paradise* directed by Charles Trego ("Island of Bali Shown on Screen," *New York Times*, 21 July 1932: 15).

46 In a Hays Office memorandum of 7 June 1950, the Production Code Administration described how it had eliminated footage from *Tabu* of barebreasted women, nude children, and a section of a dance considered sexually suggestive, because unlike *Moana*, seen as an unscripted instructional film, *Tabu* was thought to be staged: "This picture carries a seal which was granted after extensive cuts, eliminating breast shots from it. The picture was shot in the South Sea Islands and, throughout a great portion of it, there were native women with exposed breasts. It was considered that this particular film did not come within the requirement of the Code on 'natives in their native habitat,' because it is an entertainment film with nothing of the 'travelogue flavor' to it, which seems required by the spirit of the Code provision on this matter. It also appeared as though the director of the picture had not shot it indiscriminately but had very carefully selected the young girls for his cast with obviously handsome breasts. For these basic reasons, the cuts were required when the picture was presented here for a certificate" (File on *Tabu*, Hays Office files, Academy of Motion Picture Arts and Sciences Library, Los Angeles).

47 Charles Jameux, *F. W. Murnau* (Paris: Classiques du cinéma, 1965), 81–90.

48 As Lévi-Strauss himself said, "the primary function of written communication is to facilitate slavery" (Lévi-Strauss, 299).

49 Pollman, 4; Margaret J. Wiener, *Visible and Invisible Realms: Power, Magic, and Colonial Conquest in Bali* (Chicago: University of Chicago Press, 1995), 4, 269. Wiener has written a very interesting study of a similar *puputan* in 1908 which occurred at the capital of Klungkung.

50 André Bazin, "Cinema and Exploration," 1:154–55. Bazin states that in certain genres, and he refers explicitly to films portraying indigenous peoples, the actors themselves can spoil like fruit: "Little Rari [sic] of *Tabu*, they say, ended up as a

prostitute in Poland, and we all know what happens to children raised to stardom by their first film. . . . Indispensable as are the factors of inexperience and naïveté, obviously they cannot survive repetition" (André Bazin, "An Aesthetic of Reality: Neorealism [Cinematic Realism and the Italian School of Liberation]," in *What Is Cinema?*, 2:24).

The perceived fresh innocence of the indigenous actor is thus essential to the Ethnographic genre. Since the native person acting for the first time is installed in a fiction in which, whatever script he or she follows, he or she will be taken to be "real," playing him- or herself; he or she, according to Bazin's logic, does not "survive repetition." Like a child, the indigenous actor is used for his or her freshness, but at best, only once, for the "real" cannot be marketed in a star system.

51   Leprohon, 25.
52   Bazin, "Cinema and Exploration," 1:154–55.
53   See André F. Liotard, Samivel, and Jean Thévenot, *Cinéma d'exploration, cinéma au long cours* (Paris: P.-A. Chavane, 1950), 52–64; André Bazin, "Cinema and Exploration," 1: 154–55.
54   Liotard et al., 57.
55   Donna Haraway, "The Promises of Monsters: A Regenerative Politics for Inappropriate/d Others," in *Cultural Studies*, ed. Lawrence Grossberg, Cary Nelson, and Paula Treichler (New York: Routledge, 1992), 314.

6   King Kong *and the Monster*
in Ethnographic Cinema

1   Quoted in Tristan Renaud, "King-Kong: le roi est nu," *Cinéma* 218 (February 1977): 44.
2   Much of the above information on Ota Benga was communicated to me by Robert Bieder. See also Phillips Verner Bradford and Harvey Blume, *Ota Benga: The Pygmy in the Zoo* (New York: St. Martin's Press, 1992). I thank Robert Bieder for first telling me about Ota Benga.
3   J. P. Telotte, "The Movies as Monster: Seeing in *King Kong*," *Georgia Review* 42, no. 2 (summer 1988): 390.
4   Pierre Leprohon writes that cinema of exoticism "participe à la fois de la science et du rêve. . . . Sa valeur documentaire est élément de connaissance; sa poésie est aliment de rêve" (participates at the same time in science and in dream. . . . Its documentary value is the element of knowledge; its poetry is the food of dream) (Pierre Leprohon, *L'exotisme et le cinéma* [Paris: J. Susse, 1945], 12–13). *Ingagi* (1930), an infamous documentary hoax, used footage from an old Lady McKenzie expedition film and featured the sacrifice of an African woman to a gorilla, a scene staged by actresses in black face at the Selig Zoo (Gerald Peary, "Missing Links: The Jungle Origins of *King Kong*," in *The Girl in the Hairy Paw*, ed. Ronald Gottesman and Harry Geduld [New York: Avon Books, 1976], 41–42).
5   André F. Liotard, Samivel, and Jean Thévenot, *Cinéma d'exploration, cinéma au long cours* (Paris: P.-A. Chavane, 1950), 61.
6   Stephen Bann, *The Clothing of Clio: A Study of the Representation of History in*

Nineteenth-century Britain and France (Cambridge: Cambridge University Press, 1984), 22.

7   Ibid., 23.

8   Georges Canguilhem, *The Normal and the Pathological*, trans. Carolyn R. Fawcett (New York: Zone Books, 1991), 243.

9   Bronislaw Malinowski, *A Diary in the Strict Sense of the Term* (Stanford: Stanford University Press, 1989; orig. publ. 1967), 69.

10 Noël Carroll, *The Philosophy of Horror* (New York: Routledge, 1990), 31–34.

11 George W. Stocking Jr., *Victorian Anthropology* (New York: Free Press, 1987), xv.

12 See chapter 1 for Broca's analogy of the anthropological subject to the patient. Boas advised his student Margaret Mead that the anthropological method is to set "the individual against the [cultural] background"—a method which he compared to "the method that is used by medical men in their analysis of individual cases on which is built up the general picture of the pathological cases that they want to describe." See Margaret Mead Papers at the Library of Congress, Franz Boas to Margaret Mead, 15 February 1926, quoted in George W. Stocking Jr., "The Ethnographic Sensibility of the 1920s and the Dualism of the Anthropological Tradition," in *Romantic Motives: Essays on Anthropological Sensibility*, ed. George W. Stocking Jr., *History of Anthropology*, vol. 6 (Madison: University of Wisconsin Press, 1989), 243.

13 Wilson Martinez, "Critical Studies and Visual Anthropology: Aberrant vs. Anticipated Readings of Ethnographic Film," *CVA Review* (spring 1990): 34–47; Asen Balikci, "Anthropology, Film and the Arctic Peoples," *Anthropology Today* 5, no. 2 (April 1989): 4–10.

14 Jorge Preloran, "Documenting the Human Condition," in *Principles of Visual Anthropology*, ed. Paul Hockings (The Hague: Mouton, 1975), 105.

15 William B. Cohen, *The French Encounter with Africans: White Response to Blacks, 1530–1880* (Bloomington: Indiana University Press, 1980), 234.

16 Claude Lévi-Strauss, *Tristes Tropiques*, trans. John and Doreen Weightman (Paris: Librairie Plon, 1955; repr., New York: Penguin Books, 1981), 371.

17 Stephen Neale, *Genre* (London: British Film Institute, 1980), 21.

18 Carroll, *Philosophy of Horror*, 99.

19 Neale, 22.

20 As Gregg Mitman points out, Komodo dragon behavior is made into spectacle in museum dioramas through the combination of two distinct behavioral traits, both of which appear in Burden's film: the Komodo dragon's dominant head posture and the devouring motion of its jaws (Gregg Mitman, "Cinematic Nature: Hollywood Technology, Popular Culture, and the Science of Animal Behavior, 1925–1940," paper presented at the Society for Cinema Studies Conference, New Orleans, La., 10–11 February 1993). Burden, who also later produced *The Silent Enemy*, founded Marine Studios, Inc., in 1935, another pioneer venture (at least insofar as public spectacle is concerned). It was later renamed Marineland.

21 Carroll, *Philosophy of Horror*, 114.

22 American Museum of Natural History Folder on the Burden East Indies Expedition no. 3: Original Documentation.

23 Douglas Burden, *Dragon Lizards of Komodo: The Expedition to the Lost World of the*

Dutch East Indies (New York, London: G. P. Putnam's Sons, 1927), 103. Indonesian women are portrayed as animal-like, sexy, naughty "creatures" (56, 170–71). See also Burden, "The Quest for the Dragon of Komodo," *Natural History* 27, no. 1 (January–February 1927): 3–18; "Stalking the Dragon Lizard on the Island of Komodo," *National Geographic Magazine* (August 1927): 216–32.

24   See *Dragon Lizards of Komodo*, 40, 180–81, for Burden's characterization of Chu.

25   Ibid., 112.

26   Rudy Behlmer, Foreword to *The Girl in the Hairy Paw*, ed. Ronald Gottesman and Harry Geduld (New York: Avon Books, 1976), 10.

27   Burden, *Dragon Lizards of Komodo*, 90–92.

28   Behlmer, 10.

29   I thank Greg Mitman for this insight.

30   Burden, *Dragon Lizards of Komodo*, 160, 53.

31   Ibid., 57.

32   Claude Beylie, "La chasse du Comte Zaroff: la bête humaine," *L'Avant-scène* 295–96 (1–15 November 1982): 4–5.

33   Thierry Kuntzel, "The Film-Work, 2," *Camera Obscura* 5 (spring 1980): 22.

34   Ibid., 14.

35   I thank Hazel V. Carby for bringing *Island of Lost Souls* to my attention.

36   Zaroff and Moreau, however, are not without their "real life" counterparts: in the nineteenth century, the grave-robbing medical doctor/anthropologist Robert Knox, known for his motto, "Man's gift is to destroy, not to create," was forced to leave Edinburgh because his dissections offended the local populace (Stocking, 64).

37   Telotte, 395.

38   Carroll, *Philosophy of Horror*, 145.

39   Ibid., 182–93, 157.

40   Orville Goldner and George E. Turner, eds., *The Making of King Kong: The Story behind a Film Classic* (South Brunswick, N.J.: A. S. Barnes, 1975), 80.

41   Noël Carroll, "King-Kong: Ape and Essence," in *Planks of Reason: Essays on the Horror Film*, ed. Barry Keith Grant (Metuchen, N.J.: Scarecrow Press, 1984), 228.

42   James Snead, "Spectatorship and Capture in *King Kong*: The Guilty Look," *Critical Quarterly* 33, no. 1 (spring 1991): 58.

43   Stocking, *Victorian Anthropology*, 229–30.

44   Fay Wray, "How Fay Met Kong, or the Scream That Shook the World," *New York Times*, 21 September 1969, D17.

45   Merian C. Cooper, as quoted in George Turner, "Hunting 'The Most Dangerous Game,'" *American Cinematographer* 68 (September 1987): 41–42.

46   Like most films of the genre, however, *Trader Horn* depicts Africans as servile fools, evil cannibals, and bait for hungry crocodiles. Van Dyke uses the iconography of anthropology to good effect in this film: we see African "natives" pounding rice in a reconstruction of a "native village," and, in a scene in which Trader Horn confronts unfriendly Africans, the camera frames the Africans in anthropological head shots, panning from head to head. The homoerotic elements are pronounced: the bond between Trader Horn and the African "gunboy," as Trader Horn calls the solemn, tall Ranchero, is close, and as they are trying to escape the "angry savages," the wounded

Ranchero is carried to safety by Trader Horn. Trader Horn exploits Ranchero as a servant—calling him half-bulldog, half-watchful mother—and has him perform such menial chores as taking out chiggers from Trader Horn's toenails. When Ranchero dies, however, Trader Horn cradles him in his arms. This closeness is reminiscent of Daniel Defoe's *Robinson Crusoe:* Crusoe makes very little mention of his own wife, but devotes pages to the physical appearance of Friday, and goes out of his way to stress that Friday is not really black. (I am indebted to Robert Stam for this insight on *Robinson Crusoe.*)

47   Laura Mulvey, "Visual Pleasure and Narrative Cinema," in *Narrative, Apparatus, Ideology: A Film Theory Reader,* ed. Phil Rosen (New York: Columbia University Press, 1986), 203.

48   The hierarchy of observers watching Ann being filmed reinforces the subordinate position of Charlie: he is the lowest person on the ladder watching. Similarly, when Charlie muses about whether or not Denham might be willing to take his picture, another sailor replies, "Them cameras cost money. Shouldn't think he'd risk it." In light of the fact that, more often than not, Chinese characters were played by whites in Hollywood, this seemingly offhand comment is telling. "China" was a useful marker of time and difference, but not an image to be entrusted to Chinese-American hands.

49   *King Kong* opened at Grauman's Chinese Theater in Los Angeles and shared the bill with an act with a prophesizing fortune-teller: Gin Chow, Chinese philosopher ("Gin Chow at Chinese," *Los Angeles Times,* 1 April 1933).

50   Wray, D17.

51   Leprohon wrote, "Devant l'Asie, on a l'impression d'un mur. On découvre un monde fermé, impénétrable" (Before Asia, one has the impression of a wall. One discovers a closed world, impenetrable) (74).

52   David N. Rosen, "Race, Sex and Rebellion," *Jump Cut* 6 (March–April 1975): 8–10; and Snead, 53–69.

53   Snead, 64–66.

54   The bewilderment Indonesians present to the categories of race is present even today, as may be seen by the fact that V. S. Naipaul refers to Batak writer Sitor Sitomorang as a "Chinese-Negrito" and as "tribal," but never as Batak. See V. S. Naipaul, *Among the Believers: An Islamic Journey* (New York: Alfred A. Knopf, 1981), 305–17.

55   Johnson also played a Chinese in *The Mysterious Dr. Fu Manchu,* a Nubian in *The Mummy,* a Polynesian in *Moby Dick,* a Persian prince in *The Thief of Baghdad,* and a Cuban zombie in *The Ghost Breakers* (Goldner and Turner, 84). For more on Johnson's company, the Lincoln Motion Picture Company which Johnson ran with his brother George, see Donald Bogle, *Toms, Coons, Mulattoes, Mammies, and Bucks: An Interpretive History of Blacks in American Films* (New York: Continuum Publishing, 1991), 103, 110.

56   Michele Wallace, "Variations on Negation and the Heresy of Black Feminist Creativity," in *Invisibility Blues: From Pop to Theory* (London: Verso, 1990), 213–40.

57   Donna Haraway, "The Promises of Monsters: A Regenerative Politics for Inappropriate/d Others," in *Cultural Studies,* ed. Lawrence Grossberg, Cary Nelson, and Paula Treichler (New York: Routledge, 1992), 306–9.

58   Quoted in Gottesman and Geduld, "Introduction," 22.

59   Harold Hellenbrand, "Bigger Thomas Reconsidered: 'Native Son,' Film and 'King Kong,'" *Journal of American Culture* 6, no. 1 (1983): 88. Hellenbrand believes that *Native Son* by Richard Wright is a meditation on the film *King Kong* and racial stereotyping.

60   See, e.g., *Human Apes from the Orient* (American Mutoscope and Biograph, 1906), at the Library of Congress.

61   Peary, "Missing Links," 39–40.

62   See, e.g., D. W. Griffith's *Man's Genesis* (1912) for an example of a Griffith prehistoric film, or *Broken Blossoms* (1919) as an example of a Griffith racial melodrama.

63   Jay Ruby, "A Reexamination of the Early Career of Robert J. Flaherty," *Quarterly Review of Film Studies* 5, no. 4 (fall 1980): 454. Emmett J. Scott's *The Birth of a Race* (1918) was an African American response to *The Birth of a Nation* (Bogle, 102–3).

64   Jean Boullet, "Willis O'Brien, or the Birth of a Film from Design to Still," in *The Girl in the Hairy Paw*, ed. Ronald Gottesman and Harry Geduld (New York: Avon Books, 1976), 107–10.

65   At the time *King Kong* was made, O'Brien was already famous for dinosaur films like *The Dinosaur and the Missing Link* (1916) and *The Lost World* (1925), as well as for his 1930 semidocumentary film about evolution, *Creation* (Joseph E. Sanders, "O'Brien and Monsters from the Id," in *The Scope of the Fantastic—Culture, Biography, Themes, Children's Literature: Selected Essays from the First International Conference on the Fantastic in Literature and Film*, ed. Robert A. Collins and Howard D. Pearce [Westport, Conn.: Greenwood Press, 1985], 11:207–9).

66   Claude Ollier, "A King in New York," in *The Girl in the Hairy Paw*, ed. Ronald Gottesman and Harry Geduld, trans. Roy Huss and T. J. Ross (New York: Avon Books, 1976), 115.

67   Carroll, "King-Kong: Ape and Essence," 217.

68   Ibid., 219–20. Carroll, as well as Terry Heller and Gerald Peary, argue that the jungle of *King Kong* is a metaphor for the capitalist, "eat or be eaten" consumerist economy. Peary also sees Kong as a metaphor for Franklin Delano Roosevelt, a representation of the then newly elected president as a destructive force (Terry Heller, *The Delights of Terror: An Aesthetics of the Tale of Terror* [Urbana: University of Illinois Press, 1987], 46; and Gerald Peary, "The Historicity of *King Kong*," *Jump Cut* 4 [November–December 1974]: 11–12).

69   Judith Mayne argues that the savage force of the environment Kong creates is a metaphor for an image of Manhattan as chaotically destructive. See "'King Kong' and the Ideology of Spectacle," *Quarterly Review of Film Studies* 1, no. 4 (November 1976): 373–87.

70   The "entertainment of violated boundaries" occurs when elements constructed as inherent opposites—nature and society, the Primitive and the Modern—are juxtaposed. Haraway writes that the Kayapó with the camera is no longer "an entertaining contradiction," if one no longer conceives of the world as a polarized realm between nature and society. She continues, "Where there is no nature or society, there is no pleasure, no entertainment to be had in representing the violation of the boundary between them" (Haraway, *The Promises of Monsters*, 314).

71 Indeed, King Kong has become a sort of national monster fetish, everywhere reproduced and adored: King Kong names a ride in the MGM tourist park as well as a
recent sculpture on the Empire State Building. Kong is its own perfect Ethnographic
simulacrum, or, as Jean Baudrillard would say, an instance of the "hyperreal" (Jean
Baudrillard, "The Precession of Simulacra," in *Simulations*, trans. Paul Foss, Paul
Patton, and Philip Beitchman [New York: Semiotext(e), 1983], 25).

72 Jean Lévy, "King-Kong," *Minotaure* 5 (1934): 5.

73 Ibid.

74 Theodor W. Adorno, "Looking Back on Surrealism," in *The Idea of the Modern in
Literature and the Arts*, ed. Irving Howe, trans. S. P. Dunn and Ethel Dunn (New
York: Horizon Press, 1967), 220–24.

75 Perhaps another reason for the attention paid to *King Kong* by the surrealists is the
film's status as a lowbrow Hollywood production. The same sensibility led Joseph
Cornell to make *Rose Hobart* (1936), a film constructed from snippets of footage
taken from the exotic Hollywood film *East of Borneo* (1931), and led Michel Leiris to
praise *Fox Follies* (1929) as a spectacle which did not have "the slightest hint of an
aesthetic," a film which was "all popular, wonderfully cheap" (Michel Leiris, "Fox
Movietone Follies of 1929," *Documents* 1, no. 7 [December 1929], repr., *October* 60
[spring 1992], trans. Dominic Faccini: 43–46). As Ado Kyrou recommends in *Le
surréalisme au cinéma*, "The best and most exciting films [are] the films shown in
local fleapits, films which seem to have no place in the history of cinema. . . . Learn to
go see the 'worst' films; they are sometimes sublime" (cited in J. Hoberman, "Bad
Movies," in *Vulgar Modernism* [Philadelphia: Temple University Press, 1991], 13).
To praise a film like *King Kong* was to defy good taste, to embrace the common, and
to experience the sublime and oneiric in popular culture rather than in high art
venues.

76 Lévy, 5. Joseph E. Sanders saw Kong as "a monster from the Id" (214). William Grimes
sees the film as a metaphor for "repressed sexual drive." See William Grimes, "Buried
Themes: Psychoanalyzing Movies," *New York Times*, 23 December 1991, C11.

77 James Clifford, "On Ethnographic Surrealism," in *The Predicament of Culture:
Twentieth-century Ethnography, Literature, and Art* (Cambridge, Mass.: Harvard
University Press, 1988), 119.

78 Ibid., 120.

79 "King Kong," *Films in Review* (June 1975): 61. Cooper was anti-Communist and a
war fanatic; he later became the president of Pan American Airlines. For *King Kong*,
Cooper and Schoedsack arranged to borrow four planes from the U.S. Navy, and
twenty-eight different scenes in the film include footage of actual aircraft maneu-
vers. See Lawrence Suid, "King Kong and the Military," *American Classic Screen*
(July–August 1977): 14–16.

80 John Seelye, "Moby-Kong," *College Literature* 17, no. 1 (1990): 39.

81 See earlier discussion in this chapter at n. 30.

82 Lothrop Stoddard, *The Revolt against Civilization: The Menace of the Under Man*
(New York: Charles Scribner's Sons, 1923), 5–6.

83 It is interesting to note that the term so reminiscent of King Kong—the "Viet Cong"—
was not invented by the Vietnamese themselves, but by the Rand Corporation.

84   See Baudrillard, "The Precession of Simulacra," 1–80.

85   Elizabeth Alexander, *The Venus Hottentot*, The Callaloo Poetry Series, vol. 9, ed. Charles H. Rowell (Charlottesville: University Press of Virginia, 1990), 6–7.

86   Another writer who explores the voice of the African American woman exploited by anthropology is Toni Morrison, whose protagonist in *Beloved* (New York: Signet, 1991), is physically studied by anthropologists as a slave. Another writer who has explored the subjectivities of the person being filmed or studied by whites without their permission is Toni Cade Bambara in her wonderful short story "Blues Ain't No Mocking Bird," in *Gorilla, My Love* (New York: 1961; repr., Vintage Books, 1981), 127–36, which describes the response of a black family to being filmed by documentary filmmakers without their permission.

87   Reactions to the shows were often troubled and confused, relates Fusco. At Irvine, some people thought they were "real" Aborigines and became upset, or were troubled at the sight of humans in a cage. Also, many brought little gifts and food to them (Kim Sawchuk, "Unleashing the Demons of History: An Interview with Coco Fusco and Guillermo Gómez-Peña," *Parachute* 67 [September 1992]: 24).

Fusco relates that in Europe "people's behavior regressed": in England, some Englishmen made gorilla noises to them, in Spain many spectators were verbally aggressive, and Latin American tourists worried about the "negative images" of Latin America that they were portraying (C. Carr, "Is It Real or Is It . . . ? Identity and the Eye of the Beholder," *LA Weekly* (3 July–9 July 1992).

88   Gómez-Peña, quoted in Sawchuk, 25.

Conclusion

1   *The Passion of Remembrance* is the title of a 1986 film by Isaac Julien and Maureen Blackwood who were part of the black British film collective Sankofa. This film is one of many recent media works which have exploded "race" as a fixed, stable category, creating new vocabularies for confronting the politics of race and identity, as well as gender, sexuality, and desire.

2   James Baldwin and Margaret Mead, *A Rap on Race* (New York: Dell, 1971), 189.

3   Ibid., 157.

4   Ibid., 174.

5   Ibid., 187.

6   Ibid., 190.

7   Frantz Fanon, *Black Skin White Masks: The Experiences of a Black Man in a White World*, trans. Charles Lam Markmann (New York: Grove Press, 1967), 112.

8   Baldwin and Mead, 208.

9   See, e.g., David MacDougall, "Beyond Observational Cinema," in *Principles of Visual Anthropology*, ed. Paul Hockings (New York: Mouton, 1975), 109–24.

10   The effects of anthropology's "crisis" are reflected in the career trajectory of ethnographic filmmaker John Marshall. Marshall's classic *The Hunters* (1956) depicts the Ju/'hoansi people of Nyae Nyae in southern Africa (categorized as "Bushmen") as happy, isolated, pastoralist hunter-gatherers, and ignores the fact that the Ju/'hoansi

people have had contacts with other outside groups for centuries. Like *Nanook of the North, The Hunters* gives center stage to the importance of the all-male hunt. Bill Nichols has called this macho, Ernest Hemingway–style preoccupation in the works of Flaherty, Rouch, and others the "bullfight syndrome" (Bill Nichols, *Ideology and the Image: Social Representation in the Cinema and Other Media* [Bloomington: Indiana University Press, 1981], 275). Marshall himself, however, later repudiated *The Hunters* when he became aware that the film and related commercial films such as Jamie Uys's *The Gods Must Be Crazy* (1980) were being used by the South African and Namibian governments to justify the land dispossession of Ju/'hoansi people. As Tsamkxao#Oma, a Ju/'hoansi man, has explained, there are two kinds of cinema: "[One shows the Ju/'hoansi as] people like other people, who have things to do and plans to make. This kind helps us. The other kind shows us as if we were animals, and plays right into the hands of people who want to take our land" (Megan Biesele, "Reclaiming a Cultural Legacy: The Ju/'hoansi of Namibia," *Aperture* 119 [1990]: 50). Marshall attempted to correct the myths that he himself helped propagate in *The Hunters* in his later film *N!ai, The Story of a !Kung Woman* (1978), believed to be among the first ethnographic films to portray indigenous peoples as historical beings living in the present, and in his advocacy videos for the Ju/'hoansi which protest their relegation to "homelands" (reservations), the taking of their lands, their lack of political rights, and their great poverty and despair (Toby Alice Volkman, "The Hunter-gatherer Myth in Southern Africa: Preserving Nature or Culture?" *Cultural Survival* 10, no. 2 [1986]: 25–32).

11   Some have argued that Sol Worth and John Adair's project in the 1960s to study films made by Navajos initiated this trend, but Worth and Adair's "experiment" was in keeping with the classic anthropological method of using visual media to understand indigenous thought, just as Mead, for example, had earlier used stills from Flaherty's *Moana* to try to elicit information from Samoans in her 1920s fieldwork (Margaret Mead, *Blackberry Winter: My Earlier Years* [New York: William Morrow, 1972], 154). There is no acknowledgement of the political and ethical necessity of image sovereignty.

   Timothy Asch, who made ethnographic films among the Yanomami in the 1960s and 1970s, has recently written that it never occurred to him to give the camera to the Yanomami when he first began to make ethnographic films, but he has since reflected that films and video by the Yanomami would provide more accurate records of contemporary Yanomami life. Interestingly, Asch asserts that ethnographic films by indigenous peoples are likely to be of greater scientific value than films by anthropologists (Timothy Asch et al., "The Story We Now Want to Hear Is Not Ours to Tell: Relinquishing Control over Representation: Toward Sharing Visual Communication Skills with the Yanomami," *Visual Anthropology Review* 7, no. 2 [fall 1991]: 102–6).

12   Jay Ruby, "Exposing Yourself: Reflexivity, Anthropology and Film," *Semiotica* 30, nos. 1–2 (1980): 153–79.

13   Ward Churchill, *Fantasies of the Master Race: Literature, Cinema and the Colonization of American Indians*, ed. M. Annette Jaimes (Monroe, Maine: Common Courage Press, 1992), 245–46.

14   Ibid., 246.

15   Phyllis Rose discusses a number of the different interpretations of Baker in *Jazz Cleopatra: Josephine Baker in Her Time* (New York: Vintage Books, 1989).

16   "Candide," quoted in Josephine Baker and Jo Bouillon, *Josephine*, trans. Mariana Fitzpatrick (New York: Paragon House, 1988), 55.

17   Ibid., 88, 101.

18   Baker was even nominated the Queen of the Colonial Exposition in 1931, a nomination from which she had to withdraw because she was not French. In one act, Baker crooned to a white Arctic explorer, "Sail with me on a snow-white ship / To undiscovered seas" (ibid., 108). Baker also performed at the Folies-Bergère as the "native woman" Fatou who falls in love with a white colonialist (Rose, 23).

19   Baker and Bouillon, 84.

20   Ibid., 55.

21   Janet Flanner, *Paris Was Yesterday: 1925–1939* (New York: Viking, 1972), 72–73, quoted in Rose, 151–52.

22   Homi Bhabha, "The Other Question: Difference, Discrimination and the Discourse of Colonialism," in *Out There: Marginalization and Contemporary Cultures*, ed. Russell Ferguson et al. (New York and Cambridge, Mass.: New Museum of Contemporary Art and Massachusetts Institute of Technology, 1990), 85.

23   Ibid., 84.

24   Remarque, quoted in Baker and Bouillon, 86.

25   Michele Wallace, "Modernism, Postmodernism and the Problem of the Visual in Afro-American Culture," in *Out There: Marginalization and Contemporary Cultures*, ed. Russell Ferguson et al. (New York and Cambridge, Mass.: New Museum of Contemporary Art and Massachusetts Institute of Technology, 1990), 45.

26   Zora Neale Hurston, *Dust Tracks on a Road: An Autobiography* (Urbana: The University of Illinois Press, 1984), 174.

27   Zora Neale Hurston, *Mules and Men* (New York: Harper Perennial, 1990), 1.

28   Hazel V. Carby, "The Politics of Fiction, Anthropology, and the Folk: Zora Neale Hurston," in *New Essays on Their Eyes Were Watching God*, ed. Michael Awkward (Cambridge: Cambridge University Press, 1990), 79.

29   On Boas's study of isolable body movements using film, see Jay Ruby, "Franz Boas and Early Camera Study of Behavior," *Kinesis* 3, no. 1 (fall 1980): 6–11, 16.

30   Elaine S. Charnov, "Zora Neale Hurston: A Pioneer in Visual Anthropology," (paper given at the Second Annual Zora Neale Hurston Festival of the Arts and Humanities, Eatonville, Florida, 1991). I am indebted to Charnov for introducing me to this body of work.

31   Robert E. Hemenway, *Zora Neale Hurston: A Literary Biography* (Urbana and Chicago: University of Illinois Press, 1977), 111, 118.

32   Ibid., 120–22.

33   Ibid., 122.

34   Ibid., 116.

35   Ibid., 115, as quoted from Zora Neale Hurston to Langston Hughes, April 12, 1928 (James Weldon Johnson Collection, Yale); "The Florida Expedition" (typescript, American Philosophical Society Library).

36   Quoted from Sally McDougall, "Author Plans to Upbraid Own Race," *New York World Telegram*, 6 February 1935.

37   At one point in her notes Belo compares a young African American man "in trance" with the Balinese. (Jane Belo, "Notes on a Meeting on Sunday night at the Sanctified Elected Church, Beaufort, April 7, 1940," manuscript in the Margaret Mead Collection, Manuscript Division, Library of Congress, 9 April 1940).

38   Among the recordings made were the study of religious ecstasy patterns among a Baptist congregation in Beaufort; the recording of songs at Yamacraw Village in Savannah, Georgia to study how pornography in song and story developed; and singing by fish cannery workers on an island near Beaufort as well as a Baptist church in Savannah for comparison with the Commandment Keeper Church in Beaufort. (Letter of March 20, 1975 from Norman Chalfin to Joyce Aschenbrenner in the Margaret Mead Collection, Manuscript Division, Library of Congress.)

39   Zora Neale Hurston, "Ritualistic Expression From the Lips of the Communicants of the Seventh Day Church of God, Beaufort, South Carolina," manuscript in the Margaret Mead Collection, Manuscript Division, Library of Congress. See also Zora Neale Hurston, *The Sanctified Church: The Folklore Writings of Zora Neale Hurston*, (Berkeley: Turtle Island, 1981).

40   Zora Neale Hurston, "Ritualistic Expression From the Lips of the Communicants of the Seventh Day Church of God, Beaufort, South Carolina," manuscript in the Margaret Mead Collection, Manuscript Division, Library of Congress.

41   Zora Neale Hurston, untitled manuscript in the Margaret Mead Collection, Manuscript Division, Library of Congress.

42   Ibid.

43   Ibid.

44   Interview of Zora Neale Hurston by Alan Lomax as quoted in Hemenway, 168.

45   Zora Neale Hurston, letter to Jane Belo, May 2, 1940. Manuscript in the Margaret Mead Collection, Manuscript Division, Library of Congress.

46   Interview with Norman Chalfen, 14 September 1995, by the author.

47   Zora Neale Hurston, "Ritualistic Expression From the Lips of the Communicants of the Seventh Day Church of God, Beaufort, South Carolina," manuscript in the Margaret Mead Collection, Manuscript Division, Library of Congress.

48   These films of 1940 appear to be Hurston's last. In 1944, Hurston was not successful in her attempt to request from Jane Belo the use of a motion picture camera for her trip to Honduras. In her letter to Belo, she wrote, "Together we can do something that will make Dr. Margaret Meade's [sic] 'SAMOA' look like the report of the W.C.T.U." Letter from Zora Neale Hurston to Jane Belo, October 1, 1944, Margaret Mead Collection, Manuscript Division, Library of Congress.

49   Hurston, *Mules and Men*, 2.

50   Like Hurston, Dunham violated the boundaries of Primitive versus Civilized in her work and in her persona. In 1935–36, Dunham was encouraged by her mentor, anthropologist and former Boas student Melville Herskovits at the University of Chicago, to take photographs and films of Afro-Caribbean dance. Dunham's films are strictly research films in the Boasian tradition: her films of dances, shot from a distance, were meant to provide positivist records of the motor behavior of particular

cultural groups. There is little in her film work to suggest the kind of deconstructive self-reflexivity at times present in Hurston's films. However, as a dancer, choreographer, scholar, and teacher of both dance and anthropology, Dunham has provided, as Hurston did through her innovative writings, a space for a new kind of ethnography, one which she has termed "dance anthropology." Yet, as Joyce Aschenbrenner points out, Dunham could not escape the racializing criticism of white media critics. She was stereotyped like Josephine Baker as the sexy African queen. But some also referred to her as a combination of Margaret Mead and Mae West, an impersonator of a female impersonator (Joyce Aschenbrenner, *Katherine Dunham: Reflections on the Social and Political Contexts of Afro-American Dance*, Dance Research Annual 12 [New York: Congress on Research in Dance, 1981], 58). Dunham herself was perceived by dominant society as a "primitive," and her own work was labeled "primitive" dance (Aschenbrenner, 49–50). I am indebted to VéVé Clark, who lectured on Katherine Dunham's films at Yale University on 4 October 1989, for drawing my attention to this body of work.

51 Zora Neale Hurston, "What White Publishers Won't Print," in *I Love Myself When I Am Laughing . . . And Then Again When I Am Looking Mean and Impressive*, ed. Alice Walker (Old Westbury, N.Y.: Feminist Press, 1979), 170. Trinh T. Minh-ha has an interesting essay on Zora Neale Hurston. See "Outside in Inside out," in *Questions of Third Cinema*, ed. Jim Pines and Paul Willeman (London: British Film Institute, 1989), 133–49.

52 Hurston, *Mules and Men*, 245–46. See also Barbara Johnson, "Thresholds of Difference: Structures of Address in Zora Neale Hurston," in *"Race," Writing, and Difference* (Chicago: University of Chicago Press, 1986), 317–28. I agree with Johnson's reading of the conclusion of *Mules and Men* as a sly, deconstructive positioning of Hurston as anthropologist and as woman of color.

53 Conversation with Mugambi, 13 June 1995.

54 See Sol Worth and John Adair, *Through Navajo Eyes: An Exploration in Film Communication and Anthropology* (Bloomington: Indiana University Press, 1972), 157–60. The awkwardness of the Tsosie sisters reveals the gaps caused by cultural disruption, an awkwardness which anticipates Navajo filmmaker Arlene Bowman's film about her grandmother, *Navajo Talking Picture* (1986). Bowman, whose mother like the Tsosie had been sent to boarding school, was raised in Phoenix and only spoke English when she went to film her grandmother on the reservation.

55 Victor Masayesva Jr., "Kwikwilyaqa: Hopi Photography," in *Hopi Photographers/ Hopi Images*, ed. Victor Masayesva Jr. and Erin Younger, *Sun Tracks: An American Indian Literary Series*, vol. 8 (Tucson: University of Arizona Press, 1984), 10.

56 See, e.g., Dean Curtis Bear Claw's *Warrior Chiefs in a New Age* (1990), Gary Rhine and Fidel Moreno's *Wiping the Tears of Seven Generations* (1990), and Diane Reyna and Edward Ladd's *Surviving Columbus* (1992), all of which include film footage and photography by Euro-Americans such as Curtis and Joseph Dixon, but with the express aim of providing alternate readings.

57 Victor Masayesva Jr., lecture at the Walker Art Center, Minneapolis, Minn., 28 October 1994.

BIBLIOGRAPHY

"Le pied préhensile chez les aliénés et les criminels." *La nature* 1065 (28 October 1893): 339.

"Un village nègre au Champ de Mars." *L'illustration* 2729 (15 June 1895): 508.

Abu-Lughod, Lila. "Can There Be a Feminist Ethnography?" *Women & Performance: A Journal of Feminist Theory* 5, no. 1, Issue #9 (1990): 7–27.

Adorno, Theodor W. "Looking Back on Surrealism." In *The Idea of the Modern in Literature and the Arts*, ed. Irving Howe, 220–24. New York: Horizon Press, 1967.

Alexander, Caroline. "The White Goddess of the Wangora."*New Yorker* (8 April 1991): 43–76.

Alexander, Edward P. *Museums in Motion: An Introduction to the History and Functions of Museums.* Nashville: American Association for State and Local History, 1979.

Alexander, Elizabeth. *The Venus Hottentot.* Callaloo Poetry Series, ed. Charles H. Rowell. Charlottesville: University Press of Virginia, 1990.

Ames, Michael. *Museums, the Public, and Anthropology: A Study in the Anthropology of Anthropology.* Vancouver: University of British Columbia Press, 1986.

Anderson, Benedict. *Imagined Communities: Reflections on the Origin and Spread of Nationalism.* London: Verso, 1983.

Armes, Roy. *Third World Filmmaking and the West.* Berkeley: University of California Press, 1987.

Asch, Timothy, Jesus Ignacio Cardozo, Hortensia Cabellero, and Jose Bortoli. "The Story We Now Want to Hear Is Not Ours to Tell: Relinquishing Control over Representation: Toward Sharing Visual Communication Skills with the Yanomami." *Visual Anthropology Review* 7, no. 2 (fall 1991): 102–6.

Aschenbrenner, Joyce. *Katherine Dunham: Reflections on the Social and Political Contexts of Afro-American Dance.* Dance Research Annual 12. New York: Congress on Research in Dance, 1981.

Astre, Gaston. *Le Muséum d'histoire naturelle de Toulouse: son histoire.* Toulouse: Muséum d'histoire naturelle de Toulouse, 1949.

Azoulay, Léon. "Considérations physiologiques et psychologiques sur l'homme insoulevable." *Revue de pathologie comparée* (12 April 1921): 163–68.

———. "L'ére nouvelle des sons et des bruits: musées et archives phonographiques." *Bulletins de la Société d'anthropologie de Paris* 1st tome, 5th ser. (3 May 1900): 172–78.

———. "Liste des phonogrammes composant le musée phonographique de la Société d'anthropologie." *Bulletins de la Société d'anthropologie de Paris* 3d tome, 5th ser. (1902): 652–56.

Baele, Nancy. "Video Award Winners Make Compelling Series on Inuit Life." *Ottawa Citizen,* 25 May 1994.

Baker, Josephine, and Jo Bouillon. *Josephine.* Translated by Mariana Fitzpatrick. New York: Paragon House, [1977] 1988.

Baldwin, James. *The Price of the Ticket: Collected Nonfiction 1948–1985.* New York: St. Martin's/Marek, 1985.

Baldwin, James, and Margaret Mead. *A Rap on Race.* New York: Dell, 1971.

Balibar, Etienne. "Is There a 'Neo-Racism'?" In *Race, Nation, Class: Ambiguous Identities,* ed. Etienne Balibar and Immanuel Wallerstein, 17–28. London: Verso, 1991.

Balikci, Asen. "Anthropology, Film and the Arctic Peoples." *Anthropology Today* 5, no. 2 (April 1989): 4–10.

———. "Reconstructing Cultures on Film." In *Principles of Visual Anthropology,* ed. Paul Hockings, 191–200. The Hague: Mouton, 1975.

———. "Review of *Grass.*" *American Anthropologist* 82, no. 1 (1980): 229–30.

———. "Visual Anthropology: The Legacy of Margaret Mead." Paper presented at the annual meeting of the American Anthropological Association, Commission on Visual Anthropology, 1985.

Balikci, Asen, and Quentin Brown. *Ethnographic Filming and the Netsilik Eskimos.* Educational Services Incorporated Quarterly Report, 1966.

Bambara, Toni Cade. "Blues Ain't No Mocking Bird." In *Gorilla, My Love,* 127–36. New York: Random House, 1972; reprint, Vintage Books, 1981.

Bann, Stephen. *The Clothing of Clio: A Study of the Representation of History in Nineteenth-century Britain and France.* Cambridge: Cambridge University Press, 1984.

Banta, Melissa, and Curtis M Hinsley. *From Site to Sight: Anthropology, Photography, and the Power of Imagery.* Cambridge, Mass.: Peabody Museum Press, 1986.

Barnouw, Erik. *Documentary: A History of the Non-Fiction Film.* Oxford: Oxford University Press, 1983.

Barsam, Richard. *The Vision of Robert Flaherty: The Artist as Myth and Filmmaker.* Bloomington: Indiana University Press, 1988.

Barthes, Roland. *Camera Lucida: Reflections on Photography.* Translated by Richard Howard. New York: Hill and Wang, 1981.

Baudrillard, Jean. *Simulations.* Translated by Paul Foss, Paul Palton, and Philip Beitchman. New York: Semiotext(e), 1983.

Bazin, André. *What Is Cinema?* Ed. Hugh Gray. 2 vols. Berkeley: University of California Press, 1967, 1971.

Beausoleil, Jeanne. "Au service d'un idéal de compréhension internationale: les opérateurs d'Albert Kahn dans le monde." In *Le cinéma français muet dans le monde, influences réciproques: Symposium de la FIAF,* 61–69. Paris: Cinémathèque de Toulouse–Institut Jean Vigo, 1988.

———. "La planète d'Albert Kahn." *Les nouvelles littéraires* 56th year, no. 2658 (12–19 October 1978): 11.

Beausoleil, Jeanne, and Catherine Fortassier. " 'Les archives de la planète' d'Albert Kahn." *Prestige de la photographie* 3 (December 1977): 40–65.

Behlmer, Rudy. Foreword to *The Girl in the Hairy Paw*, ed. Ronald Gottesman and Harry Geduld, vi–xi. New York: Avon Books, 1976.

Belin, Esther G. "Surviving in This Place Called the United States." In *Moving the Image: Independent Asian Pacific American Media Arts*, ed. Russell Leong, 245–47. Los Angeles: UCLA Asian American Studies Center and Visual Communications, Southern Californian Asian American Studies Central, 1991.

Bender, Donald. "The Development of French Anthropology." *Journal of the History of the Behavioral Sciences* 1 (2 April 1965): 139–51.

Benjamin, Walter. *Charles Baudelaire: A Lyric Poet in the Era of High Capitalism*. Translated by Harry Zohn. London: Verso, 1983.

——. "The Work of Art in the Age of Mechanical Reproduction." In *Illuminations: Essays and Reflections*, trans. Harry Zohn. New York: Schocken Books, 1969.

Bennett, Tony. "Museums and 'the People.' " In *The New Museology*, ed. Peter Vergo, 63–85. London: Redaktion Books, 1989.

Berillon. "La fixité des races humaines et la loi de retour au type primitif." *Revue de pathologie comparée* (11 November 1919): 267–74.

Beylie, Claude. "La chasse du Comte Zaroff: la bête humaine." *L'avant-scène* 295–96 (1–15 November 1982): 4–6.

Bhabha, Homi. "The Other Question: Difference, Discrimination and the Discourse of Colonialism." In *Out There: Marginalization and Contemporary Cultures*, ed. Russell Ferguson, Martha Gever, Trinh T. Minh-ha, and Cornel West, 71–88. New York and Cambridge, Mass.: New Museum of Contemporary Art and Massachusetts Institute of Technology, 1990.

——. "The Other Question: Homi K. Bhabha Reconsiders the Stereotype and Colonial Discourse." *Screen* 24, no. 6 (November–December 1983): 18–36.

——. "Signs Taken for Wonders: Questions of Ambivalence and Authority under a Tree outside Delhi, May 1817." In *"Race," Writing and Difference*, ed. Henry Louis Gates Jr., 163–84. Chicago: University of Chicago Press, 1986.

Biesele, Megan. "Reclaiming a Cultural Legacy: The Ju/'hoansi of Namibia." *Aperture* 119 (1990): 50–57.

Bilby, Julian W., F.R.G.S. *Nanook of the North: The Story of an Eskimo Family*. New York: Dodd, Mead, 1926.

Blanckaert, Claude. "On the Origins of French Ethnology: William Edwards and the Doctrine of Race." In *Bones, Bodies, Behavior: Essays on Biological Anthropology*, ed. George W. Stocking Jr., *History of Anthropology*, vol. 5, 18–55. Madison: University of Wisconsin Press, 1988.

Blet, Henri. *Histoire de la colonisation française*. 3 vols. Paris: Arthaud, 1946–50.

Bloom, Lisa. *Gender on Ice: American Ideologies of Polar Expeditions*. Minneapolis: University of Minnesota Press, 1993.

Boas, Franz. *The Mind of Primitive Man*. New York: Macmillan, 1911.

Bocquet-Appel, Jean-Pierre. "L'anthropologie physique en France et ses origines institutionnelles." *Gradhiva* 6 (summer 1989): 23–34.

Bogle, Donald. *Toms, Coons, Mulattoes, Mammies, and Bucks: An Interpretive History of Blacks in American Films.* New York: Continuum Publishing, 1991.

Boullet, Jean. "Willis O'Brien, or the Birth of a Film from Design to Still." In *The Girl in the Hairy Paw,* ed. Ronald Gottesman and Harry Geduld, 27–49. New York: Avon Books, 1976.

Bradford, Phillips Verner, and Harvey Blume. *Ota Benga: The Pygmy in the Zoo.* New York: St. Martin's Press, 1992.

Braun, Marta. "The Photographic Work of E.-J. Marey." *Studies in Visual Communication* 9, no. 4 (fall 1983): 2–23.

———. *Picturing Time: The Work of Etienne-Jules Marey (1830–1904).* Chicago: University of Chicago Press, 1992.

British Museum. *British Museum: Handbook to the Ethnographical Collections.* 2d ed. London: Trustees of the British Museum, 1925.

Broca, Paul. "Sur les proportions relatives des membres supérieurs et des membres inférieurs chez les nègres et les Européens." *Bulletins de la Société d'anthropologie de Paris* (1867): 641–53.

Brooklyn Museum. Museum of Art at the Carnegie Institute, and Buffalo Bill Historical Center. *Buffalo Bill and the Wild West.* Brooklyn: Brooklyn Museum, 1981.

Brownlow, Kevin. *The War, The West, and the Wilderness.* New York: Alfred A. Knopf, 1979.

Burden, Douglas. *Dragon Lizards of Komodo: The Expedition to the Lost World of the Dutch East Indies.* New York: G. P. Putnam's Sons, 1927.

———. "The Quest for the Dragon of Komodo." *Natural History* 27, no. 1 (January–February 1927): 3–18.

———. "Stalking the Dragon Lizard on the Island of Komodo." *National Geographic Magazine* (August 1927): 216–32.

Calder-Marshall, Arthur. *The Innocent Eye: The Life of Robert J. Flaherty.* New York: Harcourt, Brace & World, 1963.

Canguilhem, Georges. *The Normal and the Pathological.* Translated by Carolyn R. Fawcett. New York: Zone Books, 1991.

Cantrill, Arthur, and Corinne Cantrill. "The 1901 Cinematography of Walter Baldwin Spencer." *Cantrill's Filmnotes* 37–38 (April 1982): 26–42, 56.

Canudo, Ricciotto. "Another View of *Nanook of the North*." In *The Documentary Tradition,* ed. Lewis Jacobs, 20–21. New York: W. W. Norton, 1979.

Capitan. "Présentation: à propos des déformations crâniennes dans l'art antique." *Bulletins de la Société d'anthropologie de Paris* 6th tome, 4th ser. (3 January 1895): 9–12.

Carby, Hazel V. "The Politics of Fiction, Anthropology, and the Folk: Zora Neale Hurston." In *New Essays on Their Eyes Were Watching God,* ed. Michael Awkward, 71–93. Cambridge: Cambridge University Press, 1990.

Carr, C. "Is it Real or Is It . . . ? Identity and the Eye of the Beholder." *LA Weekly* (3 July–9 July 1992): 37.

Carroll, Noël. "King-Kong: Ape and Essence." In *Planks of Reason: Essays on the Horror Film,* ed. Barry Keith Grant, 215–44. Metuchen, N.J.: Scarecrow, 1984.

———. *The Philosophy of Horror.* New York: Routledge, 1990.

Cartwright, Lisa. "Science and the Film Avant-Garde." *Cinematograph* 4 (1991): 11–20.

——. *Screening the Body: Tracing Medicine's Visual Culture*. Minneapolis: University of Minnesota Press, 1995.

Catalog. Exhibition, *La tour Eiffel*. Paris: Musée d'Orsay, 1989.

Chapman, William Ryan. "Arranging Ethnology: A. H. L. F. Pitt Rivers and the Typological Tradition." In *Objects and Others: Essays on Museums and Material Culture*, ed. George W. Stocking Jr., *History of Anthropology*, vol. 3, 3–9. Madison: University of Wisconsin Press, 1985.

Charcot, J. M., and Paul Richer. *Les difformes et les malades dans l'art*. Paris: Lecrosnier et Babé, 1889.

Charnov, Elaine S. "Zora Neale Hurston: A Pioneer in Visual Anthropology." Paper given at the Second Annual Zora Neale Hurston Festival of Arts and Humanities in Eatonville, Fla., 1991.

Chiozzi, Paolo. "Reflections on Ethnographic Film with a General Bibliography." *Visual Anthropology* 2 (1989): 1–84.

——. "What Is Ethnographic Film? Remarks about a Debate." *SVA Review* 6, no. 1 (spring 1990): 26–28.

Churchill, Ward. *Fantasies of the Master Race: Literature, Cinema and the Colonization of American Indians*, ed. M. Annette Jaimes. Monroe, Maine: Common Courage Press, 1992.

Clifford, James. *The Predicament of Culture: Twentieth-century Ethnography, Literature, and Art*. Cambridge, Mass.: Harvard University Press, 1988.

Clifford, James, and George Marcus, eds. *Writing Culture*. Berkeley: University of California Press, 1986.

Cohen, William B. *The French Encounter with Africans: White Response to Blacks, 1530–1880*. Bloomington: Indiana University Press, 1980.

Comte, Charles, and Félix Regnault. "Étude comparative entre la méthode de marche et de course dite de flexion et les allures ordinaires (Travail exécuté à la station physiologique, laboratoire du Collège de France)." *Archives de physiologies normale et pathologiques* 28th year (April 1896): 380–89.

——. "Marche et course en flexion." *Bulletins de la Société d'anthropologie de Paris* 7th tome, 4th ser. (7 May 1896): 337–41.

Comte, Charles, Félix Regnault, and presented by M. Marey. "Note." *Comptes rendus hebdomadaires des séances de l'Académie des sciences* 122 (February 1896): 401–4.

Conolly, J. *The Ethnological Exhibitions of London*. London: n.p., 1855.

Conrad, Joseph. *Heart of Darkness*. New York: Doubleday, 1950; orig. publ. 1903.

Cooper, Merian C. *Grass*. New York: G. P. Putnam's Sons, 1925.

Corliss, Richard. "Robert Flaherty: The Man in the Iron Myth." In *Nonfiction Film Theory and Criticism*, ed. Richard Meran Barsam, 230–38. New York: E. P. Dutton, 1973.

Couvares, Frank. "So This Is Censorship? Race, Sex, and Censorship in Movies of the 1930s." Paper given at the annual meeting of the American Studies Association in Costa Mesa, Calif., 7 November 1992.

Crary, Jonathan. *Techniques of the Observer: On Vision and Modernity in the Nineteenth Century*. Cambridge, Mass.: MIT Press, 1988.

Curtis, Edward S. *In the Land of the Headhunters: Indian Life and Indian Lore*. Yonkers-on-Hudson: World Book, 1915.

Dalle Vacche, Angela. *The Body in the Mirror: Shapes of History in Italian Cinema.* Princeton: Princeton University Press, 1992.

D'Anglure, Bernard Saladin. "Inuit of Quebec." In *Arctic: Handbook of North American Indians,* vol. 5, ed. David Damas, 476–507. Washington, D.C.: Smithsonian Institution, 1984.

Danzker, Jo-Anne Birnie, ed. *Robert Flaherty Photographer/Filmmaker: The Inuit 1910–1922.* Vancouver: Vancouver Art Gallery, 1980.

——. "Robert Flaherty/Photographer." *Studies in Visual Communication* 6, no. 2 (summer 1980): 5–32.

Darmon, Pierre. *La vie quotidienne du médecin parisien en 1900.* Paris: Hachette, 1988.

Dash, Julie. *Daughters of the Dust: The Making of an African American Woman's Film.* New York: New Press, 1992.

De Brigard, Emilie. "The History of Ethnographic Film." In *Principles of Visual Anthropology,* ed. Paul Hockings, 13–43. The Hague: Mouton, 1975.

——. "Review of 'From Site to Sight.' " *Visual Anthropology* 1, no. 1 (1987): 75–79.

De Heusch, Luc. *The Cinema and Social Science: A Survey of Ethnographic and Sociological Films,* vol. 16. Reports and Papers in the Social Sciences. Paris: UNESCO, 1962.

de Lauretis, Teresa. "Desire in Narrative." In *Alice Doesn't: Feminism, Semiotics, Cinema,* 103–57. Bloomington: Indiana University Press, 1984.

Demeney, Georges. *Les origines du cinématographe.* Paris: H. Paulin, 1909.

de Mortillet, Gabriel. "Photographies anthropologiques." *Bulletins de la Société d'anthropologie de Paris* 6th tome, 4th ser. (3 January 1895): 9–12.

Diawara, Manthia. "African Cinema." *SVA Review* 6, no. 1 (spring 1990): 65–74.

——. "Reading Africa through Foucault: V. Y. Mudimbe's Reaffirmation of the Subject." *October* 55 (winter 1990): 79–92.

Doane, Mary Ann. *Femmes Fatales: Feminism, Film Theory, Psychoanalysis.* New York: Routledge, 1991.

Doyle, Arthur Conan. *The Lost World.* New York: A. L. Burt, 1912.

Dubois, W. E. B. *The Souls of Black Folk.* New York: Bantam Books, 1989; orig. publ. 1903.

Duchet, Michèle. *Le partage des savoirs: discours historique et discours ethnologique.* Paris: Éditions la Découverte, 1985.

Dunlop, Ian. "Ethnographic Filmmaking in Australia: The First Seventy Years (1898–1968)." *Studies in Visual Communication* 9, no. 1 (winter 1983): 11–18.

Edwards, Elizabeth. "Photographic 'Types': The Pursuit of Method." *Visual Anthropology* 3, nos. 2–3 (1990): 235–58.

Ellis, Jack C. *The Documentary Idea: A Critical History of English-language Documentary Film and Video.* Englewood Cliffs, N.J.: Prentice-Hall, 1989.

Fabian, Johannes. *Time and the Other: How Anthropology Makes Its Object.* New York: Columbia University Press, 1983.

Fanon, Frantz. *Black Skin, White Masks: The Experiences of a Black Man in a White World.* Translated by Charles Lam Markmann. New York: Grove Press, 1967.

——. *The Wretched of the Earth.* Translated by Constance Farrington. New York: Grove Press, 1964.

Farnsworth, Clyde H. "The Day the Eskimos Were Cast into Darkness." *New York Times,*
    10 April 1992, A4.
Feldman, Alan. Notes for the Asia Society film festival, "Germany in Asia" (February
    1989).
Fienup-Riordan, Ann. *Eskimo Essays: Yup'ik Lives and How We See Them.* New Bruns-
    wick, N.J.: Rutgers University Press, 1990.
Fisher, Jean. "In Search of the 'Inauthentic': Disturbing Signs in Contemporary Native
    American Art." *Art Journal* 51, no. 3 (fall 1992): 44–50.
Flaherty, Frances. "The Camera's Eye." In *Spellbound in Darkness: A History of the Silent
    Film,* ed. George C. Pratt, 344–47. Rochester: University of Rochester Press, 1966;
    repr., Greenwich, Conn.: New York Graphic Society, 1973.
———. "Explorations." In *Film Book I: The Audience and the Filmmaker,* ed. Robert
    Hughes, 61–65. New York: Grove Press, 1959.
Flaherty, Robert. "The Belcher Islands of Hudson Bay: Their Discovery and Exploration."
    Geographical Review 5, no. 6 (1918): 433–58.
———. *The Captain's Chair: A Story of the North.* New York: Scribner's, 1938.
———. "Filming Real People." In *The Documentary Tradition,* ed. Lewis Jacobs, 97–99.
    New York: W. W. Norton, 1979.
———. "Two Traverses across Ungava Peninsula, Labrador." *Geographical Review* 6, no. 2
    (1918): 116–32.
———. *White Master.* London: George Routledge & Sons, 1939.
Flaherty, Robert, in collaboration with Frances Hubbard Flaherty. *My Eskimo Friends:
    "Nanook of the North."* Garden City, N.Y.: Doubleday, Page, 1924.
Flury, Lois. "A Magnificent Obsession." *Pacific Northwest* (January–February 1984): 24–
    43.
Folkmar, Daniel. *Album of Philippine Types (Found in Bilibid Prison in 1903): Christians
    and Moros (Including a Few Non-Christians), Eighty Plates Representing Thirty-
    Seven Provinces and Islands.* Manila: Bureau of Public Printing, 1904.
Foster, Hal. "The 'Primitive' Unconscious of Modern Art, or White Skin." In *Recodings.*
    Port Townsend, Wash.: Bay Press, 1985.
Foucault, Michel. *Discipline and Punish: The Birth of the Prison.* Translated by Alan
    Sheridan. New York: Vintage Books, 1979.
———. *Power/Knowledge: Selected Interviews and Other Writings,* ed. Colin Gordon.
    New York: Pantheon Books, 1986.
Fox, Robert, and George Weisz, eds. *The Organisation of Science and Technology in
    France 1808–1914.* Paris and Cambridge: Maison des sciences de l'homme and Cam-
    bridge University Press, 1980.
François-Franck, C.-A. *Marey 1830–1904: éloge pronome à l'Académie de médecine
    dans la séance annuelle du 17 décembre 1913.* Paris: Masson, 17 December 1912.
Frizot, Michel. *La chronophotographie: temps, photographie et mouvement autour
    de E. J. Marey.* Exposition catalog for La Chapelle l'Oratoire, Beaune (Côte-d'Or),
    27 May–3 September 1984. Beaune: Association amis de Marey, 1984.
———. *E. J. Marey: 1830–1904: la photographie en mouvement.* Paris: Centre national
    d'art et de culture Georges Pompidou, Musée national d'art moderne, 1977.

Fung, Richard. "Looking for My Penis: The Eroticised Asian in Gay Video Porn." In *How Do I Look? Queer Film and Video*, ed. Bad Object-Choices, 145–60. Seattle: Bay Press, 1991.

Gabriel, Teshome. "Ruin and the Other: Towards a Language of Memory." In *Otherness and the Media*, ed. Teshome Gabriel and Hamid Naficy, 211–19. Langhorne, Pa.: Harwood Academic Publishers, 1993.

——. "Third Cinema as Guardian of Popular Memory: Towards a Third Aesthetics." In *Questions of Third Cinema*, ed. Jim Pines and Paul Willeman, 53–64. London: BFI, 1989.

Geary, Christraud. " 'On the Savannah': Marie Pauline Thorbecke's Images from Cameroon West Africa (1911–12)." *Art Journal* 49, no. 2 (1990): 150–58.

——. "Photographs as Materials for African History. Some Methodological Considerations." *History in Africa* 13 (1986): 89–116.

Geertz, Clifford. *Works and Lives: The Anthropologist as Author.* Stanford: Stanford University Press, 1988.

Gidley, Mick. "From the Hopi Snake Dance to 'The Ten Commandments': Edward S. Curtis as Filmmaker." *Studies in Visual Communication* 8, no. 3 (summer 1982): 70–79.

Gilman, Sander L. "Black Bodies, White Bodies: Toward an Iconography of Female Sexuality in Late-Nineteenth-Century Art, Medicine, and Literature." In *"Race," Writing, and Difference*, ed. Henry Louis Gates Jr., 223–61. Chicago: University of Chicago Press, 1986.

Ginsburg, Faye. "Indigenous Media: Faustian Contract or Global Village?" *Cultural Anthropology* 6, no. 1 (February 1991): 92–112.

Ginzburg, Carlo. "Morelli, Freud, and Sherlock Holmes: Clues and Scientific Method." In *The Sign of Three: Dupin, Holmes, Peirce*, ed. Umberto Eco and Thomas Sebeok, 81–118. Bloomington: Indiana University Press, 1983.

Goldner, Orville, and George E. Turner, eds. *The Making of King Kong: The Story behind a Film Classic.* South Brunswick, N.J.: A. S. Barnes, 1975.

Gottesman, Ronald, and Harry Geduld, eds. *The Girl in the Hairy Paw.* New York: Avon Books, 1976.

Gould, Stephen Jay. *The Flamingo's Smile: Reflections in Natural History.* New York: W. W. Norton, 1985.

Greene, Naomi. *Pier Paolo Pasolini: Cinema as Heresy.* Princeton: Princeton University Press, 1990.

Greenhalgh, Paul. "Education, Entertainment and Politics: Lessons from the Great International Exhibitions." In *The New Museology*, ed. Peter Vergo, 74–98. London: Redaktion Books, 1989.

——. *Ephemeral Vistas: The Expositions Universelles, Great Exhibitions and World's Fairs, 1851–1939.* Manchester, U.K.: Manchester University Press, 1988.

Grierson, John. "Flaherty's Poetic *Moana*." In *The Documentary Tradition*, ed. Lewis Jacobs, 25–26. New York: W. W. Norton, 1979.

Griffith, Richard. "*Grass* and *Chang* (1941)." In *The Documentary Tradition*, ed. Lewis Jacobs, 22–24. New York: W. W. Norton, 1979.

——. *The World of Robert Flaherty.* New York: Duell, Sloan and Pearce, 1953.

Grimes, William. "Buried Themes: Psychoanalyzing Movies." *New York Times,* 23 December 1991, C11.

Gruber, Jacob W. "Ethnographic Salvage and the Shaping of Anthropology." *American Anthropologist* 172 (1970): 1289–99.

Guillemin, Dr. "Le transformisme intégral et la tératologie." *Revue de pathologie comparée* 18th year, no. 8 (12 November 1918): 246–47.

Hall, Stuart. "New Ethnicities." In *Black Film British Cinema,* ed. Kobena Mercer, 27–30. *ICA Documents,* vol. 7. London: Institute of Contemporary Arts, 1988.

——. "Race, Articulation and Societies Structured in Dominance." In *Sociological Theories: Race and Colonialism.* Paris: UNESCO, 1980.

Hamilton, Dr. Mlle., and Félix Regnault. *Les gardes-malades: congréationistes, mercenaires—amateurs professionnelles.* Paris: Vigot, 1901.

Hammond, Dorothy, and Alta Jablow. *The Myth of Africa.* New York: Library of Social Science, 1977.

Hammond, Michael. "Anthropology as a Weapon of Social Combat in Late Nineteenth-century France." *Journal of the History of the Behavioral Sciences* 16 (1980): 118–32.

Hanson, John Stag. "The Man Who Killed King Kong." *Movies International* 1, no. 3 (1966): 22–25, 65.

Haraway, Donna. "The Promises of Monsters: A Regenerative Politics of Inappropriate/d Others." In *Cultural Studies,* ed. Lawrence Grossberg, Cary Nelson, and Paula Treichler, 295–337. New York: Routledge, 1992.

——. "Teddy Bear Patriarchy: Taxidermy in the Garden of Eden, New York City, 1908–1936." *Social Text: Theory/Culture/Ideology* 11 (winter 1984–85): 20–64.

Harper, Kenn. *Give Me My Father's Body: The Life of Minik the New York Eskimo.* Frobisher Bay, N.W.T.: Blacklead Books, 1986.

Harris, Marvin. *The Rise of Anthropological Theory: A History of Theories of Culture.* New York: Columbia University Press, 1971.

Harvey, Joy Dorothy. "Races Specified, Evolution Transformed: The Social Context of Scientific Debates Originating in the Société d'Anthropologie de Paris 1859–1902." Ph.D. dissertation, Harvard University, 1983.

Heermann, Ingrid. *Mythos Tahiti: Südsee—Traum und Realität.* Berlin: Dietrich Reimer Verlag, 1987.

Heider, Karl. *Ethnographic Film.* Austin: University of Texas Press, 1976.

Hellenbrand, Harold. "Bigger Thomas Reconsidered: 'Native Son,' Film and 'King Kong.' " *Journal of American Culture* 6, no. 1 (1983): 84–95.

Heller, Terry. *The Delights of Terror: An Aesthetics of the Tale of Terror.* Urbana: University of Illinois Press, 1987.

Hendrick, Stephen, and Kathleen Fleming. "Zacharias Kunuk: Video Maker and Inuit Historian." *Inuit Art Quarterly* (summer 1991): 25–28.

Herbert, Robert L. *Impressionism: Art, Leisure, and Parisian Society.* New Haven: Yale University Press, 1988.

Hilton-Simpson, M. W., and J. A. Haeseler. "Cinema and Ethnology." *Discovery* 6 (1925): 325–30.

Hinsley, Curtis. *Savages and Scientists: The Smithsonian Institution and the Development of American Anthropology, 1846–1910.* Washington, D.C.: Smithsonian Institution Press, 1981.

———. "From Shell-heaps to Stelae: Early Anthropology at the Peabody Museum." In *Objects and Others: Essays on Museums and Material Culture,* ed. George W. Stocking Jr., *History of Anthropology,* vol. 3, 3–9. Madison: University of Wisconsin Press, 1985.

Hinsley, Melissa Banta, and Curtis M. Hinsley. *From Site to Sight: Anthropology, Photography, and the Power of Imagery.* Cambridge, Mass.: Peabody Museum Press, 1986.

Hoberman, J. "Bad Movies." In *Vulgar Modernism,* ed. J. Hoberman, 13–22. Philadelphia: Temple University Press, 1991.

Hollier, Denis. "The Use-Value of the Impossible." *October* 60 (1992): 3–24.

Holm, Bill, and George Irving Quimby. *Edward S. Curtis in the Land of the War Canoes: A Pioneer Cinematographer in the Pacific Northwest.* Seattle: University of Washington Press, 1980.

Holmes, Burton. *Burton Holmes: The man Who Photographed the World,* ed. Genoa Caldwell. New York: Harry N. Abrams, 1977.

Honour, Hugh. *The New Golden Land: European Images of America from the Discoveries to the Present Time.* New York: Pantheon Books, 1975.

Hurston, Zora Neale. *Dust Tracks on a Road: An Autobiography.* 2d ed. Urbana: University of Illinois Press, 1984.

———. *Mules and Men.* New York: Harper Perennial, 1978.

———. "Ritualistic Expression from the Lips of the Communicants of the Seventh Day Church of God, Beaufort, South Carolina." Manuscript in the Margaret Mead Collection, Manuscript Division, Library of Congress.

———. *The Sanctified Church: The Folklore Writings of Zora Neale Hurston.* Berkeley: Turtle Island, 1981.

———. "What White Publishers Won't Print." In *I Love Myself When I Am Laughing . . . And Then Again When I Am Looking Mean and Impressive,* ed. Alice Walker. Old Westbury, N.Y.: Feminist Press, 1979.

Hussey, Christopher. *The Picturesque: Studies in a Point of View.* London: Archon Books, 1967; orig. publ. 1927.

Hutton, Patrick H., ed. *Historical Dictionary of the Third French Republic.* Westport, Conn.: Greenwood Press, 1986.

Imperato, Pascal James, and Eleanor M. Imperato. *They Married Adventure: The Wandering Lives of Martin and Osa Johnson.* New Brunswick, N.J.: Rutgers University Press, 1992.

Institut für den wissenschaftlichen Film. "Rules for Documentation in Ethnology and Folklore." *Research Film* 3, no. 4 (1959): 238–40.

Jacknis, Ira. "Franz Boas and Exhibits: On the Limitations of the Museum Method of Anthropology." In *Objects and Others,* ed. George W. Stocking Jr., *History of Anthropology,* vol. 3, 75–111. Madison: University of Wisconsin Press, 1985.

———. "Franz Boas and Photography." *Studies in Visual Communication* 10, no. 1 (1984): 2–60.

———. "George Hunt, Collector of Indian Specimens." In *Chiefly Feasts: The Enduring*

Kwakiutl Potlach, ed. Aldona Jonaitis, 177–224. New York: American Museum of Natural History, 1991.

——. "James Mooney, Ethnographic Photographer." *Visual Anthropology* 2–3 (1990): 179–212.

——. "Margaret Mead and Gregory Bateson in Bali: Their Use of Photography and Film." *Cultural Anthropology* 3, no. 2 (May 1988): 160–77.

——. "The Picturesque and the Scientific: Franz Boas's Plan for Anthropological Film-making." *Visual Anthropology* 1, no. 1 (1987): 59–64.

Jacobs, Lewis, ed. *The Documentary Tradition.* New York: W. W. Norton, 1979.

Jameson, Fredric. "The Existence of Italy." In *Signatures of the Visible,* ed. Fredric Jameson, 155–230. New York: Routledge, 1992.

Jameux, Charles. *F. W. Murnau.* Paris: Classiques du Cinéma, 1965.

Johnson, Barbara. "Thresholds of Difference: Structures of Address in Zora Neale Hurston." In *"Race," Writing, and Difference,* ed. Henry Louis Gates Jr., 317–28. Chicago: University of Chicago Press, 1986.

Johnson, Martin. *Cannibal-Land: Adventures with a Camera in the New Hebrides.* Boston: Houghton Mifflin, 1922.

Jones, Kellie. "Pat Ward Williams: Photography and Social/Personal History." In *Pat Ward Williams: Probable Cause,* 5–8. Philadelphia: Goldie Paley Gallery, 1992.

Jordan, Pierre-L. *Premier Contact—Premier Regard.* Marseilles: Musées de Marseilles—Images en Manouvres Éditions, 1992.

Jordanova, Ludmilla. "Objects of Knowledge: A Historical Perspective on Museums." In *The New Museology,* ed. Peter Vergo, 22–40. London: Redaktion Books, 1989.

Kalb, John D. "The Anthropological Narrator of Hurston's *Their Eyes Were Watching God.*" *Studies in American Fiction* (autumn 1988): 169–80.

Kaufman, Michael T. "A Museum's Eskimo Skeletons and Its Own." *New York Times,* 21 August 1993, A1, A14.

Kavanaugh, Thomas W. "A Brief Illustrated History of the Manikins, Statues, Lay-Figures, and Life-Groups Illustrating American Ethnology in the National Museum of Natural History." Unpublished paper.

Kincaid, Jamaica. *A Small Place.* New York: Plume, 1989.

Kincaid, James R. "Who Gets to Tell Their Stories?" *New York Times Book Review,* 3 May 1992, 1.

Kinney, Leila, and Zeynep Celik. "Ethnography and Exhibitionism at the Expositions Universelles." *Assemblage* 13 (December 1990): 34–59.

Kracauer, Siegfried. *Theory of Film: The Redemption of Physical Reality.* New York: Oxford University Press, 1960.

Kroeber, Theodora. *Ishi in Two Worlds: A Biography of the Last Wild Indian in North America.* Berkeley: University of California Press, 1961.

Krouse, Susan Applegate. "Filming the Vanishing Race." In *Visual Explorations of the World: Selected Papers from the International Conference on Visual Communication,* ed. Jay Ruby and Martin Taureg, 255–66. Aachen: Edition Herodot im Rader-Verlag, 1987.

——. "Photographing the Vanishing Race." *Visual Anthropology* 3, nos. 2–3 (1990): 213–33.

Kucklick, Henrika. "Tribal Exemplars: Images of Political Authority in British Anthropology." In *Functionalism Historicized: Essays on British Social Anthropology*, ed. George W. Stocking Jr., *History of Anthropology*, vol. 2, 59–82. Madison: University of Wisconsin Press, 1984.

Kuhn, Thomas S. *The Essential Tension: Selected Studies in Scientific Tradition and Change*. Chicago: University of Chicago Press, 1979.

Kuntzel, Thierry. "The Film-Work, 2." *Camera Obscura* 5 (spring 1980): 6–69.

Kuper, Adam. *The Invention of Primitive Society: Transformations of an Illusion*. New York: Routledge, 1988.

Lajard, J., and Félix Regnault. *De l'existence de la lèpre attenuée chez les cagots des Pyrenées*, ed. Progrès médical. Paris: Lecrosnier et Babé, 1893.

———. "Poterie crue et origine du tour." *Bulletins de la Société d'anthropologie de Paris* 6th tome, 5th ser. (19 December 1895): 734–39.

Latour, Bruno. *Science in Action*. Cambridge: Harvard University Press, 1987.

Lears, Jackson. *No Place of Grace: Antimodernism and the Transformation of American Culture, 1880–1920*. New York: Pantheon Books, 1981.

Leiris, Michel. "Fox Movietone Follies of 1929." *Documents* 1 (7 December 1929); repr. in *October* 60 (spring 1992): 43–46, trans. Dominic Faccini.

Lennes, Gérard. *Histoires du cinéma fantastiques*. Paris: Éditions Seghers, 1989.

Leprohon, Pierre. *L'exotisme et le cinéma*. Paris: J. Susse, 1945.

Lévi-Strauss, Claude. *Tristes Tropiques*. Translated by John and Doreen Weightman. Paris: Librairie Plon, 1955; repr., New York: Penguin Books, 1992.

Lévy, Jean. "King-Kong." *Minotaure* 5 (1934): 5.

Liotard, André F., Samivel, and Jean Thévenot. *Cinéma d'exploration, cinéma au long cours*. Paris: P.-A. Chavane, 1950.

Loos, Adolf. "Ornament as Crime." In *The Architecture of Adolf Loos*, ed. Yehuda Safran and Wilfried Wang. London: Arts Council of Great Britain and the Authors, 1908.

Lyman, Christopher M. *The Vanishing Race and Other Illusions: Photographs of Indians by Edward S. Curtis*. Washington, D.C.: Smithsonian Institution Press, 1982.

Lyon, Luke. "History of the Prohibition of Photography of Southwestern Indian Ceremonies." Unpublished paper.

MacDougall, David. "Beyond Observational Cinema." In *Principles of Visual Anthropology*, ed. Paul Hockings, 109–24. The Hague: Mouton, 1975.

———. "Whose Story Is It?" *Visual Anthropology Review* 7, no. 2 (fall 1991): 2–10.

Mainardi, Patricia. *Art and Politics of the Second Empire: The Universal Expositions of 1855 and 1867*. New Haven: Yale University Press, 1987.

Malinowski, Bronislaw. *Argonauts of the Western Pacific*. Foreword by Sir James Fraser. New York: Dutton, 1961; orig. publ. 1922.

———. *A Diary in the Strict Sense of the Term*. Stanford: Stanford University Press, 1989; orig. publ. 1967.

Marcus, George E., and Michael M. J. Fischer. *Anthropology as Cultural Critique: An Experimental Movement in the Human Sciences*. Chicago: University of Chicago Press, 1986.

Marey, Etienne-Jules. *Le mouvement*. Paris: Masson, 1894.

———. "Physiologie générale—le mouvement des êtres microscopiques analysé pour la chronophotographie." *Comptes rendus des séances de l'Académie des sciences* (2 May 1892): 889–900.

———. "Technique physiologique—modifications de la photochronophotographe pour l'analyse des mouvements exécutés sur place par un animal." *Comptes rendus hebdomadaires des séances de l'Académie des sciences* 107 (1 October 1888): 607–9.

Marey, Etienne-Jules, and Georges Demeney. "Analyse cinématique de la course de l'homme." *Comptes rendus des séances de l'Académie des sciences* 103d tome, 2d semester (20 September 1886): 509–13.

Mark, Diane Mei Lin. "The Reel Hawaii." In *Moving the Image: Independent Asian Pacific American Media Arts*, ed. Russell Leong, 109–24. Los Angeles: UCLA Asian American Studies Center and Visual Communications, Southern Californian Asian American Studies Central, 1991.

Marks, Laura U. "Reconfigured Nationhood: A Partisan History of the Inuit Broadcasting Corporation." *Afterimage* 21, no. 8 (March 1994): 4–7.

Martinez, Wilson. "Critical Studies and Visual Anthropology: Aberrant vs. Anticipated Readings of Ethnographic Film." *CVA Review* (spring 1990): 34–47.

Masayesva, Victor, Jr., and Erin Younger, eds. *Hopi Photographers/Hopi Images*. Vol. 8. Sun Tracks: An American Indian Literary Series. Tucson: University of Arizona Press, 1984.

Matthiessen, Peter. "Survival of the Hunter." *New Yorker* (24 April 1995): 67–77.

Mauss, Marcel. "Les techniques du corps." In *Sociologie et anthropologie*, ed. Marcel Mauss, 362–86. Paris: Presses Universitaires de France, 1934.

Mayne, Judith. " 'King Kong' and the Ideology of Spectacle." *Quarterly Review of Film Studies* 1, no. 4 (November 1976): 373–87.

McBride, Bunny. "A Penobscot in Paris." *Down East: The Magazine of Maine* 36, no. 1 (1989): 62–64, 80–84.

McInroy, Patrick. "The American Méliès." *Sight and Sound International Film Quarterly* (autumn 1979): 250–54.

Mead, Margaret. *Blackberry Winter: My Earlier Years*. New York: William Morrow, 1972.

———. *Coming of Age in Samoa: A Psychological Study of Primitive Youth for Western Civilisation*. Rev. ed., New York: William Morrow, 1961; orig. publ. 1928.

———. "Visual Anthropology in a Discipline of Words." In *Principles of Visual Anthropology*, ed. Paul Hockings, 3–12. The Hague: Mouton, 1974.

Mead, Margaret, and Gregory Bateson. *Balinese Character*. New York: New York Academy of Sciences, 1942.

Mead, Margaret, and Rhoda Metraux. *The Study of Culture at a Distance*. Chicago: University of Chicago Press, 1953.

Méliès, Gaston. *Le voyage autour du monde de la G. Méliès Manufacturing Company (July 1912–May 1913)*. Paris: Association "Les Amis de Georges Méliès," 1988.

Mercer, Kobena. "Skin Head Sex Thing: Racial Difference and the Homoerotic Imaginary." In *How Do I Look? Queer Film and Video*, ed. Bad Object Choices, 169–210. Seattle: Bay Press, 1991.

Michaelis, Anthony R. *Research Films in Biology, Anthropology, Psychology, and Medicine*. New York: Academic Press, 1955.

Miller, Christopher. *Blank Darkness: Africanist Discourses in France.* Chicago: University of Chicago Press, 1985.

Minh-ha, Trinh T. "Outside in Inside out." In *Questions of Third Cinema,* ed. Jim Pines and Paul Willeman, 133–49. London: British Film Institute, 1989.

Mitchell, Timothy. "The World as Exhibition." *Comparative Studies in Society and History* 31, no. 2 (April 1989): 217–36.

Mitman, Gregg. "Cinematic Nature: Hollywood Technology, Popular Culture, and the Science of Animal Behavior, 1925–1940." Paper presented at the Society for Cinema Studies Conference, New Orleans, La., February 1993.

Mohanty, Chandra Talpade. "Under Western Eyes: Feminist Scholarship and Colonial Discourses." *boundary 2* 12, no. 1 (spring/fall 1984): 333–58.

Mohanty, S. P. "Us and Them." *Yale Journal of Criticism* 2, no. 2 (1989): 1–31.

Montandon, Georges. "Remarques sur la classification des sciences anthropologiques du Dr. Félix Regnault." *Revue anthropologique* (1931): 127–30.

Morrison, Toni. *Beloved.* New York: Signet, 1991.

Mould, David H., and Gerry Veeder. "The 'Photographer-Adventurers': Forgotten Heroes of the Silent Screen." *Journal of Popular Film and Television* 16, no. 3 (1988): 118–29.

Movie Makers, unsigned review (November 1928). "*Stark Love* and *Moana.*" In *The Documentary Tradition,* ed. Lewis Jacobs, 27–28. 2d ed., New York: W. W. Norton, 1979.

Mudimbe, V. Y. *The Invention of Africa: Gnosis, Philosophy and the Order of Knowledge.* Bloomington: Indiana University Press, 1988.

———. "Which Idea of Africa? Herskovits's Cultural Relativism." *October* 55 (winter 1990): 93–104.

Mulvey, Laura. "Visual Pleasure and Narrative Cinema." In *Narrative, Apparatus, Ideology: A Film Theory Reader,* ed. Phil Rosen, 198–209. New York: Columbia University Press, 1986.

Musser, Charles. "The Travel Genre in 1903–1904: Moving towards Fictional Narrative." In *Early Cinema: Space, Frame, Narrative,* ed. Thomas Elsaesser, 123–32. London: British Film Institute, 1992.

Naipaul, V. S. *Among the Believers: An Islamic Journey.* New York: Alfred A. Knopf, 1981.

Neale, Stephen. *Genre.* London: British Film Institute, 1980.

Nichols, Bill. *Ideology and the Image: Social Representation in the Cinema and Other Media.* Bloomington: Indiana University Press, 1981.

Niver, Kemp P. *Early Motion Pictures: The Paper Print Collection in the Library of Congress,* ed. Bebe Bergsten. Washington, D.C.: Library of Congress, 1985.

Noguès, Pierre, and Félix Regnault. "Explication mécanique des trucs de l'homme insoulevable." *Revue de pathologie comparée* (10 May 1921): 191–94.

Nordau, Max Simon. *Degeneration.* New York: H. Fertig, 1895; repr. 1968.

Nye, Robert A. "Heredity or Milieu: The Foundations of Modern European Criminilogical Theory." *ISIS: An International Review Devoted to the History of Science and Its Cultural Influences* 67, no. 238 (September 1976): 335–55.

Ollier, Claude. "A King in New York." In *The Girl in the Hairy Paw,* ed. Ronald Gottesman and Harry Geduld, trans. Roy Huss and T. J. Ross, 37–69. New York: Avon Books, 1976.

O'Reilly, Patrick. "Le 'documentaire' ethnographique en Océanie." In *Premier catalogue sélectif international de films ethnographiques sur la région du Pacifique*, 281–305. Paris: UNESCO, 1970.

Orwell, George. *Shooting an Elephant and Other Essays*. New York: Harcourt, Brace & World, 1950.

Owusu, Maxwell. "Ethnography of Africa: The Usefulness of the Useless." *American Anthropologist* 80 (1978): 310–34.

Peary, Gerald. "The Historicity of *King Kong*." *Jump Cut* 4 (November–December 1974): 11–12.

———. "Missing Links: The Jungle Origins of *King Kong*." In *The Girl in the Hairy Paw*, ed. Ronald Gottesman and Harry Geduld, 81–98. New York: Avon Books, 1976.

Perry, Benita. "Problems in Current Theories of Colonial Discourse." *Oxford Literary Review* 9, no. 1–2 (1987): 27–58.

Pines, Jim, and Paul Willeman, eds. *Questions of Third Cinema*. London: BFI, 1989.

Pitseolak, Peter. *People from Our Side: An Inuit Record of Seekooseelak, the Land of the People of Cape Dorset, Baffin Land: A Life Story with Photographs*. Edmonton: Hurtig Press, 1975.

Pöch, Rudolf. "Reisen in Neu-Guinea in den Jahren 1904–1906." *Zeitschrift für Ethnologie* (1907): 382–400.

Poe, Edgar Allan. "The Murders in the Rue Morgue." In *The Illustrated Edgar Allan Poe*, ed. Roy Gasson, 125–52. Poole: New Orchard Editions, 1976.

Pollman, Tessel. "Margaret Mead's Balinese." *Indonesia* 49 (April 1990): 1–35.

Powell, J. W. "Twenty-Third Annual Report of the Bureau of American Ethnology." *Annual Report, Bureau of American Ethnology* 23 (1901–2): xvi.

Pratt, Mary Louise. "Scratches on the Face of the Country; Or, What Mr. Barrow Saw in the Land of the Bushmen." In *"Race," Writing, and Difference*, ed. Henry Louis Gates Jr., 138–62. Chicago: University of Chicago Press, 1986.

Preloran, Jorge. "Documenting the Human Condition." In *Principles of Visual Anthropology*, ed. Paul Hockings, 103–8. The Hague: Mouton, 1975.

Prins, Harold E. L. "American Indians and the Ethnocinematic Complex: From Native Participation to Production Control." In *Eyes across the Water: The Amsterdam Conference on Visual Anthropology*, 80–90. Amsterdam: Hetepinhuis, 1989.

Proctor, Robert. "From *Anthropologie* to *Rassenkunde* in the German Anthropological Tradition." In *Bones, Bodies, Behavior: Essays on Biological Anthropology*, ed. George W. Stocking Jr., *History of Anthropology*, vol. 5, 138–79. Madison: University of Wisconsin Press, 1988.

Rafael, Vicente. *Contracting Colonialism*. Durham: Duke University Press, 1990.

Regnault, Félix. "À propos de la communication de M. Lester (sur l'anthropologie des Somalis)." *Bulletins et mémoires de la Société d'anthropologie de Paris* 8th tome, 7th ser. (1927): 188.

———. "À propos de la stéatopygie en France." *Bulletins et mémoires de la Société d'anthropologie de Paris* 3rd tome, 6th ser. (1912): 398–99.

———. "Classifications des sciences anthropologiques." *Revue anthropologique* (1931): 121–27.

———. "Conférence Lamarck: des infirmités des organes des sens dans la production des oeuvres de génies." *Bulletins et mémoires de la Société d'anthropologie de Paris* 9th tome, 7th ser. (1928): 79–81.

———. "Crânes d'Indiens du Bengale." *Bulletins de la Société d'anthropologie de Paris* 3d tome, 4th ser. (4 February 1892): 66–68.

———. "Déformations crâniennes dans l'art sino-japonais." *Bulletins de la Société d'anthropologie de Paris* 6th tome, 4th ser. (6 June 1895): 409–13.

———. "De la circoncision chez la femme." *La médecine moderne* (1893): 869–70.

———. "De la dépopulation de France." *La médecine moderne* (1893): 1256–57.

———. "De la fonction préhensile du pied." *La nature* 1058 (9 September 1893): 229–31.

———. "De la perception des couleurs suivant les races humaines." *La médicine moderne* (1893): 1062–65.

———. *Des altérations crâniennes dans le rachitisme.* Paris: Steinheil, 1888.

———. "Des anomalies osseuses chez les arriérés criminels et les brigands." *Bulletins et mémoires de la Société d'anthropologie de Paris* 9th tome, 7th ser. (1926): 92–95.

———. "Des attitudes du repos dans les races humaines." *Revue encyclopédique* (7 January 1986): 9–12.

———. "Des différentes manières de marcher." *La médecine moderne* (1893): 596–97.

———. "Des diverses méthodes de marche et de course." *L'illustration* 2765 (22 February 1896): 154–55.

———. "Des sécrétions internes comme facteur de transformisme." *Revue de pathologie comparée* (8 April 1919): 103–5.

———. "Dilation des joues: chez les souffleurs de verre et dans l'art." *La nature* 1030 (25 February 1893): 198–200.

———. "Discussion: À propos des déformations crâniennes dans l'art antique." *Bulletins de la Société d'anthropologie de Paris* 6th tome, 4th ser. (3 January 1895): 9–12.

———. Discussion for Adolphe Bloch's "De la race qui précéda les Sémiks en Chaldée et en Susiane." *Bulletins de la Société d'anthropologie de Paris* 3d tome, 5th ser. (3 July 1902): 680–82.

———. "Distinguons la race anatomique et l'ethnie psychique." *Revue de pathologie comparée* (8 February 1921): 9–11.

———. "Du pas gymnastique." *La nature* 1075 (6 January 1894): 83–86.

———. "Du rôle des montagnes dans la distribution des races." *Bulletins de la Société d'anthropologie de Paris* 3d tome, 4th ser. (7 April 1892): 221–37.

———. "Essai sur les débuts de l'art ornemental géometrique chez les peuples primitifs." *Bulletins de la Société d'anthropologie de Paris* 7th tome, 4th ser. (1 October 1896): 532–49.

———. "Étude sur Aïnos (particularités anatomiques et médicales)." *La médecine moderne* (1893): 310–11.

———. "Exhibitions foraines." *La nature* 1297 (9 April 1898): 299–302.

———. "Exposition Ethnographique de l'Afrique Occidentale au Champs-de-Mars à Paris: Sénégal et Soudan français." *La nature* 1159 (17 August 1895): 183–86.

———. "Films et musées d'ethnographie." *Comptes rendus de l'association française pour l'avancement des sciences* 2 (1923): 680–81.

———. "Forme du crâne dans l'hydrocéphalie." *Bulletins de la Société d'anthropologie de Paris* 6th tome, 4th ser. (7 February 1895): 94–97.

———. "Géographie médicale: hospitaux et maladies spéciales de l'Inde." *La médecine moderne* (1893): 638–39.

———. "Gigantisme et nanisme: des variations de format chez l'homme." *Revue de pathologie comparée* (1923): 269.

———. *Hypnotisme, Religion.* Paris: Schleicher Frères, 1897.

———. "Il convient de différencier l'ethnie linguistique de la race anatomique." *Bulletins et mémoires de la Société d'anthropologie de Paris* 10th tome, 6th ser. (19 June 1919): 55–56.

———. "La caricature dans l'art antique (déformations crâniennes)." *La nature* 1123 (8 December 1894): 21–22.

———. "La chronophotographie dans l'ethnographie." *Bulletins et mémoires de la Société d'anthropologie de Paris* 1st tome, 5th ser. (4 October 1900): 421–22.

———. "L'age de la pierre grossièrement taillée au Congo français." *Bulletins de la Société d'anthropologie de Paris* (5 July 1894): 477–80.

———. *La genèse des miracles.* Études economiques et sociales, ed. Collège libre des sciences sociales XI. Paris: V. Giard et E. Brière, 1910.

———. "La locomotion chez l'homme." *Journal de physiologie et de pathologie générale* 15th tome, no. 1 (January 1913): 46–61.

———. "La marche et le pas gymnastiques militaires." *La nature* 1052 (29 July 1893): 129–30.

———. "La mode." *La nature* 1088 (7 April 1894): 289–91.

———. "L'anthropophagie des peuples primitifs: grilles dans la grotte de Montesquieu (Ariège)." *Bulletins de la Société d'anthropologie de Paris* (1869): 606–10.

———. "La poison des flèches." *La médecine moderne* (1893): 225–26.

———. "La Polynésie française en 1892." *La médecine moderne* (1893): 4–5.

———. "La Reine du Pount (bas-relief de Deir-El-Bhan, Égypte) n'a point de stéatopygie, c'est une difforme." *Bulletins et mémoires de la Société d'anthropologie de Paris* 3d tome, 6th ser. (3 July 1913): 412–15.

———. "La réprésentation de l'obésité dans l'art préhistorique." *Bulletins et mémoires de la Société d'anthropologie de Paris* 3d tome, 6th ser. (18 January 1912): 35–39.

———. "L'art nègre." *La nature* 1219 (10 October 1896): 295–98.

———. "Le cinématographe." *L'illustration* 2779 (30 May 1896): 416–17.

———. "Le grimper." *Revue encyclopédique* (1897): 904–5.

———. "Le langage par gestes." *La nature* 1324 (15 October 1898): 315–17.

———. "Le pélerinage de Notre Dame de Lourdes." *La médecine moderne* (1893): 1160–61.

———. "Le rôle du cinéma en ethnographie." *La nature* 2866 (1 October 1931): 304–6.

———. "Le rôle mental des secrétions internes et le cerveau d'Anatole France." *Bulletins et mémoires de la Société d'anthropologie de Paris* 9th tome, 9th ser. (1928): 1.

———. "Les artistes préhistoriques d'après les derniers découvertes." *La nature* 1167 (1895): 305–7.

———. "Les attitudes dans l'art égyptien." *La nature* 1112 (22 September 1894): 261–62.

———. "Les attitudes de repos dans l'art sino-japonais." *La nature* 1154 (15 July 1895): 105–7.

———. "Les cagots et la lèpre en France." *La nature* 1022 (31 December 1892): 67–68.

————. "Les caricatures dans l'art antique (déformations craniennes)." *La nature* 1123 (8 December 1894): 21–22.

————. "Les dahoméens." *La nature* 1041 (13 May 1893): 371–74.

————. "Les déformations crâniennes dans l'art antique." *La nature* 1105 (4 August 1894): 157–58.

————. "Les déformations crâniennes dans l'art sino-japonais." *La nature* 1142 (20 April 1895): 521–22.

————. "Les mains polydactyles." *La nature* 1044 (3 June 1893): 5–6.

————. "Les monstres dans l'ethnographie et dans l'art." *Bulletins et mémoires de la Société d'anthropologie de Paris* 4th tome, 7th ser. (3 July 1913): 400–11.

————. "Les musées des films." *Biologica* 2, no. 16, supp. 20 (1912): xx.

————. "Les origines de l'art ornemental." *La nature* 1215 (12 September 1896): 227–30.

————. "Les scarifications." *La médecine moderne* (1895): 507.

————. "Les tempéraments digestifs." *Revue de pathologie comparée* (8 June 1920): 166.

————. "Les tempéraments genitaux." *Revue de pathologie comparée* (8 March 1921): 1–9.

————. "Les tempéraments rustique et affiné." *Revue anthropologique* (1938): 18–40.

————. "Les tempéraments. Leur rapport avec l'héridité, les races: comment il faut les envisager." *Revue de pathologie comparée* (14 October 1919): 21–26.

————. "Le tempérament lymphatique chez l'homme et les animaux." *Revue de pathologie comparée* (11 February 1919): 49–52.

————. *L'évolution de la prostitution.* Paris: Flammarion, 1906.

————. "L'évolution d'une image." *La nature* 1441 (5 January 1901): 84–85.

————. "L'évolution du cinéma." *La revue scientifique* (1922): 79–85.

————. "L'histoire du cinéma: son rôle en anthropologie." *Bulletins et mémoires de la Société d'anthropologie de Paris* 3d tome, 7th ser. (6 July 1922): 61–65.

————. "L'invention du cinéma." *Revue moderne de médecine et de chirurgie* vol. 4 (April 1926): 97–100.

————. "Marche et course d'après l'art antique." *La nature* 1268 (18 September 1897): 244–46.

————. "Nouvelle race d'ours des cavernes." *La nature* 720 (19 March 1887): 255.

————. "Origines de l'art ornemental." *La nature* 1201 (6 June 1896): 7–10.

————. "Ouvrages offerts." *Bulletins de la Société d'anthropologie de Paris* 4th tome, 4th ser. (15 June 1893): 381–85.

————. "Pierres ayant la forme d'organes génitaux." *Bulletins et mémoires de la Société d'anthropologie de Paris* 4th tome, 6th ser. (11 December 1913): 642–43.

————. "Pourquoi les nègres sont-ils noirs? (Étude sur les causes de la coloration de la peau)." *La médecine moderne* (2 October 1895): 606–7.

————. "Présentation: une observation de noeuvus généralisé." *Bulletins de la Société d'anthropologie de Paris* 6th tome, 4th ser. (20 June 1895): 418–19.

————. "Présentation d'une hotte primitive." *Bulletins de la Société d'anthropologie de Paris* 3d tome, 4th ser. (21 July 1892): 471–79.

————. "Quelques considérations sur l'étude des races en anthropologie et en zootechnie. I. Races et ethnies. II. Races et variétés. III. Corrélation des variétés humaines et animale sous l'influence d'un même milieu." *Revue de pathologie comparée* (10 February 1920): 2–5.

——. "Resumé et conclusions du rapport sur la valeur de l'hypnotisme comme moyen de l'investigation psychologique." In *Deuxième congrès international de l'hypnotisme . . . valeur de l'hypnotisme,* 10–12. Paris: A. Quelquejeu, 1900.

——. "Statuettes ethnographiques indiennes." *La nature* 1096 (2 June 1894): 29–50.

——. "Tempéraments dans leurs rapports avec l'alimentation et les rayons calorifiques et cliniques." *Revue de pathologie comparée* (1919): 83.

——. "The role of depopulation, deforestation and malaria in the decadence of certain nations." *Smithsonian Institution Annual Report* (trans. from Revue scientifique [Paris, 10 January 1914]: 46–48) (1914): 593–97.

——. "Un musee des films." *Bulletins et mémoires de la Société d'anthropologie de Paris* 3d tome, 6th ser. (7 March 1912): 95–96.

Regnault, Félix, and Cdt. de Raoul. *Comment on marche: des divers modes de progression de la supériorité du mode en flexion.* Paris: Henri Charles-Lavauzelle, Éditeur militaire, 1897.

Regnault, Félix, and J. Lajard. "La Venus accroupie dans l'art grec." *La nature* 1152 (29 June 1895): 69–70.

Regnault, Jules. "Le phénomène de Johnny Coulon." *Revue de pathologie comparée* (8 February 1921): 99–102.

Renaud, Tristan. "King-Kong: le roi est nu." *Cinéma* 218 (February 1977): 44.

Riaille, Girard de. "Les Nubiens du Jardin d'acclimatation." *La nature* 221 (25 August 1877): 198–203.

Richer, Paul. *Physiologie artistique de l'homme en mouvement.* Paris: Octave Doin, 1895.

Rogin, Michael Paul. Ronald Reagan, *the Movie and Other Episodes in Political Demonology.* Berkeley: University of California Press, 1987.

Rony, Fatimah Tobing. "Image Sovereignty."·*Afterimage* 21 (7 February 1994): 4–5.

——. "On Biodegradable Culture." *Artforum* (September 1991): 23–25.

——. "Those Who Squat and Those Who Sit: The Iconography of Race in the 1895 Films of Félix-Louis Regnault." *Camera Obscura* 28 (1992): 263–89.

——. "Victor Masayesva, Jr. and the Politics of *Imagining Indians*." *Film Quarterly* 48, no. 2 (winter 1994–95): 20–33.

——. "'We Must First See Ourselves': Documentary Subversions in Contemporary African-American Women's Photography." In *Personal Narratives: Women Photographers of Color.* Exhibition catalog, 11–15. Winston-Salem: Southeastern Center for Contemporary Art, 1993.

Root, Nina J., ed. *Catalog of the American Museum of Natural History Film Archives.* New York: American Museum of Natural History Department of Library Services, 1987.

Rose, Phyllis. *Jazz Cleopatra: Josephine Baker in Her Time.* New York: Vintage Books, 1989.

Rosen, David N. "Race, Sex and Rebellion." *Jump Cut* 6 (March–April 1975): 8–10.

Rosen, Phil. "From Document to Diegesis: Historical Detail and Film Spectacle." Early draft of a chapter from the forthcoming *Past, Present: Theory, Cinema, History.*

Rosenbaum, Ron. "The Great Ivy League Nude Posture Photo Scandal." *New York Times Magazine,* 15 January 1995, 26ff.

Rotha, Paul. *Robert J. Flaherty: A Biography*, ed. Jay Ruby. Philadelphia: University of Pennsylvania Press, 1983.

Rotha, Paul, with the assistance of Basil Wright. "Nanook and the North." *Studies in Visual Communication* 6, no. 2 (summer 1980): 33–60.

Rouch, Jean. "Le film ethnographique." In *Ethnologie générale*, ed. Jean Poirier, *Encyclopédie de la Pleiade*, 24:429–71. Paris: Éditions Gallimard, 1968.

———. "L'itinéraire initatique." In *CinémAction: la science à l'écran*, ed. Jean-Jacques Mensy, 5–10. Paris: Les Éditions du Cerf, 1986.

———. "Our Totemic Ancestors and Crazed Masters." *Senri Ethnological Studies* 24 (1988): 225–38.

Ruby, Jay. "'The Aggie Will Come First': The Demystification of Robert Flaherty." In *Robert Flaherty: Photographer/Filmmaker*, ed. Jo-Anne Birnie Danzker, 66–73. Vancouver: Vancouver Art Gallery, 1980.

———. "Exposing Yourself: Reflexivity, Anthropology and Film." *Semiotica* 30, nos. 1–2 (1980): 153–79.

———. "Franz Boas and Early Camera Study of Behavior." *Kinesis* 3, no. 1 (fall 1980): 6–11, 16.

———. "Is Ethnographic Film a Filmic Ethnography?" *Studies in the Anthropology of Visual Communication* 2, no. 2 (fall 1975): 108.

———. "A Reexamination of the Early Career of Robert J. Flaherty." *Quarterly Review of Film Studies* 5, no. 4 (fall 1980): 431–57.

Rupp-Eisenreich, Britta. *Histories de l'anthropologie XVIe–XIXe siècles: colloque la pratique de l'anthropologie aujourd'hui 19–21 novembre 1981, Sèvres*. Paris: Klincksieck, 1984.

Rydell, Robert. *All the World's a Fair: Visions of Empire at American International Expositions*. Chicago: University of Chicago Press, 1987.

Sadoul, Georges. *L'invention du cinéma 1832–1897*. Vol. 1: *Histoire générale du cinéma*. Paris: Éditions Denoël, 1973.

Said, Edward. *Orientalism*. New York: Random House, 1978.

Sale, Kirkpatrick. *The Conquest of Paradise: Christopher Columbus and the Columbian Legacy*. New York: Alfred A. Knopf, 1990.

Sanders, Joseph E. "O'Brien and Monsters from the Id." In *The Scope of the Fantastic—Culture, Biography, Themes, Children's Literature. Selected Essays from the First International Conference on the Fantastic in Literature and Film*, vol. 11, ed. Robert A. Collins and Howard D. Pearce, 205–17. Westport, Conn.: Greenwood Press, 1985.

Sawchuk, Kim. "Unleashing the Demons of History: An Interview with Coco Fusco and Guillermo Gómez-Peña." *Parachute* 67 (September 1992): 22–29.

Scherer, Joanna Cohan. "Historical Photographs as Anthropological Documents: A Retrospect." *Visual Anthropology* 3 (1990): 131–55.

Schneider, William H. *An Empire for the Masses: The French Popular Image in Africa, 1870–1900*. Westport, Conn.: Greenwood Press, 1982.

Schoedsack, Ernest B. "The Making of an Epic." *American Cinematographer* 64 (February 1983): 40–44, 109–14.

Schor, Naomi. *Reading in Detail: Aesthetics and the Feminine*. New York: Methuen, 1987.

Schwartz, Vanessa R. "The Public's Taste for Reality: The Morgue, Wax Museums and Early Mass Culture in Fin-de-siècle Paris." Paper given at the Annual Meeting of the Society for Cinema Studies Conference, New Orleans, La., February 1993.

Seeleye, John. "Moby-Kong." *College Literature* 17, no. 1 (1990): 33–40.

Segal, Shari, and Rhoda Metraux. "Margaret Mead: Anthropologist of Our Time (Photo Essay)." *Studies in Visual Communication* 6, no. 1 (spring 1980): 4–14.

Sekula, Alan. "The Body and the Archive." *October* 39 (winter 1986): 3–64.

Senungetuk, Joseph E. *Give or Take a Century: An Eskimo Chronicle.* San Francisco: Indian Historian Press, 1971.

Sherwood, Robert. "Robert Flaherty's *Nanook of the North*." In *The Documentary Tradition,* ed. Lewis Jacobs, 15–19. New York: W. W. Norton, 1979.

Shohat, Ella. "Imaging Terra Incognita: The Disciplinary Gaze of Empire." *Public Culture* 3, no. 2 (spring 1991): 41–70.

Silverman, Debora. *Art Nouveau in Fin-de-siècle France: Politics, Psychology, and Style.* Berkeley: University of California Press, 1989.

Smith, Donald B. *Long Lance: The True Story of an Imposter.* Lincoln: University of Nebraska Press, 1982.

Smith, Eric Alden. "Inuit of the Canadian Eastern Arctic." *Cultural Survival Quarterly* (fall 1984): 32–37.

Snead, James. "Images of Blacks in Black Independent Films: A Brief Survey." In *Blackframes: Critical Perspectives on Black Independent Cinema,* ed. Mbye B. Cham and Claire Andrade-Watkins, 16–25. Cambridge, Mass.: MIT Press, 1988.

———. "Spectatorship and Capture in *King Kong:* The Guilty Look." *Critical Quarterly* 33, no. 1 (spring 1991): 53–69.

Sontag, Susan. "Fascinating Fascism." In *Under the Sign of Saturn,* 73–105. New York: Vintage Books, 1980.

Spackman, Barbara. *Decadent Genealogies: The Rhetoric of Sickness from Baudelaire to D'Annunzio.* Ithaca: Cornell University Press, 1989.

Spindler, Paul. "New Guinea 1904–1906." *Science and Film* 8, no. 1 (March 1959): 10–14.

Spivak, Gayatri Chakravorty. "Can the Subaltern Speak? Speculations on Widow-Sacrifice." *Wedge* 7–8 (winter–spring 1985): 271–313.

———. "An Interview with Gayatri Spivak." Interview by Catherine Benamou, Judy Burns, Jill MacDougall, Avanthi Meduri, Peggy Phelan, and Susan Slyomovics. *Women & Performance: A Journal of Feminist Theory* 5, no. 9 (1990): 80–92.

Springer, Claudia. "Ethnocentric Circles: A Short History of Ethnographic Film." *The Independent* (December 1984): 13–18.

Stefansson, Vilhjalmur. *The Standardisation of Error.* London: Kegan Paul, Trench, Trubner, 1929.

Stirling, Matthew W. "Flight to the Stone Age." *Explorers Journal* 53, no. 3 (September 1975): 98–105.

Stocking, George W., Jr. *American Social Scientists and Race Theory: 1890–1915.* Ann Arbor: University Microfilms, 1961.

———. "Bones, Bodies, Behavior." In *Bones, Bodies, Behavior: Essays on Biological Anthropology,* ed. George W. Stocking Jr., *History of Anthropology,* vol. 5, 3–17. Madison: University of Wisconsin Press, 1988.

——. "Essays on Museums and Material Culture." In *Objects and Others: Essays on Museums and Material Culture*, ed. George W. Stocking Jr., *History of Anthropology*, vol. 3, 3–9. Madison: University of Wisconsin Press, 1985.

——. "The Ethnographer's Magic: Fieldwork in British Anthropology from Tylor to Malinowski." In *Observers Observed: Essays on Ethnographic Fieldwork*, ed. George W. Stocking Jr., *History of Anthropology*, vol. 1, 70–120. Madison: University of Wisconsin Press, 1983.

——. "The Ethnographic Sensibility of the 1920s and the Dualism of the Anthropological Tradition." In *Romantic Motives: Essays on Anthropological Sensibility*, ed. George W. Stocking Jr., *History of Anthropology*, vol. 6, 208–76. Madison: University of Wisconsin Press, 1989.

——. *Race, Culture and Evolution: Essays in the History of Anthropology*. New York: Free Press, 1968.

——. *Victorian Anthropology*. New York: Free Press, 1987.

Stoddard, Lothrop. *The Revolt against Civilization: The Menace of the Under Man*. New York: Charles Scribner's Sons, 1923.

Stoller, Paul. *The Cinematic Griot: The Ethnography of Jean Rouch*. Chicago: University of Chicago Press, 1992.

Suid, Lawrence. "King Kong and the Military." *American Classic Screen* (July–August 1977): 14–16.

Suleri, Sara. *The Rhetoric of English India*. Chicago: University of Chicago Press, 1992.

Tagg, John. *The Burden of Representation: Essays on Photographies and Histories*. Amherst: University of Massachusetts Press, 1988.

Taureg, Martin. "The Development of Standards for Scientific Films in German Ethnography." *Studies in Visual Communication* 9, no. 1 (winter 1983): 19–29.

Taussig, Michael. *Shamanism, Colonialism and the Wild Man: A Study in Terror and Healing*. Chicago: University of Chicago Press, 1987.

Taylor, Clyde. "The Re-birth of the Aesthetic in Cinema." *Wide Angle* 13, nos. 3–4 (July–October 1991), 12–13.

Taylor, J. Garth. "An Eskimo Abroad, 1880: His Diary and Death." *Canadian Geographic* 101, no. 5 (October–November 1981): 38–43.

Telotte, J. P. "The Movies as Monster: Seeing in *King Kong*." *Georgia Review* 42, no. 2 (summer 1988): 388–98.

Torgovnick, Marianna. *Gone Primitive: Savage Intellects, Modern Lives*. Chicago: University of Chicago Press, 1990.

Trask, Haunani-Kay. *From a Native Daughter: Colonialism and Sovereignty in Hawai'i*. Monroe, Maine: Common Courage Press, 1993.

Troy, William. "Beauty and the Beast." *The Nation*, vol. 136 (22 March 1933): 326.

Trutat, Eugène. *La photographie animée*. Paris: 1899.

Turner, George. "Hunting 'The Most Dangerous Game.'" *American Cinematographer* 68 (September 1987): 40–48.

Valladares, Michelle Yasmine. "Native American Producers Form Alliance." *The Independent* 16, no. 4 (May 1993): 5–7.

Vallois, H. V. "La Société d'anthropologie de Paris 1859–1959." *Bulletins et mémoires de la Société d'anthropologie de Paris* 1st tome, 11th ser. (1960): 293–312.

Vialle, Gabriel. "Les chasses du Comte Zaroff." *La revue du cinéma* 269 (1973): 41–43.

Volkman, Toby Alice. "The Hunter-Gatherer Myth in Southern Africa: Preserving Nature or Culture?" *Cultural Survival* 10, no. 2 (1986): 25–32.

Walker, Sheila S. "Tarzan in the Classroom: How 'Educational' Films Mythologize Africa and Miseducate Americans." *Journal of Negro Education* 62, no. 1 (1993): 3–23.

Wallace, Michele. *Invisibility Blues: From Pop to Theory.* London: Verso, 1990.

——. "Modernism, Postmodernism and the Problem of the Visual in Afro-American Culture." In *Out There: Marginalization and Contemporary Cultures,* ed. Russell Ferguson, Martha Gever, Trinh T. Minh-ha, and Cornel West, 39–50. New York and Cambridge, Mass.: New Museum of Contemporary Art and Massachusetts Institute of Technology, 1990.

Weatherford, Elizabeth. "Native American Media Makers at Work." *The Independent* 4 (1983): 17–19.

Weatherford, Elizabeth, with Emilia Seubert. *Native Americans on Film and Video.* New York: Museum of the American Indian/Heye Foundation, 1981.

Weiner, Annette. "The Ethnographer with the Movie Camera." Unpublished paper.

Wells, H. G. *The Time Machine.* New York: Random House, 1991; orig. publ. 1895.

West, Cornel. "The New Politics of Cultural Difference." In *Out There: Marginalization and Contemporary Cultures,* ed. Russell Ferguson, Martha Gever, Trinh T. Minh-ha, and Cornel West, 19–38. New York and Cambridge, Mass.: New Museum of Contemporary Art and the Massachusetts Institute of Technology, 1990.

White, Hayden. "The Value of Narrativity in the Representation of Reality." *Critical Inquiry* 7, no. 1 (autumn 1980): 5–24.

Wiener, Margaret J. *Visible and Invisible Realms: Power, Magic, and Colonial Conquest in Bali.* Chicago: University of Chicago Press, 1995.

Williams, Elizabeth A. "The Science of Man: Anthropological Thought and Institutions in Nineteenth-century France." Ph.D. dissertation, Indiana University, 1983.

Williams, Linda. "Film Body: An Implantation of Perversions." In *Narrative, Apparatus, Ideology: A Film Theory Reader,* ed. Phil Rosen, 507–34. New York: Columbia University Press, 1986.

Winston, Brian. "Before Grierson, before Flaherty: The Documentary Film in 1914." *Sight and Sound* 57, no. 4 (autumn 1988): 277–79.

Worth, Sol, and John Adair. *Through Navajo Eyes: An Exploration in Film Communication and Anthropology.* Bloomington: Indiana University Press, 1972.

Wray, Fay. "How Fay Met Kong, or the Scream That Shook the World." *New York Times,* 21 September 1969, D17.

Wright, Richard. *Native Son.* New York: Harper & Row, 1989; orig. publ. 1940.

Xert, G. "Les nouvelles galleries du muséum." *La nature* 1297 (9 April 1898): 297–98.

Newspaper and Journal Reviews

"Gin Chow at Chinese." *Los Angeles Times,* 1 April 1933.

"Imaginative Thriller." *Los Angeles Times,* 9 January 1933.

"Island of Bali Shown on Screen." *New York Times,* 21 July 1932, 15.

"King Kong." *Films in Review* (June 1975): 61.

"King Kong Lives Again." *New York Times*, 17 August 1986, 10:3.

"Museum Shreds Nude Photos of Former Students at Yale." *New York Times*, 29 January 1995, 14.

Review of *Chang*. *New York Times*, 30 April 1927, 25.

Review of *Goona Goona*. *Variety*, 17 September 1932, 18:4.

Review of *Grass*. *New York Times*, 31 March 1925, 17.

Review of *Island of Lost Souls*. *Afro-American*, 1 March 1933.

Review of *King Kong*. *Afro-American*, 27 April 1933.

Review of *King Kong*. *Journal and Guide*, 3 June 1933, 13.

Review of *King Kong*. *London Times*, 1933.

Review of *King Kong*. *New York Times*, 2 March 1933, 12:1.

Review of *King Kong*. *Newsweek* 1 (11 March 1933): 27.

Review of *King Kong*. *The Pittsburgh Courier*, 6 May 1933.

Review of *Roosevelt in Africa*. *The Moving Picture World* 6:528–29.

"Thrills in Store." *Los Angeles Times*, 14 March 1933.

INDEX

Abraham, 105

Abu-Lughod, Lila, 12

Accused/Blowtorch/Padlock (1986), 216

Adair, John, 211

Adams, Charlie, 123

Adorno, Theodor W., 185

Africa, as one pole of an oppositional paradigm, 24

African American(s): Josephine Baker as, 199–203; Hurston's research, 203–11; Other, 180

African(s), 4–5, 14, 21–26, 28, 41–42, 65, 83–90, 129–30, 189, 216; and chrono-photography, 48–59

Akeley, Carl E., 87, 102

Alexander, Elizabeth, 189–90

Allakariallak, 101–4

Allegret, Marc, 200

American Museum of Natural History, 86–87, 94–95, 98, 102, 157, 164, 210, 213

American Museum of Unnatural History, 210

Animality, 28, 114–15, 137

Anthropographie, 33

Anthropologist, as redeemer, 138. *See also* Bateson; Boas; Hurston; Mead; Stocking

Anthropology, 6–7, 10, 12–13, 24, 26, 28–30, 61–64, 161, 196–98; crisis in, 197; Culture and Personality School, 147; and decolonization, 197; and the ethnographic, 196; ethnographization of,

78; and film, 46–48, 66–71, 211–12 (*see also* Cinema, ethnographic; Film, ethnographic); and Zora Neale Hurston, 198, 203–208; and fear of hybridity, 27, 187; and medical imagery, 29, 31–35, 46; and museums, 63; and notion of vanishing native, 90–91; and romantic primitivism, 100; and idea of redemption, 131; views of race, 27 (*see also* Race(s)); and seeing, 79; through spectacle, 36–43; treatment of time, 10, 144. *See also* Boas; Ethnographic, the; Mead; Museum(s)

Anthropometry, 225–26 n. 42

Archive(s): of films, 48, 62–63, 67–71, 79–90, 236 n. 67; ideology of, 67–71

Archives de la planète, 80, 82, 195

Argonauts of the Western Pacific (1922), 14, 117

Art: "Art Science," 92; ethnographic realism, 243 n. 52; historical evidence of pathologies, 33; representation and race, 39, 203, 227 n. 53

Arunta, 65

Asch, Timothy, 196–97

Asia, in cinematic imagination, 175–76

Authenticity: and E. S. Curtis, 91; and the ethnographic present, 68; of *Grass,* 135; and work of Zora Neale Hurston, 209; indigenous people embodying, 195; of Inuit video, 124–26; and *King Kong,* 188; in *Nanook of the North,* 99–100, 113,

Authenticity (*cont.*)
116–17, 123–24, 126; politics of, 92, 95, 97
Autochromes, 81

Baartman, Saartjie, 17, 189, 226 n. 45
Bagus, Dr. Ide Gde Ing., 146
Baker, Josephine, 198–203, 215
Baktiari, 133–35
Baldwin, James, 193–94, 218
Bali, 145–48
Balibar, Etienne, 32
Balikci, Asen, 99, 108, 116, 120, 133
Bann, Stephen, 101
Barsam, Richard, 114
Batak, 3–4
Bateson, Gregory, 67, 71, 145–47
Bazin, André, 16, 131–32, 153
Bear Claw, Dean Curtis, 213
Beautiful Bermuda (1921), 84
Belo, Jane, 206, 208
Benga, Ota, 157–58, 189, 213
Benjamin, Walter, 9–10, 46, 58–59
Bérenger-Féraud, L. J. B., 27
Bhabha, Homi, 201–02
Binarisms, 84
Birth of a Nation, The, 11–12, 180
Black Skin, White Masks, 5, 16
Blonde Venus (1932), 172–73, 183
Boas, Franz, 66–67, 69; compared to Curtis, 93–94; and treatment of Eskimos, 104–05; and Zora Neale Hurston, 203–7, 209; comments on *Nanook of the North,* 77–78
Böcklin, Arnold, 181
Body(ies): anthropological interest in, 27–28; Josephine Baker as, 199; cinema of the, 111; Ethnographic, 62, 72; French, 58–62; landscaped, 79, 82; and Masayesva's film technique, 212–13, 215–16; of Native(s), 195; and racialization, 71, 215; and Regnault's work, 25–26, 49
Boundaries, performer/observer, 39–41, 169–70; violations of, 155, 165–66, 200 (*see also* Hybridity)

Braun, Marta, 47
Bride of Kong, 17, 177–78
Bring 'Em Back Alive (1932), 171
Broca, Paul, 25–27, 30, 162
Broken Blossoms (1919), 176
Brunhes, Jean, 80
Buck, Frank, 171
Buffon, Comte, 7
Burden, Katherine, 164–65
Burden, W. Douglas, 164–65, 187
Bureau of American Ethnology, 68
Burroughs, Edgar Rice, 182

Cambridge Anthropological Expeditions, 64
Camera, as rifle, 165
Camp de Thiaroye (1987), 73, 215
Cannibalism, fascinating, 9–13, 15, 24, 90, 183, 190, 217
Cannibals of the South Seas (1917), 89, 152
Canudo, Ricciotto, 115
Captain's Chair, The (1938), 121–22
Captured by Aborigines (1913), 85
Carby, Hazel V., 204
Carelli, Vincent, 197
Carroll, Noël, 169–70, 182
Cartwright, Lisa, 232 n. 25
Carver, H. P., 141–42
Censorship, 148, 212, 253 n. 46
Centaur, image of, 167
Chang (1927), 15, 133, 135–37, 154, 159
Charnov, Elaine, 205
"Chiefly Feasts: The Enduring Kwakiutl Potlatch," 98
"China Girl," 232 n. 25
Chippewa, 141–42
Christ, imagery in *The Silent Enemy,* 143. *See also* Redemption
Chronophotography, 13–15, 21, 23, 48–61, 195–96
Church, African American, 207–9
Churchill, Ward, 197
Cinema: defined, 8–9; beginning of, 25–26; controlling meaning, 90; and creation of

monsters, 189; early-twentieth-century, 9; and positivist science, 46–47, 63; and idea of redemption, 131; Regnault's views, 46–47, 62; and the return gaze, 43; successor to exhibitions, 108; as taxidermy, 88, 102; as teratology, 160. *See also* Cinema, ethnographic; Film

Cinema, ethnographic, 6–9, 12; using artifice to convey truth, 116; its context, 24; recent examples, 220 n. 16; golden age, 153; and horror film, 163; observational, 196; locus of the race of history, 170; and self-referentiality, 171; themes, 16; and visualization, 184; compared with zoos, 154. *See also* Cinema; Film

"Cinema of Exploration, The," 16

Cinématographe, 47

Cinématoscope, 47

Circle Dance (1898), 83

Civilization: as goal of race of history, 170; in *King Kong,* 165, 186; in *Trader Horn,* 173

Civilized, the, 3, 213. *See also* Modern, the

Clansman, The (1905), 180

Clemente, Steve, 177

Clifford, James, 68, 118, 186

Close-up, the, 212

Collage, a technique in *King Kong,* 182

Colonial Exposition (1931), 62

Colonialism: in America, 143; colonialization ongoing, 198; and contamination, 144–45; Dutch in Bali, 146–47, 153; and exploitation, 91; film and colonialization, 72, 84, 217; French, 56, 72–73; and guilt, 131; and Mead, 146; denied in *Moana,* 141; and Orwell, 42–43; and stereotyping, 202; in Tahiti, 144–45; and travelogues, 85; and writing, 152. *See also* Imperialism

Coming of Age in Samoa, 138

Commandment Keeper Church, 203, 206–9

Comment en marche, 59. See also *Marche en flexion*

Committee for the Research into Dementia Praecox, 146

Comte, Charles, 21, 22, 48–49

Congo (1995), 197

Consciousness, double, 4

Contamination, 144–45, 149

Cooper, Merian C., 133–37, 158–59, 165, 172

Costner, Kevin, 5, 197

Craniology, 27, 30

Criticism, film, 12

Croisiére noire, La (1926), 132–33

Culture and Personality School, 147

Culture(s): southern black, 206–11; indigenous surviving under colonialism, 91, 98; living, 206–7; as presented on film, 43, 66–67; pure and authentic, 68

Curtis, Edward Sheriff, 14, 70, 90–98, 214

Cuvier, Georges, 17, 189

Dahomeyan Ethnographic Exposition (1893), 39–40

Dance, as spectacle, 65–66

Dances with Wolves (1990), 5, 197–98

D'Anglure, Bernard Saladin, 110

Danzker, Jo-Anne Birnie, 110

Darwinian link, Kong as, 179

Darwinism, Social, 182

Death: of Inuit, 106, 109; in *Nanook,* 115–16, 131; and vanishing races, 80, 86–88, 91, 97

Decolonization, 197

Degeneration, 28

De Heusch, Luc, 100, 116–17, 122

De Mortillet, Gabriel, 28

Denis, Armand, 145, 148

Deren, Maya, 210

Dinosaurs, 180–82

Disappearing World, 70

Discourse of the self, 12–13

Disneyland, 184

Distance, viewer from image, 62

Dixon, Joseph K., 92

Doane, Mary Ann, 62

"Docteur Regnault marche," 61

Documentaires romancés, 85

Documentary, the: and authenticity, 116–17; term coined, 139. *See also* Cinema, ethnographic; Film, ethnographic
Doré, Gustave, 181
Douglas, Mary, 161
Dragon Lizards of Komodo, 164
Dubois, W. B., 4
Du Chaillu, Paul, 179
Duchet, Michèle, 7
Dunham, Katherine, 67, 210
Dutch, the, in Bali, 146–47, 153

Easy for Who to Say (1989), 72, 215
Edison, Thomas, 108
Eliade, Mircea, 244 n. 14
Empire State Building, 170, 186
Encyclopaedia Cinematographica, 69
Eskimos, imagery of, 104–5, 107–8
Esquimaux Game of Snap-The-Whip, 246 n. 32
Esquimaux Leap Frog, 246 n. 32
"Esquimaux Village," 108, 246 n. 32
Ethics, 178
Ethnicity, in Hollywood productions, 177
Ethnie, 227 n. 47
Ethnographer, the, 118, 120
Ethnographiable, 7–8
Ethnographic, the, 6–10, 15, 59, 71, 78, 104, 126, 130, 213; and anthropology, 196; Josephine Baker and, 198–203; episteme, 197; in expositions, 41–42; and Zora Neale Hurston, 204; indigenous people as, 194; and innocence, 254 n. 50; and *King Kong*, 177, 186, 189; monstrosity as, 159, 161–63, 191; objectification as, 5; Other, 58, 117, 166 (*see also* Other); present, 92, 102; three modes of representation, 195; spaces of resistance in, 217; lacking subjectivity, 203; through text alone, 89; themes in, 159; and trance in Bali, 146–47. *See also* Cinema, ethnographic; Film, ethnographic
Ethnographic/Historical, 68, 153–55, 188, 196, 198

Ethnographic Exposition (1895), 4, 15, 36, 39–40, 195, 215
Ethnographicization, 78
Ethnography, 6–7, 38; radical forms of, 210; romantic, 99–126; salvage, 78, 90–98, 126, 143. *See also* Ethnographic, the
Evolution: in Boas's thought, 78; evolutionary hierarchy, 27, 175; narrative of, 25, 41, 83, 195, 215; native(s) as existing in evolutionary time, 194–95; typology, 14. *See also* Missing link
Exotic, the, 6, 90, 132. *See also* Picturesque
Exotisme et le cinéma, le, 16, 100, 137
Expedition film. *See* Film, ethnographic
Explorations in Equatorial Africa (1856), 179
Explorer(s), 21; Flaherty as, 119–22; and treatment of Inuit, 105–7; Lévi-Strauss's views, 219 n. 8
Exposition Ethnographique de l'Afrique Occidentale (1895), 21, 36–37, 40, 45, 72; and chronophotography, 48–59
Expositions, ethnographic, 21–42; and dominance, 68; and race, 36–43. *See also* Dahomeyan Ethnographic Exposition; Exposition Ethnographique; Exposition Universelle; Pan-American Exposition; World's Columbian Exposition
Exposition Universelle (1878), 37–39

Fabian, Johannes, 10, 30, 67, 102, 118, 130
Fanon, Frantz, 4–6, 16–17, 194
Fascinating cannibalism. *See* Cannibalism
Fienup-Riordan, Ann, 107
Film: artifice in, 116; conventions of, 211–12; chronophotography as, 23; as ethnographic tool, 23; for recording facts, 193; inappropriate, 153, 216, 217; and Navajo, 211–12; as the redemption of physical reality, 131; and political physics, 144; "racial," 15, 129–134, 137, 141–44, 154, 159, 176–78, 196; Regnault's views, 45–48; as scientific, 10, 13–14, 45–48. *See also* Chronophotography; Cinema; Film, ethnographic

Film, ethnographic, 7–8, 11, 43, 196; and anthropological knowledge, 100; as art, 14; Boas and, 77–79; as entertainment, 64–65; expedition film, 164–65; as a genre, 219–20 n. 14; German style, 237 n. 73; grammar of, 212; and hybridity, 163–64; and iconography of race, 71; *King Kong*, about making, 159; Mauss's views, 69; to inspire memory, 214–15; implied narrative in, 25; origin, 14; *real*, 121; themes, 63; justifying theories, 46–48, 63, 69; and third eye, 210; as time machine, 43; as tool, 78; as voyeurism, 82. *See also* Cinema, ethnographic

Filmmaker(s): and censorship, 212; as *flâneur*, 59; as hero, 90, 170–71; as redeemer, 138; and problems of representation, 216; as surgeon, 46. *See also* Asch; Balikci; Burden; Costner; Cooper; Flaherty; Griffith; Holmes; Hurston; Johnson; MacDougal; Marshall, John; Mead; Murnau; Poisey; Regnault; Rouch; Schoedsack; Sternberg; Van Dyke; Van Valin

Films, individual. *See* individual titles

Flaherty, Robert J., 11–16, 98–126, 138–40, 195–96; as Explorer/Artist, 119, 126; as innovator, 109–10

Flâneur, 58–59

Flanner, Janet, 200

Franco-Prussian War, 61

Fraser, Sir James G., 14

Freeman, Derek, 146

Fusco, Coco, 190, 215

Gardner, Robert, 196

Gaze: allied with camera, 175–76; colonial protection from, 80; returned by colonized Native(s), 39–43; and racial identity, 55

Geertz, Clifford, 118

Gehrts, Meg, 88

Gérôme, Jean-Léon, 38

Gesture, language of, 3–4, 57–58. See also *Langage par gestes*

Ghost Dance, film as, 213

Ginsburg, Carlo, 35

Ginsburg, Faye, 8, 197

Gnosis, 24

Golden Age, 140, 147, 149

Gómez-Peña, Guillermo, 190–91, 215

Goodall, Jane, 179

"Goona goona," 148, 150

Goona Goona (1932), 145–48, 178, 186

Grass (1925), 15, 133–35, 159, 163

Great White Hunter, 90, 133, 167, 197. *See also* Roosevelt, Teddy

Greenhalgh, Paul, 37, 38

Griaule, Marcel, 69, 116, 159

Grierson, John, 139–41

Griffith, D. W., 11–12, 180

Gruber, Jacob W., 91

Guatinau, 191

Haddon, Alfred Cort, 63, 65–66

Haeseler, J. A., 70–71

Hansen, Ann Mikijuk, 124

Hansen, William, 124

Haraway, Donna, 102, 179

Harrison, Marguerite E., 133–34

Hays Office, 253 n. 46

Heart of Darkness, 121

Heart of Whiteness, 121

Hellenbrand, Harold, 179

Hemenway, Robert E., 206

Herskovitz, Melville, 67

Hilton-Simpson, M. W., 70–71

Historical/Ethnographic, 68, 78, 144, 153–55, 188, 196, 213

Historical Same/Ethnographic Other, 13, 58, 166

Historifiable, 7–8

History: banished, 109–110, 115; definitions of, 193–94; evolutionary conception of, 25; and race, 194; as (a) race, 25–30; as "sovereign science," 9; as story-telling, 194–98; writing of, 218. *See also* Time

Holmes, Burton, 83–84

Homoeroticism, 256–57 n. 46

Hoodoo, 206
Hopi, and filmmaking, 212–13
Hopi Snake Dance, 92
Horror film(s), 161, 163; and hybridity, 170; and *King Kong*, 166–70; and *The Most Dangerous Game*, 167
Hudson's Bay Company, 109
Hughes, Langston, 206
Humor, in travelogues, 84–88
Hunt, George, 94–95
Hunting, big game, 86–88. *See also Most Dangerous Game, The*
Hurston, Zora Neale, 67, 198, 203–11, 215–16
Hussey, Christopher, 79
Hybridity, 27, 159, 162, 164, 166, 187; Josephine Baker and, 200; as impure, 161; in *The Island of Lost Souls*, 169; and *King Kong*, 181, 196; of technology and style, 148

Images, and sovereignty, 211–16
Imperialism, 26, 29, 85. *See also* Colonialism
In Borneo, Land of the Headhunters (1916), 241 n. 29
In the Land of the Headhunters (1914), 14, 93–98, 131, 152, 214
Indigenous, the, 13
Indigenous people(s), 79, 85, 90, 142, 176–77, 194–95, 197. *See also* African(s), Native American(s)
Ingagi (1933), 159
Inscription, 45, 61–62, 79, 195, 234 n. 39
Institut für den wissenschaftlichen Film [IWF], 69
Inuit, 77, 99–111, 113, 122–26, 138; in *Nanook*, 77–78, 104, 110–11, 115–18, 120, 123, 126; in Pan-American Exposition (1901), 108; video produced by, 123–26
Inuit Broadcasting Corporation, 123–24, 215
Invention of Africa, The, 24
Island of Dr. Moreau, The (1896), 167

Island of Lost Souls, The (1933), 159, 167–69
Isle of the Dead, The (1880), 181
Itam Hakim, Hopiit (1985), 212
Itivimuit, 99
IWF [Institut für den wissenschaftlichen Film], 69

Jacknis, Ira, 67, 93–94
Jameux, Charles, 151
Johnson, Noble P., 177
Johnson, Osa and Martin, 88
Jomard, Edmé-François, 38
Ju/'hoansi, 260–61 n. 10
Jungle, as metaphor, 181–82

Kahn, Albert, 68–69, 80–81, 195
Kaler, I Made, 146
Kane, Elisha Kent, 106–7
Kearton, Cherry, 86
Kildea, Gary, 197
King Kong, 2, 3, 13–16, 17, 88, 133, 137, 154–55, 157–191, 196; and audience, 182–86; and *Dragon Lizards of Komodo*, 164–65; and horror films, 159–61, 166–68; and imperialism, 186–89; representation of nonwhites, 175–79; and Woman, 171–75. *See also* Kong
Knowledge, anthropological, 100
Komodo dragon, 159, 164–65
Kong, 179–89; as Darwinian link, 179; as monster, 159–64, 182, 188–89. *See also King Kong*
Kracauer, Siegfried, 100, 103, 131
Ku Klux Klan, 12
Kulturkreis school, 237 n. 73
Kunuk, Zacharias, 124–26
Kuper, Adam, 27
Kwakwaka'wakw (Kwakiutl), 67, 93–98, 214

La croisière noire, 250 n. 11
Ladd, Edward, 213
Lafitau, Joseph François, 7
Landscape(s), 82, 115

Langage par gestes, le, 48, 57–58, 62, 65, 78, 80, 195
Last of the Mohicans, The (1992), 197
Latour, Bruno, 45
Leacock, Richard, 126
Leprohon, Pierre, 16, 100, 132, 137, 153–54, 159
Leroi-Gourhan, André, 66
Letourneau, Charles, 28
Lévi-Strauss, Claude, 5, 7, 131
Lévy, Jean, 184–86
L'exotisme et le cinéma, 16, 100
Liotard, André F., 154
Locomotion studies, 33–35
Lomax, Alan, 195, 208
London, Jack, 88
Long Lance, 142–43
Loos, Adolf, 38
Lost World, The (1921), 180
Lucas, George, 197
Lyman, Christopher, 93

MacDougall, David and Judith, 8, 197
Madagascar: Manners and Customs of the Sakalava (1910), 83
Male, White, 15, 28, 144–45, 169–71, 175. *See also* Great White Hunter
Malekula, 89
Malinowski, Bronislaw, 14, 117–18, 120–22, 161
Man the Hunter, 139
Mann, Michael, 197
Marche en flexion, 49, 59–61, 72, 77, 215
Marey, Etienne-Jules, 23, 25–26, 47, 59
Marshall, Frank, 197
Marshall, John, 196, 260–61 n.10
Masayesva, Victor Jr., 212–13, 215
Mason, Mrs. Charlotte Osgood, 204–5
Massot, Claude, 122
Mauss, Marcel, 69
Maybury-Lewis, David, 197
Mead, Margaret, 67, 69, 71, 138, 145–47, 193–94, 197, 206, 208, 216, 236 n.63
Medicine, 25, 29–35, 46

Méliès, Gaston, 5
Michaelis, Anthony, 70–71
Migration, and hybridity, 187
Military Drills of Kikuyu Tribe and other Ceremonies (1914), 87
Millenium: Tribal Wisdom and the Modern World (1992), 197
Mind of the Primitive Man, The (1911), 78
Minotaure, 184
Misfortunes of Mr. and Mrs. Mott on Their Trip to Tahiti, 85
Missing link, 157, 179, 182. *See also* Evolution
Mixed race(s), 27, 162, 165–66, 200, 230 n.85. *See also* Racism
Mixture, producing monsters, 163
Moana: A Romance of the Golden Age (1926), 15, 99, 131–32, 137–43, 153, 155, 163
Modern, the, 132, 141, 144, 153; opposed to tradition, 24. *See also* Civilized, the; Modern/Primitive
Modern/Primitive, 144, 151–53, 162, 196
Monster(s): Josephine Baker as, 199; as cinema creations, 189; *ethnographiable,* 15; in horror films, 166–70; in *King Kong,* 159–64, 182, 188–89; produced by mixture, 163; subject of representation, 159
Monstrosity, 149, 151, 153, 196; as ethnographic, 159; and horror films, 163; in *King Kong,* 160; as visual, 161; in (civilized) white man, 169. *See also* Teratology
Moreno, Fidel, 213
Most Dangerous Game, The (1932), 87, 159, 166–69, 177
Mould, David H., 133
Movement, 33–35, 47
Mudimbe, V. Y., 9, 24
Mugambi, Helen Nabasuta, 211, 216
Mules and Men (1935), 204, 209–11
Mulvey, Laura, 175
"Murders in the Rue Morgue," 179
Murnau, F. W., 149–50, 152

Museum(s), ethnographic, 38, 85, 210–11;
and anthropology, 63; Boas and, 94–95;
community, 98; display, 95, 112, 181,
189; of ethnographic film, 63; a time ma-
chine, 129; world as, 32. *See also* Ameri-
can Museum of Natural History;
Archives
Musser, Charles, 83
Muybridge, Eadweard, 25–26
*My Eskimo Friends: "Nanook of the
North"* (1924), 120–21
Mythic, the, 242 n. 14
Myth of first contact, 7

Nanook of the North (1922), 11–16, 93,
99–105, 109–126, 130, 132–33, 138, 153,
160, 178, 186, 195–96, 214; analysis of
scenes, 111–16; authenticity of, 116,
123–24; Boas's comments, 77–78; *Heart
of Whiteness*, 121; history banished,
110, 115–16; inaccuracies of the film,
123; landscape in, 111, 114–15; compared with *Moana*, 139–41; and
participant-observation, 116–19; seal
hunt, 114
Nanook Revisited (1988), 122–23
Narrative, implied, 25
Nation, nineteenth-century discourses on,
26
National Geographic, 7, 10
Native American(s), 68; photographed by
Curtis, 90–98; in *Dances with Wolves*,
197–98; filming by, 211–14; surviving
European encroachment, 91. *See also*
Chippewa; Inuit; Navajo
Native Tribes of Central Australia, The
(1912), 64
Native(s), x, 5–6, 86–88; as authentic, 43;
cinematic types, 177–78; devoted, 120–
21; in evolutionary past, 194–96 (*see
also* Evolution); returned gaze, 42–43;
implicit violence toward, 86–88; in *King
Kong*, 176–78; "native villages," 36–40,
43; vanishing, 91. *See also* Primitive(s);
Race(s), vanishing; Savage(s)

Nature, La, 62
Navajo, 92, 211–12, 214
Nayoumealuk, Charles, 123
Neale, Stephen, 163
Nederlands Filmmuseum, 240 n. 23
"Negative scene of instruction," 203
Nègres, 39
Nias, 177
Noble Savage, 72, 97, 180, 194. *See also*
Savage(s)
Noogooshoweetok, 111
Nordau, Max, 28
Nordic, the, 108
Normal and the Pathological, The, 160
Normality, defined, 160–61
North American Indian, The, 90, 92
Northwest Coast Indians, 95
Nowkawalk, Moses, 123–24
Nunaqpa/Going Inland (1991), 124–26

Objectification, 5. *See also* Other; Self-
alienation
Objectivity, 210–11
O'Brien, Willis, 181–82
Observer/Observed, 216–17
Ojibwa Indians, 141–42
Ollier, Claude, 181
Ontological realism, 117
Oriental, 5
Origin of the Species, The (1859), 26, 130
"Ornament as Crime," 38
Orwell, George, 42, 87
Other, the, 4–6, 10–11, 13; African Ameri-
can as, 180; coexistence with, 191; eth-
nographic, 17, 28 (*see also* Ethnographic,
the); in Hollywood films, 177–78; post-
colonial, 15; and surrealism, 186; as
third eye, 217; values concerning, 24
Ousmane, Sembène, 73

Pan-American Exposition (1901), 108
Paradise, the lost, 147
Paris Ethnographic Exposition (1895). *See*
Exposition Ethnographique
Participant observation, 116–19

Pasolini, Pier Paolo, 242 n. 14
Pathology: monsters as pathological, 161; and race, 29–32
Peary, Robert, 105–6
Performance, as space of resistance, 217
Phillips, O. P., 68
Photography, 9, 33–35, 66, 88–89, 129; by Curtis, 90–94. *See also* Chronophotography
Physics, political. *See* Political physics
Physiologie ethniques comparées, 33
Picturesque, the, 78–80, 84, 89–90, 93, 108
Pitseolak, Peter, 110
Pöch, Rudolf, 64–66, 71
Poe, Edgar Allan, 179
Poirier, Léon, 132, 153
Poisey, David, 124
Political physics, 144–45, 153, 155, 188
Pollman, Tessel, 146
Polygenist doctrine, 27
Portrait of a Friend (1978), 194
Postmodern, the, 188
Posture, 33–34
Pratt, Mary Louise, 82
Preloran, Jorge, 162
Primitive, the, 10, 71, 78, 112, 132, 141, 153, 195; and Josephine Baker, 199–203; body, 28; as a film genre, 12; Other, 160, 253 n. 44 (*see also* Other); as pathological, 27, 32–33; Zou Zou a sign of, 202. *See also* Primitive/Modern; Primitive(s); Savage, the
Primitive/Modern, 144, 151–53, 194, 196, 198
Primitive(s), 7, 126, 139; Zora Neale Hurston as, 205; Inuit as, 99–100; Irish as, 223 n. 22; Nanook as, 104; in timeless picturesques, 13
Primitiveness, 24
Primitivism: art movement, 138, 186; and *King Kong*, 186; romantic, 100, 137
Princess Tam Tam (1935), 203
Propaganda, travelogues as, 85
Puputan, 153
Purity and Danger (1966), 161

Qaggiq/The Gathering Place (1989), 125–26
Quadra Island Kwagiulth Museum, 98

Race, 7, 10–12, 28–30; art and, 38–39; Homi Bhabha's views, 201–2; constructed nature of category, 30; discourse of, 26; and history, 25, 28, 38, 194; narrative of, 21–43; nineteenth-century discourse on, 26, 179; linked with pathology, 29–32; rhetoric of, 29; as steeplechase, 28; stereotypes, 201–2; as written in film, 45–73. *See also* Film, racial; Race(s); Racism
Race(s): Aryan, 134–35; classification, 223–24 n. 21; seen through ethnographic exposition(s), 36–43; evolutionary typology, 14, 27; and mixing, 187–88; Regnault's views, 31–33, 39–40; vanishing, 15, 67, 80, 82, 90–94, 102, 113, 141, 154, 195
Racialism, 168–69, 180
Racialization, 8, 71–73, 215; Hurston's views, 210–11; of Inuit, 103; and misrecognition, 32
Racism: and anthropological science, 32–35; of W. Douglas Burden, 165–66; in film, 84, 162, 179–80; Margaret Mead's views, 193; Zou Zou as fetish of, 202
Rango (1931), 15, 137
Reconstruction, cultural, 93–94
Redemption: anthropologist's role in, 138; and "racial films," 131–32, 141–43
Regnault, Félix-Louis, 4, 13–16, 21, 30, 77–79, 195, 215; and chronophotography, 48–63; and themes of ethnographic film, 63; ideas of race, 39–40; views on savages, 49, 56–58; and scientific inscription through film, 45–48; and teratology, 160; works described, 29
Reinhardt, Max, 202
Religions, 207. *See also* Redemption; Spirituality
Remarque, Erich Maria, 202

Representation(s), 213; art and race, 227
n. 53; of the Ethnographic, 160–61, 195;
of femininity, 62; media, and scholar-
ship, 216–17; of Samoans in *Moana*,
140–41; scientific, 45; of travel, 82; of
Woman, 226 n. 45. *See also* Art; Pictur-
esque
Resistance: acts of, 70; a mode of the third
eye, 213–14; spaces of, 217
Return of the Jedi, The (1983), 197
Revillon Frères, 109, 113
Revolt against Civilization, The, 188
Reyna, Diane, 213
River of Doubt, The (1913–14), 241 n. 29
Robeson, Paul, 203
Roosevelt, André, 145, 147–48
Roosevelt, Teddy, 86
Roosevelt in Africa (1910), 86
Rosen, Phil, 9
Rouch, Jean, 8, 73, 116, 122, 126, 194, 197
"Round the World Films," 85
Rousseau, Jean-Jacques, 7
Ruby, Jay, 7

Said, Edward, 5
Salvage ethnography. *See* Ethnography,
salvage; Race(s), vanishing
Samoa, 139–40
Savage, the, 9, 71, 162, 213; in expositions,
37, 41; and female gender, 172–75; and
movement, 49, 77; as a term, 222 n.3;
vanishing, 91. *See also* Primitive, the;
Savage(s)
Savagery, 3; and Asia, 175–76; and dark
skin, 177; in *The Most Dangerous
Game*, 166
Savage(s), x, 3–5, 7, 10, 12, 23, 36, 59–61,
161; Australian aborigines as, 64–65;
Josephine Baker as, 200, 202; in *King
Kong*, 176–77; people of color as, 217;
Regnault's views, 49, 56–58; undanger-
ous in travelogues, 85. *See also* Primi-
tive(s); Savage, the
Schoedsack, Ernest B., 133–37, 158–59
Scholarship, media, 216–17

Schomburgk, Hans Hermann, 241 n. 33
Science: and Inuit, 105–7; and *langage par
gestes*, 57–58; and race, 29–30, 46–48.
See also Anthropology; Cuvier; Exposi-
tions; Mead; Pathology; Racism;
Regnault
Seeing, 23, 41, 79, 181, 184. *See also* Gaze;
Representation; Third eye
Self/Other, 4, 6, 12–13, 41. *See also* Other,
the
Self-reflexivity: in anthropology, 7; in
Dunham's work, 263–64 n. 50; and Zora
Neale Hurston, 210
Sembene, Ousmane, 215–16
Senungetuk, Joseph E., 99
Sex and the hunt, 165
Sexuality. *See* Gender; Voyeurism
"Shooting an Elephant," 42
Sights of Suva (1918), 84
Silent Enemy, The (1930), 141–43
*Simba, The King of Beasts, A Saga of the
African Veldt* (1928), 88, 90
Simpson, Lorna, 72, 215
Sitten und Gebrauchen am Senegal
(1910), 83
Slyomovics, Susan, 6
Social Darwinism, 233 n. 37
Société d'anthropologie de Paris, 26–27, 29
Société préhistorique française, 25
Sorcerer, 94
Sovereignty, image, 211–16
Sound, in film, 142–43
Specimens, people as, 25
Spectacle, 63, 89, 154, 189–91
Spectatorship, 207
Spencer, Walter Baldwin, 64–65
Spirituality, 212–13, 215–16
Spivak, Gayatri Chakravorty, 24
Spotted Elk, Molly, 142–43
Stark Love (1927), 131–32
Starting Fire with Gunpowder (1991), 124
Steeplechase, as metaphor, 28
Stefannson, Vilhjalmur, 116–17
Stereotype(s), 72, 99, 197, 202–3, 221 n. 25
Sternberg, Josef Von, 173–74

St. Louis Fair (1904), 213
Stocking, George W., Jr., 7, 27, 78, 138
Stoddard, Lothrop, 188
Story-telling, 194–98
Studies, time motion, 23
Subject/Object, 207, 209–11
Suleri, Sara, 80, 90
Surrealism, 184–86, 259 n. 75

Tabu: A Story of the South Seas (1931), 15, 99, 144, 149–153, 155, 162, 173, 178, 186
Tahiti, 144–45
Taqramiut Nipingat, Inc., 123
Tarzan, 5, 10
Tarzan of the Apes (1912), 180
Taureg, Martin, 63
Taxidermy, 14, 195; cinematic, 79, 88; the irony of reality, 116; vs. the monster, 153–54; *Nanook of the North* as, 100–104; and redemption, 131; as representation, 101–2, 244 n. 10; and teratology, 166
Teratology, 159–60, 166–67. *See also* Monstrosity
Themes, of ethnographic film, 63
Third eye, the, 6, 13, 16–17, 198, 213–15; James Baldwin possessing, 194; defined, 4; and ethnographic spectacle, 41; Hurston's, 207, 209–11; as Other, 217
Third World, 71
Thompson, Samuel, 206
Through Navajo Eyes, 211–12
Time: controlled by film, 48; as creator of meaning, 130; definitions of, 193; mourned in *Tristes Tropiques*, 163; "naturalized-spatialized," 130; and political physics, 144; timelessness, 68, 78; and redemption, 129–155. *See also* Ethnographic, present; Evolution; History
Time Machine, The (1896), 129–30, 179
Time motion studies, 13–14. *See also* Chronophotography
Tirailleurs, 72–73
Tourism. *See* Travelogues

Tourist, x, 83–84
Trader Horn (1931), 88, 172–73
Tradition, 24
Trance and Dance in Bali (1936), 146, 208
Transformations, 206–7
Transformisme, 26, 223 n. 20
Travelogues: commercial, 82–83; and dominance, 82; Kahn archival footage, 81; racial content, 84
Tristes Tropiques (1955), 5, 131, 162
Tsosie, Maryjane, 212
Tupi, 6
Turner, Terry, 197
Tylor, E. B., 63
Types, anthropological, 66

U'mista Cultural Centre, 98

Van Dyke, W. S., 144, 172
Vanishing races. *See* Race(s), vanishing
Van Valin, William, 108–9
Varanus komodensis, 164
Veeder, Gerry, 133
Ventriloquism, ethnographic, 154–55
Verne, Jules, 182
Verner, Samuel P., 157
Visualism and modernity, 30
Visualization, in *King Kong*, 184–86
Visual media. *See* Chronophotography; Cinema; Film; Photography
Voyeurism, 39, 66, 82, 113, 140

Wallace, Michele, 203
Wallace, Minik, 106–7, 157, 178, 189, 213
Washington, Reverend George, 207
Waterton, Charles, 101, 116
Webster, Gloria Cranmer, 98
Wells, H. G., 129–30, 135, 179
West Africans. *See* African(s)
Western, the, 13
Westernization, and contamination, 149
Where do we come from? What are we? Where are we going? (1897–98), 140
White Goddess of Wangora, The (1913), 241 n. 33

White Shadows in the South Seas (1929), 144–45, 149, 153, 173
Wild Man, myth of the, 187
Williams, Pat Ward, 216
Woman, 62; as constructed in *King Kong* and similar films, 171–75, 178, 186; Native, 82, 102, 140, 148, 177–78; as spectator, 62; West African, 54; White, 171–76, 178, 180–81; Wolof, 21, 23. *See also* Baker; Body(ies); Voyeurism
World's Columbian Exhibition (1893), 79

Worth, Sol, 211–12
Wright, Richard, 204

"The Year of the White Bear," 190–91
Yeibichai dance, 92–93, 214
Yellow Robe, Chauncey, 142–43

Zoo(s), 68, 157–58; and cinema, 154
Zou Zou (1932), 200–201
Zou Zou, as sign, 202–203

Fatimah Tobing Rony teaches Asian American Studies
at the University of California, Los Angeles.

Library of Congress Cataloging-in-Publication Data
Rony, Fatimah Tobing.
The third eye : race, cinema, and ethnographic spectacle /
by Fatimah Tobing Rony.
Includes bibliographical references and index.
ISBN 0-8223-1834-2 (cloth : alk. paper). —
ISBN 0-8223-1840-7 (pbk. : alk. paper)
1. Motion pictures in ethnology.   2. Indigenous peoples
in motion pictures.   3. Visual anthropology.   I. Title.
GH347.R55 1996
305.8'00208—dc20   96-13255 CIP